Working
Writing

Working Writing

Greg Larkin

Northern Arizona University

Charles E. Merrill Publishing Company
A Bell & Howell Company
Columbus   Toronto   London   Sydney

Published by
Charles E. Merrill Publishing Company
A Bell & Howell Company
Columbus, Ohio 43216

This book was set in Melior and Standard Typewriter.
Production coordinator: Pamela Hedrick
Copy editor: Beth Riegel Daugherty
Cover designer: Cathy Watterson
Cover photographer: Dallas Chamber of Commerce

Library of Congress Catalog Number: 84-43015
International Standard Book Number: 0-675-20237-X
Printed in the United States of America
1 2 3 4 5 6 7 8 9 10—90 89 88 87 86 85

FOR SIGNE
and OUR SEVEN

Contents

Appendices

Preface

As Henry David Thoreau reminds us, "That government is best which governs least." I think the same applies to textbooks, too many of which are bulky and boring. If I did not quite succeed in making this text short, I hope I made up for it by making it interesting.

The central belief behind this text is that writers in the working world are not fillers of forms or followers of formulas. The effective technical writer does not so much find ready-made patterns to imitate as create original documents to satisfy the demands of a specific situation requiring communication. Therefore, I have built this book around typical communication situations, most of which actually happened to me before I quit working and became a teacher.

In addition to on-the-job influences, I must confess some scholarly influences as well. I have followed with interest and enthusiasm the rise of the process orientation in composition theory and pedagogy over the past twenty years. A host of writers, such as Janet Emig, James Kinneavy, Ross Winterowd, and Linda Flower, among others, have written persuasively on this subject and have certainly influenced how I think about composition and how I teach it. In one sense, all I have done in this book is systematically apply process theory to technical writing.

You have probably heard the old parable, "Give a person a fish and you feed for a day; teach a person to fish and you feed for a lifetime." Students will find no fish in *Working Writing*, no long lists of steps to create the perfect process paper, no collection of essays to copy. Instead, students will become apprentices, looking over the shoulders of journeyman writers who are struggling with communication tasks. The apprentice does not merely learn about writing and does not merely study the final products the master has created. Instead, the apprentice participates with the writer in the false starts, the motivations, and the increasing awareness of actual circumstances that lie behind every effective piece of writing. Of course, the apprentice is given regular chances to examine the master's work. Even more important, however, the apprentice is placed in many situations and told to communicate, just as the practicing writer is placed in situations and communicates. To borrow a distinction from second language learning, I want students of *Working Writing* to not just *learn* about writing or about technical formats, but to *acquire* the ability to write. If they do acquire that ability, they will also acquire the ability to generate appropriate forms and formats for themselves, following models when they can, but not being afraid or unable to head out on their own when they have to—which they usually will.

I cannot conclude without offering thanks to the many people who have made this book possible, especially my many students who are becoming writers and my many friends who are already practicing writers in business, industry, and government. I have enjoyed working closely with both groups for many years.

I would also like to thank all the many helpful people at Charles Merrill Publishing Company, who offered me constant good advice and even better criticism. I especially want to thank my copy editor, Beth Riegel Daugherty, who suggested innumerable improvements and had to suffer through reading the whole manuscript not once but several times. I am indebted to these reviewers who offered specific comments that helped shape the final text: Phillip Sparks, Nashville State Technical Institute; Kathleen Forrest, Onandaga Community College; William F. Woods, Wichita State University; David K. Farkas, University of Washington; George E. Kennedy, Washington State University; and William O. Coggin, Bowling Green State University.

Finally, I cannot adequately thank my wife and children, who had to put up with the clack of the computer keyboard from behind closed doors for over a year. As the saying goes about the chicken, the pig, and breakfast, from my students, friends, and editors there was contribution, but from my family there was total commitment.

UNIT
I

Writing in the
Working World

1

Communication on the Job

> The communicator must have certain fundamental communication skills to solve problems and make a career out of a job.

This chapter introduces you to the writing situations typical of the working world of business, industry, and government. You may find that the sorts of communication demanded on the job differ from some writing assignments given in school. For instance, school assignments often focus on length. Most students have heard the command, "Write a 500-word essay" or "Write a ten-page report." Students may think teachers care more about length than content and try to hit the magic "500-word" or "ten-page" limit exactly.

In the working world, however, length is not arbitrarily set beforehand. Instead, content and context determine the length. In fact, content and context determine most things in professional writing. As a result, many things you worry about on school writing assignments become unimportant in professional writing. This chapter explains what *is* important in writing on the job.

EFFECTIVE WRITING

Just what is expected in professional, on-the-job writing? Writers in business, industry, and government want to have these qualities of effective writing in their documents:

▶ *Clearly Defined Purpose:* The reader then knows exactly what response is expected. Some typical purposes for writing include persuading, informing, instructing, and recommending.

▶ *Adequate Factual Support for Purpose:* The reader not only knows what to do after reading, but also feels inclined to do it. The reader is neither deluged with facts, nor left wondering about the specifics of the situation.

▶ *Clear and Appropriate Organization:* The reader can progress without having to stop to interpret apparent jumps or gaps in development.

▶ *Clear Sentences:* The reader can understand the relationship of each sentence to the one that follows.

▶ *Concise Presentation:* The reader senses that every necessary point is handled as briefly as possible.

▶ *Effective Language:* The reader is not distracted by such things as awkward or unclear sentences; poor word choice; incorrect grammar, spelling, or punctuation; and various nonstandard language forms.

▶ *Appropriate Use of Standard Formats:* The reader recognizes and feels comfortable with the expected forms for business letters, abstracts, proposals, progress reports, documentation, and other formats typical of writing in business, industry, and government.

This text covers the specific processes and guidelines for incorporating these qualities of good writing into your writing.

SOLVING PROBLEMS

Chris Todd has worked for over a year in the accounts payable department of a major international company. Many of the companies from which Chris receives invoices offer a small discount if payment is made within ten days. Chris monitors the exact payment and discount terms on the invoices and processes them efficiently. But after a year and a half, Chris no longer feels challenged or fulfilled by this responsibility. She wants more from her job.

To advance, Chris must manage these discounts skillfully, which requires the ability to plan and communicate. Only through effective communication can Chris distinguish herself from other workers who simply process invoices.

For instance, Chris knows she has to use her communication skills, not her mathematical or accounting abilities, to solve a problem with a supplier. For six months, Acme Rubber Company has been sending its invoices later and later. They offered a generous 3 percent discount for invoices paid within ten days, but the invoices were dated six to eight days before Chris received them. She did her job as well as she could, always watching carefully for Acme invoices and processing them immediately, even hand carrying them to the mailroom. Yet soon she received an invoice from Acme Rubber billing her back for the last discount she had deducted. Acme's invoice stated that her payment had not been received within the specified ten days.

Chris' problem with Acme is not unusual. Simply getting your job done is often not enough. Efficient processing of invoices cannot solve Chris' problem wth Acme Rubber Company any more than writing a set number of pages or words produces an effective piece of writing. Besides getting your job done or your paper written, you have to communicate. No matter how efficiently Chris processes her invoices, she cannot solve her problem with Acme Rubber Company without communication.

If Chris is content to stay where she is in her company, she can continue to process invoices as efficiently as she can, watch for special discounts, and hand carry correspondence to the mailroom. But if she wants to move up, she has to communicate; that is, she must stop working around problems and start solving them.

Communicating to Solve Problems

A communicator is a problem solver, not someone content to work around problems. Although a problem may continue unresolved, usually it must be resolved immediately if the job is to be done at all. Every job involves these situations going beyond the normal day-to-day routine, and the worker who communicates to resolve such situations is effective (and promotable).

Look at the following situations and identify the job, what must be done to accomplish that job, and the communication required.

> Brad Green, an electrician, was awarded a contract to install outside lighting on and around a new apartment building. Brad completed the job ahead of schedule, but several of the fixtures he installed proved defective. Mr. Smith, the contractor who hired Brad, is worried that the replacement fixtures may not arrive in time to be installed by the promised completion date.

What is Brad's job? To install the outside fixtures and replace the defective ones.

What must he do to get the job done? Know how to install fixtures quickly and efficiently, which includes a knowledge of basic electrical wiring, handling and hookup of fixtures, testing the system, trouble shooting, etc. Brad can do all these things, because he is a skilled electrician. But that is not the whole issue here. In this case, Brad needs to be a skilled communicator, too.

What does Brad have to communicate to get the job done? His electrical skills have little value if he cannot reassure the contractor that he will complete the job on time and arrange with the supplier to replace the defective fixtures immediately. Therefore, Brad faces at least two communication tasks:

- Inform the contractor of the projected arrival date of the replacement fixtures, and reassure him that they will be installed before the deadline.
- Inform the supplier about the defective fixtures, arrange for their return, and even more important, insist on the immediate shipment of the replacement fixtures.

No matter how good an installer Brad is, he probably will not work for Mr. Smith again if he does not communicate effectively with both Mr. Smith and the fixture supplier. To get the job done, Brad must communicate.

Job Analysis   Here are several other job situations to analyze. In each case, answer these questions:

- What is the person's job?
- What must the person do to get the job done?
- What does the person have to communicate, and to whom?

Gloria Kramer is a technical writer for Automated Systems, Inc., a large manufacturing company specializing in sophisticated medical hardware. Before Automated Systems can market its machines, it has to file a lengthy series of explanatory documents with the state office of consumer affairs. Gloria heads a team of engineers responsible for writing these documents. She herself is not a trained engineer, but she is responsible for the final documents, without which the company cannot sell its equipment.

Sheila Murphy, a manager for her government agency, is in charge of the daily functioning of her office. Her supervisor, the agency head, is ultimately responsible for all the affairs of the agency. The agency head makes policy decisions that Sheila must implement in her office. Recently the agency telephone bill has increased drastically. The agency head asks Sheila to find out why.

Ted Fanning is the chief of a drilling crew for a large oil company. Lately, many of the company's drilling rigs have experienced costly downtime because of torsional failures in tool joints. The head office wants to know what is wrong and what can be done to correct the problem.

Rob Stevens is a rancher in Wyoming. He has begun to lose more and more of his stock to grizzly bears, wolves, and coyotes. The grizzlies are a protected species and many environmental groups are urging protection for wolves and coyotes as well. Rob cannot legally kill grizzlies, and wolves and coyotes may soon join the list of protected species.

To sum up, then, every job (beyond the most menial, dead-end kind) requires two interrelated sets of skills:

- The job skills themselves—the knowledge and abilities required to get the job done.
- Communication skills—the knowledge and abilities required to solve problems that inevitably arise.

Furthermore, job skills and communication skills often become even more closely related.

> The further one goes up the ladder in any job or with any company, the more one's job skills become, by definition, communication skills.

The plumber, earning $14.74 an hour, knows how to sweat a joint. Performing this physical process efficiently is one of the plumber's job skills. The shop manager, earning $35,000 a year, also knows how to sweat a joint, but more important, he knows how to explain to an angry customer why the joint the plumber sweat still leaks. The shop manager also knows how to tell the plumber to fix the joint correctly. The shop manager's job is not to fix pipes, but to communicate with customers and plumbers. Finally, the owner, earning 15 percent of the value of every job done by his workers, even though he may or may not remember how to sweat a joint, certainly knows how to prepare a bid (a form of communication) and how to present it in an acceptable format. For the owner and the shop manager, the job *is* communication—solving problems, getting contracts, keeping customers happy, and obeying building regulations. Communication allows the plumbers to continue fixing leaks, and the managers to continue managing the day-by-day business of the shop.

These job descriptions do not mean that owners are better than plumbers, but that the two jobs involve different sets of problems, require different skills, and present different challenges. This text addresses the problems, skills, and challenges of the person whose job requires communication. By using the techniques presented in this text, the communicator can solve problems by communicating effectively. (Although this text concentrates on written communication, most of the techniques that make writing effective also apply to oral communication. See appendix III.)

Analyzing a Problem's Parts

The best way to solve any communication problem is to break it down into its parts. Most large problems consist of several smaller problems, which when solved provide a solution to the original larger one. Generally, problems can be divided into three types:

> ▶ *Problems of Fact:* Establishing verifiable information and acceptable definitions of terms.
>
> ▶ *Problems of Interpretation:* Establishing clear and logical relationships among pertinent facts and acceptable definitions. These relationships allow the reader to draw conclusions based on the available facts and definitions.
>
> ▶ *Problems of Value:* Establishing hierarchies of importance, so that choices can be made when different sets of facts, definitions, and interpretations are mutually exclusive.

Let's examine these three types of problems in a specific context.

A coal company has the opportunity to lease 20,000 acres in southwestern Wyoming for exploratory drilling. The overall problem is, should they lease the property or not?

To make an intelligent decision, the coal company must analyze the overall problem by breaking it down into its relevant parts:

Problems of Fact
- What costs will be incurred if the property is leased?
- How much will be paid to the party from whom the land is leased? How and when will these payments be made?
- What are the property's geological features?

Problems of Interpretation
- Do the geological studies indicate a high-grade coal area?
- Have other mining companies been successful in the same area?
- How long before the mine becomes profitable?

Problems of Value
- Will the value of the coal justify the impact of a large-scale mining operation on the environment?
- Will the length of time required for the mine to become profitable be too long to make it an attractive investment?

Several important relationships become apparent through such an analysis. First, questions of interpretation and value imply factual questions that must be answered before one can interpret and evaluate. Second, once facts are established, interpretation and evaluation naturally follow.

Problem Analysis Following are a few additional problems for you to analyze. First, list as many smaller problems as you can, and then group them logically.

> The board of directors of a large bank is considering a loan application from a man who wants to open a new restaurant. The board's problem is whether to grant the loan.

> The National Park Service has received a request from a group of Boy Scouts to go on a 70-mile hike in the Grand Canyon National Park. The problem is whether to issue the scouts a permit for the hike.

> Brent Schwinn, owner of a construction company, has just received an unusually low quotation on some lumber he needs for a house he is working on. Brent's problem is whether to buy the lumber at such a low price, and if so, how much to buy.

Analyzing a Problem's Context

These three communication situations are typical of the problems encountered in business, industry, and government. Through careful analysis, the communicator begins to solve the problems; however, he cannot effectively analyze them in isolation. Problems always exist in a context, which must be taken into account as they are solved and the appropriate documents written. The context of any communication situation can be divided into three parts—the purpose, the audience, and the author, as shown in the following diagram.

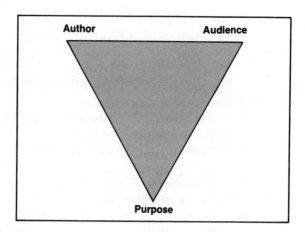

The effective writer must thoroughly understand the context of the writing. Otherwise, even the most careful analysis of the problem does not lead to effective communication. For instance, we all get the runaround occasionally. We want some product, information, or service, but no one seems able to help. Everyone involved gets frustrated, but the problem is no closer to a solution. Usually this situation results from not knowing the right person to talk to, the right questions to ask, or the right language to use. In other words, we do not know the context. We waste a lot of time talking to the wrong people, asking the wrong questions, and using the wrong words. In short, we get the runaround. Often, it's our own fault, because we have not done our contextual homework.

To communicate in business, industry, and government, the writer must know the purpose, the audience, and his or her own position before beginning to communicate. Careful contextual planning takes a little time, but ultimately saves everyone hours of frustration and wasted effort. In many cases the resulting improved communication may save both the writer and the company money and improve both of their professional images.

Contextual Analysis   Unfortunately, no systematic and universally applicable process for contextual analysis exists. The writer must assess purpose, audience, and her own role in each communication situation and must also realize that the three are delicately interrelated. Sometimes appealing to the audience is most important, but sometimes the purpose determines who the audience is and what stance the author wants to take. Still other times the author's attitude determines what audiences to address and for what purposes. As a writer drafts a document, she must carefully consider all three contextual elements, both in themselves and in their relationships to each other.

A writer considering contextual analysis in the following specific situation must decide whether to write a directive, a request, or a suggestion.

George Morris works as a district supervisor for the Fish and Wildlife Service. One of the offices in his district, Bright Falls, has needed an additional car for some time, and George has been unsuccessfully petitioning the General Services Administration to get one. George finally received a directive from General Services stating he could not get another car for the district, but that he could transfer the extra car in the Cottonwood office to Bright Falls. Now George has to figure out how to effect the transfer.

DRAFTING THE DOCUMENT

George's first thought is that the General Services directive clearly states his own purpose—he must direct the transfer of the car. So he drafts a memo to the Cottonwood office:

```
        By order of General Services Administration, car
#001-700 will be placed at the disposal of the Bright
Falls office immediately.
```

This memo has a very clear purpose, but George realizes that the Cottonwood office might be offended by such a brusque directive. In other words, George decides to consider his audience, not just his purpose. He knows that Tom Malohney, the office chief at Cottonwood, is a bit of a rebel who dislikes following orders for orders' sake only. However, he also knows that Tom is sensible, and he usually plays ball if given logical reasons. So George decides not to mention the General Services directive, but give reasons for the transfer instead. His second draft begins

```
        Over the past two years the Bright Falls office has
added three new people, while the Cottonwood office has
subtracted one. However, the motor pools based at each
office have remained the same, so that six people now
share two cars at Bright Falls, while three people each
have their own cars at Cottonwood.
```

George likes this start, but he does not know how to move into the actual purpose. He has adapted well to his audience, but overly muted the purpose. He thinks of his own role in the situation—he *is* the district supervisor; he *can* command—so he adds the following sentence to his second draft:

```
        Therefore, I have decided to transfer car #001-700
from Cottonwood to Bright Falls.
```

But now George remembers Tom's well-known dislike of directives. George does not want to pull rank on Tom, because while doing so might get the immediate job done, it could also harm their long-term relationship. So George tones down his directive to a suggestion. In other words, George decides to take a less commanding authorial stance:

```
    Therefore, I would like to suggest that we transfer
car #001-700 from Cottonwood to Bright Falls.
```

But what if Tom does not agree with this suggestion? George decides his personal suggestion may be so weak that it sacrifices the whole purpose of the memo.

George is experiencing a typical writing problem: contextual elements pull in different directions, and he needs to balance them. George decides to let the suggestion be the General Service Administration's, not his. He thus plays the role of a transmitter of information rather than a director of policy:

```
    Therefore, the General Services Administration has
recommended that we transfer car #001-700 from Cottonwood
to Bright Falls.
```

Then George decides to emphasize his helplessness—Bright Falls needs the additional car and General Services gives him only one way to get it. George opts against a dictatorial stance, and takes a stance supportive of Tom, but shows he must ultimately bow to other pressures:

```
    Therefore, the General Services Administration has
recommended that we transfer car #001-700 from Cottonwood
to Bright Falls. I know your people are used to having a
car apiece, but I don't know what else we can do.
```

Checking this latest draft against his sense of Tom as his audience, George decides the conclusion may invite Tom to offer an alternative. So he decides to be a little more forceful at the end, although not on the basis of his supervisory position. To allow Tom some latitude, George decides not to mention when the transfer should occur. He knows Tom will grudgingly accept the transfer in principle, and then, with Tom on his side, George can go into detail about the actual transfer. To introduce those details before getting Tom's general approval would probably take more time and effort than using separate letters for each purpose. His analysis of audience and author's role causes George to modify his original purpose; he breaks it into two bite-sized chunks that Tom can swallow more easily. So George winds up with

> Over the past two years the Bright Falls office has
> added three new people, while the Cottonwood office has
> subtracted one. However, the motor pools based at each
> office have remained the same, so that six people now
> share two cars at Bright Falls, while three people each
> have their own cars at Cottonwood. Therefore, the General
> Services Administration has recommended that we transfer
> car #001-700 from Cottonwood to Bright Falls. I know your
> people are used to having a car apiece, but I don't know
> what else we can do. General Services insists that this
> is the only solution. However, I'll keep pressing for
> another district car to replace the one you're losing.

EVALUATING THE DRAFT

In the process of drafting this memo, George did not focus exclusively on purpose, audience, or his own role, but tried to balance all three. Once a writer analyzes the context and determines the basic content of a piece of writing, he must constantly monitor the emerging document:

▶ Have I analyzed the problem correctly and completely?
▶ Have I left out any important facts?
▶ Is my interpretation of the facts sound?
▶ Am I coming across with the degree of authority I want to project?
▶ Have I appealed to the qualities important to my audience?
▶ Will my audience clearly see the result I'm expecting?

Of course, these are only a few examples of the many context-based questions possible.

Other important questions are language-based:

▶ Is my choice of words right?
▶ Are my sentences too long or too short?
▶ Are my sentences too complex or too simple?
▶ Are my paragraphs logical, orderly, and helpful?
▶ Does my document move clearly from point to point?
▶ Are my graphic aids clear and useful?
▶ Are my grammar, spelling, and punctuation correct?

Again, these are only a few of the language-based questions the writer could ask.

The writer can answer all these questions only by referring back to the analyses of the problem and its context. For instance, you can only determine whether your choice of words is right by looking at your subject, your audience, and the image you want to project. Basically, all the questions about the emerging document boil down to one: "Am I doing the job I set out to do in this piece of writing?"

However, this crucial question has one important qualification. As one writes a document and begins to evaluate it, she may discover flaws in the initial plan. Thus, the writer should never regard the initial assessment of the problem or its context as absolutely final. When necessary, the writer should reassess the problem or its context. The writer must also remember that the order he or she follows when analyzing the problem is not necessarily the order to use when presenting it in the final document. The writer must take into account the demands of the situation as well as the analysis of the problem itself to create the document's best organization.

> Writing is a fluid and dynamic process that the writer must approach openly and creatively.

To see how one keeps the writing process open, analyze these early drafts by answering the following questions:

Purpose
- What is the author's purpose?
- How is the author attempting to achieve that purpose?
- What can the author do to better achieve that purpose?

Audience
- What is the author's assessment of the audience?
- What is the author doing in the draft to reach that audience?
- What can the author do to reach that audience more effectively?

Author
- What stance is the author taking?
- What is the author doing in the draft to project that stance?
- What can the author do to improve that stance?

Ed Post is the environmental coordinator for a mining company. A coalition of local ranchers and environmental activists has written an open letter to the newspaper opposing the expansion of the company's mining operations in the area. The president of the company has asked Ed to respond by writing an open letter to the newspaper stating the company's view of the proposed expansion.

Ed's draft (so far) is this:

My fellow citizens:

We at Donner Mining share your concern about the
environment. But we must point out that we have a valid
license to expand the mine. If our company is to survive
these hard economic times, we have to expand. Otherwise,
we will have to close the mine. Since many people in this
town are employed by the mine, our closing would have a
bad impact on the town's economy. So while we share your
concern about the environment, we hope you recognize that
there are compelling economic issues at work here, too.

Bob Price is operations manager for a bank that has just opened a
new branch office south of town. Bob has advertised for bids for the
janitorial services in the new branch. He received five bids and has awarded
the contract to one company. He must now write an official acceptance
notice.

Bob's draft (so far) is this:

I am happy to inform you that your company has been
selected to clean the bank. Please sign and date the
enclosed contract. We'll expect you to show up Monday,
January 3, to begin cleaning. Please observe the bank's
security procedures very closely. We look forward to a
long and happy relationship.

Sarah Frederick is a personnel officer with the state government. She
has recently received an angry letter of complaint about the alleged rude-
ness of a state driver's license examiner. State policy is to respond to all
such allegations.

Sarah's draft (so far) is this:

We appreciate your letter of the 21st expressing
dissatisfaction with the conduct of Mr. Jones of the
driver's license division. Naturally, we are anxious for
your dealings with the state government to be pleasant.
However, since your letter expresses more anger than
specific facts about Mr. Jones' supposed improper
actions, we can do little for you. If you care to file a
formal complaint, you can pick up the necessary form at
the county clerk's office. But if you don't have anything
specific to complain about, I would advise you to save
everybody a lot of trouble by just forgetting it.

By checking the document as one goes, the writer can monitor how effectively the problem is being addressed and how appropriate the document is for the particular situation. In addition, by analyzing the draft in progress, the writer often arrives at new insights about the problem and the situation, which in turn allow her to make beneficial changes. Finally, the writer may also polish and correct surface blemishes.

SUMMARY

Professional writers in business, industry, and government are, above all, problem solvers, and problems demand, above all, communication. Effective problem solvers, or communicators, analyze problems clearly, recognize the contexts within which those problems exist, and monitor their own performances while writing.

However, writers do not necessarily first analyze the problem, then devise a strategy for dealing with it, and finally monitor the success or failure of that strategy. The communication process is much too fluid for any such linear development.

EXERCISES

1. In the examples featuring Brad Green, Gloria Kramer, Sheila Murphy, Ted Fanning, and Rob Stevens, analyze the problem(s) each one faces. That is, what questions of fact, interpretation, and value must each individual answer before communicating?

2. For the same examples named in question 1, what is the context within which the individual's problem exists? That is, what audience(s) does the individual need to address, what authorial role(s) does the individual want to adopt, and what purpose(s) does the individual want to accomplish?

3. Again, for each of the examples named in question 1, select one specific context—a unified audience, purpose, and authorial role—and write a draft. You may supply appropriate "factual" details as needed.

4. Does the draft you wrote for question 3 seem based on an adequate analysis of the problem? Does it appropriately address the situation? Is the language appropriate to the problem and the situation? Is the language correct? Using the list of effective writing qualities at the beginning of this chapter, how good do you think your draft is? What can you do to improve it?

5. Read George Morris' complete draft again, and then apply the questions in question 4 to it.

6.   Bill Murphy works as legal counsel for an oil company. He has been negotiating permits from private landowners for the right to do exploratory drilling on their land. Mr. Tom Fenton has requested certain changes in the permit before he will sign it. Bill thinks the proposed changes could make his company liable so he does not want to allow Mr. Fenton's changes.

Bill needs to reply to Mr. Fenton, his primary audience. However, Bill also realizes his company is eager to drill in that particular area and will be upset if Bill fails to get the permit signed. Thus, Bill has a secondary audience for his letter—his employers. He knows they are looking over his shoulder to see how effectively he handles the situation with Mr. Fenton. Bill needs to keep his employers' wishes in mind as he writes his letter, applying the cover-your-ass principle known as "CYA."

Bill considers the following points about his primary audience as he makes his initial analysis:

- Mr. Fenton owns the property Bill's company wants to explore.
- Bill believes Mr. Fenton feels protective about his property, but will let the exploration go forward if he is paid enough.
- Mr. Fenton's proposed changes indicate he is cautious, exacting, and difficult to deal with.

Bill must consider these and many other qualities of his primary audience as he drafts his letter.

Bill also considers the following points about his secondary audience as he initially analyzes his writing task:

- Bill's company is in the business of drilling for oil. They want to drill in every promising location.
- Bill's company will take a calculated risk if it offers a good chance for profit.
- Bill's company does not like to take big chances for small profits.

Bill must consider these and many other qualities of his secondary audience as he writes his draft.

Bill has several possible purposes for his letter:

- He can refuse Mr. Fenton's suggested changes and insist he accept the permit as is. (But Bill remembers his company wants to drill, so Bill rejects this purpose. It fits his primary audience, but not his secondary one.)
- He can accept Mr. Fenton's suggested changes. (But Bill thinks the changes are not wise for his company, so he rejects this purpose, also. Again, it fits Bill's primary audience, but not his secondary one.)
- He can persuade Mr. Fenton to modify some of his suggested changes. (Bill accepts this purpose because he thinks it will cause Mr. Fenton to modify some of his suggestions and to sign the permit.)

Bill has considered both his audiences to generate an effective strategy for his letter.

Just as Bill has two audiences, so too he has a dual role as author:

- He needs to be conciliatory and understanding, so he does not offend Mr. Fenton; yet he cannot be too mild and lead his company into an unwise agreement.

- As an individual, he understands Mr. Fenton's suggestions, but as a company employee, he must insist on certain points.

Bill hopes Mr. Fenton responds positively to his personal appeal and his employers are impressed with his company loyalty.

Making use of all this information, write Bill's letter to Mr. Fenton. Be prepared to defend every aspect of your letter.

7. Here are several other problems to study. In each case, determine the possible audiences, purposes, and authorial roles inherent in the situation. Then determine which audiences, purposes, and authorial roles fit together and which approach to take. Finally, generate a first draft of a document.

> Mary Thomas is a buyer for an electrical contractor. She has two sources for 3/0 wire. The first, Miller Electric Products, offers quick delivery and high quality products, but has high prices. The second, Discount Electric Products, has low prices, but offers inferior materials and slow delivery. Mary's company needs to replace a large order of 3/0 wire they just shipped to a customer.

> Floyd Martin is the area engineer for the U.S. Army Corps of Engineers. As part of his responsibility, he explains government policies to the many contractors hired by the Corps. One of the government's policies about contractors is that a deficiency in part of a job may result in a withholding of all payment until it is corrected. A contractor in Floyd's district writes to ask why he has not received a check for the completed part of a job. Floyd's records include several unresolved deficiency reports from field engineers.

> Lee Naylor, an inside salesman for a building products distributor, is responsible for keeping the company's warehouse adequately stocked. Company policy requires that he record each purchase he makes to avoid duplicate orders. In a rush, Lee places a large order for outlet boxes and forgets to record it on the inventory card. A few days later, the warehouse chief notices that outlet boxes are running low, checks the inventory card, finds no order placed, and orders a large shipment of inventory boxes. A week later two large shipments of outlet boxes are delivered, more than the company can sell in a year. Company policy is never to hold any item in stock for more than six months.

8. Think of some writing you actually need to do, but not necessarily a school assignment. For instance, you may need to apply for a job, write a merchant asking for your money back, write a "letter to the editor," write to your parents for more money, etc. Apply the principles presented in this chapter to that piece of writing—analyze the problem and its context, write a draft of the document, and evaluate its effectiveness.

FOR FURTHER READING

Bazerman, Charles. "What Written Knowledge Does: Three Examples of Academic Discourse." *Philosophy of the Social Sciences* 11 (September 1981): 361–87.

Berthoff, Ann. *The Making of Meaning: Metaphors, Models and Maxims for Writing Teachers.* Montclair, N.J.: Boynton Cook, 1981.

Bitzer, Lloyd. "The Rhetorical Situation." *Philosophy and Rhetoric* 1 (Winter 1968): 1–14.

Booth, Wayne. "The Rhetorical Stance." *College Composition and Communication* 14 (October 1963): 139–45.

Corder, Jim. "Rhetorical Analysis of Writing." In *Teaching Composition: 10 Bibliographical Essays.* Ed. Gary Tate. Fort Worth: Texas Christian University Press, 1976.

D'Angelo, Frank. *A Conceptual Theory of Rhetoric.* Cambridge, Massachusetts: Winthrop, 1975.

Dillon, George. *Constructing Texts.* Bloomington: Indiana University Press, 1981.

Emig, Janet. "Writing as a Mode of Learning." *College Composition and Communication* 28 (May 1977): 122–128.

Gibson, Walker. *Tough, Sweet, and Stuffy: An Essay on Modern American Styles.* Bloomington: Indiana University Press, 1966.

Ong, Walter. "The Writer's Audience Is Always a Fiction." *PMLA* 90 (January 1975): 9–21.

Richards, I.A. *The Philosophy of Rhetoric.* New York: Oxford University Press, 1936.

Zoellner, Robert. "Talk-Write: A Behavioral Pedagogy for Composition." *College English* 30 (January 1969): 267–320.

2

The Rhetoric of Communication

Although you may have heard *rhetoric* defined strictly in the negative sense of manipulation, rhetoric is actually the skillful and effective use of language—in this text, particularly written language—to achieve some purpose. As discussed in chapter 1, the context of any communication situation involves three major elements: purpose, audience, and author. These three elements make up the rhetoric of communication. Although discussed separately, these rhetorical elements function interdependently in any piece of writing.

> Modifying one rhetorical element—purpose, audience, or author—means modifying the other two as well.

PURPOSE

In any writing situation the writer must identify a rhetorical purpose—decide *why* she needs to communicate. Exactly what result does the writer expect from the audience? The effective writer in business, industry, and government usually wants to explain the purpose as clearly and quickly as possible. Ideally, at the beginning of the piece of writing, and certainly by the end, the audience should know exactly what the writer expects of them, and feel motivated enough to do it.

> For the past twenty years Tom Finney has been given an extra day off at Thanksgiving because he works in Madison, Wisconsin, three hours away from his family in Chicago. Although everyone else in the company must be back on the job the Friday after Thanksgiving, Tom has that day off too, giving him a four-day weekend. But this year the company has hired a new branch manager who knows nothing of Tom's special arrangement. Because the branch manager is new and does not want to set a precedent, he is cool to the whole idea. Finally, he requires Tom to draft a formal request for the special day off.

Analyzing Purpose

This situation is fairly simple. Tom's purpose is to recommend an action, in this case that he be allowed an extra day off. In support, Tom can note a fact— he has had this day off for over twenty years—and an interpretation—this long history is more important than any negative precedent the extra day off might set. That is, Tom can justify an existing policy, rather than recommend a new one. This slight modification in purpose might mean the difference between Tom's retaining a *long-standing* extra day off and his being refused a *new* request for an extra day.

Compare the following excerpts from two versions of Tom's formal request:

Purpose #1: To justify an existing policy.

```
My having the Friday after Thanksgiving off has been
allowed and accepted in the past for the following
reasons:
```

Purpose #2: To recommend a new policy.

```
There are several important reasons I should be allowed
to take off the Friday after Thanksgiving.
```

Different Purposes

No matter which way Tom decides to write his request, its overall purpose is clear. But to best fulfill this overall purpose, Tom must effectively use several types of support at particular points in his document:

- Factual Support: Informing the manager about the past situation.
- Interpretive Support: Explaining why the situation was allowed in the past.
- Evaluative Support: Defending the previous manager's policy of allowing the extra day.

Tom should consider all these areas of support, but he may not use them all in the final document because his exact strategy will be determined not only by purpose, but by audience and author's role as well.

In a more complex situation the possible supports and their interrelationships multiply rapidly.

Zelda Stern works in the mayor's office. The city has grown by 40,000 people in the past ten years, and the city's personnel and services have grown right along with the population. The old city hall is too small to accommodate the city government any more. The ideal property for the new city hall has been occupied by a furniture store for over seventy years, but the city decides to use the principle of eminent domain to get it. The owner of the furniture store disputes both the city's right to do so and its suggested compensation. So the whole matter winds up in court. Zelda has to draft a report outlining the city's position. Although Zelda works for the mayor, she is sympathetic to the furniture store owner.

In this complex situation, Zelda can frame her report from any one of several angles:

- Factual Purpose: To inform the court of the city's reasoning.
- Interpretive Purpose: To explain why the city chose that particular property for the new city hall.
- Evaluative Purpose: To justify the city's proposed action.

Since lawyers will probably justify the city's plan, Zelda's report should either inform or explain. As part of her overall informative or explanatory purpose, Zelda considers and incorporates some other types of support:

Factual
- To review the situation.
- To report on previous examples of eminent domain elsewhere.
- To compare and contrast the chosen property with other possible sites for the new city hall.

Interpretive
- To choose among alternative ways of handling the store owner's refusal to cooperate.
- To show that the compensation offered the store owner is fair.

Evaluative
- To defend the city's decision.
- To establish that the city's needs have priority over the individual store's needs.

In other words, Zelda must identify both the overall purpose of her document and its interlocking supports. She has several options for the overall purpose and many additional options for supports. Of course, Zelda cannot choose any purposes in isolation. She must also consider both her audience and her own role.

Using Purpose Analysis Look at the following problems and identify possible overall purposes and supports.

Robert Andrew is an accountant for a small steel products fabrication company. He likes his work and does an excellent job. In fact, he has done so well that another company in the same industrial park has offered him a similar job at a considerable increase in pay. Robert has been trying for several years to have his salary upgraded to an acceptable level, but although he gets a small raise each year, he never catches up to where he feels he should be.

Robert decides to write to his current employer. What overall purposes and supports might he have?

> Mertyle Lovelace is a claims adjuster for a large moving company. She has received an irate letter from a client who was forced to pay $314 in delivery charges before the local moving company would deliver his belongings from storage to his new house. The client points out that the terms of his contract state "door-to-door service," implying that delivery to the house is included in the basic price of the move. Therefore, the local agent had no right to collect additional fees.

Mertyle must answer the client's letter. What overall purposes and supports might she have?

AUDIENCE

Audience is also an important rhetorical element in any writing situation. The writer must first determine to whom she is writing and must then gather all the pertinent information about that audience.

Stated and Unstated Audiences

Usually, at least one audience's identity is inherent; however, the writer must not assume that the most obvious audience is the only or the most important audience. In fact, in business, industry, and government, the stated audience is often not the primary one, as the following example illustrates.

> Brian Long works in the purchasing department of Deleo's Office Supply, a small electronics manufacturing company specializing in various pieces of office equipment, such as word processors and calculators. For years Brian's company has had an open order with Ace Electronics to supply transistors and other parts. Over the past two years, however, Brian has noticed a steady deterioration in the quality of Ace's parts. He has suggested several times that Deleo's switch to another parts supplier. He has even documented the increasing number of defective parts from Ace, but management wants still more evidence, both about Ace and about any proposed alternative supplier.

Brian decides to report the results of his research to Ace Electronics and send a copy to his employers, his *real* primary audience in this case.

CYA   Brian also has a third audience in mind as he writes this report. He knows his company is being increasingly criticized; some defective parts from Ace are going out in Deleo's products, which are then returned. In a few cases, some of Deleo's customers have opted for other manufacturers. Brian anticipates that sooner or later someone at Deleo's will be blamed for the continued use of defective Ace parts, and he wants his report on file so *he* will not be the one held responsible. By considering the implications of his writing and its possible future audiences, Brian protects himself, known throughout business, industry, and government as cover your ass (CYA).

Another important fact about audiences in business, industry, and government creates the need for CYA. Because often *everything* is filed, one must anticipate that some audiences, not intended or even considered, may eventually read one's writing, perhaps years later. Documents in business, industry, and government have no set limit to their useful (or troublesome) life. Writers need to keep this fact in mind as they consider audience.

Analyzing Audience

After the writer identifies the audiences, he must carefully analyze them. Many approaches to audience analysis are possible, but as useful as any are the reporter's tried and true *who, what, when, why, where,* and *how.* The writer wants to know as much as possible about the audience, and so asks

- ▶ Who are they?
  - Intelligence and training levels?
  - Biases?
  - Attitudes?
  - Values?
- ▶ What are they?
  - Position in their company?
  - Responsibilities?
  - Contacts with others?
  - Degree of influence?
- ▶ When will they read the document?
  - As part of a busy day?
  - Under time pressure?
  - At the beginning or end of the document's circulation?
  - After or before the document's contents have been approved or implemented?
- ▶ Why will they read the document?
  - For information only?
  - To make a decision?
  - To review and edit?
  - To pass on to someone else?
- ▶ Where will they read the document?
  - In a busy office?
  - In the train or subway?
  - In a meeting?
  - At home?

▶ How will they read the document?
   Quickly, skimming for main ideas only?
   With careful attention to every detail?
   Eager to find fault or be sympathetic?
   As part of a larger picture or in isolation?

Questions like these, that establish a clear view of the audience, allow the writer to adapt to that audience. Of course, this list, though lengthy, does not exhaust the possibilities. Nor does a given situation necessarily demand that all these questions about audience be answered. The crucial fact about the audience in one situation may be insignificant in another. And certainly a writer considering audience must also consider purpose and author's role. A given purpose and author's role influence who the audience is and how best to approach it.

Applying Audience Analysis

Audience analysis helps the writer define the audience, and more important, then shape the document to fit. The following situation demonstrates both audience analysis and application of that analysis to the resulting document:

Carmelo Ruiz is a professor of economics at the university. Some burglars apparently have a key to his office and periodically enter at night to steal books, paper, and other items. Carmelo has written to the physical plant several times requesting that a new lock be installed on his office door. So far he has received no response, and no new lock either. He calls physical plant on the phone, but they claim they never received any request from him. They also inform him that there is a three-month backlog on work orders. Carmelo gets angry and decides to write to the president of the university.

```
     I must complain about the outrageous lack of
cooperation I have been receiving from the physical
plant. Its lack of service seems typical of this sorry
university. I am writing to see if you can intercede for
me with them.
```

At this point Carmelo stops his draft because he recognizes two points about his audience:

1. The middle sentence about "this sorry university" will probably offend the president, who may get upset at Carmelo rather than help him solve the problem.

2. The last sentence, about the president's interceding with the physical plant, makes Carmelo realize that even though he is addressing the president, his primary audience is still the physical plant.

Therefore, Carmelo decides to be more subtle. Instead of directing the president to the physical plant, he uses the president as a weapon against the physical plant. Carmelo begins another draft of his letter, directed to the physical plant itself, with a carbon copy to the president. As he writes, Carmelo thinks particularly about the degree of influence the president may have over the physical plant, the information he needs to include to get the president interested in this situation, and the action he wants the physical plant to take, especially since they will know the president is getting a copy of the letter.

```
        Over the past six months I have repeatedly had my
office burglarized. I have lost some university property,
and all the items in my office, the most valuable of
which are also university property, are in great danger.
I have made two formal requests to you to change the lock
on my office door, but so far there has been no action.
When I called today, your secretary stated it would be at
least three months before the new lock would be
installed. I am concerned that this delay may result in
the loss of valuable university property and I hope that
by informing you of this danger I will have done all I
can to avoid this loss to the university.
```

Carmelo hand carries this letter to the physical plant and sends the president's copy through the campus mail system. His hunch is that this letter, carbon copied to the president, will make the physical plant move his request to a higher priority. Two days later a physical plant locksmith installs a new lock on Carmelo's door. The university mail service is so slow, the president does not get his copy until four days after it was sent.

Using Audience Analysis   Here are a few examples for you to analyze in terms of audience. Which of the reporter's questions about audiences *(who, what, when, why, where, how)* are most important for the writer to know the answers to? What additional facts about the audience would be relevant in each of the following situations?

Jeff Daniels is a consulting engineer who has just been hired by a manufacturing plant to assess its entire production system. The head of the plant wants a full report from Jeff within thirty days.

What does Jeff need to know about the head of the plant as he works on his report? What other audiences should Jeff have in mind as he researches, organizes, and drafts his report?

Gayle Smith is a public relations officer with a large night club in Las Vegas. She has received a tourist's letter of complaint about the service and entertainment of the club, passed on to her by the editor of a local newspaper's ombudsman service. The newspaper editor invites Gayle to respond to the tourist's complaint, promising to print both the tourist's letter and Gayle's response in the paper.

What audiences does Gayle have to consider in her response? Which audience is most important to her? What does Gayle most want to know about her audiences as she considers her response?

AUTHOR

Still another rhetorical element the writer must carefully consider is his own stance, angle, or attitude toward the problem and the audience. In many cases the author purposely manipulates that stance so it most effectively communicates the purpose to the audience at hand.

Analyzing Author

To analyze one's own stance, the writer asks the same *who, what, why, when, where,* and *how* questions asked about the audience, but changes them to apply to the writer:

▶ Who am I?
  Intelligence and training?
  Biases?
  Attitudes?
  Values?

▶ What is my role as writer?
  Position?
  Responsibilities?
  Contacts with others?
  Degree of influence?

▶ When will I write the document?
  Under pressure?
  With enough time?
  Under close supervision?
  At the beginning or end of a project?

▶ Why will I write the document?
  To inform?
  To persuade?
  To review?
  To evaluate?

▶ Where will I write the document?
   In a quiet office?
   In a train or subway?
   In the library?
   At home?

▶ How will I review my own document?
   Quickly skimming only for main ideas?
   With careful attention to every detail?
   Eager to find fault or with sympathy?
   As part of a team or individually?

Manipulating Stance

Again, this list of author-based questions is by no means exhaustive. Many possibly relevant points about the author exist, and only in the context of a specific situation can the author identify those points. Only by considering the full situation can the author effectively begin to manipulate his stance, as in the following example.

> Charles Merriweather is a salesman for a national wood products distributor. He has been working for over a year on a multi-million dollar sale of lumber to a developer of a large housing project. At first it appeared that Charles had the sale, but recently he has seen signs that something may be wrong. Unknown to Charles, the developer has closed a deal with another supplier. Charles' boss, Harrison Buford, has just learned of the closed deal with the other distributor. To save both Charles and the company lost time and further embarrassment, Harrison must tell Charles that the deal is off.

Harrison begins his draft as follows:

```
    As president of Shaker Wood Products, I am ordering
you to drop the Coco Palms sale. We've spent over a year
on it with no result and I suspect that you're just being
strung along. Why don't you get on to something
productive?
```

In this draft Harrison takes the role of Charles' boss, which he is, and simply orders him off the sale. However, to do so without any clear reason makes him seem arbitrary and unfair. Such an approach will surely harm Charles' ability to make further sales, either by causing him to lose confidence or to get angry, or both.

Harrison needs to be a friend to Charles at this time, not a boss. Harrison wants to be positive and optimistic, so he reworks his draft to take a more upbeat authorial stance:

> After careful consideration, this office has decided we have an excellent opportunity to make an important breakthrough sale to Pioneer Homes. I've been getting some signals that suggest the Coco Palms deal is off anyway, as I believe you have, too. So let's put that one behind us for a while and concentrate on the Pioneer deal, which looks like a real hot one.

Using Author Analysis   Here are some examples for you to analyze in terms of authorial stance. How does the author want to come across in each situation?

Huong Doan worked for the U.S. government in Viet Nam and later moved to Los Angeles. She had not heard from her parents or brothers and sisters since the fall of Saigon. Now she has received a letter from her father. She writes to the U.S. Immigration and Naturalization Department requesting permanent visas for her entire family.

Frank Charles is the immigration officer who must write back to Huong Doan. What authorial stance does he want to adopt?

Tip Fenter is the office manager for a large department store. Recently his company expanded their offices by about 50 percent, adding a new wing to their building. Unfortunately, the roof of the new wing leaks. Despite two phone calls, Mr. Fenter has not been able to get the builder out to repair the roof.

Mr. Fenter decides to write a formal letter to the builder. What authorial stance should he take?

SUMMARY

Inherent in any problem requiring communication is a rhetorical situation, which includes the purpose for the communication, the audience to whom the communication is directed, and the authorial stance of the writer. Effective writers carefully analyze these three rhetorical elements and incorporate an accurate understanding of the specific purpose, audience, and authorial stance into their writing of the document. Furthermore, the effective writer realizes that these three elements of rhetoric do not stand in isolation, but are instead dynamically related. Modifying any one rhetorical element has an important impact on the other two.

EXERCISES

1. This chapter contains several sample writing situations. Pick one of them and draft the piece of writing required, supplying any necessary facts on your own. Record the changes you make as you go along, and explain each in terms of the underlying rhetorical elements.

    As a variation, create several sets of facts for a different situation and write a draft for each set. How does each set of facts cause you to modify the purpose, audience, and authorial stance in the document itself?

2. The following two letters are based on the situation involving Gayle Smith, the public relations officer for the Las Vegas night club, in the audience section of this chapter.

Dear Let Emma Help,

   I am furious. We had our tickets for Frank Sinatra's new show purchased ages in advance. Then last night my family and I still had to cool our heels in line at the Thunder Club for hours. We finally struggled to the front of the line half an hour after the show was supposed to start. We were rudely turned away from the door at that point on the grounds that all the tickets were sold out. When I showed him our <u>reserved</u> tickets, he said we showed up too late so our tickets were sold to someone else. Our vacation is ruined.

                                      Furiously yours,

                                      Clarence Tom

                                      Clarence Tom

Dear Emma,

   The Thunder Club strives to keep its customers happy. When I checked into Mr. Tom's complaint, which you passed on to me, I found he left a few important details out of his account.
   Our ticket office has two clearly marked lines, one for those still needing to buy tickets and one for those holding reserved seats. On the night in question, the opening of Mr. Sinatra's new show, many more people had reservations than showed up to buy tickets at the door.

Hence, the reservations line was much longer than the new ticket line. Mr. Tom was directed by one of our staff to the reservations line, but he insisted on getting in the shorter line. At ten minutes to show time we automatically make available the seats of any parties who have not claimed their places. Thus, people ahead of Mr. Tom in the new ticket line were sold tickets for those reserved seats not claimed in the reservation line. When Mr. Tom got to the front of the new ticket line all the unclaimed seats, including his own, had been sold.

We are sorry that Mr. Tom and his family missed the show. I will be happy to issue him complimentary tickets for Mr. Sinatra's show on any night that he and his family wish.

Sincerely,

Gayle Smith

Gayle Smith,
Public Relations,
The Thunder Club

Outline the rhetorical situation for each of these two passages—that is, define and characterize the purpose, audience, and author's attitude in each. Cite specific passages from the letters to support your analysis.

3. Able Plumbing is expanding its business and needs to buy several new typewriters. The purchasing department has gathered some information on the various typewriters available:

Model #	Cost	Service Contract	Delivery	Guarantee	Features
2700	$570	$100/year; covers repair parts only	3 days	2 years	basic; no frills
3100	$650	$200/year; covers all repair expenses	1 week	5 years	correcting key
4000	$770	$150/year; covers repair parts only	2 weeks	5 years	limited word processing; can type multiple copies of same letter

a. You are the sales manager of the company that markets model 2700. Write a sales letter to Able Plumbing. Or, do the same for either of the other models.
b. You are an employee of Able Plumbing. Write a memo to your boss recommending the purchase of model 2700. Or, do the same for either of the other two models.
c. You are the manager of Able Plumbing. You have selected model 2700. Write a letter to the sales manager of that company informing her of your choice. Or, do the same for either of the other two models.
d. You are the manager of Able Plumbing. Select one of the three models and write a letter to the sales managers of the other two companies informing them that you are not going to buy their products.

FOR FURTHER READING

Bitzer, Lloyd and Black, Edwin, eds. *The Prospect of Rhetoric*. Englewood Cliffs, N.J.: Prentice-Hall, 1971.

Cooper, Charles and Odell, Lee, eds. *Research on Composing: Points of Departure*. Urbana, Illinois: NCTE, 1978.

Ehninger, Douglas. "On Systems of Rhetoric." *Philosophy and Rhetoric* 1 (Summer 1968), 131–44.

Fogarty, Daniel. *Roots for a New Rhetoric*. New York: Russell and Russell, 1968.

Freedman, Aviva and Pringle, Ian, eds. *Reinventing the Rhetorical Tradition*. Conway, Arkansas: L & S Books, 1980.

Graves, Robert, ed. *Rhetoric and Composition: A Sourcebook for Teachers*. Rochelle Park, N.J.: Hayden, 1976.

Johannesen, Richard, ed. *Contemporary Theories of Rhetoric: Selected Readings*. New York: Harper and Row, 1971.

Joos, Martin. *The Five Clocks*. New York: Harcourt, Brace, and World, 1961.

Kinneavy, James. *A Theory of Discourse*. Englewood Cliffs, N.J.: Prentice-Hall, 1971.

Larson, Richard. "Discovery through Questioning: A Plan for Teaching Rhetorical Invention." *College English* 30 (November 1968), 126–34.

Murphy, James, ed. *The Rhetorical Tradition and Modern Writing*. New York: MLA, 1982.

Winterowd, W. Ross, ed. *Contemporary Rhetoric: A Conceptual Background with Readings*. New York: Harcourt Brace Jovanovich, 1975.

3

Molding Form to Fit Audience

W hen a person feels like eating, he goes to a restaurant. The particular restaurant a diner chooses depends on many circumstances: how much time and money he has, how fancy he wants it to be, and a host of other factors. But no matter what restaurant the diner enters, he expects to find certain things: tables, chairs, napkins, utensils, cooks, and, of course, food.

> Readers are like diners in a restaurant; they come in expecting certain general features.

Later in this chapter, you will look at some of the specialized writing formats typically used by writers in business, industry, and government, and determine the appropriate audience for each. First the discussion focuses on the general format necessary for on-the-job writing.

THE GENERIC DOCUMENT AND ITS PARTS

Figure 3–1 defines each part of the generic document and indicates each part's general location and length. The figure indicates relative length only—the position of a document's parts and the proportion of those parts to the whole remain the same, however, no matter how long the document, whether one or five hundred pages.

With these basic relationships established, now consider each of these parts and its use in more detail.

The Abstract

The abstract, sometimes called the executive summary, condenses the entire document and is placed at the beginning, before the document itself. The two main audiences for the abstract are researchers or reviewers, and administrators. Anyone having to gather sources on a given subject appreciates the abstract because she can get the document's main idea and major supporting points in a paragraph or a page. If any of this information looks interesting or relevant, the reader can then read the full document, knowing she will find useful information. If, on the other hand, the reader does not find the abstract interesting or relevant, she may skip the document without worrying about missing something important. The abstract allows a reader to evaluate large numbers of sources in a short time.

The administrator also focuses on the abstract, but for different reasons. Charged with making big money decisions quickly, the administrator's two

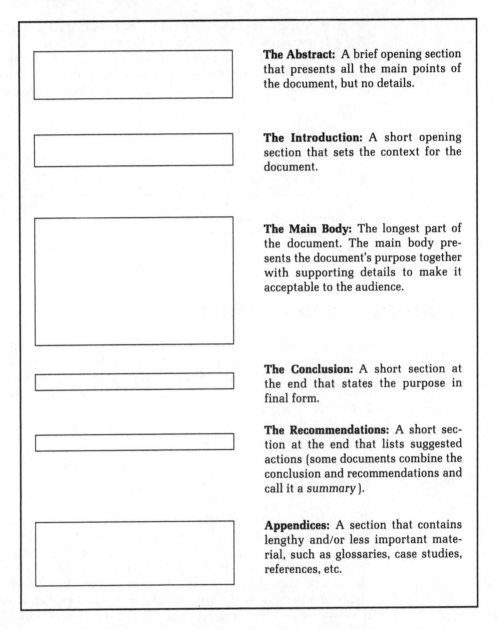

The Abstract: A brief opening section that presents all the main points of the document, but no details.

The Introduction: A short opening section that sets the context for the document.

The Main Body: The longest part of the document. The main body presents the document's purpose together with supporting details to make it acceptable to the audience.

The Conclusion: A short section at the end that states the purpose in final form.

The Recommendations: A short section at the end that lists suggested actions (some documents combine the conclusion and recommendations and call it a *summary*).

Appendices: A section that contains lengthy and/or less important material, such as glossaries, case studies, references, etc.

Figure 3–1. The Generic Document and Its Parts.

catch words are *time* and *money*. The administrator depends on the abstract to give him enough information to make a decision, but to present it briefly enough for him to make that decision quickly. In most cases, an administrator does not read the whole document. In fact, the administrator often reads *only* the abstract.

These two readers' needs determine the abstract's two crucial requirements: completeness and brevity. In the abstract, both the document's main point and supporting points must be clear. It neither provides details nor indicates general areas of interest. Instead, the abstract condenses. Two sample abstract sentences follow, along with comments on their effectiveness.

> This paper will examine the nesting habits of the
> mallard.

This sentence introduces an area of interest rather than condenses what the document actually says. An abstract should state the specific points *about* mallard nesting habits made in the document. It should not merely indicate the area discussed. An improved version might be

> The mallard makes small secluded nests with plenty of
> water and cover nearby.

Here is another example of a passage from an abstract.

> In 1976 the U.S. Fish and Wildlife Service's Animal
> Damage Control program spent $8.9 million in seventeen
> western states to kill 83,790 coyotes. During this same
> year, 3,200 ranchers filed loss reports with rates above
> 5 percent, 43,200 reported loss rates below 5 percent,
> and 29,500 reported no losses at all. Of the 8.87 million
> sheep in the U.S. that year, coyote losses were estimated
> at 4.2 percent.

These details belong in the main body. The abstract should stick to main points. An improved version might be

> In 1976 the U.S. Fish and Wildlife Service spent a lot of
> money to kill a small number of coyotes bothering a small
> number of ranchers.

One can write an effective abstract by reducing each paragraph or section of the original document to one sentence. The writer then combines these sentences, using appropriate transitions. To make the abstract approximately 250 words (the standard length), the writer reduces every *paragraph* to a sentence (for short reports), or every *section* to a sentence (for longer reports).

By reducing paragraphs or sections to sentences and arranging these sentences in a hierarchy, the writer can generate different versions of the same abstract, varying in length and level of detail. Sentences that make specific points are indented to the right of sentences that make more general points. This system generated an abstract for a short article by J.B.S. Haldane on size.

The paragraph by paragraph reduction of this article yields the following sentences arranged in a general to specific hierarchy from left to right:

1. Different animals are naturally different sizes, each of which automatically carries with it a different form.

    2. For instance, a man sixty feet tall would weigh a thousand times as much as a man six feet tall, but his bones would be only ten times bigger; hence, he could not support his own weight without a change in form.   .

    3. To use an example from zoology, a gazelle, a rhinocerous, and a giraffe are in the same order, but each has a body and legs adjusted to carry its own weight, given its height.

        4. Air resistance is proportional to surface area, not to weight; hence small animals are not injured by a fall.

        5. Surface tension, which coats an object with water, affects small animals much more than it does large ones, because small animals have a much larger surface-to-weight ratio.

    6. A very small animal can get by with simple bodily systems; a tenfold increase in size requires new forms to serve the thousandfold increase in volume.

    7. The larger one becomes, the more complicated one's bodily systems must be to serve the larger bulk.

8. A given form can only increase in both size and efficiency for a short while before an entirely new form is required to serve the new size.

For a short abstract (probably the case for such a short article), the writer draws a vertical line to the right of the numbers representing the first level. The resulting abstract combines sentences 1 and 8:

```
Different animals are naturally different sizes, each of
which automatically carries with it a different form. A
given form can only increase in both size and efficiency
for a short while before an entirely new form is required
to serve the new size.
```

On being the right size

J.B.S. Haldane

The most obvious differences between different animals are differences in size, but for some reason the zoologists have paid singularly little attention to them. In a large textbook of zoology before me I find no indication that the eagle is larger than the sparrow, or the hippopotamus bigger than the hare, though some grudging admissions are made in the case of the mouse and the whale. But yet it is easy to show that a hare could not be as large as a hippopotamus, or a whale as small as a herring. For every type of animal there is a most convenient size, and a large change in size inevitably carries with it a change of form.

Let us take the most obvious of possible cases, and consider a giant man sixty feet high—about the height of Giant Pope and Giant Pagan in the illustrated *Pilgrims Progress* of my childhood. These monsters were not only ten times as high as Christian, but ten times as wide and ten times as thick, so that their total weight was a thousand times his, or about eighty to ninety tons. Unfortunately the cross sections of their bones were only a hundred times those of Christian, so that every square inch of giant bone had to support ten times the weight born by a square inch of human bone. As the human thigh-bone breaks under about ten times the human weight, Pope and Pagan would have broken their thighs every time they took a step. This was doubtless why they were sitting down in the picture I remember. But it lessens one's respect for Christian and Jack the Giant Killer.

To turn to zoology, suppose that a gazelle, a graceful little creature with long thin legs, is to become large, it will break its bones unless it does one of two things. It may make its legs short and thick, like the rhinoceros, so that every pound of weight has still about the same area of bone to support it. Or it can compress its body and stretch out

its legs obliquely to gain stability, like the giraffe. I mention these two beasts because they happen to belong to the same order as the gazelle, and both are quite successful mechanically, being remarkably fast runners.

Gravity, a mere nuisance to Christian, was a terror to Pope, Pagan, and Despair. To the mouse and any smaller animals it presents practically no dangers. You can drop a mouse down a thousand-yard mine shaft; and on arriving at the bottom, it gets a slight shock and walks away, provided that the ground is fairly soft. A rat is killed, a man is broken, a horse splashes. For the resistance presented to movement by the air is proportional to the surface of the moving object. Divide an animal's length, breadth, and height each by ten; its weight is reduced to a thousandth, but its surface only to a hundredth. So the resistance to falling in the case of the small animal is relatively ten times greater than the driving force.

An insect, therefore, is not afraid of gravity; it can fall without danger, and can cling to the ceiling with remarkably little trouble. It can go in for elegant and fantastic forms of support like that of the daddylonglegs. But there is a force which is as formidable to an insect as gravitation to the mammal. This is surface tension. A man coming out of a bath carries with him a film of water of about one-fiftieth of an inch in thickness. This weighs roughly a pound. A wet mouse has to carry about its own weight of water. A wet fly has to lift many times its own weight, and as everyone knows, a fly once wetted by water or any other liquid is in a very serious position indeed. An insect going for a drink is in as great danger as a man leaning out over a precipice in search of food. If it once falls into the grip of the surface tension of the water—that is to say, gets wet—it is likely to remain so until it drowns. A few insects, such as water-beetles, contrive to be unwettable; the majority keep well away from their drink by means of a long proboscis.

Of course tall land animals have other difficulties. They have to pump their blood to greater heights than a man, and, therefore, require a larger blood pressure and tougher blood-vessels. A great many men die from burst arteries, especially in the brain, and this danger is presumably still greater for an elephant or a giraffe. But animals of all kinds find difficulties in size for the following reason. A typical small animal, say a microscopic worm or rotifer, has a smooth skin through which all the oxygen it requires can soak in, a straight gut with sufficient surface to absorb its food, and a single kidney. Increase its dimensions tenfold in every direction, and its weight is increased a thousand times, so that if it is to use its muscles as efficiently as its miniature counterpart, it will need a thousand times as much food and oxygen per day and will excrete a thousand times as much of waste products.

Now if its shape is unaltered its surface will increase only a hundredfold, and ten times as much oxygen must enter per minute through each square millimetre of skin, ten times as much food through each square millimetre of intestine. When a limit is reached to their absorptive powers their surface has to be increased by some special device. For example, a part of the skin may be drawn out into tufts to make gills or pushed in to make lungs, thus increasing the oxygen-absorbing surface in proportion to the animal's bulk. A man, for example, has a hundred square yards of lung. Similarly, the gut, instead of being smooth and straight, becomes coiled and develops a velvety surface, and other organs increase in complication. The higher animals are not larger than the lower because they are more complicated. They are more complicated because they are larger. Just the same is true of plants. The simplest plants, such as the green algae growing in stagnant water or on the bark of trees, are mere round cells. The higher plants increase their surface by putting out leaves and roots. Comparative anatomy is largely the story of the struggle to increase surface in proportion to volume.

Some of the methods of increasing the surface are useful up to a point, but not capable of a very wide adaptation. For example, while vertebrates carry the oxygen from the gills or lungs all over the body in the blood, insects take air directly to every part of their body by tiny blind tubes called tracheae which open to the surface at many different points. Now, although by their breathing movements they can renew the air in the outer part of the tracheal system, the oxygen has to penetrate the finer branches by means of diffusion. Gases can diffuse easily through very small distances, not many times larger than the average length travelled by a gas molecule between collisions with other molecules. But when such vast journeys—from the point of view of a molecule—as a quarter of an inch have to be made, the process becomes slow. So the portions of an insect's body more than a quarter of an inch from the air would always be short of oxygen. In consequence hardly any insects are much more than half an inch thick. Land crabs are built on the same general plan as insects, but are much clumsier. Yet like ourselves they carry oxygen around in their blood, and are therefore able to grow far larger than any insects. If the insects had hit on a plan for driving air through their tissues instead of letting it soak in, they might well have become as large as lobsters, though other considerations would have prevented them from becoming as large as man.

For a longer abstract, the writer moves the vertical line to the right of the numbers representing the next level of abstraction. The resulting abstract includes sentences 1, 2, 3, 6, 7, and 8:

```
Different animals are naturally different sizes, each of
which automatically carries with it a different form. For
instance, a man sixty feet tall would weigh a thousand
times as much as a man six feet tall, but his bones would
be only ten times bigger; hence, he could not support his
own weight without a change in form. To use an example
from zoology, a gazelle, a rhinocerous, and a giraffe are
in the same order, but each has a body and legs adjusted
to carry its own weight, given its height. A very small
animal can get by with simple bodily systems; a tenfold
increase in size requires new forms to serve the
thousandfold increase in volume. The larger one becomes,
the more complicated one's bodily systems must be to
serve the larger bulk. A given form can only increase in
both size and efficiency for a short while before an
entirely new form is required to serve the new size.
```

For an even longer abstract, the writer puts all the sentences together. This system allows the writer to adjust the abstract's length while preserving the original document's most important parts.

EXERCISE

Select any article or book part not abstracted anywhere else (to your knowledge). Write an abstract for it. Hand in a copy of the article or book part with your abstract.

The Introduction

The first item in the document itself is usually the introduction, which prepares the reader for the main body's details. Most introductions have four main parts:

1. *The Interest Getter:* A brief item designed to involve the reader with the subject. Anecdotes, striking statistics, questions, and quotations are all effective interest getters.

2. *The Background:* Helpful or even necessary information that does not belong in the main body of the report. Such information should not extend over 10 percent of the document's total length. (Lengthy background material should appear in an appendix.) Historical sections, definitions of terms, and settings of scope are examples of background material.

3. *The Purpose:* The main point of the whole document. The purpose is stated clearly and briefly, at either the start or the end of the introduction.

4. *The Plan of Development:* A brief prediction of the major sections in the main body of the report, usually presented as the last item in the introduction.

The following introduction illustrates these four parts.

```
     Trying to keep abreast of rapid developments in the
technical and scientific fields challenges the
educational community. Being current is nowhere more
important than in the high school physics course. A
recent effort to modernize high school physics courses
uses lasers to demonstrate basic physics principles. This
report explores the feasibility of building and using a
low-cost home-built laser to demonstrate basic physics
principles. This report includes three sections: laser
theory and operation, requirements necessary for using
any laser to demonstrate basic physics principles, and a
comparison of four low-cost home-built lasers to see
which one, if any, best suits this application.
```

At the end of a brief introduction, the reader should know what the document aims to do, any necessary background information, and the plan of development.

EXERCISE

1. Identify the exact passages in the sample introduction that fulfill each of the four parts of an introduction.

2. Write an introduction for any one of the writing situations presented earlier in this book. Remember to take into account the rhetorical demands of the situation you choose.

3. Write an introduction for a subject of your own choice. Remember, you cannot do this successfully until you have analyzed the situation and generated an appropriate strategy to fit the rhetorical demands of your document.

Many writers confuse the introduction with the abstract. The abstract *condenses* the whole document, whereas the introduction *predicts* its shape and content. Unlike the introduction, the abstract includes any recommendations and conclusions. The abstract aims at audiences who may not read the whole document, whereas the introduction aims at audiences who plan to read it all.

The Main Body

The document's main body will be analyzed in detail in the next chapter.

The Summary

A document may end with only conclusions, with only recommendations, or with both (a summary).

A conclusion reemphasizes the document's main point, without making recommendations. It is usually not aimed at an administrative audience, which would have read the conclusions in the abstract. The conclusion states the document's purpose, recapitulates its major supporting points, and thus reaffirms the successful achievement of the purpose. The report about using lasers to demonstrate basic physics principles ended with this conclusion:

```
        A low-cost home-built laser is a feasible way to
demonstrate basic physics principles in the high school
classroom. Specifically, the dye laser meets all six
requirements for this application: it produces a visible,
continuous, and low-intensity beam, and it is portable,
cheap, and easy to construct.
```

The recommendations section of a document is usually reserved for the end, and lists the actions that the document's main body argues for. If the writer of the report about lasers and basic physics principles wanted his report to spur the school district to buy or build a laser, the report might end with a recommendation section:

```
    1. The Hart Prairie District should budget $100 to build
       a dye laser for introductory physics classes this
       fall.
    2. The Hart Prairie District should contact teachers
       interested in using this laser so that scheduling and
       storage can be arranged for maximum efficiency and
       safety.
    3. The Hart Prairie District should hire a competent
       builder to begin work on the laser as soon as the $100
       is approved.
```

By putting these two sections together, the writer summarizes the report:

<u>Summary</u>

<u>Conclusion</u>

A low-cost home-built laser is a feasible way to demonstrate basic physics principles in a high school classroom. Specifically, the dye laser meets all six requirements for this application: it produces a visible, continuous, and low-intensity beam, and it is portable, cheap, and easy to construct.

<u>Recommendations</u>

1. The Hart Prairie District should budget $100 to build a dye laser for introductory physics classes this fall.
2. The Hart Prairie School District should contact teachers interested in using this laser so that scheduling and storage can be arranged for maximum efficiency and safety.
3. The Hart Prairie District should hire a competent builder to begin work on the laser as soon as the $100 is approved.

If the writer were aiming at an administrative audience, the entire summary would appear up front, in the abstract.

The Appendix

The final section of a document, the appendix or appendices, usually contains materials too long and/or too unimportant to be included in the main body. Such items generally function as additional reading, rather than as an integral part of the report itself. Many readers do not read an appendix at all, but some, especially those interested in all the smallest details, will pore over it.

From one to all of the following items may appear in an appendix section:

- Bibliography
- Glossary
- Questionnaires used as part of the research for the document
- Case studies
- Technical data
- Schematics and flow charts

An appendix can include almost anything the writer thinks some readers might find relevant. Except for the bibliography, any item in the appendix could appear in the report's main body, but in an abbreviated form. Excessive length and relevance to only some readers qualify an item for the appendix instead of the main body. For example, the report on lasers had two appendices, a bibliography and a ten-page, fully detailed technical description of a dye laser. Most readers did not need those two items, but some did. The technical description was particularly lengthy, and in the main body, it would have slowed down many readers. Such a description interests the laser expert or the technician hired to build one, but neither of these readers is the main audience for the report.

The generic document as outlined illustrates the basic parts found in a document. But rarely does a generic document fit an actual writing situation exactly, just as rarely does a diner enter a "food" restaurant. Instead, when one feels like Chinese food, one goes to a Chinese restaurant. Because certain types of food are typical of Chinese restaurants, one expects to find them there. In other words, each sort of restaurant, and each sort of writing, has its own menu by which eaters and readers can predict what is coming, and be guided in their eating and reading accordingly.

> The job of a writer is to know her audience and to prepare a document appropriate to that audience.

AUDIENCE TYPES

In business, industry, and government, various writing situations exist (comparable to various sorts of restaurants) that have certain forms (comparable to different dishes at a restaurant) associated with them. When the reader recognizes a certain situation, he expects the sorts of documents often associated with that situation. On the other hand, the writer must recognize the situation and the audience and prepare the document usually associated with both. Four typical writing situations and their usual audiences follow.

The Novice

The novice is a beginner. Novices read for information, because they know very little about a subject. They often read simply out of curiosity. However, people taking their first jobs in a field, or people promoted to positions broader than their training, are required to read material beyond their knowledge, and thus read at least part of the time as novices. The word does not imply a pejorative: everyone is a novice in most subjects. Readers need to know when they are novices and read accordingly, and writers need to know when their readers are novices and write accordingly. In the oil business, a consumer filling up her car is a novice.

The Administrator

The administrator reads to make decisions. Decision makers usually decide not only what they themselves are going to do, but also what many other people are going to do. The administrator is a busy person whose administrative reading is strictly business. Decision makers are influenced by the cost of what they read about. They do not like decisions that cost money, but given the right motivation (the chance to make more money by spending some), they decide to spend. The writer must realize, however, that sometimes an administrator is also a novice about a subject's specifics, even though he has to make a decision about that subject. In the oil business, an executive vice-president, charged with making sure the oil company makes a profit, is an administrator.

The Expert

The expert is the advanced thinker, totally up-to-date on a particular subject. Because of the time and effort required, few people are experts in more than one or two things. (Unfortunately many people *think* they are experts in everything. Often they fool not only themselves but others, too.) About her own subject, the expert is much more knowledgeable than the novice and much less pragmatic than the administrator. The expert generally takes more interest in theory than in its application. In the oil business, a geologist, who knows how to locate oil but whose chief concern is not how much it costs to get it out, is an expert.

The Operator

The operator does the work assigned by others (usually administrators). He likes to follow directions and takes pride in doing a job right. On the job, the operator reads not for interest, profit, or knowledge, but strictly for what to do and how to do it. The operator does not want responsibility or choices. He wants unambiguous instructions. In the oil business, an oil rig laborer, running the machinery according to instructions, is an operator.

These four audiences represent extremes. In a real writing situation, the writer must remember that such categories may overlap. For instance, one person may read a document from several points of view, or a single document may be read by several readers, each reading from a different point of view. The final document, then, must serve all these readers, or at least establish priorities among their needs.

EXERCISE

The distinctions among these four general audiences are summarized in table 3-1 (see pages 48 and 49).

Continue table 3-1 by filling in the blanks after each question and under each audience. In doing so, you will begin to sketch out the specific forms associated with each one. Be prepared to defend your answers.

Answers to these questions show how much the audiences differ. These different audiences expect forms geared to their needs. Specific forms and their typical audiences are the subject of chapter 4.

SUMMARY

A general format for reports includes the following sections.

- The Abstract: A brief condensation of the entire report, placed before the document itself, where busy executives and researchers can read it instead of the entire document.
- The Introduction: Beginning the document itself, it prepares the reader for the document's main body. It usually consists of an interest getter, a background statement, a purpose, and a plan of development.
- The Main Body: The lengthy section in the middle of the report that contains the evidence and arguments to support the document's purpose.
- The Conclusion: A restatement of the main and supporting points at the end of the report.
- The Recommendations: A short numbered section listing the specific actions the writer wants the reader to follow.
- The Summary: A combination of the Conclusion and the Recommendations.
- The Appendix: A section following the report itself, containing material that is lengthy, of interest to few readers, or extremely detailed or technical.

The writer should consider using special forms appropriate to particular situations and audiences. The writer may address

- The Novice, a reader without much prior experience of or knowledge about the subject.
- The Administrator, the busy executive who reads quickly to make decisions.
- The Expert, a well-informed reader who reads to increase his knowledge and expertise.
- The Operator, a reader who follows others' instructions and reads to find out what to do.

Table 3-1. Audience Types.

Question	READER			
	Novice	Administrator	Expert	Operator
1. Who is audience?	Beginner; Layman	Decision maker; Executive	Scientist; Devotee	Doer; Technician
2. Why will they read my report?	Job requirement; Interest	To make a decision	For more knowledge	To find out what to do
3. Do they need introductory or background material?				
4. Do they need definition of terms?				
5. What level and type of language is needed?				

Table 3-1. continued.

6. Do they need illustrations? If so, what kinds?				
7. What level of detail is needed?				
8. What parts of generic document should be used?				
9. How should report be organized? What should main idea be?				
10. What result does my report aim for?				

EXERCISE

Find several pieces of writing, using newspapers, magazines, technical journals, or documents from a job you have held. For each piece of writing, answer the following questions:

1. What is the context of the piece of writing? Specifically, what is the purpose, who is the audience, and who is the author?

2. Do the purpose, audience, and author fit together smoothly? Justify and/or suggest improvements in any part of the document.

3. Does the piece of writing use any of the forms discussed in this chapter, such as introduction, appendix, etc.? If so, are they used effectively and appropriately? What improvements would you suggest?

4. How effective is the document, judged by the criteria listed in chapter 1? What specific improvements would you suggest?

FOR FURTHER READING

Adams, James. *Conceptual Blockbusting: A Pleasurable Guide to Better Problem Solving.* San Francisco: W.H. Freeman, 1974.

Cowan, Gregory and Cowan, Elizabeth. *Writing.* New York: John Wiley and Sons, 1980.

Cowley, Malcolm, ed. *Writers at Work.* New York: Viking, 1958.

Crowhurst, Marion and Piche, Gene. "Audience and Mode of Discourse Effects on Syntactic Complexity in Writing at Two Grade Levels." *Research in the Teaching of English* 13 (May 1979): 101–09.

D'Angelo, Frank. *Process and Thought in Composition.* 2nd ed. Cambridge, Massachusetts: Winthrop, 1980.

Faigley, Lester. "Generative Rhetoric as a Way of Increasing Syntactic Fluency." *College Composition and Communication* 30 (May 1979): 176–81.

Gorrell, Robert, ed. *Rhetoric: Theories for Application.* Champaign, Illinois: NCTE, 1967.

Halloran, Stephen. "Classical Rhetoric for the Engineering Student." *Journal of Technical Writing and Communication* 1 (1971): 17–24.

Moffett, James. *Teaching the Universe of Discourse.* Boston: Houghton Mifflin, 1968.

Sawyer, Thomas. "Real Life Writing and Speaking: Not Hot-House Exercises." *IEEE Transactions on Education* E-17 (August 1974): 164–66.

Sparrow, W. Keats and Cunningham, Donald, eds. *The Practical Craft: Readings for Business and Technical Writers.* Boston: Houghton Mifflin, 1978.

Wells, Walter. *Communications in Business.* Belmont, Calif.: Wadsworth, 1977.

4

Basic Formats
for
Communication

A s chapter 3 showed, writing in business, industry, and government often incorporates certain familiar features. Not all types of writing use these features, but many technical reports do.

> A trained reader looks for standard and expected patterns, and a trained writer provides them.

Much school writing may also fit one of these familiar patterns, so that once you master the patterns, your writing efforts should become less troublesome and more productive.

Chapter 3 examined the typical parts of any report. This chapter presents four types of reports often used in business, industry, and government writing. Each type and a specific example of each is presented. In each case, a brief analysis of how and why the specific example varies slightly from the generalized form is also presented. Even more specialized documents considered in units 2 and 3 incorporate the underlying patterns detailed in this chapter.

THE THESIS REPORT

In a thesis report, the writer establishes the report's structure and scope in a central statement that he supports throughout the document. This central statement is by definition arguable, neither an obvious matter of indisputable fact nor a mere opinion that cannot be successfully defended or verified. For instance, the statement, "The process of refining crude oil into usable products is difficult, time consuming, and costly," is a simple and undisputed matter of fact; it might work for a long, simply factual school paper, but would be superfluous in the working world. Or the statement might serve as the thesis for a description of an oil refinery to a lay audience or novices. However, if the audience wanting a description of an oil refinery were potential investors, this thesis would not work because that audience implies a specific rhetorical purpose with many limitations and special demands. Similarly, using the description for public relations would imply a specialized document, not at all like a typical school report.

At the other extreme, a statement such as "The oil industry does not care about the consumer," is an opinion impossible to prove. How can a writer prove caring or not caring? Such a statement is an emotional charge, not a supportable thesis.

The writer supports the thesis with a variety of evidence spread fairly evenly through the text. Such factual evidence as statistics, professional opinions, surveys, observations, experiments, and all sorts of test data can be used to support a thesis. In short, the author organizes the strongest possible evidence into the pattern most supportive of the thesis. (For more on this point, see chapter 13.) The author also blends her remarks smoothly into these documented factual materials. (For more on this point, see chapter 14.) The thesis report is a well-reasoned and supported argument. The facts supporting the thesis are based on carefully gathered and documented information. The thesis itself and the author's commentary running through the report are interpretations and conclusions drawn from the available facts.

The article "Things Go Better with Coconuts" is an example of a thesis report. It appeared in a specialized journal dealing exclusively with nutrition. Many readers of this journal, administrators concerned with nutrition problems on a worldwide scale, face problems in their own parts of the world similar to those described in the article. Thus, the writer wants not only to describe her solution to her problem, but also to suggest that similar solutions might work on similar problems anywhere in the world.

EXERCISE

1. What is the thesis of "Things Go Better with Coconuts"?

2. What arguments does the author use?

3. What is some of the specific evidence provided?

4. What other arguments or evidence might the author consider adding to support the thesis?

5. What seems to be the rhetorical situation behind the article? What does the writer do to fit the article to its audience?

6. How effective is this article in terms of the criteria listed in chapter 1? What are its particular strong and weak points? How could it be improved?

THE REPORT OF ORIGINAL RESEARCH

The report of original research includes a central statement of a research problem and a methodology, often in the form of a study or experiment designed to solve that problem. After the problem itself is fully explained, sometimes a review of the literature, or an account of various previously completed studies on the same or a closely related problem, is presented. This section places the writer's approach in context. Following the discussion of previous work, the writer presents his own method of studying the problem. The remaining sections usually include results, where the writer describes the factual outcome of

Things go better with coconuts—Program strategies in Micronesia

Nancy Rody

Politics, economics and cultural traditions are considered factors in projects to increase consumption of indigenous foods.

Summary

A two-year nutrition education program was initiated in the U.S. Trust Territory of the Pacific Islands with the objective of promoting the increased utilization of indigenous foods and discouraging the use of expensive and nonessential imported foods. Program emphasis was placed on practical methods of changing nutrition practices and attitudes. Motivational techniques employed resulted in the reduction of soft drink importation and an increase in breastfeeding. Extent of behavioral change was measured directly by tax receipt data for soft drink consumption and through clinic observation for changes in infant feeding practices. By enlisting the active participation of honored persons and institutions and recognizing popular political views, support was achieved which enhanced efforts to modify food behavior through change in personal values.

PARADISE LOST

In the isles of Micronesia where island peoples once lived an idyllic existence reaping the fruits of the land and the sea, Micronesians now consume fish which is caught in waters off their shores, frozen, transhipped to the United States or Japan for canning, and sent back to the islands to be sold for very high prices (1).

Micronesia, with a population of approximately 120,000, is a U.S. Trust Territory comprised of 2,000 islands scattered across the Western Pacific. Twenty-five years ago most indigenous peoples

lived primarily on a crop gathering and fishing subsistence level. The traditional diet appeared to have been quite adequate as evidenced by the reported general good health of the population at that time (2).

Interviews with district physicians indicate that nutrition problems are on the increase, particularly in those areas undergoing rapid urbanization. A 1975 nutrition study in the populous district of Ponape surveyed the problems in detail. The report indicated that although at birth and shortly after, most of the children are of average weight, by two years of age 50% of these children are below average weight for that age. Ponape children are infested with a great number of intestinal parasites which take a significant amount of whatever food the child consumes. In 1975 about one-third of all hospitalized children were infested with intestinal parasites; and just under one-half of all the children had a respiratory infection, quite often a common result of roundworm infestation. Additionally, these children are also subject to nonspecific dysenteries with resultant dehydration. In Ponape, one or two children die of kwashiorkor each year, and many more suffer from the effects of chronic undernutrition. Ponape children grow and develop slowly, are chronically ill, and have little resistance to infectious disease (3).

The World Health Organization has reported an increasing prevalence of diabetes mellitus around the world, particularly in areas where there has been economic development (4). Diabetes is the third leading medical cause of death in the Northern Marianas, the most "modern" of the districts of Micronesia (5).

A health screening in 1977 of all children in Palau, the district largest in land mass, indicates greater occurrence of dental caries for young children as contrasted with their older siblings. Incidence of one or more caries was 12% for high school freshmen, 23% for children in grades one through eight, and 47% among preschoolers (6). During the same year a similar study was conducted in the Northern Marianas, and the findings there were very much the same as those in Palau. Children six to seventeen years old averaged 1.4 teeth extracted for each filling placed (7).

The increase in nutrition-related health problems is thought to be the result of migration from outlying islands to heavily populated district centers where western commercial influence is dominant and wages are low in relation to imported food prices. Because of the high price of canned food and relatively low salaries, families are sometimes only able to buy rice, but no fish or meat (8). There is little concept of budgeting, and money is often wasted on low nutrient density foods such as sugar and soft drinks. The Director of Health Services for Micronesia has indicated that malnutrition may soon become the most extensive and serious health problem affecting the preschool child in Micronesia (9).

Despite widespread concern about nutrition-related disease and malnutrition, little has been done throughout the area to put into effect any comprehensive plan to alleviate the problem other than some well-intentioned, stop-gap government group feeding programs that serve imported foods. These programs have real potential for abuse, and they tend to undermine traditional values of cultural integrity and self-reliance in Micronesia.

NUTRITION EDUCATION BEGUN

A nutrition education program was initiated through the Yap District Health Department with the objective of promoting the increased utilization of locally produced foods and discouraging the use of expensive and nonessential imported foods. Yap District is a group of 17 inhabited islands located in the Western Caroline Islands of Micronesia. The District consists of two distinct groups of islands: the four high volcanic islands of Yap proper and the numerous low sandy coral atolls of Yap's outer islands. Each of these two areas has a distinct culture unique in language, dress, social structure, and problems. The district center, Colonia, is located in the central high island group and is the site of the island port, governmental offices, hospital, major stores, mis-

sions, and schools. Roads are limited, of poor quality, and may be impassable in the rainy season. Many villages are not connected to the road and can only be reached by foot. One island is accessible by boat only, and another by a lengthy log footbridge from the main island. Life centers around the village, the extended family, and its lands. More than any other district of Micronesia, the approximately 7,500 people of Yap depend on the land and sea for their food staples: fish, coconuts, taro and other tubers, various types of bananas and seasonal fruits. In recent years there has been a steady migration to the Yap district center, the focal point of the developing cash economy. Food imports were found to have increased 253% in Yap over the two-year period, 1974 to 1976 (10). However, the Yapese consider themselves the elite of Micronesia in that they still place high value on the preservation of their traditional culture, including long revered food customs. They are a very conservative people, inclined to look cautiously on outside influence.

The outer islands are largely coral and sand with limited agricultural possibilities. Staple foods are coconut and breadfruit. Since these islands are subject to periodic typhoons which heavily damage breadfruit and coconut trees, the sea has been the most reliable source of food until the advent of trading ships laden with rice. The closest outer island to Yap proper is 100 miles; the farthest is 500 miles. The district's erratic field-trip ship service is the only form of inter-island transportation. This government operated ship stops at the islands several times each year to transfer supplies and permit officials such as physicians to visit.

Mean annual income is less than $2,000 per household, averaging ten to thirteen members. The prices of most imported foods are prohibitively high. A 1976 survey indicated that imported food prices in Yap's district center average 74% above retail food prices in Guam, and that Guam's food costs, in turn, are higher than any of the 50 U.S. states (11). Prices in village stores are higher than in the district center due to additional transportation costs and because sales are usually made on credit. The most popular imported foods are polished rice, sugar, soft drinks, bread made from bleached flour, noodles, and canned fish. Because many of these foods are imported from Eastern countries, they are not enriched with vitamins and minerals lost in processing.

Costs of local agricultural and fisheries products are very low in relation to imported food prices, but these commodities have not been readily available. The Trust Territory Government is attempting to develop cash crops, such as copra and black pepper, for export, but no program has been initiated to reduce the importation of foods.

An average of 95% of the Trust Territory budget is derived from U.S. grants (12). This situation is reflected in a serious imbalance of external trade. Exports, primarily copra, have not kept pace (1951—$2.2 million, 1976—$4.8 million) with the rapidly increasing rate of imports (1951—$8.9 million, 1976—$38.4 million) (13). Most of these imports consist of consumer goods, particularly foodstuffs, much of which could be produced locally. The United Nations Visiting Mission to the Trust Territory reported that "such a trend in no way encourages the population to make maximum use of the Territory's own resources but leads it to rely increasingly on the purchase of foreign products, financed from the outside. Obviously, this situation has repercussions at the political level" (12).

The nutrition education program was implemented in Yap by a single nutritionist and has been in effect for two years. It has attempted to couple conventional educational techniques—instruction with posters, flannelgraphs, and flipcharts—with more unorthodox methods that together will achieve the desired change in food attitudes and practices.

THINGS GO BETTER WITH COCONUTS

A nutrition project with the objective to promote the popularity of coconut juice instead of soft drinks was developed in 1975. This objective was chosen due to the great concern of Yap District physicians and dentists over the high sugar intake which they observed throughout the local population. Individual diet histories accomplished by the nutritionist in Yap indicated that it was not at all unusual for an average Yapese adult to consume daily several soft drinks and as much as a half pound of sugar mixed with coffee, tea, milk, or plain water. The health staff felt that this intake was contributing to the increasing incidences of diabetes, obesity, and dental caries.

Project promotion materials included a locally produced comic book and bar graph charts illustrating the relative nutritive value of coconut juice and soft drinks. Attention was given in these materials to the fact that the sale of coconuts, a local product, is advantageous to the Yapese economy. This economic incentive to realize proportionately greater profits was discussed individually with storekeepers and potential coconut suppliers.

The largest grocery store in Colonia agreed to stock coconuts and to display posters that promoted drinking-coconuts alongside advertisements for soft drinks in the store. Other stores soon followed suit and made their own signs. The island's only newspaper carried a photo of coconuts with a purloined caption indicating that they are "real" while a well-known soft drink was captioned, "It's the artificial thing!" Most young Yapese adults are literate, and the slogans soon became popular catch-phrases around the district.

A political cartoon feature, which was not originated by the nutrition program, appeared in the newspaper soon after the promotion campaign began. It depicted a canned soft drink as a character representing unpopular foreign political influence while a coconut character represented Yapese sentiments. This cartoon motif became a regular feature of the paper.

As a result of the campaign, most stores on the four main islands now keep cold drinking-coconuts in their refrigerators. Coconuts are sold for 20 or 25 cents, half the price of soft drinks. Several individual stores report average sales of 1,000 coconuts weekly per store on the main island even though the total population is less than 4,000. Some storekeepers say they sell more coconuts than soft drinks. Coconuts are now served regularly in the most prominent local restaurant and as refreshments at the majority of official functions. They are also sold in the concession of the two local movie theaters.

A problem was encountered by several storekeepers in obtaining sufficient coconuts to meet the demand of their customers. Coconuts are quite plentiful on Yap, but they were not usually marketed by farmers except as copra, the dried meat of the mature nut. Recognizing this, some secondary school employees organized groups of teenage boys to climb family owned trees and husk the available green nuts. The boys found this after-school enterprise very profitable to the extent that one energetic young man managed to save enough money for a vacation trip to Canada.

Based on district tax receipts, imports of soft drinks to Yap in 1974 totaled $450,216. In 1975, the total was $198,447. Complete figures on the import value of soft drinks in 1976 are not yet available, but through the third quarter the total was $88,478. Tax receipts do not show any significant increase in the importation of any other substitute beverage. These figures coupled with storekeepers' reported high volume sales of coconuts indicates that the decreased imports of soft drinks can be attributed at least in part to the sale of coconuts. The population of Yap has increased approximately 6% during the time importation of soft drinks has decreased, and the retail cost of soft drinks has increased by ten cents per can. These factors indicate an even greater per unit reduction in soft drink consumption than can be determined from import value alone.

Although economics undoubtedly accounted for much of the increasing popularity of coconuts, other factors also contributed to the success of the campaign. My observation is that change originating from older values was accepted by the community and was not seen as something imposed from the outside. Attitudes were also probably influenced through political associations which were reinforced by events such as the appearance of the newspaper cartoon.

OTHER PROGRAM STRATEGIES

Another focus of the Yap nutrition program appealing to the "old ways" and the "virtues of tradition" has been to encourage breastfeeding and the use of inexpensive local foods for babies. A video tape was made with local people explaining the advantages of breastfeeding and the disadvantages of bottle feeding. It was narrated by highly respected local women in the three languages of the district. This video tape is shown in the hospital clinic waiting room at regular intervals. An illustrated booklet on breastfeeding is given to all prenatals seen at the clinic, and an illustrated baby feeding "calendar" is given to all postpartums. These educational guides have been prepared in the vernaculars of the district. Almost all women in Yap come to the hospital for their birth deliveries.

Using a battery operated projector, a filmstrip featuring a well-known and widely respected Yapese woman breastfeeding her baby is shown at meetings with village mothers. A radio spot consisting of a dialogue between two fathers commenting on the money that can be saved by breastfeeding was aired regularly. Training in the advantages of breastfeeding has been provided to health department personnel, and they are encouraged to promote breastfeeding among their own families and in their home villages. Health curricula developed for secondary school classes encourages breastfeeding through activities such as calculating the cost of bottle feeding for one year and experiments with spoiled milk. The hospital clinic nutritionist provides individual counseling to mothers who have problems with breastfeeding.

A second video tape was made to demonstrate the preparation of homemade baby food from local foods. This tape featured a well-known, highly educated Yapese woman as the principal actor, narrator, and role model. It is also shown in the clinic. The baby feeding calendar given to postpartums at the hospital illustrates the use of local foods for infants. Training on baby food preparation was provided to health department personnel. Training was made available to the general public through a demonstration of how to make baby food from local food using a simple hand grinder. This demonstration was given inside the largest food store in the district center on government "payday." Samples of this food were given away after the demonstration. Illustrated handouts headlined "Someone Is Paying $4.80 Per Pound For Bananas," describing the relative merits of commercial baby food and home prepared baby food, were available at the demonstration. The content of the pamphlet was later published in the only local newspaper. Store management cooperation for the demonstration was facilitated through the use of a food grinder that is sold by the store.

Evaluation of the infant nutrition facet of the program has been confined to clinic observation. Two years ago more than 75% of the women seen in clinic were bottle feeding their infants and they were often actively encouraged to do so by health department personnel. Bottle feeding was considered a status symbol, the "modern" thing to do. Mothers were bottle feeding their infants mixtures of over-diluted milk, flour and water, or fruit-flavored soft drinks. Women who breastfed their infants were often ashamed to do so in public, not for reasons of modesty, as women traditionally go bare-breasted in Yap, but because they were considered old-fashioned. Now more than 50% of the mothers can be observed in the clinic waiting room breastfeeding, and those who have a bottle may try to conceal it. Documentation of the extent of use of local foods for infant feeding is difficult due to the lack of household surveys. However, clinical counseling nutrition records show that at least half of the mothers are utilizing indigenous foods for infant feeding.

IMPLICATIONS

The favorable response to the Yap nutrition education program appears to be based on the highly visible participation of respected local persons and institutions and the appeal to Yapese pride in traditional ways. The program reinforces nationalistic tendencies and certain valued cultural traditions. Realistic methods by which this developing area in Micronesia can meet its health needs, despite limited resources, are the major focus of all nutrition education activities. The sole budget item for the first year of this two-year program was the nutritionist's salary; the second-year budget was increased by $1,200 for material and publication costs. Program strategy is based on practical methods of altering personal attitudes and practices for long-term benefit rather than on isolated remedial programs such as free food distribution. Behavior is based on learned values. Motivation to change behavior occurs only when opportunity is given to each individual to attain sufficient knowledge to make responsible value judgments. This premise has guided the development of Yapese nutrition programs.

The coconut juice vs. soft drink project is a case history which could have application in many parts of the tropical world. A value-based and emotionally appealing campaign could promote the popularity of coconut or other local juices in many areas where they are readily available as a tasty, money-saving substitute for high sugar drinks. Long-term evaluation is necessary to measure realistically the health, economic, and social impact of the program.

Family income is inadequate to purchase sufficient quantities of canned milk and processed infant foods in many developing areas. There is a great need for more aggressive advertising campaigns utilizing persuasive, imaginative techniques to promote the use of breast milk and homemade infant food resources in these areas.

REFERENCES

1. McHenry, D. F., Micronesia: Trust betrayed, Carnegie Endowment for International Peace, New York, 1975, p. 8.
2. Murai, M., Nutrition Study in Micronesia, U.S. National Research Council, Pacific Science Board, Atoll Research Bulletin no. 27, 1954.
3. Demory, B. G. H., An Illusion of Surplus: The effect of status rivalry upon family food consumption, Ph.D. dissertation, University of California, Berkeley, 1976, pp. 53–54.
4. Mitchel, H. S. et al., Nutrition in Health and Disease, J. B. Lippincott Co., Philadelphia, 1976, p. 396.
5. U.S., Trust Territory of the Pacific Islands, Department of Health Services, Northern Mariana Islands Comprehensive Five Year Health Plan 1977–1982, Saipan, 1977, unpublished.
6. U.S., Trust Territory of the Pacific Islands, Department of Health Services, Dental Study (TTPI): Paulau District Department of Health Services, Saipan, 1977, unpublished.
7. U.S., Trust Territory of the Pacific Islands, Department of Health Services, Dental Study (TTPI): Northern Marianas Department of Health Services, Saipan, 1977, unpublished.
8. Hezel, S. J., and C. B. Reafsnyder, Micronesia: A changing society, Micronesian Social Studies Program, Trust Territory of the Pacific Islands Publications, Saipan, 1973, p. 33.
9. Kincaid, P. J., Trust Territory of the Pacific Islands Nutrition Survey, U.S., Trust Territory of the Pacific Islands, Health Council, Saipan, 1973, foreword.
10. U.S., Trust Territory of the Pacific Islands, Office of Economic Development, Estimated Dollar Value of Non-Government Imports, Yap District, 1977, unpublished.
11. Rody, N., Yap's food prices 74% higher than Guam's, The Carolines Observer, 1 (No. 1):8, 1976.
12. Labby, D., The Demystification of Yap, University of Chicago Press, Chicago, 1976, p. 8.
13. Smith, U. N., Trust Territory: Foreign trade analysis, U.S., Trust Territory of the Pacific Islands, Department of Resources and Development, Economic Development Division, Saipan, June, 1977, unpublished.

the study; discussion, where the writer presents his judgments about the quality or proper interpretation of the results; and conclusions or recommendations, where the writer lists the major points of value gained from the study.

The report of original research usually includes little documented evidence other than in the review of the literature. The writer often uses headings and subheadings to divide the report into distinct sections. The report develops logically, but it does not so much flow as move through distinct stages. If the thesis report works like an automatic transmission, the report of original research works like a standard shift.

The main information in the report of original research is located in two places: the review of the literature and the results sections. As much as possible, the writer places information in tabular form: charts, tables, graphs, etc. Opinions are included only in the discussion, results, and conclusion sections.

"The Effects of a Collegiate Wrestling Season" originally appeared in a journal specializing in sports medicine. The audience is thus a group of specialists in a narrow field. They do not require general background information, but are instead interested in the scientific details, the methodology, and the conclusions of the article. The article is presented in a typical scientific format, allowing the expert audience the fastest possible entry into the meat of the subject.

EXERCISE

1. What is the main point of this report of original research?

2. Where is the review of the literature and how does the writer relate it to the rest of the report?

3. How effective is the research design? How effectively is this design presented in the methods section?

4. Where do the authors express opinions and judgments about the results of their research? How effectively do the authors express these opinions and judgments?

5. Do the authors present any recommendations? Do these recommendations follow from the research itself? How effectively do the authors present these recommendations?

6. What seems to be the rhetorical situation behind the article? What do the writers do to fit the article to its audience?

7. How effective is this report in terms of the criteria listed in chapter 1? What are its particular strengths and weaknesses? How could it be improved?

The effects of a collegiate wrestling season on body composition, cardiovascular fitness and muscular strength and endurance

J.M. Kelly, B.A. Gorney and K.K. Kalm

Exercise Physiology Laboratory
St. Cloud State University
St. Cloud, Minnesota 56301

Wrestlers, body densitometry, Vo_2 max, isokinetic strength, minimal wrestling weight, perceived minimal weight

ABSTRACT. The purposes of this investigation were: (1) to study the body composition, cardiovascular fitness and muscular strength and endurance of collegiate wrestlers during the course of a season; (2) to determine if selected regression equations used to predict minimal wrestling weight were accurate; (3) to determine if the wrestlers who participated in the study had an accurate perception of their ideal minimal wrestling weights. Body composition (body densitometry), aerobic power (Vo_2 max), and muscular strength and endurance (isokinetic) were measured during pre, peak, and post-seasons. The fact that very few significant changes occurred in these measurements during the course of the study appears to be the result of year-round training on the part of the athletes studied. Their peak-season percent body fat (8.36%) was very similar to that reported in other studies involving mature wrestlers. Rapid weight loss through dehydration appeared to be the preferred method of weight reduction among these athletes.

As the sport of wrestling has grown in popularity, so has the concern of many individuals directly and indirectly involved with it. This concern usually manifests itself in the process of "making weight." It is not uncommon for wrestlers throughout the country to lose from 10 to 12 pounds of their body weight in the few days preceding each match (12) so that they might compete in lower weight classes in hopes of wrestling small opponents. Since this practice is so common, the possible advantages are nullified and the risk of health impairment increased.

Although the sport of wrestling has recently been the focus of considerable research, it is commonly recognized that securing more scientific information in this sport is of great importance. The purposes of the present study were: (1) to study the body composition, cardiovascular fitness and muscular strength and endurance of collegiate wrestlers throughout the course of a wrestling season; (2) to determine if selected regression equations used to predict minimal wrestling weight and body fat were suitable for predicting the minimal wrestling weights of the subjects used in the present study; (3) to determine if the wrestlers who participated in the present study had an accurate perception of their minimal wrestling weights.

From J. M. Kelly, B. A. Gorney, and K. K. Kalm, "The Effects of a Collegiate Wrestling Season on Body Composition, Cardiovascular Fitness, and Muscular Strength and Endurance," *Medicine and Science in Sports and Exercise,* 10, ii (1978), 119–22. Copyright © 1978 by *Medicine and Science in Sports and Exercise.* Reprinted by permission.

METHODS

Subjects

Nineteen subjects from the 1975–76 St. Cloud State University wrestling team were selected by the coach as those who would most probably serve as the nucleus for the varsity team. For various reasons, only 13 completed the 3 phases of the investigation which included: (1) Pre-season (data collected in September); (2) Peak-season (data collected in January and February); (3) Post-season (data collected 5 weeks following the season's conclusion).

Six of the selected wrestlers qualified for the NCAA Division II Wrestling Tournament, two were finalists and three received All-American honors. The informed consent was obtained following a detailed explanation of the study and the risks involved in it. The data were collected between 6:30 a.m. and 10:00 a.m. to allow for as much overnight rehydration as possible. Efforts were also made to reduce the possibility of extreme dehydration by avoiding the 48 hour time period preceding each match.

Anthropometric Measurements

All of the selected anthropometric measurements were repeated at least twice so that two measurements for each variable were obtained that differed by no more than 2 mm except for the skinfolds which differed by no more than 1 mm. Height and weight were also recorded: height to the nearest .25 inch and weight to the nearest 0.05 kg. The same individual took each measurement and had previously demonstrated an objectivity coefficient of over .90 between his measurements and the measurements of an experienced investigator. A sliding wooden anthropometer caliper was used to measure the body diameters, which were later satisfactorily rechecked with the caliper recommended and designed by Tipton and his associates (15). The selected diameters were as follows: biacromial, chest width, chest depth, bi-iliac, bitrochanteric, elbow, knee, ankle, and wrist. The diameters were measured according to the specifications of Tcheng and Tipton (15) except for the elbow and knee (2). The circumference measurements were obtained with the use of a Lufkin physician's metal retractable tape and were as follows: the neck, chest, bicep, waist, thigh and calf, and were measured according to Behnke and Wilmore (3). The skinfolds were measured with a Lange skinfold caliper and included the subscapular, tricep, chest, pectoral, suprailiac, abdominal and thigh. The skinfolds were measured as reported in a previous publication (16).

Body Composition

Body composition was assessed for all subjects by the hydrostatic weighing technique. Residual volume was determined by the "closed circuit oxygen-dilution method" as described by Wilmore (17). Both the body density and residual volume

technique were reported previously (16). The residual volume was measured only during the peak-season because of an equipment malfunction. When repeat measurements were taken on seven of the nine varsity wrestlers several months following the season only a small mean difference (24 ml) was observed. The correlation between the original and repeated values was .989. This stability of the residual volume in the present study is supported by other studies involving wrestlers (1,14). Percent fat and lean body mass were calculated from the formula developed by Brozek et al. (5).

Muscular Strength and Endurance

A Cybex II dynamometer was used to measure isokinetic strength and muscular endurance. An attempt was made to measure those muscle groups that were used most extensively in wrestling. A battery of 29 muscular strength and endurance tests were administered to each subject. The dominant side was used in each test. With the exception of grip strength, each test included a fast speed component (180°/sec) and a slow speed component (30°/sec). The battery of tests included: (1) Shoulder Flexion-Elbow Extension and Shoulder Extension-Elbow Flexion, (2) Hip Flexion, (3) Shoulder Horizontal Flexion and Extension, (4) Knee Flexion and Extension, and (5) Grip Strength.

To standardize the experiments and localize the contractions to the proper muscle groups the subjects were required to participate in a practice session on a day prior to the day of testing. During the tests the subjects were encouraged to exert maximal force throughout the desired range of motion. Motivation was held as constant as possible during each of the tests that were administered. The dynamometer was positioned to the proper length and height for each of the subjects and maintained constant for each of the testing sessions. The protocol for the testing was as follows: (1) five maximal contractions throughout the described range of motion at 180° per second; (2) two minutes rest; (3) repeated maximal contractions throughout the range of motion at 30° per second until the subject's force decreased to 50 percent of the initial maximum force; (4) two minutes rest; (5) repeated maximal contractions throughout the range of motion at 180° per second until the subject's force diminished to 50 percent of the initial maximum force.

Cardiovascular Fitness

A continuous-type treadmill test to exhaustion (Wilmore, personal communication) was used to measure maximal oxygen uptake. After a 5 minute warm-up walk and run the treadmill speed was set at 3.5 miles per hour and zero percent grade. The elevation of the treadmill was increased by 2.5 percent each minute until a 5 percent grade was reached. At that time the treatment speed was increased to 6 miles per hour and the grade continued to be increased by 2.5 percent each minute until exhaustion. The majority of the athletes were fatigued within 8 to 10 minutes while the longest effort required 12 minutes. The subjects breathed through a Hans Rudolph Low Dead Space Valve (No. 2700) into a Parkinson-Cowan, CD4, gas meter and a mixing chamber. Gas samples were collected during the last 30 seconds of each minute by drawing them from the mixing chamber into sampling bags by an electric pump. The concentrations of oxygen and carbon dioxide in each bag were analyzed with Beckman OM-11 and LB-2 analyzers. The analyzers were calibrated at the beginning and at the end of each test using cylinders of standard gas, periodically analyzed by the Scholander technique.

RESULTS AND DISCUSSION

Body Composition and Anthropometry

Age, height, weight, and body diameters for the 13 wrestlers who completed all phases of the study are presented in Table 1. Table 2 includes circumference and skinfold data from each testing period while Table 3 presents the body densitometry data. A repeated measures analysis of variance was employed to determine statistical significance. The F ratios ranged from 0.004 for LBW to 1.462 for the suprailiac SF thicknesses and failed to reach the required 0.05 level of significance (3.40).

The small sample size undoubtedly made it difficult to detect possible differences, but the data do indicate that the body composition and anthropometric measurements of the wrestlers in the present study remained very stable throughout the entire wrestling season.

Because 3 of the 13 wrestlers who completed the study did not compete on the varsity, it was felt that they should be removed and the data be examined again. One of the remaining 10 varsity wrestlers

Table 1. *Age, Height, Weight, and Body Diameters for the Pre-season Test on 13 Collegiate Wrestlers.*

Variable	Mean	S.D.
Age (Years)	20.31	1.32
Height	174.48	7.42
Weight (Kilograms)	78.65	15.77
Diameters[a]		
Biacromial	41.59	2.10
Chest Width	29.54	1.83
Chest Depth	20.37	2.08
Bi-iliac	27.89	2.08
Bitrochanteric	32.49	2.69
Right Elbow	7.19	.41
Left Elbow	7.33	.33
Right Wrist	5.98	.36
Left Wrist	5.92	.38
Right Knee	9.38	.58
Left Knee	9.42	.67
Right Ankle	6.90	.50
Left Ankle	6.92	.54

[a]Anthropometric measurements and height measured in centimeters.

chose not to complete the testing and was also eliminated. Finally, it was felt that the heavyweight should also be removed because he carried far more fat than did the other varsity wrestlers. The data for the 8 varsity wrestlers appear in Table 4. Although the 8 varsity wrestlers were somewhat leaner than the entire group (8.4–10.4%) these data also indicate that the body composition and anthropometric measurements of these university wrestlers remained stable throughout the course of the study. The fact that the mean weight varied by no more than 2.4 pounds from September to March was extremely interesting and is probably the result of year round training. This trend was also apparent when we looked at the data of the 6 national qualifiers separately. Their data were almost identical to the data on the 8 varsity wrestlers.

The mean, peak-season percent fat (8.4%) for the varsity wrestlers in the present study is very similar to that reported in other studies involving mature wrestlers (7,11,14). This is considerably higher than the minimal wrestling weight recommended by Tcheng and Tipton (15). Their recommendation, however, was based upon anthropometric measurements rather than body densitometry. In view of the findings from these studies, it is felt that the 5% value should be looked upon as the extreme minimal fat weight rather than a desirable or optimal fat level.

Table 2. *Body Circumference and Skinfold Data for 13 Collegiate Wrestlers.*

	Pre		Peak		Post	
Variable	Mean	S.D.	Mean	S.D.	Mean	S.D.
Weight (Kg)	78.65	15.77	77.10	15.48	78.68	14.68
Circumferences[a]						
Neck	39.59	2.35	40.74	2.68	41.25	2.18
Chest	97.35	7.92	98.09	7.33	98.22	6.26
Waist	82.54	10.50	80.31	9.99	83.32	9.10
Bicep	32.71	3.51	32.32	2.94	32.69	2.94
Thigh	57.64	7.01	56.39	6.37	57.68	6.24
Calf	38.19	2.98	37.68	3.30	37.88	2.96
Skinfolds[b]						
Subscap.	11.96	5.54	10.50	5.37	11.50	5.18
Tricep	7.12	5.17	6.77	3.99	7.23	3.94
Pectoral	7.50	5.40	6.15	4.12	6.73	3.77
Chest	10.35	6.43	8.08	5.32	9.46	4.94
Suprailiac	20.62	11.30	12.27	7.58	17.54	7.14
Abdominal	18.42	9.01	12.73	8.46	16.00	7.55
Thigh	13.15	7.38	10.54	8.42	11.77	7.37
Total SF	89.12	48.55	67.04	42.30	81.73	40.23

[a]Circumferences reported in centimeters. [b]Skinfolds reported in millimeters.

Table 3. *Body Densitometry Data for 13 Collegiate Wrestlers.*

	Pre		Peak		Post	
Variable	Mean	S.D.	Mean	S.D.	Mean	S.D.
Body Density	1.0704	.0130	1.0765	.0130	1.0709	.0130
RV[a]			1111.0	270.0		
Weight[b]	173.0	34.7	169.6	34.1	173.1	32.3
LBW[c]	149.6	22.0	150.6	22.6	150.2	22.1
% Fat	12.8	5.3	10.4	5.4	12.6	5.2
DMWW[d]	157.5	23.3	158.5	23.8	158.1	23.3
Total Skinfolds	89.1	48.6	67.0	42.3	81.7	40.2

[a]RV = Residual Volume, reported in milliliters (BTPS). [b]Weight — reported in pounds. [c]LBW = Lean Body Weight, reported in pounds. [d]DMWW = Determined Minimal Wrestling Weight, reported in pounds.

Table 4. *Body Densitometry Data for 8 Varsity Wrestlers.*

	Pre		Peak		Post	
Variable	Mean	S.D.	Mean	S.D.	Mean	S.D.
Weight[a]	159.1	21.7	156.7	22.5	158.9	21.1
Body Density	1.0753	.0042	1.0815	.0040	1.0760	.0050
LBW[b]	141.8	17.8	143.1	20.0	142.2	19.9
DMWW[c]	149.3	18.8	150.6	21.0	149.7	20.1
% Fat	10.8	1.7	8.4	1.8	10.5	2.1
Total SF	68.1	14.9	49.6	13.2	62.6	15.1

[a]Weight reported in pounds. [b]LBW reported in pounds. [c]DMWW reported in pounds.

Over half of the wrestlers in the present study made weight by losing several pounds (up to 11 pounds) in the last few days preceding their matches throughout the regular season. In fact, four of the national qualifiers each lost a minimum of 9.5 pounds (one lost 20 pounds) within a few days preceding the national championships. Two of these athletes made it to the finals and advanced to the Division I meet while another received All-American honors. Each of these four individuals wrestled in a weight category that was equal to or below his lean body weight. These weights were determined by densitometry when the subjects were in a hydrated state two weeks preceding the tournament. None of these wrestlers were below 6.2% fat at that time. It is presumed, therefore, that dehydration was utilized to a great extent in making weight. This practice, while recognized by many health authorities as undesirable, is probably used to a great extent in collegiate wrestling and supports the recent findings of Zambraski et al. (18).

An effort was made to measure body density during times when dehydration would be at its minimum. Serious errors in establishing fat content can be made if body densitometry is done when in a dehydrated state. Furthermore, establishing minimal wrestling weight by skinfold measurements can also lead to distorted minimal wrestling weights if done while in a dehydrated state. Both procedures tend to make the athlete appear to be less fat than what is actually the case.

Three regression equations were examined to determine if they would be useful in predicting the body composition of the wrestlers in the present study. The fat values obtained from the equations were correlated with the percent body fat values obtained through body densitometry. The actual values were then plotted against the derived values by the least squares linear regression technique in an effort to determine which yielded the best prediction of body fat for the 19 wrestlers used in the present study. The correlation and standard error of the estimates were as follows: (1) Forsyth-Sinning-3 (14) $r = .87 \pm 3.83\%$; (2) Tcheng-Tipton Skinfold (15) $r = .88 \pm 2.08\%$; and (3) Wickkiser-Kelly (16) $r = .90 \pm 2.85\%$.

The Cheng-Tipton Long Form equation for determining minimum wrestling weight (MWW) (15) was also studied. True MWWs (LBW + 5% fat)

for wrestlers in the present study were calculated from their LBWs determined by hydrostatic weighing and correlated with values derived from the Cheng-Tipton equation. This resulted in a high correlation (.94) which can be explained by the extreme heterogeneity of the data. However, when the standard error of the estimate (3.54 kg) was taken into consideration, it was found that the equation could mispredict minimal wrestling weight by as much as 15 pounds at the 95% confidence level. This standard error of the estimate (3.54 kg) approximates the value (3.63 kg) reported by Tcheng and Tipton (15). In this case, each of the three previously mentioned equations designed to predict body fat proved to be better predictors of body composition and MWW (LBW + 5% fat) than did the Tcheng-Tipton equation. The fact that these equations were based upon skinfold measurements and were independent of body size apparently explains their accuracy. The present study, therefore, tends to support the work of other investigators and indicates that data obtained from these equations should be used by coaches and officials as valuable screening information rather than absolute values (9,14,15).

During the pre-season, each wrestler was asked to estimate his optimal wrestling weight. Optimal weight was defined as the lightest effective weight that a wrestler could reach without sacrificing strength, endurance or quickness. The estimates were correlated with densitometrically determined weight classes optimally (MWW) suited for each wrestler (LBW + 5%). A high correlation (.97 $\pm$ 2.59 kg) resulted from this procedure. This however, was anticipated because of the small number of subjects and wide range in body weight. This same rationale explains the high correlation (.94) obtained when estimates from the Tcheng-Tipton equation were subjected to the same procedure. This suggests that these mature wrestlers had a reasonably accurate perception of their MWW. It should be pointed out, however, that the majority of these wrestlers perceived MWWs that contained 8–10% body fat rather than the 5% levels used in this study. The remaining weight was lost through dehydration.

Muscular Strength and Endurance

Very few significant changes in muscular strength and endurance occurred during the course of the study. This most likely resulted because of the superb condition of these athletes at the beginning of the study. Significant differences were found in only 7 of 29 variables that were selected to measure muscular strength and endurance. For convenience, only the variables in which significant changes occurred are presented in Table 5. A repeated measures analysis of variance was employed to determine if the mean differences were significant. The .05 level (F = 3.40) of significance was used for this purpose. The Scheffe test was utilized to determine which differences were significant. Only one significant difference in muscular strength and one in muscular endurance were found between the pre and peak-season testing. The endurance variable was significantly increased while the strength variable was significantly decreased. This would indicate that very little change occurred in muscular strength or endurance as a result of the wrestling season. However, when the post-season data were compared with the pre and peak-season data, five out of the seven strength tests conducted at 180° per second were found to be significantly greater in favor of the post-season. For some reason the athletes were stronger when their muscle groups moved at a rapid speed during the post-season testing than they were during the pre or peak-season testing. This may have resulted from an increase in weight training following the season on the part of some wrestlers. It is interesting to note that there were no concomitant changes in the strength tests that were conducted at a slower speed (30° per second).

In general, these findings support the conclusion of two unpublished theses (Hassman, R. P., U.

of Oregon, 1961) and (Polo, J. F., Montana State U., 1964). Both found significant strength gains following the season.

Cardiovascular Fitness

Because we were unable to complete the postseason max Vo₂ testing on the two national finalists, their values are not included within the data presented in Table 6. The peak season Vo₂ max values for these two athletes were 71.5 and 62.4 ml/kg/min respectively.

Repeated measures analysis of variance was used to determine if any of the mean differences were significant. The F-ratios were very low (.03-1.25) indicating that the cardiovascular fitness variables studied in this investigation remained very stable throughout its course. This finding was in harmony with the results of the body composition and muscular strength and endurance testing and probably reflects the intense year round training that the majority of these athletes underwent.

The mean Vo₂ max value of 61.0 ml/kg/min for the 11 wrestlers appearing in Table 6 is almost identical with that reported by Nagle et al. (60.9) in their study of Olympic contenders (11). Both of these values, however, are considerably higher than the values reported by Gale and Flynn (7) (54.3 ml/kg/min). This difference may partially be explained by comparing the testing protocol employed in these studies. The testing procedure was very similar in both the present study and in the study by Nagle and his associates, while the protocol used by Gale and Flynn required a much longer time to administer

Table 5. *Muscular Strength and Endurance Data for 13 Collegiate Wrestlers.*

Variable	Pre Mean	S.D.	Peak Mean	S.D.	Post Mean	S.D.	Fᶜ
Endurance 180°/secᵃ							
Knee Ext	35.9ᵈ	7.9	48.8	11.0	46.5	8.6	4.81
Strength 30°/secᵇ							
Shld Ext-El Ext	182.6ᵉ	25.7	147.6	19.1	160.7	26.4	4.74
Strength 180°/sec							
Shld Flex-El Ext	55.8	17.7	57.8	17.7	76.5ᶠ	14.2	4.09
Knee Flex	57.5	17.7	60.6	14.5	84.6ᶠ	25.4	4.98
Knee Ext	83.3	13.7	87.6	22.6	117.3ᶠ	35.6	4.55
Hip Flex	75.0	21.0	81.3	17.9	112.5ᶠ	21.8	8.86
Shld Ext-El Flex	80.3	24.0	82.9	26.9	108.8ᶠ	22.0	3.58

ᵃUnits reported in number of repetitions. ᵇUnits reported in foot-pounds of force. ᶜF-ratio of 3.40 significant at p < .05. ᵈPeak significantly greater than pre. ᵉPre significantly greater than peak. ᶠPost significantly greater than pre and peak.

which could have resulted in lower values than are normally obtained in tests designed to reach maximal values more abruptly (6,10).

When the peak mean for the 6 national qualifiers (65.7 ml/kg/min) was compared with the rest of the team (61.0) it was interesting to note the substantial difference. Although the sport of wrestling requires many other attributes in addition to aerobic power, the data from the present study would tend to support the contention that cardiovascular conditioning is an extremely important component of wrestling success.

When the wrestlers reported for the peak-season evaluation, the investigators were surprised to observe such a small drop in weight from September (159.1 pounds) to February (156.7 pounds). However, when these weights were compared with the weight classes in which these athletes competed, it became clear that the majority of the wrestlers lost large quantities of weight (up to 11 pounds) during the day preceding each match).

Because the athletes were apparently in a hydrated state for the peak-season treadmill testing, it was felt that this did not provide a clear picture of what their aerobic capacities were when they stepped on the mat. With this in mind, four of

the national qualifiers were asked to simulate a wrestling match by weighing-in, in the morning, and running to exhaustion on the treadmill, five hours later. This was done because in collegiate wrestling it is common practice for athletes to have five hours between weigh-in and competition. The results of this experiment appear in Table 7. Each of the subjects completed this phase of the study within two weeks of the national competition. While it is recognized that five hours of rehydration is not long enough for a wrestler's body to return to the normal hydrated state, the wrestlers in the present study were able to lose from 3.7 to 9.5% of their body weight without causing a significant change in aerobic power. This data would tend to support the findings of several related studies (4,8,13).

CONCLUSION

The peak-season percent body fat (8.36%) for the wrestlers in the present study is very similar to that reported in other studies involving mature wrestlers. It would appear that this may be an optimal fat level for most mature wrestlers and that the 5% level should be looked upon as the extreme minimal fat weight rather than a desirable or optimum level.

Table 6. *Cardiovascular Fitness Data for 11 Collegiate Wrestlers.*

Variable	Pre Mean	S.D.	Peak Mean	S.D.	Post Mean	S.D.
Weight (kg)	79.1	16.5	77.2	15.8	79.1	15.2
Height (inches)	68.8					
$\dot{V}_E$ STPD	119.9	14.9	126.8	19.2	119.3	13.2
$\dot{V}o_2$max ml/kg/min	58.6	6.4	61.0	5.8	57.2	7.2
RER (max ex)	1.14	.04	1.14	.04	1.11	.07
Max HR	192.5	6.9	188.2	5.1	193.1	6.8

Table 7. *Simulated Match Data.*

Subject	Normal Peak-Season Weight (pounds)	Weigh-in (pounds)	5 Hours Later (pounds)	Base-Line[a] $\dot{V}o_2$ max ml/kg/min	Simulated Match $\dot{V}o_2$ max ml/kg/min
1	152.5	142.0	149.1	67.4	71.5
2	161.0	150.0	157.1	68.4	66.4
3	176.7	167.0	173.4	62.4	59.8
4	210.1	190.0	199.2	59.6	58.9
Mean	175.0	162.3	169.7	64.5	64.2

A larger number of the wrestlers in the present study made weight by losing up to 11 pounds in a few days preceding each of their matches. While this may be an undesirable practice, it is probably widespread throughout collegiate wrestling. Rapid weight loss through dehydration appears to be the preferred method of weight reduction among wrestlers and appears to be a result of the rules governing the sport.

ACKNOWLEDGMENTS. This study was partially supported by a St. Cloud State University Faculty Research Grant. The authors wish to express their appreciation to Mr. Randal Kolb for his valuable assistance with the statistical analysis of the data.

REFERENCES

1. Bachman, J. D. and S. M. Horvath. Pulmonary function changes accompany athletic conditioning programs. *Res. Quart.* 39:239, 1968.
2. Behnke, A. R. and J. Royce. Body size, shape and body composition of several types of athletes. *J. Sports Med. and Phys. Fitness.* 6:75-88, 1966.
3. Behnke, A. R. and J. H. Wilmore. *Evaluation and Regulation of Body Build and Composition.* Englewood Cliffs: Prentice-Hall, Inc., 1974.
4. Bock, W., E. L. Fox and R. Bowers. The effects of acute dehydration upon cardiorespiratory endurance. *J. Sports Med. and Phys. Fitness.* 7:67-72, 1967.
5. Brozek, J., F. Grande, J. T. Anderson and A. Keys. Densitometric analysis of body composition: revision of some quantitative assumptions. *Ann. N. Y. Acad. Sci.* 110:113-140, 1963.
6. Froelicher, V. F., H. Brammell, G. Davis, I. Noguera, A. Stewart and M. Lancaster. A comparison of three maximal treadmill exercise protocols. *J. Appl. Physiol.* 36:720- 725, 1974.
7. Gale, J. B. and K. W. Flynn. Maximal oxygen consumption and relative body fat of high-ability wrestlers. *Med. Sci. Sports.* 6:232-234, 1974.
8. Henschel, A., H. L. Taylor and A. Keys. Performance capacity in acute starvation with hard work. *J. Appl. Physiol.* 6:624-633, 1954.
9. Landwer, G. E., G. O. Johnson and R. W. Hammer. Weight control for high school wrestlers. *J. Sports Med.* 3:88-94, 1975.
10. McArdle, W. D., F. I. Katch, and G. S. Pechar. Comparison of continuous and discontinuous treadmill and bicycle tests for max Vo_2. *Med. Sci. Sports.* 5:156-160, 1973.
11. Nagle, F. J., W. P. Morgan, R. O. Hellickson, R. C. Serfass and J. F. Alexander. Spotting success traits in olympic contenders. *Phys. Sports Med.* 3:31-34, 1975.
12. Ribisl, P. M. and W. G. Herbert. Effects of rapid weight reduction and subsequent rehydration upon physical working capacity of wrestlers. *Res. Quart.* 41:536-541, 1970.
13. Saltin, B. Aerobic and anaerobic work capacity after dehydration. *J. Appl. Physiol.* 19:1114-1118, 1964.
14. Sinning, W. E. Body composition assessment of college wrestlers. *Med. Sci. Sports.* 6:139-145, 1974.
15. Tcheng, T. K. and C. M. Tipton. Iowa wrestling study: anthropometric measurements and the prediction of a 'minimal' body weight for high school wrestlers. *Med. Sci. Sports.* 5:1-10, 1973.
16. Wickkiser, J. D. and J. M. Kelly. The body composition of a college football team. *Med. Sci. Sports.* 7:199-202, 1975.
17. Wilmore, J. H. A simplified method for determination of residual lung volumes. *J. Appl. Physiol.* 27:96-100, 1969.
18. Zambraski, E. J., C. M. Tipton, T. K. Tcheng, H. R. Jordan, A. C. Vailas and A. K. Callahan. Iowa wrestling study: changes in the urinary profiles of wrestlers prior to and after competition. *Med. Sci. Sports.* 7:217-220, 1975.

THE PROBLEM/SOLUTION REPORT

The problem/solution report falls into two parts, with the emphasis on the latter. The first section presents a problem, and the second section presents a solution to that problem. The documentation in the report falls mainly in the solution section, since the problem stems from personal experience in a particular job and hence requires little documentation. Once the writer defines the problem, however, she defends the solution with all the documented information she can muster. The following article is an example of a problem/solution report.

Temporary installation reduces sewer failure problems

Clarence W. Myrold, P.E.

It took only 97 days from design to on-line when a major Detroit sewer failed.

An impermanent installation rescued the City of Detroit, Mich., when a major sewer that serviced more than 150,000 persons failed.

The failure of a major 11-ft. diameter sewer posed a serious health hazard to several communities and a military base northeast of Detroit. Because of this, the mayor requested urgent action. Detroit was declared a disaster area by the governor of Michigan, who demanded an accelerated, flexible, and integrated solution.

This major sanitary sewer services an area of approximately 55 sq. miles in the northeastern suburbs of Detroit, Mich., including the communities of Mt. Clemens, Fraser, Clinton Township, Harrison Township, and the northeast portion of the City of Sterling Heights. Emergency pumping operations were initiated by the owner. Further action included immediate restoration of the decommissioned and evacuated Hayes/18 Mile Pumping Station and reactivation of the existing Selfrige Air Force Base Treatment Plant to isolate a portion of the upstream flow, stabilization of the failed interceptor and surrounding subsoils utilizing a special grout mixture of water, cement, and flyash, and design and construction of a temporary bypass and pumping station with capacity to carry peak flows.

Considering the complexity of the Temporary Bypass and Pumping Station installation, it is unique that only 97 calendar days were required from design to activation. The temporary bypass was actually in operation earlier, accepting flow from the emergency pumps within the sewer.

SEWER BUILT ON A LAKE BED

Original construction of the existing 11-ft. inside diameter interceptor sewer consisted of a secondary lining of poured-in-place concrete, with a minimum wall thickness of not less than 14 inches with a primary lining of rib and wood lagging consisting of 4-inch thick boards set between typical 4-foot spaced ribs.

The mining machine utilized was designed to bore a tunnel 14.5 feet in diameter utilizing dewatering wells in advance of the mining operations with the bulk of the mining operations carried out under air pressure. In general, the design invert is approximately 60 feet below ground surface.

The geologic setting in which this project is located consists of a glacial lake-bed environment. The lacustrine deposits of sand and clay are bordered by the Birmingham Moraine several miles to the west and the Mt. Clemens Moraine a short distance to the east. Both of these water-laid moraines trend in a northeast to southwest direction. A Pleistocene age delta has been deposited by the predecessor of the present Clinton River as it crossed the Birmingham Moraine. This delta created large sand deposits along the north side of the present Clinton River. The area between the Clinton River and the project site appears to represent a transitional area between the deltaic deposits and the lacustrine deposits of sand and clay.

The cause of the failure has not been fully established. Determination of such is not within the scope of this review. However, it is known that shortly after midnight July 29, 1978, Fraser police officers on routine patrol noted that the pavement on 15 Mile Road, in the vicinity of Hayes Road, was buckling and settling. Eventually, the subsidence of 15 Mile Road was highly evident as the eastbound lane ultimately settled approximately 3.5 feet below the level of the westbound lane and open fissures developed along and adjacent to the sewer center-line. Later investigation indicated that the interceptor was completely filled with soil at one point.

EMERGENCY RELIEF IS PROVIDED

The initial main thrust of the owner, the Detroit Water and Sewerage Department (DWSD), was directed at the rapid construction of an emergency relief around the failed interceptor. However, it was recognized that this system would not provide adequate service for a sufficient period of time to effect repairs to the failed section of the interceptor. On this basis, the DWSD began preparations to build a major, although semi-permanent, pumping station together with its by-pass and stand-by electrical protection, of sufficient capacity to carry peak flows.

The design, construction, and construction management during this time of stress provided numerous examples of cooperation nationwide. To expedite delivery of sheet piling from North Carolina and Mississippi, men stood in front of weigh stations waving the trucks through. When requested by the consultants, pumps and other equipment from Connecticut, Texas, Indiana, and New York were diverted to the project. A major electrical control panel was designed in three days and subsequently constructed by the supplier in 12.

Around the clock construction included driving sheet piling at night utilizing emergency flood lights. This proved to be an extremely difficult task. Initially, it was considered feasible to drive the sheet piling utilizing a vibratory driver, possibly in conjunction with predrilling operations. However, due to the extremely compact nature of the subsoils found at the lower depths, the performance of the vibratory hammers was not satisfactory. The sheet piling was ultimately driven utilizing a Link-Belt 660 diesel hammer in conjunction with a program of augering and jetting adjacent to the piles as they were being driven.

Innovative features created by necessity include: 1) two 48-inch diameter wet taps into the existing sewer approximately 60 feet below grade, which are the largest known; and 2) the completed operational pumping station at the time of its construction was the largest submersible sanitary pumping station in the world. The magnitude of the project can be further shown in that the daily ground water discharge from the 51 wells required to dewater the area to construct the Temporary By-pass and Pumping Station and stabilize the failed sewer was calculated as sufficient to supply 20,000 homes.

The completed by-pass system is performing satisfactorily and is meeting or exceeding the requirements set forth by the DWSD. The Pumping Station includes six 6,000-gpm submersible pumps for a total capacity of 36,000 gpm, which are electrically sequenced to provide both conservation of electrical energy and to provide uniform wear of the pump units. In addition, two 750 kw emergency generators provide further stand-by protection.

CAN BECOME PERMANENT

The structures involved were designed in such a manner that although they are presently considered temporary (two to five year design life), certain additional expenditures would allow their designation to be extended to that of a permanent facility.

The failed zone of the existing tunnel sewer was isolated and stabilized from the operational system by means of bulkheads constructed both upstream and downstream of the failed zone, installation of dewatering wells along the present tunnel sewer, and the injection of cementious grout into the fissured subsoils.

Based on records maintained during the grout stabilization program a total of 16,946 cu. ft. of grout was injected into the subsoils surrounding the interceptor. This total represents an average application rate of approximately 30 cu. ft. of grout per lineal foot of sewer along the stabilized area west of Hayes Road and approximately 46.4 cu. ft. per lineal foot of sewer east of Hayes Road.

The site was restored to the point that 15 Mile Road may be reopened to normal traffic and permanent repairs to the tunnel sewer may be implemented as soon as plans and funding are available.

A potential disaster involving the health, welfare, and personal loss to more than 150,000 residents of several communities, as well as disruption of an established military base, was averted by the rapid application of engineering principals and prompt construction which minimized the effects of a major sanitary trunk sewer failure. The actual cost of approximately $12 million was also within the preliminary project estimate, not to exceed $13 million.

The solution section resembles the thesis report, while the problem section is similar to the problem definition in the report of original research. The problem/solution report, in effect, personally introduces a problem and presents the solution to that problem in the form of a thesis report.

This article originally appeared in a periodical read primarily by practicing engineers responsible for job-site performance. The audience, then, contains many technicians or operators responsible for getting things done. Thus, this article presents more background information and less scientific notation. The author is reporting a success that he expects the audience members to be able to apply to their own problems.

EXERCISE

1. What problem does the report deal with?

2. What is the solution to the problem?

3. Does the solution seem to be a good one? Do you see any objection to it? Do you see any better solution?

4. What seems to be the rhetorical situation behind the article? What does the writer do to fit the article to its audience?

5. How effective is this report in terms of the criteria listed in chapter 1? What are its particular strengths and weaknesses? How could it be improved?

THE THEORY/APPLICATION REPORT

The theory/application report uses a two-part structure superficially like that of the problem/solution report. However, in the theory/application report the documented information is primarily in the first section, which functions like the review of the literature section in the report of original research.

Once the writer documents the theory, he moves on to apply it, point by point, to a particular situation. Like the problem section in the problem/solution report, the application section is usually personal or job oriented. Thus, the theory/application report centers information in the theory section and opinions in the application section. Structurally, then, the theory/application report is the opposite of the problem/solution report.

The following article, which describes some sophisticated test equipment, originally appeared in a specialized engineering journal and was later reprinted in a less specialized journal. The authors appeal to three audiences in this article: engineers, who want to see how this particular equipment works; experts, who want to know the theory behind the equipment; and administrators, who want to know whether this equipment can solve their problems.

Acoustic emission testing of FRP equipment—I

T. J. Fowler and R. S. Scarpellini

Monsanto Co.

This nondestructive technique is rapidly gaining acceptance as both a proof and an in-service inspection test. Part I describes the concept; Part II presents test procedures.

Acoustic emission testing is a recently developed method for determining the structural adequacy of fiber-reinforced plastic (FRP) structures. It is particularly valuable because many of the nondestructive test methods used for metals are unsuitable with FRP. In many cases, it has been able to identify defects not detected by other methods and to furnish insight into failure mechanisms.

Acoustic emission offers a number of advantages over conventional visual inspection methods, which tend to be subjective. For testing of in-service equipment, visual examination requires an empty, decontaminated vessel stripped of external insulation. In contrast, plant acoustic emission tests are normally carried out with process fluids flowing, and plant downtime is reduced or eliminated. The need for decontamination is eliminated and only minor removal of insulation is required. In addition, acoustic emission testing has the advantage of providing information on the structural adequacy of the entire piece of equipment.

To facilitate exchange and development of nonproprietary information on the application of acoustic emission to FRP equipment, the Committee on Acoustic Emission of Reinforced Plastics (CARP) has been formed under the auspices of The Society of the Plastics Industry (SPI). It includes FRP equipment manufacturers, research organizations, resin

and glass suppliers, acoustic emission instrumentation suppliers, and FRP users.

WHAT IS ACOUSTIC EMISSION

Acoustic emission is the term used to describe elastic stress waves produced in solids as a result of the application of stress. The waves are generated by rapid release of energy within the material. In FRP composites, acoustic emissions are generated by cracking of the matrix, debonding of the matrix from the fibers, laminate separation, fiber pullout and breakage of the fibers. The acoustic emission generated during stressing of equipment is detected by sensitive piezoelectric transducers attached to the surface. Measurement is accomplished in a number of ways, as shown in Fig. 1:

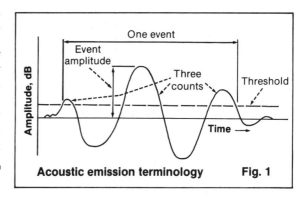

Acoustic emission terminology   **Fig. 1**

• Counts—Acoustic emission is normally measured in counts, the number of times the amplitude of the signal from the transducer exceeds a set threshold. The number of counts is the measure of the total acoustic emission.

- Events—Acoustic emission occurs in "bursts" of continuous counts, called events. Each event can be recorded and analyzed.
- Amplitude—The maximum signal amplitude during an individual event is normally measured in decibels and is referred to as the event amplitude.

BEHAVIOR OF FRP

Fig. 2 is a representative acoustic emission plot for a composite material, showing total counts vs. loading, in accordance with ASTM-D638 test procedures. The curve illustrates a number of important facets of FRP acoustic emission behavior. As with most materials, the total emission count increases at an accelerating rate with the addition of load. The massive emissions that occur near failure are of little practical interest; and for field tests, emissions at service loads are of much greater value.

The onset of emission will normally occur in the strain range of 0.001–0.005, the exact value depending on type of resin, and the construction and quality of the laminate. This strain range corresponds with the onset of fiber/matrix debonding and resin microcracking [1-4], and is well below the ultimate strain of either the resin or glass. The initial cracking is due to stress magnification between and around the fibers [5].

As a general rule, the percentage of ultimate load corresponding to initiation of emission is in the 25–50% range, depending on the type of construction. The fraction of ultimate load for first emission, or for a given number of counts, will decrease with an increasing amount of random glass. Random glass tends to emit sooner than unidirectional fibers (either parallel or perpendicular to the direction of stress). Combinations of different types of construction (for example, random and longitudinal) and woven roving, will tend to emit sooner than constructions having only random fibers.

CREEP

Above a particular level of load, acoustic emission will continue when the load is held constant (see Fig. 3). The continuing emission at 1,200 and 1,600 lb should be noted. Emissions during a load-hold are indicative of *creep*, and a time plot can be used to determine if the creep deformation is becoming unstable. Creep is the result of continuing damage resulting from stress redistribution caused by visco-elastic flow of the matrix [6].

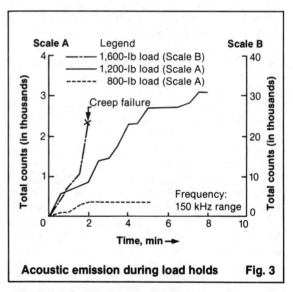

Acoustic emission during load holds   **Fig. 3**

AMPLITUDE DISTRIBUTION

A histogram of the amplitude of events can help to define defects in equipment [7]. The two histograms shown in Fig. 4 are for the load ranges 4% to 50% of the failure load, and 4% of failure load to failure. The load was applied in a series of steps to 25, 50,

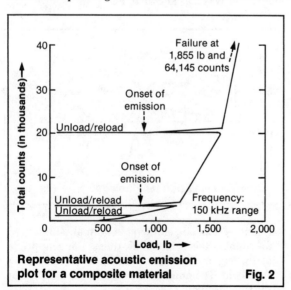

Representative acoustic emission plot for a composite material   **Fig. 2**

75 and 100% of the failure load, with intermediate unloadings to a nominal stress of approximately 4% of ultimate. The equipment threshold was set at 40 dB.

For the lower load range, the events tend to be of low amplitude. It is believed that these correspond to fiber/matrix debonding and matrix cracking. For the higher load range, high-amplitude events occur that are believed to correspond to fiber breakage. As would be expected, an increasing proportion of high-amplitude events occur as the specimen approaches failure. An amplitude histogram can be used to estimate the percentage of ultimate load being carried by a structure.

For some types of FRP construction, the failure histogram is bimodal, with one peak at the threshold level and another corresponding to fiber breakage in the 70-to-80 dB range. It has been reported [8] that in addition to distinguishing between fiber breakage and other failure mechanisms, an amplitude distribution plot can detect delamination failures. Delaminations tend to give a cluster of events centered in the 50-to-60 dB range.

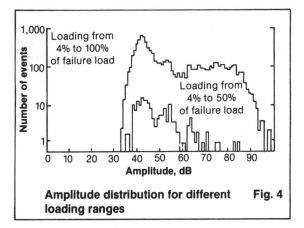

Amplitude distribution for different   **Fig. 4**
loading ranges

SPECTRAL ANALYSIS

As is the case with amplitude distribution analysis, spectral analysis of frequencies can be used to provide information regarding the mode of FRP fracture [9–12]. However, attenuation is dependent on frequency and thus poses difficulties when spectral analysis techniques are applied to full-scale equipment. During the course of a test, the ratio of total low-frequency (50 kHz) to total high-frequency (150 kHz) counts declines, as shown in Fig. 5. A number of authors [9, 10] have reported that interfiber failure has a spectral peak at a lower frequency than does fiber fracture. This is confirmed by Fig. 5.

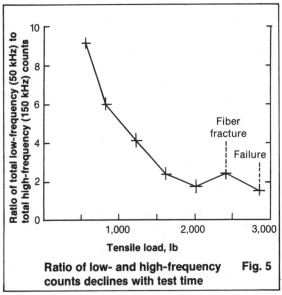

Ratio of low- and high-frequency   **Fig. 5**
counts declines with test time

FELICITY EFFECT

An unusual feature of FRP emission relates to the *Kaiser* effect, which occurs during an unload/reload cycle. It is the phenomenon whereby emissions do not occur until the previously attained maximum load is reached. FRP exhibits the Kaiser effect up to a percentage of ultimate load. However, above this load, emission will begin at loads lower than the previously attained maximum. This is known as the *Felicity* effect.

If a FRP specimen is held at load for a long period of time, the Felicity effect will be present. This occurs because of the redistribution of residual internal stresses during the unload period. The result of the redistribution is that additional microfailures will occur during reloading. Redistribution begins as soon as load is removed, and for initial loads close to ultimate, the Felicity effect is observed without a hold in the unloaded condition.

Because of the Felicity effect it is possible to test in-service vessels without exceeding the maximum operating load, thus eliminating the risk of permanent damage.

The ratio of the load at onset of emission to the previously attained maximum load is known as the Felicity ratio. This is a measure of the total amount of damage. The lower the number, the greater the damage [13].

ATTENUATION
Wave propagation and attenuation studies conducted on FRP show that high-frequency emissions are attenuated faster than low-frequency emissions [14]. Apparently, transmissibility increases with an increasing percentage of glass, and with the hardness of the resin. In addition, continuous fibers transmit better than chopped fibers. Because continuous fibers provide good transmissibility in one direction, a filament-wound vessel will have different attenuation characteristics in different directions.

Part II (in the Nov. 17 issue) will present acoustic emission test procedures for FRP equipment.

REFERENCES
1. Owens, M. J., and Smith, T. R., *Proc. 6th Inter. Reinforced Plastics Conference,* British Plastics Federation, London, 1970.
2. Howe, R. J., and Owen, J. M., *Proc. 8th Inter. Reinforced Plastics Conference,* British Plastics Federation, London, 1972.
3. Garrett, K. W., and Bailey, J. E., The Effect of Resin Failure Strain on the Tensile Properties of Glass Fiber Reinforced Polyester Cross-Ply Laminates, *J. of Materials Science,* Vol. 12, 1977.
4. Norwood, L. S., and Millman, A. F., Strain Limited Design Criteria for Reinforced Plastic Process Equipment, 34th Annual Technical Conference, Reinforced Plastics/Composites Institute, The Society of the Plastics Industry, New Orleans, 1979.
5. Kies, J. A., U.S. Naval Research Laboratory Report No. 5752, 1962.
6. Rotem, A., and Baruch, J., Determining the Load-Time History of Fiber Composite Materials by Acoustic Emission, Technion-Israel Institute of Technology, Haifa, Israel, MED Report No. 44, March, 1974.
7. Rotem, A., and Eliezer, A., Fracture Modes and Acoustic Emission of Composite Materials, *J. of Testing and Evaluation,* Vol. 7, No. 1, January, 1979.
8. Wadin, J. R., Listening to Composite Materials. Acoustic Emission Applications, Dunegan/Endevco, San Juan Capistrano, Calif., April, 1979.
9. Wolitz, K., Brockmann, W., and Fischer, T., Evaluation of Glass Fiber Reinforced Plastics by Means of Acoustic Emission Measurements, 4th Acoustic Emission Symposium, High Pressure Institute of Japan, Tokyo, September, 1978.
10. Crostack, H. A., Basic Aspects of the Application of Frequency Analysis, *Ultrasonics,* Vol. 15, p. 6, November, 1977.
11. Egan, D. M., and Williams, J. H., Jr., Acoustic Emission Spectral Analysis of Fiber Composite Failure Mechanisms, NASA Contractor Report 2983, 1978.
12. Henneke, E. G., Signature Analysis of Acoustic Emissions from Composites, NASA Grant NSG 1238, 1978.
13. Fowler, T. J., and Gray, E., Development of an Acoustic Emission Test for FRP Equipment, Preprint 3583, ASCE Convention and Exposition, Boston, April, 1979.
14. Pollock, A. A., and Cook, W. J., Acoustic Emission Testing of Aerial Devices, Southeastern Electric Exchange, Engineering and Operating Division in Annual Conference, New Orleans, April, 1976.

Acoustic emission testing of FRP equipment—II

T. J. Fowler and R. S. Scarpellini

*Monsanto Co.**

Test methods and rejection criteria for FRP vessels are presented. Sample results provide insight into what to expect.

The fundamentals of acoustic emission behavior of FRP equipment have already been discussed. This concluding article applies these fundamentals in actual test procedures.

SOURCE LOCATION

With metals, acoustic emission sources can be located by use of multiple sensors and a triangulation-type approach. The arrival time of a given event is compared between different sensors, and the source calculated.

The triangulation technique is feasible for small test samples of FRP. However, for full-size structures, it has proven unsatisfactory. The location of defects in FRP is normally based on the "area of interest" method. This takes advantage of the attenuation characteristics of FRP.

A low-frequency channel monitors a large area of the equipment, while high-frequency channels monitor local areas of interest. An active high-frequency channel indicates that the defect is within the vicinity of one of the transducers feeding into the channel. Switching between the transducers can better define emission location. Transducers may be moved during a test.

The results reported here are based on tests of glass-reinforced polyester, epoxy and vinyl ester systems, and asbestos-reinforced furan. Dunegan/Endevco equipment was used for the testing that employed one low-frequency channel (50 kHz) and 7 high-frequency channels (150 kHz). Work by other

*To meet the authors, see *Chem. Eng.*, Oct. 20, p. 148. This article is an update of a paper presented at a NACE seminar in New Orleans, Oct./Nov. 1979. The paper is included in NACE publication, "Managing Corrosion with Plastics—Vol. IV," December 1979.

authors [1-6] indicates that the results obtained are applicable to other systems.

. . . a typical FRP tank setup for acoustic emission testing [has] sensors [that] are attached to the vessel with adhesive tape, and a grease-like acoustic couplant [that] provides a link between the FRP and the transducer. Transducers are normally mounted on areas that are expected to be highly stressed by the test load, or have a history of being problem areas (for example, nozzles, lugs, and knuckle regions). Circuit continuity and transducer response are checked out by using an artificial pulser placed near each transducer in turn. The pulse will normally be seen on two channels—the one being checked, and the low-frequency channel.

Transducer spacing is determined via an attenuation check. This is carried out by moving the pulser away from the transducer in 2-in. increments, both horizontally and vertically, until no signal (less than 30 dB) is detected. For a pulser giving a 70-dB signal 1 in. away, transducer spacings should be about three times the zero-signal distance.

Prior to testing, background noise should be checked. This is normally accomplished by recording emissions for 10 to 15 min prior to loading. Background noise can become significant below 20 kHz. Accordingly, the preamplifier filters and transducers are selected so that only emissions above this value are monitored. Occasionally, the low-frequency channel will pick up background noise during a test. Typical noise sources are compressors, forklift trucks, etc. Provided that the practices enumerated below are observed, the high-frequency channels are normally immune to background noise.

- Vessels should be filled through a drowned nozzle. Free-falling liquid and splashing can create false

emissions. Care should be taken to avoid entraining large quantities of gases in the filling medium.
- Cables should be taped to, or clear of, equipment.
- Mount equipment on rubber pads if possible.
- In some cases, agitated vessels can be tested with the agitator running, but check background noise first.
- When analyzing test results, discount false emissions caused by valve openings and closings, traffic over cables, steam traps, etc.

VESSEL AND TANK TESTS

New vessels are normally monitored during the initial hydrotest in the fabricator's shop. As appropriate, the vessel can be retested after shipping and placement. A typical load-time sequence is shown in Fig. 2. As can be seen, loading is increased in a series of steps up to the design load.

In contrast to metal equipment, FRP equipment should not be overloaded during hydrotest. In metals, beneficial residual secondary stresses result from overloading. This is not the case with FRP; permanent damage, which can be detrimental to long-term life, can result from overloading. The hold periods are used to assess creep. For vessels subject to vacuum, a similar load sequence is used.

The loading sequence shown in Fig. 3 is used for questionable or unacceptable new tanks. In this case, the equipment is unloaded and reloaded. This procedure permits assessment of the Felicity ratio.

In-plant tests can be carried out with process fluids or by a hydrotest. Use of process fluids has a number of advantages, including reduction or elimination of plant downtime, and elimination of the decontamination requirement. Fig. 4 shows the load sequence for an in-service vessel. In this case, loading starts from the 60% level.

In order to take advantage of the Felicity effect, in-service vessels are operated for one week prior to testing at 60%, or less, of the normal capacity. For in-service tanks, the Felicity ratio is calculated directly from the test loading sequence, as the load at onset of emission divided by the maximum operating load. This permits a redistribution of stress and ensures that the acoustic emission test will detect existing damage.

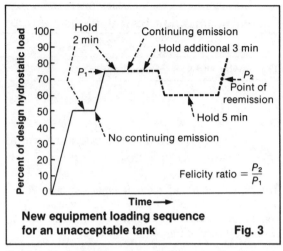

New equipment loading sequence for an unacceptable tank **Fig. 3**

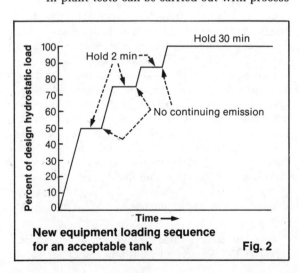

New equipment loading sequence for an acceptable tank **Fig. 2**

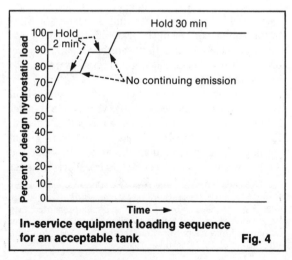

In-service equipment loading sequence for an acceptable tank **Fig. 4**

For a test to be meaningful, loads must be of the same magnitude and in the same direction as in-service loads. Nozzles and equipment supports are frequently designed to resist mechanical loads. Accordingly, external loads should be applied when it is desired to check these items. Simulated mechanical loads can be applied in a number of ways, including sandbags, the weight of an individual, jacks and springs.

VESSEL REJECTION CRITERIA

Fig. 5 shows emissions from a vessel tested to failure. The notations superimposed on the plot indicate areas of maximum emission. It should be noted that virtually no emission occurs below 18 ft of water. At this point, the emissions take off sharply. This clear delineation between no emission and significant emission is characteristic of FRP vessel tests and is a clear indication of the onset of damage. Therefore, it makes little difference whether the rejection limit is set at 1,000, 5,000, or 10,000 counts.

With increasing load, an increasing number of high-amplitude events are observed. For example, only 9 events greater than 70 dB were observed during loading up to 18 ft. In contrast, 20 events greater than 70 dB were noted in loading from 18 to 19 ft. Events greater than 70 dB are indicative of glass breakage.

For depths of water greater than 20 ft, emissions continued throughout the 1 to 12-min hold periods. A Felicity ratio of 0.88 was observed during the 19-14-19-ft unload/reload cycle.

Based on such tests of FRP tanks and vessels, the following rejection criteria, in order of importance, are proposed for new vessels [7].

1. Total counts in excess of 5,000 on either of the two counters. This assumes that all active 150-kHz channels are switched into the same counter.
2. More than 10 events of over 70 dB amplitude.
3. During a load-hold, emissions last beyond two min.

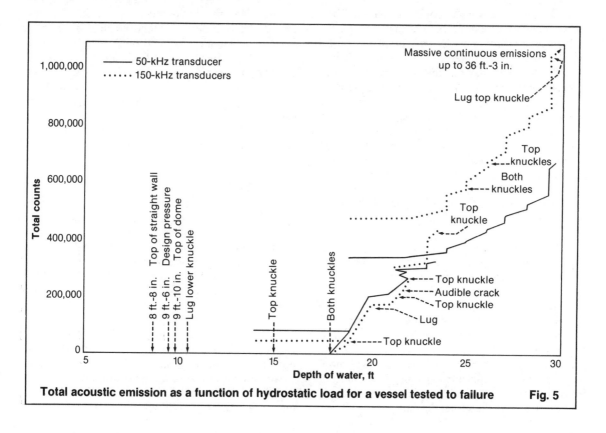

Total acoustic emission as a function of hydrostatic load for a vessel tested to failure   **Fig. 5**

4. A Felicity ratio of less than 0.95. The Felicity ratio is measured during reloading, and is defined as load at onset of emission, divided by the maximum load previously attained.

The above criteria apply to the specific Dunegan/Endevco equipment configuration used for these tests. For other instrumentation, some modification may be needed.

The first criterion can be considered as an indication of cumulative damage. The second is a measure of fiber breakage. The third relates to creep stability, and the fourth is a measure of previous damage.

For vessels already in service, Criteria 3 and 4 are of prime importance. Criterion 1 is of less importance, with 2,500 total counts being the test ceiling (instead of 5,000). Criterion 2 will very seldom govern.

TEST RESULTS

Acoustic emission should not be considered as a replacement for visual inspection. Visual inspection and acoustic emission testing are complementary to one another. Each can reveal unique information.

Table I summarizes the authors' experience with acoustic emission testing of new equipment. With the three exceptions noted below, all vessels listed in Table I passed visual inspection prior to testing. A number of vessels required retest or test following shipping. This accounts for the total number of tests being greater than the number of equipment items. Defects were found in a number of the new vessels. The majority of these defects were repairable. Typical defects include: cracked flanges, nozzles and sumps; air entrapment; and secondary joint failure.

Detection of repairable defects in the vessel manufacturer's shop is of benefit to both the vendor and the purchaser, and shop repairs are generally easier, and of better quality, than field repairs.

Because of air entrainment, 3 vessels failed visual inspection. The air bubbles were located on the outside of the vessel, in low-stressed areas. The acoustic emission test showed that the structural properties had not been degraded to an unacceptable level and, because the entrained air was not critical from a corrosion viewpoint, it was possible to accept the vessel despite the visual defects.

Table I. *Acoustic emission tests of new tanks and vessels.*

Number of equipment items	62
Number of tests	78
Acceptable tests	41
Failed visual inspection but acceptable by acoustic emission	3
Failed test—repairable	9
Failed test—unacceptable	1
Failed test—acceptable for operation at lower pressure	1
Tested in field following shipping—acceptable	16
Tested after repair of shipping damage	
a. Acceptable	3
b. Unacceptable	1

Table II shows the authors' experience with in-service tanks and vessels. Such vessels are retested at periodic intervals, so the number of tests exceeds the number of equipment items. It should be noted that the tests revealed defects in over half of the vessels. Of these, one-third were repairable, and two-thirds were taken out of service. Typical defects include internal corrosion and erosion, mechanical damage, delamination, weathering, and inadequate repairs. It is often difficult to repair defects and/or damage to in-service vessels. Unless internal damage is caught early, chemicals will penetrate the resin-rich interior liner and permeate the structural fiberglass. When this occurs, excessive amounts of materials must be removed, and repairing is uneconomical.

PIPE TESTS

Seventy tests have been run on pipes and/or pipe assemblies. The majority of these tests (49) have been directed toward development of test criteria and methods. The remaining 21 tests revealed defects in approximately one-quarter of the assemblies.

Procedures for testing pipe are similar to those for testing tanks and vessels. The pipe is filled with water or process fluids and monitored during pressurization and load-holds. As is the case with vessels, the maximum test pressure should not exceed the maximum pressure encountered during operation. For large-diameter pipe, the deadweight of the fluids can result in significant stresses at the supports. Accordingly, support areas should be monitored during pipe filling.

Table II. *Acoustic emission tests of in-service tanks and vessels.*

Number of equipment items	340
Number of tests	407
Acceptable tests	204
Failed test—repairable	80
Failed test—unacceptable and replaced	60
Failed test but operating at reduced levels or out of service	58
Unacceptable tanks tested to destruction	5

Many pipe systems use cemented socket and spigot joints. Frequently, excess nonstructural cement is present at the edge of the joint, and this fractures during the first pressure cycle. Because of this, it is recommended that, for pipe systems with cemented joints, emissions during the first pressurization cycle be discounted. This first pressurization is normally a rapid increase in pressure, immediately followed by unloading. The second pressurization is monitored for emissions, and pressure is increased in a series of steps with intermediate load holds. The load levels and hold times should be similar to those used for vessels.

Attenuation through a joint is normally severe. Accordingly, it is advisable to mount transducers on both sides of a flanged or socket and spigot joint. For large-diameter pipe with butt and strap joints, transducers can be mounted directly on the strap.

In piping systems, joints and flanges are particularly troublesome. Very little trouble has been experienced with straight pipe. However, tees and elbows have, on occasion, shown signs of distress at pressures below the rated level.

REFERENCES

1. Carlyle, J. M., Acoustic Emission in Fiber Reinforced Composites, Department of the Navy Report No. NADC-75082-30, 1975.
2. Jessen, E. C., and De Herrera, A. J., Prediction of Composite Pressure Vessel Performance by Application on the Kaiser Effect in Acoustic Emissions, ASME Paper H300-12-2-037, June, 1975.
3. Rotem, A., and Eliezer, A., Fracture Modes and Acoustic Emission of Composite Materials, *J. of Testing and Evaluation*, Vol. 7, No. 1, January 1979.
4. Hamstad, M. A., and Chiao, T. T., Structural Integrity of Fiber/Epoxy Vessels by Acoustic Emission, SAMPE *Quarterly*, October 1976.
5. Harris, D. O., Tetelman, A. S., and Darwish, F. A. I., Detection of Fiber Cracking of Acoustic Emission, Dunegan/Endevco Technical Report DRC-71-1, San Juan Capistrano, Calif.
6. William, R. S., and Reifsnider, K. L., Investigations of Acoustic Emission During Fatigue Loading of Composite Specimens, *J. of Composite Materials,* Vol. 8, October 1974.
7. Fowler, T. J., and Gray, E., Development of an Acoustic Emission Test for FRP Equipment, Preprint 3583, ASCE Convention and Exposition, Boston, April 1979.

EXERCISE

1. What is the theory presented in this pair of reports?

2. To what specific problem or situation is this theory applied?

3. Does the application seem to follow the theory? Do you see any possible objections to the proposed application?

4. What seems to be the rhetorical situation behind the article? What do the writers do to fit the article to its audiences?

5. How effective is this report in terms of the criteria listed in chapter 1? What are its particular strengths and weaknesses? How could it be improved?

SUMMARY

In business, industry, and government, writers combine related sets of information and opinions in several typical formats: the thesis report, the report of original research, the problem/solution report, and the theory/application report. Knowing these four patterns and using them when appropriate can help a writer decide on the writing's scope and strategy.

EXERCISES

1. Read the following questions. Which type of report would each question probably generate? Also indicate a possible situation and audience appropriate to each report. Be prepared to explain and defend your choices by indicating the structure and scope you expect in the reports.
   a. Can I use a laser to demonstrate basic physics principles?
   b. Will the Wankel engine reduce automobile exhaust fumes?
   c. Should seat belts be mandatory?
   d. What species of sea gull is eating all the prawns at the Kahuku aquafarm?
   e. Can Rogerian psychology be used to reduce tension between labor and management?
   f. What methods can women use to be assured of fair treatment by their employers?
   g. Do first-grade children learn better in an open classroom or in the traditional closed classroom?

2. Write four questions of your own, one for each of the four general report types.

3. Read the article on drilling for oil and answer the questions that follow it. This article was originally published in *World Oil*, published by and aimed at people in the oil industry.
   a. Which of the four patterns does the article most closely fit?
   b. In what ways does it differ from the general pattern? Can you account for these variations on the basis of the rhetorical situation inherent in the article?
   c. How effective is the article? Can you make any suggestions to improve it?

4. Examine several magazines to find at least one article for each of the patterns described in this chapter. In a brief report, answer the questions in number 3 about each article.

5. Select one of the patterns identified in this chapter and use it to write an article or report of your own. Do not worry if your report varies in some ways from the general pattern, but do be prepared to justify those variations.

Solving drilling problems in the Baltimore Canyon

Vernon H. Goodwin, III and Terry Lucht

*Senior Drilling Engineer and Drilling Engineer,
Production Engineering Services, Continental Oil
Co., Houston*

Editor's Note

*In early 1978, after all litigation was finally
removed and the path opened to drilling in
the Baltimore Canyon, Continental Oil Co.
(Conoco) spudded the area's first well on
April 10. Hudson Canyon Block 590-1 was
located some 75 miles offshore New Jersey in
242 feet of water (Fig. 1).*

*Not only the petroleum industry, but also
the government and the public alike had hopes
that this area in the U.S. North Atlantic would
prove to hold vast reserves of oil and gas to
help ease the nation's current energy dilemma;
however, only two mentionable gas finds have
been reported out of the 14 wells drilled and
tested to date. Conoco had interest in three
of the 14 wells drilled, including serving as
operator on the Hudson Canyon well to be
discussed.*

*Unfortunately, Conoco's first wildcat
was one of the dry ones. The company spent a
total of $4 million in its attempt and reported
"no significant shows."*

*Conoco employed the semi-submersible
Diamond M New Era to drill the wildcat. The
rig's special outfitting and its logistics package
are discussed in addition to specifics of the
drilling and operational events occurring at
the well site.*

Several important lessons were learned from the
drilling of the first well in the Baltimore Canyon.
Problems encountered by Continental Oil Co. during
the drilling of Hudson Canyon Block 590-1 well offshore New Jersey included: a mislocated guide base,
crossthreaded casing joints, a poor cement job, misrun surveys, excessive bit wear and wellhead con-

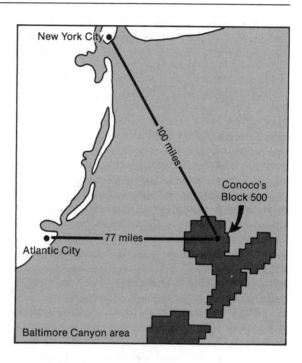

**Figure 1. Conoco's Hudson Canyon Block 590-1
well was located 75 miles offshore New Jersey in
242 feet of water. Rig was on location from April
9, 1978, to June 9, 1978.**

nector failure. While these problems caused lost
time, operation recommendations were made which
hopefully will eliminate similar problems on future
wells in the area.

MOBILIZATION

The drilling rig commenced mobilization at Sabine
Pass on March 14, 1978. Sixteen days were required
to complete the following:

- Steam boiler system installation (basic winteriza-
tion)
- Central deck drain installation (in compliance with
environmental regulations)

- Oil mop installation for the deck drainage system
- Shunt installation for cuttings and mud to a depth of 40 feet subsea (USGS permit regulations)
- BOP stack maintenance
- Equipment loading (Conoco's equipment)

Rig departed Sabine Pass on March 30, 1978, and arrived on location at Hudson Canyon Block 590 on April 9. Towing time was 10 days and 7 hours with a 5,700-hp combination boat. Although the rig is self-propelled, insurance and basic maritime safety necessitated this tow-assist movement.

LOGISTICS

The drilling rig was 77 air miles due east of Atlantic City, N.J., and 185 miles south-southwest by boat from Davisville, R.I. The Rhode Island docking facility is an old Navy "Sea-Bee" facility dating from World War II. It has an extremely large concrete-asphalt storage area, spacious docking facilities and 40 feet of water depth at the dock. Numerous service companies and all the oil companies drilling in the Mid-Atlantic area employ this facility for material transfer. Because of the distance, Atlantic City was the chief supervisory operating center.

Two 206-foot combination anchor-handling and supply boats (5,700 hp) serviced the rig from the Rhode Island base, a 12-hour run in good weather. This run was approximately 3 to 4 hours longer than necessary due to U.S. Navy restrictions on routes of travel. Deck cargo was rigged for one hook pickup employing prefabricated metal containers for pallet material and other small, hard-to-handle materials. The 13⅜-inch and 9⅝-inch casing was all preslung for ease of handling in rough weather.

An 80-foot, single screw, 345-hp converted fishing trawler was used as a standby boat. Aboard this vessel was numerous safety equipment including a rubber dingy with an outboard motor to assist a man overboard.

An IFR-equipped Bell 212 helicopter was operated strictly for Conoco operations based in Atlantic City. All personnel on Conoco flights were required to wear cold water survival jackets as an added safety feature in the event of an emergency ditching. In 40° F water, survival time ranges from a few minutes to over four hours. Numerous periods of dense fog lasting six or seven days resulted in unfly-able conditions throughout much of May and early June. On one occasion a workboat was used to change out the rig crews, as no crewboat was available in the area.

Only the Conoco drilling superintendent and the contractor's rig manager lived in Atlantic City. All other personnel commuted from the Gulf Coast area due to the high experience levels required for this crucial operation.

COMMUNICATIONS

Communications consisted primarily of a low-band company radio with sets located on the rig, workboats, standby boat, Atlantic City base, Davisville base, and a repeater in Southhampton, N.Y., to talk to workboats in transit to and from the rig. Also a leased long-line telephone circuit connected Atlantic City to Davisville direct.

The second line of communications was the UHF telephone installed on the rig, receiving in Atlantic City. Atmospheric conditions frequently interrupted this mode.

The third line of communication was the MARISAT satellite. This utilized transmission to a satellite and back to a receiving station in Connecticut capable of teletype, voice or data transmission. This was used primarily to receive daily weather and to DART electric logs into Houston for immediate evaluation. Teletype machines were also installed in Atlantic City and Davisville to receive weather and transact other business.

DRILLING

After arrival on location, running anchors (eight primary with no piggybacks) and finding the bottom free of obstructions, a temporary guidebase (TGB) was landed April 10. The 36-inch hole was drilled through the TGB and 30-inch casing was run to 347 feet KB (kelly bushing), 33 feet below TGB, where a bridge was encountered and the casing pulled and set back in the moonpool. Two unsuccessful attempts to stab the drill string into the TGB confirmed that it had tilted. Guidelines breaking on the attempts, the location was abandoned.

Rig was moved 50 feet and second location spudded April 14. A 36-inch hole was drilled to 515 feet KB with no TGB used. The 30-inch structural pipe was run to 497 feet and cemented when hard fill prevented washing casing to 515 feet. The strength of the 30-inch casing was not believed great enough, with the pipe set 31 feet above the sea floor, to support the weight and bending moment of the 18¾-inch blowout preventer (BOP) stack. The 30-inch casing was cut 9 feet below the sea floor and the location abandoned April 16.

Rig was again moved 50 feet to a third location and spudded April 17 (Fig. 2). A 36-inch hole

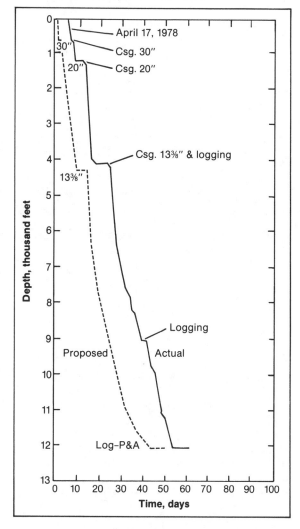

Figure 2. *After abandoning two locations, a third hole was successfully drilled to 12,000 feet TD. Three strings of casing were run—30-inch, 20-inch and 13⅜-inch. Curve reflects number of feet actually drilled/day.*

was drilled to 525 feet and the 30-inch structural casing was run and cemented at 519 feet KB. A 17½-inch hole was drilled to 1,129 feet, underreamed to 26 inches, and 20-inch casing was run and cemented at 1,112 feet KB with 850 sacks of cement. An 18¾-inch 10,000 psi subsea BOP stack was landed on the 20-inch casing and used to drill the remainder of the hole. A 12½-inch hole was drilled to 4,015 feet, and after running logs, the hole was opened to 17½ inches and 13⅜-inch casing was run and cemented at 3,963 feet KB with 2,700 sacks of cement. A 12¼-inch hole was drilled to 8,899 feet where a correlation logging run was made. Drilling continued to 12,000 feet total depth (TD). After logging operations at TD were completed, the well was plugged and abandoned.

Plugging was accomplished with Class H cement. A total 200 sacks were used across the 13⅜-inch casing shoe at 3,963 feet, a cement retainer directly above at 3,810 feet, 50 sacks above retainer, and 50 sacks set at surface from 550 feet to 335 feet KB. At this time, attempts to pull the BOP stack and riser with surface hydraulic controls failed. The 13⅜-inch, 20-inch and 30-inch casing strings were then cut simultaneously 15 feet below the mudline. The BOP stack and riser were pulled with the 20-inch and 13⅜-inch casing stubs suspended in the collet connector. The collet connector was manually released at the surface and the casing stubs recovered. The 30-inch running tool, with 17½-inch stabilizer made up below, was used to stab into and recover 30-inch casing and permanent guidebase, abandoning the well with no obstructions left on the sea floor. Abandonment operations were completed June 8, and the rig released June 9. (See Table 1 for full account of rig time.)

DRILLING OPERATIONAL PROBLEMS

Temporary guidebase (TGB) failure Sea bottom conditions resulted in failure of the TGB. Coarse-grained sand at the sea floor was washed out while drilling the 36-hole, and the TGB shifted and settled. This prevented reentry with the drill string and/or casing. The TGB was abandoned on the sea floor after the guidelines broke while attempting to run 30-inch. No trace of the base was found by visual diver inspection using a hand-held camera and light.

Table 1. *Rig Time Analysis, Hudson Canyon Block 590-1.*

Operation	Actual Time (hrs.)	% Total	
Moving on/off	18.5	1.26	
Rigging up/down	19	1.30	
Surveying	46	3.14	
Drilling	521	35.61	
Reaming	59	4.03	
Redrilling	18	1.23	
Tripping	184.75	12.63	
Circulating	48	3.28	
Test equipment	52	3.55	
Logging	89.5	6.12	
Running casing	70.5	4.82	
Cementing/WOC	36.5	2.49	
Repairing rig	60	4.10	
Fishing	33	2.26	
W.O.W.	71	4.85	
Waiting on service company	13.5	0.92	
Waiting on orders	6	0.41	
Change BHA	12.5	0.85	
Handling BOP stack and riser	56.5	3.86	
Other miscellaneous	46.75	3.20	
	1463	100.00	
"Time Lost Due to" Data	Actual Time	% Total Lost Time	% Total
Drilling first two unusable holes	166	47.16	11.35
Misrun surveys (2 hrs)	11.5	3.27	0.79
Rig repair	60	17.05	4.10
Fishing (cut casing and stuck pipe)	7.5	2.13	0.51
W.O.W.	71	20.17	4.85
W.O. service co. (AZ casing cutter)	13.5	3.84	0.92
W.O. orders	6	1.70	0.41
Other (manually disconnect collet connector, lay down cut casing)	16.5	4.69	1.13
	352	100.00	24.06

30-inch casing—hole loss   After moving the 50 feet, a second 36-inch conductor hole was drilled and the 30-inch casing was run and cemented. Diver measurement confirmed that the permanent guidebase was 33 feet above the sea floor.

As the possible bending moments with the 28¾-inch BOP stack attached to this guidebase exceed the casing string's collapse resistance, the casing was cut and the hole abandoned.

Although heavier walled, 30-inch casing with increased collapse resistance could be used, the distance from the permanent guidebase to the nearest pipe supporting point remains critical. In areas of large tide variation, some success has been achieved with large skirted temporary guidebases and over drilling the 36-inch hole.

20-inch casing—lost time due to weather   The 20-inch casing used was buttress. To run the 811 feet of casing with a mild pitch and roll causing cross-threading of several joints required 13½ hours. Considerable time could have been saved had a different coupling been available.

Cement setting time   A Gulf Coast type cement composition proved to have extremely long setting times of 48 to 72 hours. Both a 40° F mixing water temperature and the addition of a fluid loss additive with a lightweight cement combined to produce poor results on conductor and surface casing jobs. It was recommended that only Class H cement with 3% $CaCl_2$ be used on the 30-inch casing to provide rapid thickening time in cold water and give additional support to the pipe. If possible, all cements should be pilot tested at a lab using the cement after it has arrived on the rig. If time is not available to send in the cement during spud, the conductor and surface pipe cements should be pilot tested on the rig to check for setting time and contamination.

Survey failures   A total of 9½ hours was lost due to misrun single shot surveys. The film was either not exposed properly or was lodged in the camera and was not removed when retrieval was attempted. It is believed the problem could be eliminated by storing, loading and unloading the camera in the company representative's office. Less moisture and the warmer temperature of the office should allow the film to be more easily removed.

Excessive bit wear   Bit number 15 (API Type 5-1-7) had 22 broken teeth and 9 lost teeth after 59 hours on bottom while cutting 842 feet of hole. A shock sub was run with bit number 16 (API Type 5-2-7)

producing a bit run of 106½ hours and 1,421 feet of hole cut with only two broken teeth and one tooth lost. Extreme surface vibration was experienced often throughout bit run number 15 while bit number 16 had very little surface vibration using a shock sub. Bit numbers 15 and 16 drilled from 8,899 feet to 11,161 feet. Correlating lithology and drilling rates, button bits and a shock sub could have been used cost effectively below about 7,500 feet.

Wellhead connector failure   The wellhead connector would not release when pulling the stack to abandon the well. The casing had to be cut with the stack attached. The cut was made 12 feet below the mudline through the 13⅜-inch, 20-inch and 30-inch casing strings in 1 hour and 52 minutes in a single cut. The 13⅜-inch and 20-inch stubs were then pulled with stack as the 20-inch and 30-inch were not locked together. After manually releasing the connector at the moonpool, the connector was examined and found all threaded connections on the ring hydraulic jacks were corroded and could be broken by hand. This connector was completely overhauled in late March 1978, and an incorrect alloy fitting was used when replaced. Approximately 29 hours rig time was lost attempting to unlatch the stack and rigging up to lay down cut-off joints.

FOR FURTHER READING

Applewhite, Lottie. "Examination of the Medical/Scientific Manuscript." *Technical Writing and Communication* 9 (1979): 17–25.

Blicq, Ronald. *Technically Write! Communication for the Technical Man.* Englewood Cliffs, N.J.: Prentice-Hall, 1972.

Brunner, Ingrid; Mathes, J.C.; and Stevenson, Dwight. *The Technician as Writer: Preparing Technical Reports.* Indianapolis: Bobbs-Merrill, 1980.

Dodds, Robert. *Writing for Technical and Business Magazines.* New York: John Wiley and Sons, 1969.

Estrin, Herman. "An Engineering Report Writing Course that Works." *Improving College and University Teaching* 26 (1968): 28–31.

Halloran, S. Michael. "Teaching Writing and the Rhetoric of Science." *Journal of Technical Writing and Communication* 8 (1978): 77–88.

Holtzman, Paul. *The Psychology of the Speakers' Audience.* Glenview, Illinois: Scott, Foresman, 1970.

Mathes, J.C. and Stevenson, Dwight. *Designing Technical Reports: Writing for Audiences in Organizations.* Indianapolis: Bobbs-Merrill, 1976.

McKee, Blaine. "Do Professional Writers Use an Outline When They Write?" *Technical Communication* 19 (1972): 10–13.

Miller, Walter James. "What Can the Technical Writer of the Past Teach the Technical Writer of Today?" *IRE Transactions on Engineering and Speech* 4 (1961): 69–76.

Pearsall, Thomas. *Audience Analysis for Technical Writing.* Encino, California: Glencoe Press, 1969.

Sullivan, Jeremiah. "The Importance of a Philosophical 'Mix' in Teaching Business Communications." *Journal of Business Communications* 15 (1978): 29–37.

5

Graphics

Effective writing in business, industry, and government usually implies effective graphics. Technically oriented audiences often take a Missourian attitude—"Show me!" is the name of the game. Often the best way to show is by presenting data in the form of graphs, diagrams, flow charts, and other graphics. Basically, *graphics* refers to any of the document's nonprose elements, such as tables, charts, pictures, maps, etc. The writer has a twofold goal in creating graphics: (1) to make the data stand out on the page and (2) to make the data support the main purpose of the document as clearly and strongly as possible. Effective graphics accomplish both these goals.

GRAPHIC EFFECTS

Many technical pieces of writing have two main kinds of material: 1) prose, the text or written part of the document and 2) supporting graphic material. Generally speaking then, the text or prose contains directional material—ideas, conclusions, opinions, observations, recommendations, etc. The graphic portion of the document contains informational material—details that support the opinions and conclusions in the form of tables, charts, graphs, pictures, etc.

The text and the graphics support each other. Ideally, the reader grasps the writer's ideas and opinions from the text, and turns to the graphics for support of those ideas and opinions. The graphics in turn send the reader back to the text for more ideas. The reader moves back and forth down the page, first looking at text and then at graphics. The reader clearly understands the main idea from the text and sees support for the main idea in the graphics. The writer organizes the document so that the facts in the graphics clearly support the main idea.

For this mutually supporting graphic and text relationship to work most effectively, the graphic must be visible simultaneously with the relevant text. The reader should not have to hunt around for a supporting graphic—it should jump out. Pagination, graphic size, and layout sometimes make it difficult to keep text and graphic together; however, the writer can usually achieve this important goal by planning ahead and being creative.

Conversely, the graphic must not be so detailed that the reader forgets the point of the text. Graphics are not ends in themselves. The text is primary—it contains the main point. Graphics must do their job and then get out of the way to let the text take over again.

The text does not support the graphics—the graphics support the text.

This graphic and text relationship also implies that whenever possible, details should appear in graphic form. The reader should never have to plow through long and dense passages of prose that could appear as graphics instead.

GRAPHIC FORMATS

Many different graphic formats can be used to support the text's main ideas. However, the ideal graphic format depends on the type of data being presented.

Tables

The table presents large amounts of data in a simple, brief, and clear linear format. The same data in prose would be bulky, confusing, and inaccessible. Tables help the reader grasp relationships that might be invisible in prose. Also, tables allow the writer to focus attention on specific pieces of data while retaining a clear presentation of the whole.

You can clearly see the uses and advantages of tables by comparing the following two versions of a memo, the first in an ineffective prose format, and the second in an effective prose and tabular format.

```
        As requested by Tom Lindsey, we have analyzed the
sales records of our statewide branches. We have based
our calculations on the total inventory on hand as of
March 1, 1985. We find that some stores are doing very
well, while others are struggling just to break even. A
few are not even managing to do that. The White Plains
store is doing the best job. Its sales volume for the
first quarter is 678,000 dollars, up over 25 percent so
far this quarter. Its current inventory of 450 thousand
dollars' worth seems adequate, yet not overly large.
Comparing its sales volumes for the fourth quarters of
1984 vs. 1983, we find a gain from 459,000 dollars to
543,000 dollars. The Yonkers store is not doing so well.
First quarter sales, at 80,000 dollars, are up only 2
percent from last quarter. As a result, it has a large
inventory of several items, some of which have not sold a
single unit since Christmas. Yonkers' total inventory is
currently worth 220,000 dollars, almost three times its
first quarter sales total. Comparing its sales volumes
for the fourth quarters of 1984 vs. 1983, we find a
slight drop, from 83,000 dollars to 78,000 dollars.
Tarrytown is in between the two other stores. At 477,000
dollars' worth, sales are up 15 percent, and inventories
are down, too. In fact, it probably doesn't have enough
on hand to meet the usual Easter demand. Comparing its
sales volumes for the fourth quarters of 1984 vs. 1983,
we find a gain from 378,000 dollars to 417,000 dollars.
```

We would recommend that three-quarters of the excess
inventory from Yonkers be transferred to Tarrytown. We
should also do a marketing analysis to see if perhaps the
Yonkers store ought to be eliminated altogether.

The problems in this memo are not ones of content or organization, but of
format. The following version adds no new information, but simply changes
from a prose to a combination prose/tabular format:

RE: Statewide Sales Report and Recommendations

At the suggestion of Tom Lindsey, we offer the following
recommendations for our three New York branches:

1. White Plains—Retain as is.
2. Tarrytown—Absorb extra inventory from Yonkers.
3. Yonkers—Begin marketing analysis for possible
   closure.

The following information supports these recommendations:

Store	Sales Figures (Thousands of Dollars)			
	Current Inventory	1st Qtr 1985	4th Qtr 1984	4th Qtr 1983
White Plains	450	678	543	459
Tarrytown	140	477	417	378
Yonkers	220	80	78	83

EXERCISE

Use the qualities of effective writing presented in chapter 1 to evaluate these two
versions of the memo. Which version do you think is better? Defend your answer with
specific evidence.

In summary, tables allow the reader to interpret data quickly and efficiently. The writer supports the text's conclusions by referring to appropriate
tables. Tabular data supports the prose.

Table Format   The formats of tables are governed by precise rules designed to
enhance their effectiveness as supportive material. (See figure 5-1 for examples
of how these rules are followed.)

Mean Penetration Depth (δ_{90}) of Resin Around Southern Pine Earlywood and Latewood Adhesive Bonds as Related to Reaction Time Prior to Application of Resin				
Reaction Time (Hr.)	**Depth of Penetration**			
	Earlywood		**Latewood**	
	Mean (μm)	**Range** (μm)	**Mean** (μm)	**Range** (μm)
0.00	260	(20)	143	(0)
0.50	285	(30)	—	—
1.50	280	(40)	145	(60)
2.50	150	(30)	140	(80)
3.50	123	(30)	102	(40)
4.25	48	(0)	32	(10)

Glutamate Content of Certain Foods*				
Product	**Percent of Protein in Food**	**Percent of Glutamate in Protein**	**Protein-bound Glutamate (Grams per 100 Grams of Food)**	**Free Glutamate (Grams per 100 Grams of Food)**
Cow's milk	3.5	23.4	0.819	0.002
Human milk	1.4	16.4	0.229	0.019
Camembert cheese	17.5	27.4	4.787	0.600
Parmesan cheese	36.0	27.4	9.847	0.600
Eggs	12.8	12.4	1.583	0.023
Chicken	20.6	16.1	3.309	0.044
Beef	18.8	15.1	2.846	0.033
Pork	15.2	15.3	2.325	0.023
Peas	23.8	23.5	5.583	0.200
Corn	10.0	17.7	1.765	0.130
Tomatoes	1.0	23.8	0.238	0.140
Spinach	2.3	12.6	0.289	0.039

*From Baker, et al., 1977; Giacometti, 1979; and International Glutamate Technical Committee, 1974.

Figure 5-1.   Sample Tables.[1]

[1]Table on penetration of resin from M.S. White, G. Ifju, and J.A. Johnson, "Method for Measuring Resin Penetration into Wood," *Forest Products Journal,* 27, vii (1977), 54. Copyright © 1977 by the Forest Products Research Society. Reprinted by permission. Table on glutamate content from "Monosodium Glutamate (MSG)," *Food Technology,* Oct. 1980, 50. Copyright © 1980 by the Institute of Food Technologists. Reprinted by permission.

1. Self-sufficient tables (those that can be understood on their own) are placed in a box and given a number (see figure 5-1). The writer numbers such tables consecutively in a document and gives them explanatory titles.

2. Tables dependent on the prose text for their interpretation are not placed in a box or given a number. Instead they are integrated into the text itself. (The table in the previous memo is an example.)

3. Vertical columns and horizontal lines are identified at the top and left sides, respectively. The writer makes the headings grammatically parallel.

4. The heading in the top left-hand corner always refers to the vertical column on the extreme left. Hence, comparisons among items in the table are always made vertically. Details about any one item in the table are always visible horizontally.

5. Clear abbreviations and symbols are used in the column and line headings to keep them as brief and uncluttered as possible. The writer uses internal footnotes to present additional information about headings or titles. These footnotes use symbols or letters (*, †; a, b) rather than numbers.

6. The data in each vertical column are presented in the same units, identified at the top of the column.

7. The data's source is indicated with a footnote at the top of the table or appropriate column, referring the reader to the bottom of the table for details.

Compare the following paragraph with the same information in a tabular format:

```
        XYZ College admits foreign students in several ways.
Students can be admitted if they are in the upper 50% of
their secondary school class, have a TOEFL score of 500
or better, an ACT Composite Score of 18 or better, an SAT
Combined Score of 850 or better, or a secondary school
GPA of 2.5 out of 4.0. Freshmen can also be admitted to
the English Language Institute if they have a TOEFL score
between 400 and 500 or a Michigan score of 65 or better.
Transfer students can be admitted if they have 18 hours
or more of college level academic courses with a GPA of
at least 2.5 out of 4.0, a TOEFL score of 550 or better,
an ACT Composite Score of 20 or better, or an SAT
Combined Score of 950 or better. Returning students can
be admitted if they had a GPA on leaving XYZ of 2.5 or
better, a GPA at another university or college of at
least 2.5 out of 4.0, or they can be admitted
provisionally for one semester, during which they must
get a GPA of at least 2.5 in order to be allowed to
register for a second semester.
```

Admit Code	Admission Standards
1	Freshmen–Regular Standing
01	–TOEFL Score of 550 or better
02	–ACT Composite Score of 18 or better
03	–SAT Combined Score of 850 or better
2	Freshmen–English Language Institute
01	–TOEFL Score between 400 and 500
02	–Michigan Test Score of 65 or better
3	Transfer Students–Regular Standing
01	–18 or more hours of college level academic courses in English with GPA of at least 2.5 out of 4.0
02	–TOEFL Score of 600 or better
03	–ACT Composite Score of 20 or better
04	–SAT Combined Score of 950 or better
4	Transfer Students–English Language Institute
01	–TOEFL Score between 400 and 500
02	–Michigan Test Score of 65 or better
5	Returning Students
01	–GPA on leaving XYZ of 2.5 or better
02	–After leaving XYZ, GPA at another college or university in English of at least 2.5 out of 4.0
03	–Provisional admittance for one semester–2.5 GPA in first returning semester required in order to register for the following semester

Title: XYZ College–Undergraduate Admissions Standards for Foreign Students

EXERCISE

1. Compare and contrast the two versions of the admissions materials. Which version provides more information? Which information is more accessible to the reader? Is the paragraph poorly written? Could the table be improved?

2. Construct a table from the following data about the Funhouse Preschool:
   Young children can attend Monday and Wednesday
   Prekindergarten children are aged 3.5 to 4.5 years
   Cost for first grade is $175 per month
   Cost for young children is $58 per month
   Day care is 7:30 a.m.–5:30 p.m.
   Prekindergarten children may attend five mornings per week
   Kindergarten meets five half days per week
   Materials for kindergarten cost $50 per month
   Five afternoons per week cost $127 per month
   Only children aged 3.5–4.0 years can attend two mornings per week
   Day care is available fo prekindergarten children
   Prekindergarten children can attend three mornings per week
   Only children aged 4.0–4.5 years can attend three mornings per week
   Cost of two mornings per week is $65 per month
   First grade meets five days a week
   Cost of three mornings a week is $82 per month
   Kindergarten children are aged 4.5–5.5 years
   Kindergarten costs $138 per month
   Prekindergarten children can attend two mornings per week
   Young children can attend Tuesday and Thursday
   Prekindergarten five mornings per week costs $127 per month
   Prekindergarten children can attend three mornings per week
   Day care costs $283 per month
   Prekindergarten children can attend five afternoons per week

3. When would the table you created in question 2 be useful? Imagine a likely audience, purpose, and author's stance for this situation. Write an appropriate document. Be sure to incorporate the table.

Graphs and Charts

Graphs and charts present numerical data pictorially, helping readers visualize relationships among those data.

Graphs Basically, the graph is a two-dimensional field used to plot the relationships among two interrelated sets of data. The most common sort of graph has the familiar X and Y axes, with data of one sort on the X axis and data of another related sort set on the Y axis. Such a representation allows the reader to see at a glance not just the data, but more important, the relationship between the two sets of data. For any value on either axis, the reader can quickly derive the related value or values on the other axis (see figure 5–2).

In creating graphs, the writer must select an appropriate scale for both axes. One too small distorts overall patterns, with even small variations appearing to cause large changes on the graph. One too large has the opposite effect, as even large variations in data will appear to have little impact on the basic shape of the graph.

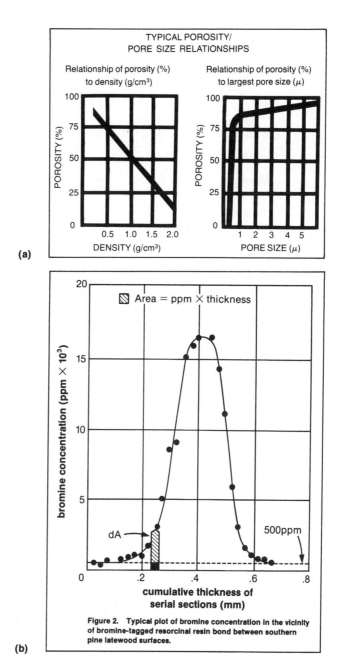

(a)

(b)

Figure 5-2.   Sample Graphs.[2]

[2]**(a)** Graphs on Typical Porosity/Pore Size Relationships from *What is GORE-TEX® expanded PFTE?* (Newark, Del.: W.L. Gore Associates, 1980), 1. Copyright © 1980 by W.L. Gore Associates. Reprinted by permission.   **(b)** Graph on Cumulative Thickness of Serial Sections (Figure 2) from M.S. White, G. Ifju, and J.A. Johnson, "Method for Measuring Resin Penetration into Wood," *Forest Products Journal*, 27, vii (1977), 53. Copyright © 1977 by the Forest Products Research Society. Reprinted by permission.

Charts While the graph illustrates relationships, the chart illustrates comparisons, usually among several sets of information. Figure 5–3 illustrates a combination of a graph and three bar charts (used to show relative quantities).

Many other sorts of charts are possible, including the pie chart, the pictorial chart, which uses drawings to represent numerical information, and the map chart, a schematic representation of a geographical area, on which various pictures, drawings, or other devices are superimposed (see figure 5–4).

Photographs, Drawings, and Diagrams

When supporting material is pictorial rather than numerical, writers choose photographs, drawings, and diagrams as their graphic aids. All three use the same key principles:

1. All pictorial representations should conform to the general principles for any graphic aid:

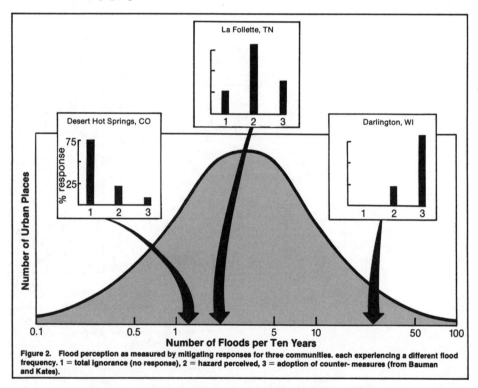

Figure 2. Flood perception as measured by mitigating responses for three communities. each experiencing a different flood frequency. 1 = total ignorance (no response), 2 = hazard perceived, 3 = adoption of counter- measures (from Bauman and Kates).

Figure 5–3.   Graph and Charts.[3]

---

[3]Graph and Charts on Number of Floods per Ten Years (Figure 2) from John E. Costa, "The Dilemma of Flood Control in the United States," *Environmental Management*, 2, iv (1978), 316. Copyright © 1978 by Springer-Verlag New York Inc. Reprinted by permission.

▶ Provide a detailed view of something difficult or impossible to convey in prose

▶ Clearly support the text

▶ Be visible simultaneously with the text they support

2. The details of the pictorial aid should be clear, especially those most relevant to the point being made. In a photograph, clarity is achieved through good lighting, wisely chosen camera angle, and an absence of irrelevant background detail. Drawings and diagrams use the same basic elements to achieve clarity: focus on relevant details and intelligent selection of presentation angle.

3. Many pictorial graphic aids can be further clarified by superimposing explanatory labels to identify key parts. As always, the writer's goal is to direct the reader's attention.

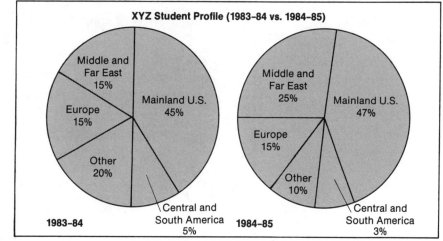

(a)

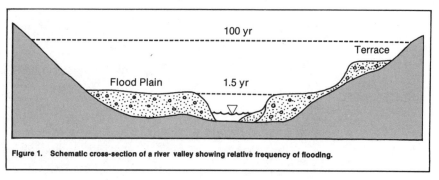

Figure 1.   Schematic cross-section of a river valley showing relative frequency of flooding.

(b)

Figure 5-4.   Sample Charts.[4]

[4](b) Schematic chart of Flood Plain (Figure 1) from John E. Costa, "The Dilemma of Flood Control in the United States," *Environmental Management*, 2, iv (1978), 315. Copyright © 1978 by Springer-Verlag New York Inc. Reprinted by permission.

Photographs, drawings, and diagrams each have unique features. The writer considers these features when selecting which one of the three graphic aids to use.

Photographs Photographs are the most realistic and dramatic representation of physical features. In a good photograph the reader can see exactly what the writer is talking about.

The range of photographic possibilities has greatly increased. Today's photographer has many special lenses that allow shots not possible before. Furthermore, cameras can be fastened to other equipment, such as microscopes and telescopes, to provide pictures not visible to the unaided human eye.

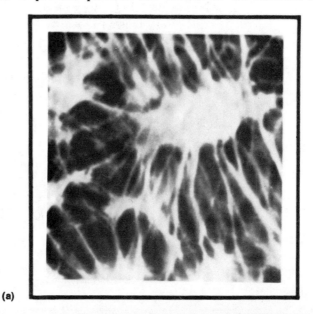

(a)

(b)

Figure 5-5. Sample Photographs.[5]

[5](a) Photograph of stained glass from *What is GORE-TEX® expanded PFTE?* (Newark, Del.: W.L. Gore Associates, 1980), 1. Copyright © 1980 by W.L. Gore Associates. Reprinted by permission. (b) Photograph of Navy plane from Harold Andrews, "Naval Aircraft: X-26," *Naval Aviation News,* July–August, 1983, 17. Copyright © 1983 by Naval Aviation News. Reprinted by permission.

Finally, cameras can go places the human eye cannot normally go. For instance, photographs can be taken from a plane looking at the earth below or show magnified views of objects which would otherwise be indiscernible to the human eye (see figure 5-5).

Drawings Sometimes the writer wants to represent something that cannot be produced in the real world and so cannot be photographed. Other times a photograph is too expensive or time consuming. Then the writer uses a drawing. For instance, a cross section or cutaway view of a machine, while possible to photograph, requires ruining the machine—the only way to photograph a cross section of a coffee maker is to cut one in half!

Drawings may also be preferable to photographs when the writer wants to show things that cannot be photographed, such as a memory, or nonexistent or imaginary items, such as an artist's rendition of a proposed building (see figure 5-6).

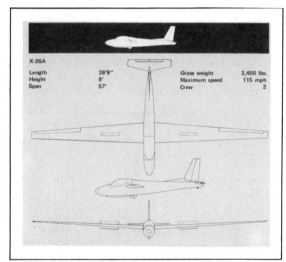

(a)

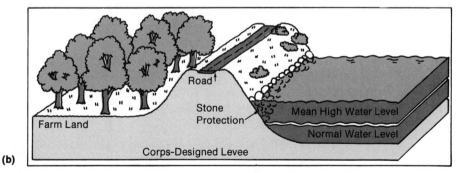

(b)

Figure 5-6. Sample Drawings.[6]

[6]**(a)** Drawing of X-26A from Harold Andrews, "Naval Aircraft: X-26," *Naval Aviation News,* July–August, 1983, 17. Copyright by Naval Aviation News. Reprinted by permission. **(b)** Drawing of a cross-section from "William G. Stone Lock and Port of Sacramento," *Explore 6: The California Coastline: The Sacramento-San Joaquin Delta* (San Francisco: Army Corps of Engineers), 3. Copyright by the Army Corps of Engineers. Reprinted by permission.

Diagrams Finally, sometimes writers want to show, not physical objects, but ideas. A diagram is a symbolic representation well-suited to the presentation of ideas. For instance, a flow diagram of a company's corporate structure symbolically represents the power relationships among employees. Another common diagram, based on a physical object, is the exploded view, which does not aim to picture the object, but to show the working relationships among its parts. Other typical examples of diagrams include blueprints, wiring schematics, and maps (see figure 5-7).

All these graphic aids have the common purpose of illustrating and supporting conclusions, recommendations, and interpretations the writer places in the text. The writer selects the exact graphic aid by considering the situation behind the writing—especially the purpose, audience, and author's role.

EXERCISE

1. Examine the article entitled "Ice Bridging" and answer the following questions about it:
   a. How important to the article are the graphic aids?
   b. How well does the writer integrate the graphic aids into the text?

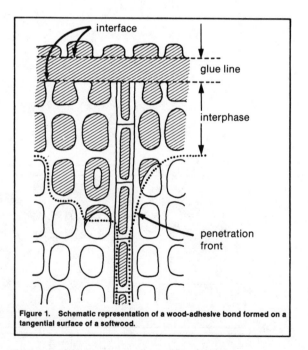

Figure 1. Schematic representation of a wood-adhesive bond formed on a tangential surface of a softwood.

Figure 5-7. Sample Diagram.[7]

---

[7]Diagram (Figure 1) from M.S. White, G. Ifju, and J.A. Johnson, "Method for Measuring Resin Penetration into Wood," *Forest Products Journal,* 27, vii (1977), 52. Copyright © 1977 by the Forest Products Research Society. Reprinted by permission.

    c. What would be the effect if the graphic aids were removed?

    d. Could the graphic aids be turned into prose and used in the text without harming the article's quality? Defend your answer.

    e. Should the author improve the graphic aids? Which ones? And how?

2. Find any magazine article that includes several of the graphic aids discussed in this chapter. After carefully examining the article, answer the questions presented in question 1.

3. Think of any writing you need to do that would benefit from any of the graphic aids discussed. Prepare the graphic aid first, and then write the prose around that graphic aid. What advantages are there to preparing the graphic aid first? Does preparing it first imply that it is more important than the prose?

GRAPHIC AIDS IN PROSE

The writer can incorporate some graphic devices into the prose itself. Such devices are designed to make the conclusions, opinions, and recommendations of the text jump out at the reader:

single-sentence paragraphs

headings and subheadings

numbering systems

CAPITAL LETTERS

boldface type

<u>underlining</u>

white space

lists

EXERCISE

Which of these devices do you see at work in each of the following memos? In each case, explain the device's effect. Do you see any places where the writer could use more of the devices listed or change devices effectively? Remember that the basis for all your answers and suggested improvements must be the rhetorical situation behind the document.

```
This memo details our progress to date on the Switzer
Project. Last month we surveyed the grounds and laid out
the initial forms. We have hired ten extra men for the
coming month, which should be the most demanding. We will
probably lay all the concrete within the next two weeks
and be ready to start putting up the walls before the
month is out. We anticipate finishing the job on
schedule, in early July.
```

```
MEMO
TO:  Chief Muldoon,
       Sechrist Police Dept.
FROM: Sgt. Murphy,
        Legal Liaison Office
RE:  Sechrist Police Dept. Library
```

We would like to request that you authorize a full-time library director for the 1985 fiscal year, at a salary not to exceed $18,000.

The Division of Corrections has far more than that available in its payroll budget as a result of staffing changes, it has a serious need, and it has the opportunity, through an improved library, to dramatically increase the effectiveness of overall operations. These factors are detailed below. For the past several years, increasing numbers of officers in the department have taken advantage of the library's services. The recent court ruling allowing officers to act as their own counsel will surely increase those numbers further. Therefore, we are constantly upgrading the library's holdings of case histories.

Naturally, a well-run library does not happen by accident, nor continue to be well-run without a competent director. For the past year, Officer Montoya has directed the library, along with her full-time patrol duties. However, Officer Montoya will be leaving us this fall. The danger is that the library will fall into disuse or stagnation, just when it should be expanding to serve the increasing numbers of officers likely to be using it. It is essential that the library preserve its ability to offer expert help to the many officers desiring it. To do so the library must have an expert director.

I feel justified in withholding payment on this month's bill for the following reasons:
I. The charge of $35.47 is for the first repair to the vacuum cleaner; however, as soon as I got it home, it refused to work, so I took it back, but when I got it home a second time it STILL didn't work, so I took it back a third time, but when I got it home it still didn't work, so I refuse to pay my bill until it does work.

> I am requesting that 25 out of the present 45 temporary programmers be retained until at least October 28, 1983. Their jobs will be terminated on September 30 if they are not given an extension for at least one more month. Several important fiscal year projects have to be completed before Oct. 31 (a Monday). The regular programmers will not be able to get it all done in time. By extending these positions, the budgets can be prepared and delivered by November, as they are supposed to. The 25 employees for the extra month will cost $46,567.

SUMMARY

The final draft of a business document usually contains two major parts:

▶ Directional material, or text: The writer's own opinions, recommendations, and conclusions
▶ Informational material, or graphics: The factual support for the writer's opinions

These two elements should be mutually supporting. The text leads the reader to the graphics; the graphics support the text. To accomplish this, graphics should always be visible simultaneously with the relevant text. The most useful graphic aids include the following:

- Tables
- Graphs
- Charts
- Photographs
- Drawings
- Diagrams

The writer should also use graphic effects to attract the reader's attention to the document's main and supporting points. The writer can use

single-sentence paragraphs
headings and subheadings
numbering systems
CAPITAL LETTERS
boldface type
<u>underlining</u>

white space
lists

to make main points more highly visible.

Ice bridging

First LT Mark L. Prahl

When the temperature plunges below zero, the 23d Engineer Company puts Mother Nature to work.

An ice bridge built in Alaska by the 23d Engineer Co. The 23d built three ice bridges during Brim Frost 83.

It doesn't take magic for a man, a jeep or even a 27-ton bulldozer to cross deep water in winter. All it takes is ingenuity, hard work and some frigid weather to make an ice bridge.

The first step in building an ice bridge is site reconnaissance because there are important location characteristics to consider in positioning the bridge.

The river channel should be straight and fairly wide, more than 60 feet if possible. Areas with unstable currents or temperatures, such as rapids and hot springs, are avoided. Normally, a straight, wide channel will have a slower flow and a level ice surface, and the channel should lie so prevailing winds won't drift snow across the bridge. Routing the bridge between sandbars yields shorter, stronger spans.

The area upstream is also examined. There should be no significant inflow channels directly upstream (closer than 2 km) which may disrupt normal flow.

The bridge should be as close to existing roads as possible because it merely continues those roads. However, for safety, ease of construction and maintenance, the crossing location has a higher selection priority than its distance to roads, as long as the bridge is easily accessible to wheeled vehicles.

A final primary consideration is the near and far banks. A gradual slope to the stream is best because it ensures ease of access by vehicles. If the banks are too steep, ramps are built from the banks to the stream.

After the bridge location has been chosen, the final check before construction is measuring (profiling) the ice. The profile is the most important step in ice bridging and must be conducted diligently and without shortcuts. All safety precautions must be observed and immediate aid ready in case of ice failure while crews are working.

A profile crew is two or more people, with the lead person tied to the rest of the crew by a line. The lead man bores test holes at 10-foot intervals with an auger or ice-chopper. As he crosses the river, the following persons (the recording crew) belay him and are prepared to assist if he breaks through. Data is recorded for each hole, including its location, ice thickness, snow cover, channel depth and ice quality.

If the profile crew encounters ice 4-inches thick or less, they don skis or snowshoes for safety before continuing. Ice less than 3 inches is too thin; a different site or a standard fixed bridge must be used.

When the profile is complete, all information necessary to decide on accepting the ice bridge location has been collected and construction may begin.

A profiling crew testing ice thickness.

Ice bridge construction is the process of artificially increasing the rate of ice formation on the bridge surface.

The first step is dealing with snow covering the crossing strip. The snow is cleared in a lane 30 meters wide. The roadway is standard military road width, but a 30-meter lane ensures plenty of ice to support it. The snow may be cleared entirely off of the bridge or be compacted to no more than 2 inches thick. Compacting may be done with snowmobiles, skis, or snowshoes. Any snow removed from the bridge must be distributed to avoid snow berms higher than 12 inches on the edges of the bridge.

Whether the snow is cleared or compacted, the next step is flooding. Hand-operated or gas-powered ice augers are used to drill 12-inch wide holes in the ice on the downstream side of the bridge. The river or lake becomes the water source for a pumping operation.

"We pump water up from below and flood the ice about an inch deep, let it freeze, then flood it again, until we get the thickness we want," explains SFC Lincoln V. Thompson, operations and training NCO, 23d Engineer Company (Combat) (Heavy), 172d Infantry Brigade. "We've crossed a D7 'cat' on 32 inches of ice and it weighs 54,200 pounds with its bullblade."

The 23d Engineer Company uses three commercial, electric submersible pumps (each powered by a five-kilowatt generator), or gasoline-powered centrifugal pumps to raise layers of water.

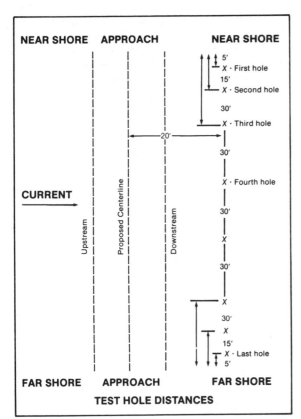

A typical arrangement of profile holes.

"The commercial pumps are better for this job than the centrifugal ones," says Thompson. "The electric pumps are self-priming and won't freeze in extreme cold. We just drill a hole in the ice, drop it in and start pumping."

"How fast we can build a bridge depends on temperature and how long the bridge must be," explains CPT Christopher M. Turletes, 23d Engineer Company commander. "We figure one squad with one pump can freeze 100 feet of bridge per hour at –10°F."

With the slowness of clearing snow and freezing water, ice bridging can't be considered a hasty crossing for combat use.

"Tactically, ice bridges are used on main supply routes and lines of communication," says Turletes. "They are deliberate crossings used when the area beyond is secured and ready to be opened for resupply."

Like the pumps they use, some of the 23d Engineer Company's ice-bridging techniques deviate from standard Army procedure.

"We've built a lot of ice bridges and done considerable research with the Corps' Cold Regions Research Laboratory (CRRL)," explains Turletes. "There's also a lot of research being done commercially on the North Slope with ice bridges, and we've used that, too."

"Figures in TM 5349, *Arctic Construction,* indicate a 200-foot width for ice bridges," Turletes says. "Of course, the wider the bridge, the stronger it is. But the TM tends to be conservative. Our experience and CRRL's research shows that an ice bridge over 14 inches thick is strong enough to resist bending, and that 30 meters is a good width to work with."

Some experts recommend replacing three or four inches of snow on the bridge as a treadway.

"Snow is an insulator and tends to protect the ice bridge from cold air," says Turletes. "After the bridge is constructed, we replace no more than one inch of snow for a wearing surface."

Other experts advocate freezing timbers into the ice to reinforce the bridge.

"Our research and experience shows that logs, planks and straw don't really strengthen an ice bridge," says Turletes. "They are darker, absorb solar heat and could weaken the bridge. We often use logs for ramps and treadways, but not frozen into the ice itself."

After the 23d Engineer Company builds their ice bridges, they maintain several safety factors. "When in doubt, profile," is the rule. They measure the ice thickness every eight hours not only to monitor the thickness of the ice, but also the distance to the bottom of the channel. "If the ice builds up too thick below, the water dams up behind the bridge and the pressure can cause shears at any weak point," says Thompson.

The 23d Engineer Company built three ice bridges at Fort Greely, Alaska, during exercise Brim Frost 83. Their mission during the exercise was to operate, maintain and upgrade the exercise's main supply route.

CASE IN POINT

The Letter of Application and Résumé

The writer just beginning her career writes nothing more important than a letter of application and résumé, which together form the standard job-seeking package. Furthermore, nothing is more essential to a well-written letter and résumé than effective graphics.

When preparing a letter of application and résumé, remember these considerations:

1.   The letter and résumé are you—they are all the prospective employer sees. He judges your employability based on these two items alone. If you are not going to do your best on them, you might as well head for the unemployment line, or try for a job where you have a known "in" through a relative or friend. In open, genuine job competition, the sloppy writer does not have a chance.

2.   The best approach to use in the letter is to let the employer know exactly how you can help her. The point then becomes not how great you are, but how much you can do for the employer. This is a small but important distinction, for the letter writer always treads the thin line between bragging and relating job qualifications to job demands. Keeping the focus on "what I can do for you" keeps you on the good side of the line.

3.   The letter and résumé are relatively set forms that you must personalize even as you follow. You want the prospective employer to remember your letter and résumé because they are unique, but in a positive sense. You must mold form to situation, as discussed in chapter 3. Many employers receive hundreds or even thousands of applications a year. Yours must be memorably good.

4.   The relationship between the letter and the résumé is the same as that between a document's text and the supporting graphics—the letter explains your qualifications and claims you and the job were made for each other; the résumé provides the supporting details for those assertions.

5.   The letter and the résumé should be concise. The letter should be a single page. The résumé should also be concise, but may take more than one page. It is more important to give a full picture of your relevant experiences and qualifications than it is to be brief. However, avoid padding the résumé. Its purpose is to support your application, not give your life history. For each possible item, ask yourself, "Will this information improve my chances of getting the job?" The more relevant qualifications you have, the longer your résumé should be.

6.   The letter and résumé must be perfect. They should be typed. (The résumé can be professionally printed.) Above all, they must be neat and correct in every detail. Nothing is easier than for an employer to reject a letter and résumé for mechanical flaws. Such flaws say loud and clear, "I'm too lazy and

incompetent to get even this letter and résumé right, and I'll be the same kind of employee."

Specific instructions for writing the letter follow:

1. The first paragraph should contain two points:

a. *Tell how you learned about the job.* If you do not know there *is* a job, there is little reason to write. A letter asking for a job will probably not be specific enough to interest anyone. Most employers do not look for employees in a general sense; instead, they look for qualified people to do specific jobs.

Also, many employers spend a lot of money advertising their job openings. They want to know which ads are doing the job and which are not.

Finally, if you know some good name to drop, this is the place to do it—just do not overdo it.

b. *Make specific application for a specific job.* Many employers have lots of openings simultaneously. As explained earlier, the employer wants to know exactly what you think you can do for him. You will not be hired just to work, but to do a specific job.

2. The second paragraph is the longest in the letter, and has just one function: *to elaborate on your pertinent qualifications.* In this paragraph you literally convince the prospective employer that you have had the experience to do the job she needs done. Also, you convince the employer to examine your résumé. (Many résumés are never even looked at.)

3. In the final paragraph you *request some specific action by the prospective employer.* You may request an interview or further application materials. If you will be in the vicinity of the employer's office, you may indicate specific dates and say you will call for an appointment when you are in town. The bottom line of the letter and résumé is getting an interview. Rarely do employers hire people straight from the letter and résumé. Instead, employers use them as screening devices, refusing almost all applicants, and offering interviews to the few they consider serious contenders for the job.

Remember these key points when preparing the résumé:

1. Put as much as possible in a block format. Avoid prose sections unless absolutely necessary. Use phrases, and be sure to break the entries up with white space, headings, and other graphic effects to make each item stand out individually.

2. Outside of material that must be arranged chronologically, try to place your strongest supporting material first and weaker items later. For instance, if your main qualification is educational, list your education early in the résumé. If your main qualification is work experience, list vocational experiences before educational ones. Lead from your strength.

3. The four major areas to include are personal, education, vocational, and references.

Under personal you may list such things as height, weight, health, marital status, etc. Recent laws make it illegal for a prospective employer to hold such things as divorce, number of children, etc. against you. In fact, you are not required to list anything you think may be held against you. The recent trend is to list as few things as possible in the personal section, and to place it last in the résumé. In general, though, it is wise to provide as much information about yourself and your life-style as you feel comfortable with. For instance, you might list a few hobbies or interests under the personal section. Increasingly, employers realize that they hire human beings, not just workers.

Under education list all your college or university schooling, starting with the most recent first and going back to list your high school by name and city. You can list any specific post-high school courses relevant to the job. Most employers are also interested in any special honors you achieved at school, as well as things like school clubs, athletics, service organizations, etc.

Under vocational list your work experience in reverse chronological order. Important items to list for each job include the following:

- Dates you held the job
- Exact title of the job
- Duties (be as specific as you can)
- Name of supervisor

Be sure to use a block format rather than a long section of prose the reader can easily skip over. Other items you may want to include are your salary and your reason for leaving the job.

Under references list three to five people whom you have asked to write letters on your behalf. You should provide an exact address for each reference, so that the prospective employer can contact these people if he wants to. The references should be from as wide a range of backgrounds as possible. For instance, you might ask some former teachers, as well as former employers. Of course, make sure the persons you ask can give you positive recommendations. Most people will tell you honestly if they feel they cannot do so.

If you have a reference file set up somewhere, such as at a college or university placement office, you may leave out the list of references, state that "References are available upon request," and include the address of the placement office.

Other items that may be placed in the résumé are a statement of career objectives, specific skills, and a picture of yourself at your responsible and employable best.

Letter and Résumé for Ross Daniels

213 S. Main St.
Charlotte, NC 28472
June 30, 1983
(704) 774-1756

Mr. Malcolm Shavers
Hearthstone Manufacturing
P.O. Box 43
Raleigh, North Carolina 28670

Dear Sir:

I was very interested to read your advertisement for
computer programmers in the June issue of Computer World.
I believe I am qualified for the position of
Programmer-II, and I would like to apply for the job.

My qualifications include both educational and vocational
experience. I have a B.S. in computer science from
Northwestern University. While going to school, I worked
part time in the university computer center as a student
assistant. Upon graduating four years ago, I worked full
time as a computer operator for the accounting division
of the Walgreen's regional office in Muncie, Indiana.
Last year I decided to return to North Carolina, where I
took a position as an accounting and data entry clerk at
Pierce and Fennell, Inc. in Charlotte. I believe my
experience will allow me to adapt very quickly to your
particular system, and to become a productive and
valuable employee with a minimal amount of training time.

I would appreciate the chance to meet with you personally
to discuss my qualifications for the job. I am available
for an interview at your convenience, and can be reached
at the address or telephone number listed above. Thank
you for your consideration.

Sincerely,

Ross Daniels

Ross Daniels

encl.

June 30, 1983

RÉSUMÉ FOR
ROSS DANIELS

ADDRESS: 213 S. Main St.   PERSONAL DATA: 6′2″ tall
            Charlotte, NC 28472   210 lbs.
TELEPHONE: (704) 774-1756   Married

PROFESSIONAL OBJECTIVE

A computer programmer position leading to opportunities in
systems analysis or management.

SKILLS

Hardware   Languages   Operating Systems

Univac 90/80   BASIC   VS-9
IBM 5100   COBOL   CP-5
SIGMA VI   ASSEMBLER
                      RPG

EDUCATION

B.S. in Computer Science, 1979, Northwestern University.
GPA: 3.6 out of 4.0
Key courses: BASIC Programming   COBOL Programming
              Information Systems   RPG Programming
              Assembler Language   Operating Systems
              Data Base Management   FORTRAN
Honors: Dean's list, 4 semesters
          Pinkney Scholarship, 4 semesters

High School Diploma, 1975, Ygnacio Valley H.S.,
   Concord, California

VOCATIONAL

May, 1982—present Accounting and Data Entry Clerk,
   Pierce and Fennell, Inc., Charlotte, North Carolina.
   Supervisor: Ted Clemmons
   Duties: Primary responsibility for accounts receivable
            system of over 2000 accounts maintained on
            computer. Designed a client information maintenance
            and retrieval system which was recently added to
            the current operating system.

May, 1979-May, 1982 Computer operator, Walgreen's Drug
   Stores, Regional Office, Muncie, Indiana.
   Supervisor: Martha Carey
   Duties: Processed bank reconciliations and posted ledgers.

```
January, 1978-May, 1979      Student Assistant, Northwestern
   University Computer Services Center, Evanston, Illinois.
      Supervisor:  Jaime Baca
      Duties:  College of Engineering Lab Supervisor,
               Computer Lab Assistant, Computer operator.

REFERENCES (by permission)

Martha Carey
Accounting Section Chief
Walgreen's Drug Stores
Regional Offices
121 Miller Ave.
Muncie, Indiana 47301

Professor John Siemons
Computer Sciences Dept.
Northwestern University
Evanston, Illinois      56704

Jaime Baca
Operations Manager
Computer Services Center
Northwestern University
Evanston, Illinois 56704
```

2

WRITING ASSIGNMENT

Select any job you are now applying for, or one you will be applying for soon. Prepare a letter and résumé you could use to apply for this job. Or, if you wish, imagine you are just about to graduate from the college or university you now attend. Prepare a letter and résumé for the job you plan to apply for when you graduate.

FOR FURTHER READING

Anton, Jane; Russell, Michael; and the Research Committee of the Western College Placement Association. *Employer Attitudes and Opinions Regarding Potential College Graduate Employees.* Hayward, California: Western College Placement Association, 1974.

Brusaw, Charles; Alred, Gerald; and Oliu, Walter. *The Business Writer's Handbook.* New York: St. Martin's, 1976.

Comarov, Avery. "Tracking the Elusive Job." *The Graduate,* Knoxville, Tennessee: Approach 13–30 Corp., 1977.

Day, Robert. *How to Write and Publish a Scientific Paper.* Philadelphia: ISI Press, 1979.

Jordan, Stello; Kleinman, Joseph; and Shimberg, H. Lee, eds. *Handbook of Technical Writing Practices.* New York: Wiley-Interscience, 1971.

MacGregor, A.J. *Graphics Simplified: How to Plan and Prepare Effective Charts, Graphs, and Other Visual Aids.* Toronto: University of Toronto Press, 1979.

Michelson, Herbert. *How to Write and Publish Engineering Papers and Reports.* Philadelphia: ISI Press, 1982.

Murphy, Herta, and Peck, Charles. *Effective Business Communication,* 3rd ed. New York: McGraw-Hill, 1980.

Pearsall, Thomas, and Cunningham, Donald. *How to Write for the World of Work,* 2nd ed. New York: Holt, Rinehart and Winston, 1982.

Treece, Malra. *Successful Business Writing.* Boston: Allyn and Bacon, 1980.

Turnbull, Arthur, and Baird, Russell. *The Graphics of Communication,* 4th ed. New York: Holt, Rinehart and Winston, 1980.

Wilkinson, C.W.; Clarke, Peter B.; and Wilkinson, Dorothy C. *Communicating Through Letters and Reports,* 7th ed. Homewood, Illinois: Richard D. Irwin, 1980.

UNIT II

The Writing Process

6

An Overview of the Writing Process

T he writer can analyze his problem and its rhetorical context, select an appropriate form, and generate relevant graphic aids, and still not have written a thing.

> The worst enemy of the writer is the blank page.

If the writer stares at the blank page, waiting for the perfect words to come before putting anything down, the page will probably remain blank.

Effective writers do not create final copy in one step. Instead, they engage in a series of thinking and writing activities that lead to the final document. These activities are collectively referred to as the writing process. However, this process is recursive, not linear. That is, any of the activities that make up the process may be engaged in at any time and in any order. The writing process is a series of possible activities, rather than a blueprint or list of mandatory steps.

PREWRITING

Researchers have recently confirmed that most good writers do not simply take up the pen and write out the final document. Instead, they go through various preparatory activities, collectively called prewriting. Some forms of prewriting, known as heuristics, are rather rigid, patterned activities that systematically direct the writer through a predetermined set of actions. At the opposite extreme, other forms of prewriting, known as discovery techniques, are unstructured activities that encourage the writer to range freely through the topic. Other varieties of prewriting fall between the totally structured and the totally unstructured. But writers use all prewriting activities to get themselves started. Almost anything can be a valuable prewriting activity if it succeeds in getting the writer to put something down on that blank page.

During the prewriting stage, writing is a learning process. The writer discovers exactly what she wants to say through writing. These discoveries are crucial during prewriting, although they may occur later in the writing process as well. But at this early stage in the writing process, the writer needs ways to generate ideas about the situation behind the writing. The writer does not worry about efficiency at this stage, but wants to generate a mass of material from which to select later on. A good writer works from an abundance of material, not a scarcity, because she knows it is easier to cut than to add later.

The following specific heuristics and discovery techniques are especially helpful in generating material on technical subjects.

Heuristics

Two heuristics, *particle, wave, and field* and *the pentad,* have proven particularly effective in getting writers started.

Particle, Wave, and Field   The particle, wave, and field approach was formalized by Young, Becker, and Pike, in their text *Rhetoric: Discovery and Change* (see For Further Reading at end of this chapter). Their full system is much more subtle and complex than the simplified version presented here.

To employ the particle, wave, and field approach as a heuristic for prewriting, the writer analyzes the problem or writing situation from three distinct viewpoints. First, the writer looks at the writing in isolation, or as a particle. What makes this piece of writing unique? From the particle perspective the problem and its rhetorical situation are analyzed in themselves.

In the wave presentation, the writer analyzes the problem as part of a series or sequence. How has the problem or situation changed over time? What sequence of events, or chain of causes and effects has led to the situation as it now stands? In short, in the wave perspective the writer examines the problem in a developmental context.

Finally, in the field perspective the problem is analyzed in its full context. What are the implications of the problem on the world around it? What are the cultural and situational contexts in which the problem is set? How is the problem connected to things outside itself? Looking from a field perspective is in some ways the opposite of viewing the problem in isolation.

Let's apply each perspective to the following situation:

> Tom Johnson handles the payroll, accounts receivable, and accounts payable at the local hospital. His office is in the process of switching over from manual operation to a newly purchased computer to issue all checks and keep all records. Some of the hospital employees are nervous about how the computer will affect their jobs.

Tom wants to reassure the employees about how the computer will be used, what it can and cannot do, and how it will affect various hospital functions. But he does not know exactly what he needs to say, to whom, and in what format. He decides to apply particle, wave, and field before he communicates anything to anyone.

Particle Perspective
• First, Tom isolates factors about the situation itself.

> *The computer will help keep records accurately and be able to retrieve them. It will print all the checks, automatically taking out the proper amounts for taxes, insurance, and other deductions, and deposit funds directly into appropriate employee or supplier accounts. It can keep a running account of all expenditures and accounts payable and receivable, and can process all insurance claims and checks, crediting each to the proper account.*

Wave Perspective
• Then Tom looks at the situation's history.

> *Over the past ten years, hundreds of human errors about proper income tax withholding, proper discount on supplier invoices, and crediting checks to the right patient's account have occurred. The old manual system often requires a week to generate payroll checks.*

Field Perspective
• Finally, Tom looks at the context of the situation.

> *Computer technology surrounds me and the employees every day, from video games to bank statements. The hospital upgrades all its medical equipment constantly, striving to be up to date.*

These jottings are not even a first draft for Tom, but they are ideas that will help him start one. They are not complete or in the order Tom will eventually use them. Tom will probably think of other ideas later to add to the ones listed. But still, particle, wave, and field has started Tom thinking logically about his writing problem. He now has some useful insights into the problem itself, its development, and its context. With these seed ideas Tom is more prepared to generate a rough draft than he was before. Through the particle, wave, and field heuristic Tom has begun to discover what he wants to tell the hospital employees and how to go about telling them.

Pentad   Another useful heuristic device, formalized under the term *pentad* by Kenneth Burke, has been long familiar to the journalist as the five Ws: *who, where, when, what,* and *why* (see Burke, *A Rhetoric of Motives,* in the For Further Reading section at the end of this chapter). Burke introduces different terminology for the traditional five Ws:

▶ Act: What was done?
▶ Agent: Who did it?
▶ Agency: By what means was it done?
▶ Scene: Where and when was it done?
▶ Purpose: Why was it done?

Burke's terms stress the human element in communication. For instance, the word *act* implies a humanly motivated happening, while *what* may refer to an unmotivated event resulting from physical laws. A tree falling in the forest is a physical event, which could be considered under the reporter's *what*, but not under Burke's *act*; however, a logging company that fells trees for profit is humanly motivated, and hence performs an *act*. Similarly, the *who* question for the reporter could include a fungus that weakened the tree and caused it to fall, but the term *agent* for Burke implies more than a physical cause. For all the terms, Burke focuses on human involvement in the rhetorical situation.

Before attempting to write a rough draft, Tom applies the pentad to his communication about the new computer:

- Act: A computer will be installed. This act is in the future, not completed yet.
- Agent: The hospital board of directors, putting increasing pressure on the hospital manager to change, wants the computer installed. Thus, the agent in this case is coming from the top down—with authority.
- Agency: Tom realizes that the way the act is done is everyone's main concern. No one disagrees with the act itself, but people are nervous about how it will be accomplished.
- Scene: The decision-making *where* and *when* do not concern most of Tom's audience. However, the installation and start-up *where* and *when* concern many of Tom's fellow workers at the hospital.
- Purpose: Red ink and inefficiency motivate the decision. The new computer will not replace anyone; rather, the computer should benefit all employees and the hospital itself.

With this pentad analysis, Tom can formulate a rough plan for communicating with the hospital employees. First he will establish the common ground they all share: the desire to improve efficiency and cut costs. Then he will show that installing a computer—exactly this sort of computer, at exactly this time, to do exactly these things—will accomplish these goals. Furthermore, Tom wants to show that the decision-making process was carried out according to established hospital guidelines, and that no employees or jobs are threatened. In other words, not merely the computer itself, but the agency behind it is also on the employees' side. By considering human *agency*, rather than the abstract *how*, Tom has discovered a major strategy for his document.

Using both particle, wave, and field and the pentad, Tom has generated a lot of information pertinent to his task. He does not have a rough draft; he may not even use some of the material generated, and he will certainly reorganize it at later stages of the writing process. However, Tom has started his writing task, and he knows he has examined the problem systematically. Although he does not close his mind to new ideas and approaches, he is confident he has made a significant beginning.

Discovery Techniques

Like heuristics, the purpose of discovery techniques is to get the writer started. However, discovery techniques are more exploratory and less formalized than heuristics. Two proven discovery techniques are freewriting and word listings.

Freewriting   Like most prewriting techniques, freewriting has a long tradition; however, its most influential modern exponent is Ken Macrorie, especially in his book *Telling Writing* (see Macrorie entry in the For Further Reading section at the end of this chapter). In freewriting, the author simply takes pen in hand and begins to write, not attempting logic, organization, grammatical correctness, or much of anything else. The only rule is to *keep writing*; do not stop for anything. Even if one writes "I don't know" or "stupid, stupid, stupid" over and over again, the writer does not allow the pen to stop moving. Freewriting gets the juices flowing, allows the mind to put on paper what's locked inside. Again, writing *anything* on paper is more productive than staring at the blank page. Through freewriting the writer often discovers what he wants to say about a given subject.

Let's apply freewriting to the following situation:

Fred Smithson is the environmental coordinator for a road contractor. Fred's company is in the preliminary stages of building a new road to connect two existing roads. Especially in winter, fatal accidents often occur at corners A and B (see map).

In the 1920s the county could not get the rights to build across the property between points A and B, so they built the road around the prop-

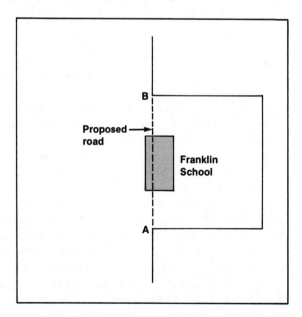

erty. In 1951 the county acquired the property, but in the midst of the postwar baby boom, used it for a school instead of a road. Now the county cannot fill all its elementary schools, so the time seems right to consolidate schools, eliminate Franklin School, and build the needed road.

However, local parents have voiced considerable opposition. The county has therefore decided to hold an open meeting, allow the road contractor and the parents' spokesperson fifteen minutes apiece to make a statement, and then open the meeting to questions and answers.

As environmental coordinator, Fred Smithson must prepare the road contractor's statement. Fred knows how to build roads and how to minimize their negative effects on the environment, but he knows nothing about upset parents. He feels helpless because he does not know what to say in this situation. So he begins by freewriting:

> *I know how to build roads, first the excavating, then the grading, etc., etc., but that's not what's wanted at this meeting. The parents are afraid to move their kids. Can I give them any advantage back in return? Like more safety on the highways. Statistics of numbers of accidents at the corners that the new road will eliminate. The new road will actually be a benefit environmentally because it will lessen the decelleration and acceleration along that stretch of road, thus lessening pollutants. But evidence, evidence, I've got to have facts to make all the believable—to motivate acceptance from the parents.*

Fred literally casts about for points to make, and he discovers several. His passage contains no facts, but does point out promising leads that Fred can pursue; he believes he can get the facts to support those leads. In addition, Fred has discovered a trade-off strategy, which he may or may not use in the final presentation.

Word Listing   Word listing is another useful discovery technique. It is similar to word association: a psychological examiner says a word and the client responds with the first word that comes to mind. By concentrating on the communication situation, the writer may come up with some important words that then stimulate her thinking. These key words can be listed or grouped into related clusters. Such clusters may trigger further insight into the problem and perhaps even the beginnings of an organization for the document.

After doing a little research, Fred decides to use the word list approach:

> *Safety*
> *1978: 25 accidents*
> *7 fatalities*
> *1979: 22 accidents*
> *9 fatalities*

Parents

children crossing street

familiar with old road

Environment

EPA standards for SO_2, NO_2, particulates

accelleration test

May 1980 study

   7.0 ppm SO_2

   5.7 ppm NO_2

   10.0 ppm particulates

   too high

Through the word listing and grouping, Fred generates a basic organization for the details that he will use to write the rough draft of his statement. He could not have simply written a rough draft off the top of his head. He needed the freewriting and the word listing to discover what he had to say and to generate a basic organization. The prewriting techniques allowed Fred to break his initial efforts into manageable steps. What he could not do all at once he could do in gradual steps.

Other Prewriting Techniques

Although many other possible ways of getting started exist, only two more established approaches, the rhetorical situation and the introduction, can be looked at here. These techniques are not as systematic as heuristics or as flexible as discovery techniques. They too have as their primary goal getting the writer to generate useful materials, not final copy. From the materials generated through prewriting activities, the writer can glean the beginnings of a rough draft.

Rhetorical   As discussed in chapters 1 and 2, every communication situation consists of purpose, audience, and author. The writer may analyze these three elements as a way to start composing.

The Rio Poco Mining Company is exploring possible new areas for copper mining. The State Department of Environmental Quality monitors such activities closely and requires a semiannual progress report detailing the company's activities during the previous six months and outlining the proposed activities for the next six months. Andy Rice has just been hired as Rio Poco's Environmental Engineering Specialist and is responsible for writing the report's basic text every six months and forwarding it to Rio Poco's president for review before it goes to the Department of Environmental Quality.

Before beginning his first report, Andy analyzes his rhetorical situation:

> *Purpose:* I want my semiannual reports to accomplish a meeting of the minds between economic and environmental concerns. I believe mining can be done on a sound economic <u>and</u> environmental basis. My job is to reassure both audiences that the company's past actions met both objectives, and that they will continue to do so.
>
> *Audience:* I recognize two major audiences. The stated audience is the Department of Environmental Quality, which wants to ensure that the mining activities of the Rio Poco Mining Company in no way endangers the state's environment. Thus they will tend to be critical, conservative, and disinterested in the economic aspects of mining.
>
> On the other hand, I know the report's first audience is my own president, who can make any alterations he wishes and make my first report my last. I have met the president only once, but he seemed reasonable and open-minded, although primarily interested in the mines' financial success.
>
> *Author:* I am a new employee; I need to prove myself by doing an especially thorough job on this first report. I wish to come across as dedicated to Rio Poco's interests and as professionally competent to protect the environment around the mines.

By sketching out his purpose, audience, and authorial role, Andy has developed a clear idea of where both he and his report stand. Andy realizes he has to keep his rhetorical situation uppermost in his mind as he writes the rough draft.

Introduction   A writer can also get started on a writing project by drafting an introduction. This draft may or may not open the final document. Remember, at this point in the writing process, the writer simply wants to get started, not produce final copy.

The general introduction format, as discussed in chapter 3, consists of four parts that do not have to appear in exactly this order:

- ▶ Interest getter: A short statement to get the audience involved, such as a short quotation, a striking statistic, or an anecdote
- ▶ Background: Presentation of the context of the document, such as a historical sketch, a review of related literature, or the establishment of key priorities
- ▶ Purpose: A clear, short statement of the overall point of the document
- ▶ Plan: A brief statement of the organization of the document

With the rhetorical situation in mind, Andy decides to sketch out his introduction. He could actually draft one in prose form, or just list the four elements and his plan for fulfilling each:

> Interest getter: Former Governor Jones' statement that mining will never come to Penschal County.
> Background: A brief history of Rio Poco's efforts to get a permit to mine in Penschal County.
> Purpose: To detail the last six months' activities of the Rio Poco Mining Company in Penschal County, to show that the mine is both making a profit and protecting the environment.
> Plan: A geographical survey of the county, mine by mine. Each mine to be discussed under four headings: 1) activities; 2) results; 3) environmental safeguards; and 4) future plans. A summary of all four areas to conclude the document.

> In the prewriting portion of the writing process, the writer gets started, not finished.

Prewriting is not an attempt to generate even a rough draft. Instead, at the outset the writer concentrates on gathering and organizing the available facts on the problem and its context. The writer may not use any of the discussed prewriting techniques, may use them singly or in combination, or may use different ones at different times. It is even possible that much later in the writing process, the writer will come back to certain prewriting activities. Writing situations are much too individual to be approached the same way every time.

WRITING

At some point the writer must stop prewriting and begin writing. This statement does not imply that once writing begins, all prewriting ends. On the contrary, whenever the writer gets stuck, he may want to prewrite again on that sticking point. Or the writer may just skip the sticking point to keep on writing and not lose momentum. No absolute rules for writing the rough draft exist. Ideally the materials generated through prewriting help the writer complete a rough draft. Sometimes the writer follows prewriting materials almost word for word. Other times, she may ignore them altogether. When that happens, the writer may come back to the prewriting materials later or abandon them entirely.

> The writer should write the first draft quickly. The writer uses prewriting techniques to generate materials, and the first draft to work with those materials.

The final, perfect copy comes later, after the rewriting stage. Emphasizing speed, the writer can start writing at the beginning, the middle, or the end of the document. It does not matter as long as he starts writing. The writer uses the materials generated in prewriting as a guide and storehouse of information, but never as a deadening final word on anything.

Andy Rice of the Rio Poco Mining Company, having outlined his introduction as one of his prewriting techniques, decides to start his rough draft by writing the introduction.

```
        A little over six years ago Governor Babbington
Jones emphatically stated, ''Commercial mining will never
come to Penschal County!'' Today, commercial mining has
come to Penschal County—it's Governor Jones who has gone.
        All of us at Rio Poco Mining are proud of what we're
doing in Penschal County—proud of the income we're
generating for the county and state, and proud of our
traditional concern for the environment. We're determined
that nothing will change our company's commitment to
economic growth and to environmental protection and even
enhancement.
        The report that follows details the Rio Poco Mining
Company's first six months of operation in Penschal
County, showing clearly that the mine is generating
revenue and protecting the environment. First, the report
presents a mine-by-mine analysis of the company's
activities, second, it reports exact tonnages from each
mine and calculations of value, both in absolute terms
and in tax revenues, third, it explains the environmental
safeguards the company has undertaken in detail, mine by
mine, and fourth, it details the company's plans for the
next six months.
        The overall picture is one of health for the Rio
Poco Mining Company and for Penschal County.
```

Andy completes the rough draft of his report, using the facts he has gathered over the past months. He still does not have a final version ready for his president to review, but he does have an organized and workable draft that he can polish in the rewriting stage.

REWRITING

The final stage of the writing process is rewriting, or performance monitoring. At this point, the writer performs two important, different, and often overlapping functions on the first draft: revision and editing. Revising and editing may take place simultaneously, and usually occur over several drafts. A skillful rewriting job is not a once-through proposition.

Revision

In revising, the writer checks the document's logic, organization, and coherence. In other words, the writer checks the *content* to make sure the document fulfills its purpose, reaches its intended audience, and projects its author appropriately. The writer attempts to see the piece of writing anew, from a different perspective, through different eyes; hence the term *revision*.

The writer should try to get some help in finding this more objective viewpoint by taking the document to other people—co-workers, colleagues, other individuals respected in the profession—for their opinions. If time allows (and unfortunately it often does not), the writer puts the document aside for a day or a week and then comes back to it with fresh sight. The writer should then think about possible changes as a result of feedback and distance, but of course, he need not accept other opinions or make any changes after a week. The final decisions and the final shape of the document belong to the author— at least until it is passed to the next level for review. The president may not like Andy Rice's approach and may change it; however, Andy has the right and the responsibility to have the document the way he wants it when it leaves his hand.

Editing

In editing, the writer concerns herself with precise language and details. The writer scrutinizes every word, every sentence, every mark of punctuation to make sure she has made the best possible choices. Everything from spelling to paragraphing is checked and rechecked. *Now* the writer grooms and polishes the piece of writing to perfection.

> Usually, the writer does not polish until the end of the writing process, when she knows the document says what she wants it to say.

There is no use stopping to polish a sentence in the rough draft, when you may take that very sentence out in the revision stage. Still, as mentioned earlier, the writer should not insist that the process follow an absolute sequence. If the writer notices a word or sentence in the first draft that obviously needs improvement, it might be well to fix it on the spot, or at least mark it for fixing later, because otherwise the change could be forgotten. The point is, the writer does not concentrate on editing problems in the first draft, but if she notices some, she can correct them. Similarly, while polishing or editing, the writer may have a major insight and decide to make major changes in the document. Ideally, this would not happen, but realistically, it does, so make the changes rather than submit a piece of writing you know needs basic improvements.

After finishing the first draft of his report, Andy Rice rewrites it. He puts the first draft aside for a week and then comes back to it. At the revising level, he discovers his draft condescends to the State Department of Environmental Quality and is tedious and repetitious. Andy thinks his constant harping on the company's concern with the environment may raise more suspicions than it will allay fears. Andy decides on a softer sell; rather than proclaim his company's environmental concerns, he lets the facts talk for him. Facts do not usually talk for themselves, but he knows he can give them a voice by careful organization and development. He remembers Shakespeare's famous line "The lady doth protest too much, methinks" and decides that since Rio Poco is in fact innocent of any environmental wrongdoing, he does not need to protest its innocence. At the editing level, Andy realizes that the items in his series should be separated by semicolons, not commas, and he cuts unnecessary language.

The new introduction for the final version of his report to the president reads

```
        The first six months of the Rio Poco Mining
Company's activities in Penschal County have ended.
Initial efforts in the exploratory phase indicate that
the venture will be even more successful than we had
hoped.
        The Rio Poco Mining Company is proud of its record
of cooperation with the people and the environment around
it. In this spirit, we are pleased to present the
following report detailing our first six months of
operation, specifying what we're gaining from Penschal
County, and what we're giving back in return. The report
consists of four sections: 1) a mine-by-mine analysis of
the exploratory and other activities carried out during
the last six months, including exact tonnages removed
from each site; 2) an economic accounting for the funds
put into and taken out of the mine; 3) an environmental
accounting for each mine's activities; and 4) a
prospectus for the next six months.
```

THE NEED FOR THE WRITING PROCESS

Many writers in business, industry, and government do not have or take the time to use the writing process described in this chapter. This fact suggests several important conclusions.

Since business, industry, and government are not generally known for effective writing, perhaps more on-the-job writers *ought* to use such a process. Even a brief examination of "real world" documents suggests that many writers write once only, off the tops of their heads.

Business writers usually explain that they do not use a writing process because first, they do not know one, and a close second, they do not have time.

Although an argument can be made for ineffective writing costing time and money later, these writers have a point: often writing tasks are assigned the day after they are due, and even when the lead time seems ample, professionals can rarely sit for uninterrupted hours working on a single piece of writing. The writers in business, industry, and government are also engineers, technicians, or persons involved with several other functions besides writing. Thus, they have many tasks and people other than writing and writers to contend with. These facts suggest that the more internalized the writing process becomes, the more quickly and efficiently one applies it. The less effective the writer, the less he knows and applies the writing process, the more troublesome are the real drawbacks typical of most business writing environments.

Like any skill, writing becomes easier and the results better if one takes a systematic approach and if one practices. The time and effort needed to learn the writing process more than pay for themselves, in increased ease of writing and improved quality of the final product.

SUMMARY

Effective writing does not result either from writing down on paper the first ideas and phrases one can think of or from staring at a blank page for hours until one gets the ideas and wording just right. Instead, good writing comes from flexibly applying the writing process, which includes three major stages: 1) prewriting, when the writer carefully explores the subject matter, analyzes the problems, and considers the context; 2) writing, when the writer uses the insights gathered in the prewriting stage as guides and raw materials for an initial draft; and 3) rewriting, when the writer reexamines the basic approach taken to the problem, modifies it if necessary, and carefully polishes the language to fit as nearly as possible the plan, purposes, and audiences of the document, and checks to make sure the rules of correct grammar and mechanics have been followed. Although these three stages may overlap and interweave considerably, they all do take place sometime before the document is completed.

EXERCISES

1. Using the situation described for Tom Johnson, Fred Smithson, or one from an earlier chapter, take the document through all three stages of the writing process until you have a final version, supplying any "facts" as needed. Evaluate the final version using the qualities of effective writing listed in chapter 1. How good is your final version? What further improvements can you make?

2. Think of any writing you actually have to do right now—a letter home, an application for a scholarship, a consumer complaint, a gripe at the dorm, etc. Right now, without any thought or planning, write a version of this document off the top of your head. Then, consider a second piece of writing and generate it using the

writing process outlined in this chapter. Which version do you think more effectively fulfills the qualities of good writing listed in chapter 1?

3. In this chapter you followed Andy Rice through the entire writing process. Study Andy's prewriting, writing, and rewriting of the introduction to his report. Describe and explain every change Andy made as he went along. Also, describe and explain any changes Andy should have made, but did not. Finally, generate an even more effective introduction for Andy.

FOR FURTHER READING

Beach, Richard. "Self-Evaluation Strategies of Extensive Revisers and Non-Revisers," *College Composition and Communication* 27 (May 1976): 160–64.

Braddock, Richard; Lloyd-Jones, Richard; and Schoer, Lowell. *Research in Written Composition.* Urbana, Illinois: NCTE, 1963.

Burke, Kenneth. *A Rhetoric of Motives.* Berkeley: University of California Press, 1969.

Elbow, Peter. *Writing with Power: Techniques for Mastering the Writing Process.* New York: Oxford University Press, 1980.

Faigley, Lester and Witte, Stephen. "Analyzing Revision." *College Composition and Communication* 32 (December 1981): 400–14.

Gregg, Lee and Steinberg, Erwin, eds. *Cognitive Processes in Writing.* Hillside, New Jersey: Erlbaum, 1980.

Harrington, David, et al. "A Critical Survey of Resources for Teaching Rhetorical Invention: A Review Essay," *College English* 40 (February 1979): 641–61.

Lauer, Janice. "Heuristics and Composition." *College Composition and Communication* 21 (December 1970): 396–404.

Macrorie, Ken. *Telling Writing,* 3rd edition. Rochelle Park, N.J.: Hayden, 1980.

Miller, Susan. *Writing: Process and Product.* Cambridge, Massachusetts: Winthrop, 1976.

Murray, Donald. "Write before Writing." *College Composition and Communication* 29 (December 1978): 375–82.

Sommers, Nancy. "Revision Strategies of Student Writers and Experienced Adult Writers." *College Composition and Communication* 31 (December 1980): 378–88.

Young, Richard; Becker, Alton; and Pike, Kenneth. *Rhetoric: Discovery and Change.* New York: Harcourt, Brace and World, 1970.

7

The Language
of
Communication

```
Memo to:  Tim Merton
From:  Phyllis Leon
Re:  Attached Proposal

    Your immediate action on this proposal is requested
as we are holding the cars with the intent to purchase or
lease contingent upon your approval of the project and
delivery of a replacement unit at Seaside Branch with a
24-hour refusal notice.
```

Help! That is probably the only appropriate reaction to this memo's sentence. Even if Phyllis Leon adequately analyzed the purpose, audience, and authorial stance before writing, her memo does not perform adequately. No doubt she has something definite, even urgent, in mind. But the reader, Tim Merton, cannot interpret that urgent message. Perhaps he can read the attached proposal itself and then go back and figure out the memo. But if that's the case, it would be better not to attach a cover memo at all. What goes wrong with the language of so much writing in business, industry, and government? Is there a systematic way for writers to avoid inflicting such dense prose on their readers?

Preview Questions

1. Just what is a good sentence?
2. Can a given idea be written in only one good sentence?
3. Should the same idea always be expressed in the same sentence, no matter what the rhetorical situation?
4. Do all good sentences have something in common?

The writer wants to put his piece of writing in the best possible language. But as discussed in chapter 6, lengthy puzzling over the ideal sentence structure on the first draft only harms the draft's content, perhaps fatally. The writer must write the first draft quickly, but that very speed often results in weak sentences. With the methods explained in this chapter you can improve weak sentences. But remember, you cannot improve an unwritten sentence. So first get something worth improving down on paper. *Then* start the improving.

To make genuine improvements instead of superficial changes, the effective writer must first understand the qualities of good prose. Then the effective writer must be able to read her prose objectively to spot any places where its language deviates from those qualities. Finally, the writer must be able to correct the deficiencies she sees. But effective writers go beyond the mere correction of errors to use the rewriting stage of the writing process to generate excellent language from the good language of the earlier version. The writer who limits rewriting to the mere fixing of errors places a low ceiling on his writing. The best rewriting concentrates positively on creating the best language, not negatively on repairing the worst. This chapter presents effective language from many angles, but concentrates on two: the grammatical (sentence structure and punctuation) and the rhetorical (adapting to audience and achieving coherence). Throughout the writing process, and especially in rewriting, the grammatical and the rhetorical overlap. Almost always, the writer must consider both at once when attempting to rewrite her prose. The rest of this chapter examines the basic English sentence structure and then presents several approaches for monitoring and revising language.

BASE SENTENCES

In English the normal sentence pattern is Subject (S), Verb (V), and Object (O):

Subject	Verb	Object
The company	drilled	a well.

Strictly speaking, sentences only joining the subject to a noun that renames the subject or an adjective that describes the subject do not have an object at all, but a complement. Consider the following two sentences:

He is my friend.
They became angry.

In these examples, *friend* and *angry* are complements. But what is important for writers, as opposed to grammarians, is that although objects and complements serve different grammatical functions, their positions in normal word order are the same.

Word Order

Occasionally, a sentence may not require a subject, a verb, an object or a complement, but the missing element or elements do not change the normal order of the remaining words in the sentence. If, on the other hand, the normal word order is changed,

Subject	Object	Verb
The company	a well	drilled.

the reader still understands the sentence, but wonders why written so strangely it is. The reader may think the unusual word order attempts to communicate some special message.

> A good sentence is one in which the main idea is perfectly clear, with no unusual or misleading features to distract the reader's attention.

If a reader has to spend time and effort puzzling over an unusual form, that form should reveal some special meaning that could not be conveyed through a different but more normal form.

However, not all good sentences have to be as simple as "The company drilled a well." Sentence clarity is a function not of simplicity, but of internal structure and relationships. "The company a well drilled" is not hard to read because it is less simple than "The company drilled a well." The two sentences are equally simple. But one uses an abnormal word order (for English), while the other uses the normal English word order, which allows the reader to grasp the relationships among the parts of the sentence quickly. If the relationships are clear, even an extremely complex sentence may be quite clear. If the subject, verb, and object relationships are not clear, then even a simple sentence may not be clear.

EXERCISE

Indicate the subject, verb, and object in each of the following sentences:

a. The young executive with the expensive tastes foolishly wasted all of his company's money.

b. In summary, we recommend that well number 20–C be redrilled.

c. The Houston Sewer Authority, as part of its program to reduce pollution in the Brazos River, built the Pasadena tunnel, which intercepts twelve major surface sewers and diverts them into the Alamo Street interceptor, a tributary feeding into the Bird Island treatment plant.

Sentence Content

Merely placing a subject, verb, and object in normal order does not guarantee a good sentence. Many sentences, especially ones written quickly on first drafts, have a grammatical subject, verb, and object in proper order, but none of these correspond to what the sentence is about conceptually. In other words, the grammar of the sentence leads one way, but the content of the sentence leads another way. Consider the following example:

```
    It was a half-hour drive until we came to a
beautiful park.
```

The grammatical structure of this sentence is

Grammatical Subject	Verb	Object
It	was	a half-hour drive until we came to a beautiful park.

But conceptually, the sentence is not about an *it*. Similarly, the active verb in the sentence is not *was*, nor is the receiver of the action, or object, *a half-hour drive*. Conceptually, the sentence's underlying structure is as follows:

Conceptual Subject	Verb	Object
We	drove	to a beautiful park in a half-hour.

The word *it* in the grammatical subject position in the original sentence fails to name the conceptual subject, the actual doer of the sentence, *we*. The same discrepancy exists for the grammatical verb, *was*, and the action actually performed in the sentence, *drive*, and the grammatical object, *drive*, and the actual receiver of the action in the sentence, *park*. These discrepancies between grammar and content are detailed in the following chart:

	Subject	Verb	Object
grammatical positions	it	was	drive
underlying concepts	we	drove	park

This inconsistency is at the root of many unclear or bad sentences.

By selecting one word or phrase that names the actual doer in the sentence, and placing that same word or phrase in the grammatical subject position, the writer can generate simple and clear sentences. In the example, if the writer chooses to fill in *we* for the subject, *drive* for the verb, and *park* for the object, the resulting base sentence would be "We drove to a beautiful park in a half-hour." The point is, the writer identifies the conceptual subject, verb, and object and then puts accurate words and phrases in subject, verb, and object positions. Then, with the three key words of the sentence in place, the writer can build the rest of the sentence on an accurate and clear base.

EXERCISE

For each of the following sentences identify the grammatical subject, verb, and object. Then identify the conceptual subject, verb, and object. Are the grammatical positions consistent with the underlying ideas? If not, rewrite the sentences to make the grammar and the ideas consistent. The first one has been done for you to help you see the systematic process of generating base sentences.

At this time, it is the opinion of our gas sales personnel that our purchaser, Oregon Natural, would purchase the additional seven to eight MMCFD.

	Subject	Verb	Object
grammatical positions	it	is	opinion
underlying concepts	personnel	believes	purchaser

words added to complete the
sentence:
at this time
our gas sales
that our

final sentence: At this time, our gas sales personnel believe that our purchaser, Oregon Natural, would purchase the additional seven to eight MMCFD.

b. There is some question as to the validity of this recoverable reserve estimate due to the lack of well control in Jones' map.

c. It has recently come to light that you have been in direct contact with the architect engineer.

d. For the past two months we have been attempting to have the sink in the Coconino building completed.

e. The objective in this data acquisition was to address the following considerations that are of primary importance in the study.

f. It is important to note that a firm commitment for one compressor and a tentative commitment for a second compressor could be made with some company.

g. It would also require some modification by our company and I don't have any idea of the cost of modification.

h. The new computer terminal is required to be compatible with any system to be installed in Cleveland.

i. As you were informed by telephone on 30 September 1982, there exists a warranty on that item.

j. You broke the bell of one section of pipe while digging; however, examination revealed the pipe cracked prior to excavation.

k. It is further recommended that well #402 be plugged and abandoned.

l. Furthermore, it is requested that the division office anaylze this project as expeditiously as possible due to the possibility of acquiring rig #5.

m. It is desirable to obtain this workover rig to provide the capability to workover wells as required immediately prior to, as well as during, this fiscal year.

n. If additional wells are to be drilled in this area, there will be additional expenditures of $75,000 for each well.

o. If a location is encountered where a sufficient source of commercial electric power is nearby, not requiring an initial investment of more than $50,000, then conversion should be considered.

p. It has come to our attention that the logging operation on the Cascade Range provides for the use of a borehole geometry tool. It is the opinion of this office that sufficient information can be gathered with the 4-arm caliper tool.

q. It is recommended in this memo that risers, which visual inspection indicates could be a potential problem, reference the photographs in this year's and last year's reports, should be either ultrasonically or radiographically inspected.

r. One area stressed by the Marine Board that could be improved on in our operations is visual inspections of platforms.

s. Because of a lack of continuity of effort there was no follow-up to this program and it was not implemented.

t. Therefore it is requested that your office consider development of a program that would qualify the extent of corrosion on platforms with emphasis on the splash zone.

u. There apparently was a communication problem on lease numbers made with our people in Spokane who are in charge of making the royalty payments.

v. There is a definite need for the shop to have at least four spare tractors.

w. It took the combined efforts of hundreds of scientists and technicians working as a team for our first space laboratory to be launched.

SENTENCES IN CONTEXT

However, merely joining the grammar and the ideas into a single base sentence does not necessarily mean that the best sentence has been found. If writers could automatically craft the perfect sentence by merely matching grammar and ideas, the writing of effective sentences would be a purely mechanical process—complicated to be sure, but still one that could be reduced to a set of absolute rules. But as we have seen in chapters 1 and 2, the process of communication is above all a human process, always involving a rhetorical context that must be taken into account before the best sentence can be written. What is best in one rhetorical context will probably not be so in another. Joining grammar and ideas is necessary to create effective sentences, but it is only the first of several steps. The whole process of writing effective sentences can be illustrated with another simple sentence:

```
There was a bicycle moving quickly down the highway.
```

If you completed the previous exercise, you can pick out the grammatical and conceptual subject, verb, and object:

	Subject	*Verb*	*Object*
grammatical positions	there	was	bicycle
underlying concepts	bicycle	moved	highway

Filling in the minimal words yields the following grammatical sentence:

```
A bicycle was moving quickly down the highway.
```

Now you have a clear base sentence, which is a good place to start the second stage of the rewriting process. To complete the second stage the writer must think about his audience, purpose, and authorial stance. To improve a base sentence any further, the writer must examine the context in which the sentence appears. Individual sentences taken out of context, such as those in the exercise, cannot be improved beyond the base sentence form. Even more important, once the sentence is put into a context, the base sentence might *not* be the best sentence, i.e., the sentence whose language most perfectly fits the context. Writing effective sentences is a more subtle task than merely joining grammar and ideas.

Note the effect context has on judgments about sentence quality by placing the base sentence, "A bicycle was moving quickly down the highway," into its original context:

> Ida Johnson is driving her son home from basketball practice. She comes to a busy highway, onto which she must turn left to get home (see map). As the map shows, the highway turns sharply to the left just where Mrs. Johnson is stopped at a stop sign. Traffic is heavy and Mrs. Johnson slowly inches forward to get a better view of the oncoming traffic down the highway to her left. She is not yet on the highway when suddenly she sees a bicycle quickly approaching her car, on the highway's right edge. She stops immediately, and the bicycle swerves in an attempt to miss her, but the bicycle just grazes the front of her car. The rider loses control, and then crashes in the middle of the road. An oncoming car, unable to avoid the bicycle and rider sprawled in the middle of the highway, runs over them, killing the bicycle rider. The bicycle rider's family sues Mrs. Johnson.

Mrs. Johnson hires a lawyer who requires her to write her account of the accident. After using several prewriting techniques, Mrs. Johnson generates the following first draft:

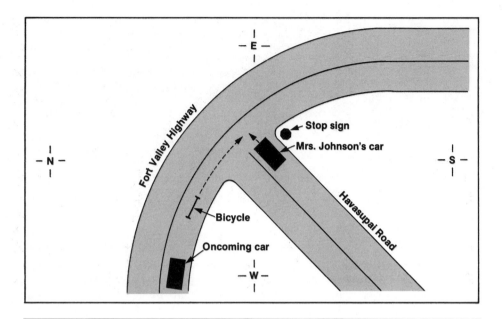

> On January 8, 1983, I was attempting to make a left
> turn from Havasupai Drive onto Fort Valley Road when I
> was hit by a bicycle coming from my left, going east down
> Fort Valley Road. The rider of the bicycle was thrown by
> the impact out into the street, where an oncoming car ran
> over her. There was a large crowd around the victim.
>   When I came up to the stop sign at the corner I
> stopped completely and then slowly moved forward so I
> could see when I could make my left turn. I could not
> turn, so I inched forward very slowly. <u>There was a</u>
> <u>bicycle moving quickly down the highway.</u> The rider
> swerved toward the highway to avoid me, just grazed the
> front of my car, lost control of her bicycle, and crashed
> and landed in the middle of the highway. There was a car
> coming down the highway which ran the rider over and
> killed her. My car was still well out of the highway.

The sentence "There was a bicycle moving quickly down the highway"
can be rewritten as the base sentence "A bicycle was moving quickly down the
highway." Because it is more concise, the base sentence is a slight improvement
over the original. But this slight theoretical advantage does not mean that the
base sentence is better when placed in context. As discussed in chapter 6, the
revision process involves both grammatical (or editorial) changes and conceptual (or re-vision) changes. If Mrs. Johnson rewrites her explanation looking
only for grammatical errors, she will not fix this sentence, because it is not
wrong. Mrs. Johnson will not improve her writing much by just fixing wrong
sentences. The sentence in question is not wrong or awkward, but it implies

Mrs. Johnson saw the bicycle all along and knowingly inched out into its path. Mrs. Johnson wants to make it clear she did not pull into the bicycle's path; rather, the bicycle ran into her while she was still out of the highway. Therefore, in this context, Mrs. Johnson adds a clarifying phrase to her original sentence, not to improve its grammar, or to make it less awkward, which would be editing, but to improve its effectiveness, which is re-vision. Since this clarification is so important to her defense, she adds it to the front of her sentence:

```
Before I got to the highway, a bicycle was moving quickly
down the highway.
```

Reviewing this new sentence, Mrs. Johnson sees that it places *bicycle* in the subject position, but she wants to emphasize not the bicycle but that *she saw* the bicycle. Therefore she decides to take *bicycle* out of the subject position and replace it with *I*. Similarly, she is most concerned with her seeing at this point, so she decides to change the verb from *was moving* to *saw*, since that is what she did. This re-vision results in the following sentence:

```
Before I got to the highway, I saw a bicycle moving
quickly down the highway.
```

(Note that Mrs. Johnson did not even see or need to see that the earlier sentence had a dangling modifier. Her re-vision automatically eliminated that problem without her even knowing it. This is why editing is normally saved for the very end of the writing process.) Re-vision will not eliminate all editing problems, but it often eliminates some. Also, there is no particular virtue in editing sentences or phrases that do not make it into the final version.

Finally, Mrs. Johnson dislikes the sound of the two *highways* in the same sentence. Fixing this requires an editorial change rather than a re-vision. To change it, Mrs. Johnson can simply substitute the word *road* or some other synonym for one of the *highways*. However, thinking about this simple editorial change, she realizes she also wants to emphasize that the bicycle ran into her and not she into the bicycle. Changing emphasis is a matter of re-vision, not mere editing. Therefore, instead of just inserting the synonym *road*, she changes her sentence to

```
Before I got to the highway, I saw a bicycle moving
quickly toward me.
```

This entire defensive line of reasoning has been built into the sentence's language through re-vision and editing. With the defensive posture now firmly in mind Mrs. Johnson decides to emphasize a new point, that the bicycle was going too fast, so she substitutes *speeding* for *moving quickly*:

```
      Before I got to the highway, I saw a bicycle
speeding toward me.
```

The process of rewriting has considerably improved the grammar and content—in a word the language—of this particular sentence, especially when viewed in context:

```
     I could not turn, so I inched forward very slowly.
Before I got to the highway, I saw a bicycle speeding
toward me. The rider swerved toward the highway to avoid
me.
```

Thus, the best sentence does not exist in isolation or out of context. Even in context, it results from carefully balancing the demands of audience, purpose, and authorial stance, along with the grammatical and conceptual demands of the sentence. Grammatical rewriting can generally be handled through relatively mechanical editorial changes. Conceptual rewriting generally requires a more thoughtful contextual analysis. For instance, the best sentence for the audience might not fit the desired tone, so a compromise has to be worked out. Above all, once the writer establishes the basic grammar of the sentence, she must make the remaining choices conceptually and contextually, not grammatically. To some extent, grammar can be handled in isolation, but content cannot.

CRAFTING SENTENCES

The crafting of basic sentences may be summarized in the following steps. Most effective writers do not consciously work through these steps because the steps have become second nature. In other words, the effective writer writes, rather than follows a series of steps. Nonetheless, a beginning writer can profit from such a list. An unpracticed writer may have to work methodically through each step, but will soon internalize the process.

   I. Establish the base sentence.
      A. Find the grammatical subject, verb, and object of the first draft sentence.
      B. Find the conceptual subject, verb, and object of the first draft sentence.
      C. Complete the base sentence using the conceptual subject, verb, and object as the key words.

II. Mold the base sentence to reflect the desired emphasis of the sentence in its context.
   A. Analyze the context.
      1. Purpose
      2. Audience
      3. Authorial stance
   B. Manipulate the structure and/or words of the base sentence to fit the purpose, audience, and authorial stance.

Several examples that illustrate these steps follow.

I. The additional eight million cubic feet per day would, according to Mr. Smith, be purchased by Oregon Natural.
   A. subject = eight million cubic feet
      verb = would be purchased
      object = Oregon Natural
   B. subject = Oregon Natural
      verb = would purchase
      object = eight million cubic feet
   C. Base Sentence: Oregon Natural would purchase the additional eight million cubic feet per day.

II. A. The writer is urging his company to invest in more natural gas wells.
      1. The purpose of the document that includes this sentence is to convince the company to acquire the new well, on the grounds that extra gas can be sold at extra profit.
      2. The audience, an executive in the writer's company, is afraid their company will purchase too many wells and thus oversupply themselves with natural gas.
      3. The writer is not in a position of enough authority in his company to demand that the new well be bought; thus, he must be clear and forceful, but not overly aggressive.
   B. Final Resulting Sentence: Mr. Smith of our marketing department is confident Oregon Natural will purchase another eight million cubic feet per day.

      With the same base sentence, notice how a different context demands a different final revised sentence.

II. A. The writer is questioning his own marketing department's assertion that the company can sell an additional eight million feet of natural gas.
      1. The purpose of this second document is still to convince the company to purchase the new well; however, the writer wants to have the record state clearly that the recommendation is based on the marketing department's go ahead. (The writer wants to practice CYA.)
      2. The audience is Mr. Smith, head of marketing, with whom the writer disagrees.

3. The writer is in a peer or lateral relationship to Mr. Smith; thus he can be relatively chatty and informal.

B. Final Resulting Sentence: Your earlier report, on which I am basing my recommendation, stated that Oregon Natural would take an additional eight million cubic feet per day.

EXERCISES

1. In each of the following passages, pick out at least one sentence that seems to have a faulty sentence base. Does anything in the context of the passage justify the apparently faulty base? If not, improve the sentence and explain your changes.

```
INTEROFFICE MEMO

     If Thursday, May 22, at 4:00 p.m. for our final
committee meeting to consider a final draft is
unaccommodatable for you, please call me.
```

```
MEMO TO FILE

Subject:  Future Corrosion and Mechanical Engineers
          Meetings


     This memo is in response to the attached letter from
R.C. Johnson, which solicited comments on how to improve
the effectiveness of the Corrosion and Mechanical
Engineers meetings. The following contains our comments
on each of the items listed at the end of R.C. Johnson's
letter:

     1. Consideration of recent company-wide meetings
indicates the presentations by Research personnel have
consistently been of much benefit to us, and we are
utilizing information from these presentations (settling
tanks with Vortex design, inhibitors for hot deep wells,
corrosion and stress-corrosion resistence and
metallurgy).
     2. We recommend that regional corrosion engineers
meetings be initiated; we believe that all of our
district offices will benefit from a meeting discussing
monitoring techniques used by each district. Furthermore,
if all presentations are reviewed or selected from those
given at regional meetings, ''show and tell''
presentations should be eliminated. For this to be
effective, of course, all regions will need to have these
meetings.
```

3. Concerning company-wide meetings, we feel that the current type of meeting on a nine-month frequency should achieve the goals of these meetings.

4. An alternative may be to alternate the current type of meeting with a smaller work session including only research, regional and general office staff, with six months between each meeting. In any case we wish to reserve the right to have district personnel attend the company-wide meeting on a selective basis, that is to make specific presentations of widespread interest and importance or to participate in discussions essential to district corrosion problems.

Department of Community Affairs
363 West State St.
Provo, Utah 84601

Dear Mr. Smith:

Reference is made to your letter dated 23 May informing this office that in accordance with the provisions of the U.S. Office of Management and Budget Circular A-95 Revised and Chapter 85, Utah Laws of 1936, the Project Modification for the Hobbs Canyon project was being processed. The State Identifier number for this project is OSRC-FY-79-1865.

A meeting to discuss the status of this project was held with Springville Township officials on 10 November 1979. Should you have any questions or desire additional information please contact Ms. Tracy Jones of the Provo office at 375-1950.

Sincerely,

---

2. Earlier in this chapter you read Mrs. Johnson's first draft of her defense in the case of the cyclist who was run over. How effective is this first draft? Does it satisfy the criteria of good writing as listed in chapter 1? What specific improvements would you suggest? If necessary, rewrite Mrs. Johnson's entire draft.

3. Take any magazine, newspaper, or book you wish. Examine a passage for any sentences that appear to have faulty bases. Does the context of the entire passage justify the apparently faulty base? If not, correct the sentences in question, explaining your rationale in terms of purpose, audience, authorial stance, and/or stylistic or grammatical considerations.

4. You are the manager of the Peabody Telephone Supply Company. You have ordered 10,000 feet of 300-pair cable at a cost of $1200/foot. Unknown to you, one of your employees has also ordered 10,000 feet of the same cable, so 20,000 feet of the cable have been delivered instead of 10,000.

   a. Write a letter to the Python Cable Company, the supplier of the cable, requesting permission to return the extra 10,000 feet of cable for full credit.

   b. Write a memo to the employee who ordered the extra cable, explaining that all orders must be cleared through the branch manager and entered in the permanent record so such duplication can be avoided.

   c. You are the president of Python Cable Company. Write back to the manager of the Peabody Telephone Supply Company refusing his request to return the cable, but retaining his good will and his future business.

FOR FURTHER READING

Bartholomae, David. "The Study of Error." *College Composition and Communication* 31 (October 1980): 253-69.

Christensen, Francis. "A Generative Rhetoric of the Sentence." *College Composition and Communication* 14 (October 1963): 155-61.

D'Eloia, Sarah. "The Uses—and Limits—of Grammar." *Journal of Basic Writing* 1 (Spring-Summer 1977): 1-20.

Faigley, Lester. "Names in Search of a Concept: Maturity, Fluency, Complexity, and Growth in Written Syntax." *College Composition and Communication* 31 (October 1980): 291-300.

Flower, Linda. "Writer-Based Prose: A Cognitive Basis for Problems in Writing." *College English* 41 (September 1979): 31-49.

Kroll, Barry. "Error-Analysis and the Teaching of Composition." *College Composition and Communication* 29 (October 1978): 242-48.

Lanham, Richard. *Revising Prose.* New York: Charles Scribner's Sons, 1979.

Macrorie, Ken. *Searching Writing.* Rochelle Park, New Jersey: Hayden, 1980.

McCarron, William. "Confessions of a Working Technical Editor." *The Technical Writing Teacher* 6 (1978): 5-8.

Williams, Joseph. "The Phenomenology of Error." *College Composition and Communication* 32 (May 1982): 152-68.

Winterowd, W. Ross. "The Grammar of Coherence." *College English* 31 (May 1970): 328-35.

Witte, Stephen and Faigley, Lester. "Coherence, Cohesion and Writing Quality." *College Composition and Communication* 32 (May 1981): 189-204.

8

Beyond the Base Sentence

T he qualities of effective writing listed in chapter 1 could be reduced to the 4 Cs. The language of all professional writers in business, industry, and government should be

▶ Clear
▶ Concise
▶ Coherent
▶ Correct

Before one can attain these 4 Cs, one must control the base sentences as discussed in chapter 7. But monitoring the base sentences does not result in clear, concise, coherent, and correct writing. The missing element is style. *Style* is an elusive term, but basically it refers to the total impact of a piece of writing, or the way it comes across.

> To create an effective style the writer must mesh the 4 Cs with the rhetoric of the particular writing situation.

The writer controls her style by controlling a multitude of individual language features in the piece of writing: word choice, sentence structure, organization, graphic aids, and a host of others. The total impact of all these features constitutes the writing's style. The writer aims to create a unified style in which tone, word choice, organization, and so forth, all fit smoothly together for a unified effect. Or, if there is a discrepancy among certain features of the document, the writer controls even that discrepancy for a definite purpose.

This chapter examines the first three of the 4 Cs: clarity, conciseness, and coherence. Correctness is addressed separately in chapter 9. By looking at a particular quality of good writing in detail, you can see how a writer attains each of these desired qualities.

CLEAR

Clear language means only one thing, and that one thing is obvious. "They are cleaning women" is not clear because it could mean at least two different things. "If the Limpscaw Method is requested for the Z options and the mode is distributed, then those transactions qualifying for a particular Z option are taken to room 101" is not clear because it is not obvious that it means anything at all. But a writer may know language should be clear and know what clear language is and still be unable to write clearly.

To write clearly, the writer must develop four distinct skills in the writing process. The writer must

▶ Know exactly what he wants to say, or must discover it through the writing process

▶ Choose the exact words, sentences, and organizational patterns to fit what she wants to say

▶ Read his writing from the audience's perspective

▶ Modify her writing to fit the audience

These four abilities can be applied to the following situation.

John Clann heads purchasing for the telephone company. One of the district offices requested figure 8 telephone cable with a three-eighth inch support wire. John thinks this is unusual, and he doubts that the cable is really what the office wants. He wants to communicate his concern without seeming ignorant and without making the requesting office seem ignorant, either. Of course he also does not want to order something he'll only have to try to return later.

To be clear, John must decide exactly what he wants to say. Does he wish to challenge the order? Question it? Reject it? If, in an attempt to be diplomatic, John writes the following, his readers may not be offended, but they almost certainly will not know exactly what he wants either.

```
        Your purchase order #2103 for 10,000 feet of figure
    8 telephone cable with three-eighth inch support wire is
    a little strange.
```

Does this sentence mean that the *order* is strange? Or does it mean that the office's ordering such cable is strange? Or that the cable itself is strange? Or something else altogether? The reader cannot tell. Hence the writing is unclear. Perhaps John has not thought enough about what he wants to say and does not yet know what to write.

Thinking further, John decides he wants to question the ordering office so that they will rethink the order—is the cable exactly right for the application they have in mind? Thus John rephrases his sentence as follows:

```
        Your purchase order #2103 requires an unusual item:
    10,000 feet of figure 8 telephone cable with a three-
    eighth inch support wire.
```

At this point John has decided exactly what he wants to say and has stated it in the exact words to convey only that meaning. Now John must think of the situation's rhetoric to see if his audience will understand the statement as he intends. Is the tone clear? Will the office become defensive because John has used such accusing words as **your** *purchase order, requires,* and *unusual*? John decides to depersonalize his opening sentence to make it clear he is not accusing, only inquiring.

```
     Purchase order #2103 calls for a special item:
10,000 feet of figure 8 telephone cable with a three-
eighth inch support wire.
```

Now John feels confident that he knows what he wants his sentence to say, he has selected words to say exactly what he wants, and his audience will understand him. The same analysis John has applied to one sentence can be applied to a paragraph, a letter, a report, or any piece of writing, no matter how long or short. For instance, what appropriate revisions can you suggest for the next few sentences of John's letter?

```
     This cable will have to be specially made, which
will make it impossible to be returned to the supplier.
Therefore, I think you should use another more standard
cable. This way you could still use the cable even if the
thing you think you want it for does not work out.
```

EXERCISES

1. Analyze the following passages for clarity. Improve each by 1) deciding exactly what the passage is trying to say; 2) selecting language that states the meaning without ambiguity; and 3) shaping that meaning to fit the audience and situation implied. In some cases you may think of several implied audiences and situations, and hence come up with several different versions of a single passage. Be prepared to explain the differences behind the various versions.

   a. Listed below are the five rigs that we request to be worked over.

   b. It should be noted that these test programs are only useful in debugging the top half of the system.

   c. We have processed an employee change authorization form changing her place of employment from Concord to Walnut Creek.

   d. The formats for data on the magnetic tape are standard throughout the PBX industry.

   e. As applied to deposit of a customer's payment on an invoice, we operate through a network of sixty-five branch banks all over the western United States.

2. Here is a specific situation and a longer piece of writing for you to analyze and improve in clarity.

> Frank Morris is coordinator of data processing for a large company that is switching over to a new centralized word processing system. He wants to call a meeting to introduce and explain the new system to representatives from each section of the company. He thinks it essential to explain the system to at least one person from each section, so that person can in turn spread the word to others in his or her section. However, Frank does not have the authority to command attendance at his meeting.

Frank's first draft of the memo announcing the meeting follows:

```
To:  Section Chiefs
From:  Frank Morris

     The new ZBC 1000 is here! It is going to be the only
way to get anything typed in this office after January
15, 1985. If your section has no one who can use the
system, you won't get anything typed.
     A meeting is scheduled to be held in room 2701 on
January 4, 1985 to discuss and review any proposed
implementation plan outlining the tasks and
responsibilities of each section to complete the
switchover by January 15. It is imperative that a
representative from each section attend this meeting to
be sure his responsibilities are fully comprehended and
are achievable as outlined in my implementation plan.
```

CONCISE

Effective writing in business, industry, and government is concise. Concise does not necessarily mean short. Rather, conciseness is a ratio of content to length. The writer ultimately wants to reduce the length as much as possible, while still retaining clarity. Generally, if two passages are equally clear, the shorter version is better. (Remember, however, that clarity includes appropriateness to the intended audience, which might on occasion make a longer passage better than a shorter one.) But if two passages are not equally clear, then the clearer one is better, even if longer. Conciseness is important, but it cannot substitute for clarity.

Usually, however, conciseness and clarity do not oppose each other. Look again at John Clann's letter questioning his office's purchase order for telephone cable. After getting his first sentence exactly the way he wanted it, John completed the memo as follows:

```
      Purchase order #2103 calls for a special item:
10,000 feet of figure 8 telephone cable with a three-
eighth inch support wire.
      This cable will have to be specially made, which
will make it impossible to be returned to the supplier.
Therefore, I think you should use another more standard
cable. This way you could still use the cable if the
thing you think you want it for does not work out.
```

John's memo is reasonably clear, but it is not concise. John could say the same thing with equal or greater clarity and in fewer words.

The exact causes of word bloat, excess verbiage, or just plain long-windedness, are not easy to identify. However, in general, wordiness is indicative of two broad problems: redundant or unnecessarily complicated choice of words, and inherently wordy sentence structures. John's memo provides several examples of each problem. Let's analyze just one sentence of the memo for conciseness.

```
      This cable will have to be specially made, which
will make it impossible to be returned to the supplier.
(19 words)
```

This sentence is wordy because John cast it in an inherently wordy sentence structure: it contains two clauses (separated by the comma), when it needs only one. You can see the wordiness more clearly by identifying the main idea in each clause:

1. The cable has to be specially made.
2. The cable cannot be returned to the supplier.

In other words, the first clause specifies a quality of the cable—it has to be specially made. The second clause tells a result of that quality—it cannot be returned. If John changes the first clause, he can join it to a more concise second clause.

```
      Since the cable will have to be specially made, it
will be impossible to return to the supplier. (17 words)
```

This new structure allows the writer to make several small changes, such as shortening the verb in the main part of the sentence from *to be returned* to *to return*.

Still, John can make the sentence even more concise by seeing that *specially made* as a quality of the cable can be expressed in an adjectival phrase, instead of a clause.

> ```
>         This specially made cable will be impossible to
> return to the supplier. (12 words)
> ```

This sentence is great in terms of conciseness, but John should notice that he has now lost the emphasis on causality achieved by *since* in the previous version. This version just mentions that the cable is specially made; it does not point out that because it is special, it is impossible to return. The new sentence's conciseness costs it some clarity. If John knows his audience will understand that the cable's specialness makes it impossible to return, then he can use this concise form. But if John wants to be sure his audience understands that special cable cannot be returned, then he should go back to the previous version and try another way to be more concise. Clarity in this rhetorical context must precede conciseness. John tries another version.

> ```
>         This cable, being specially made, cannot be returned
> to the supplier. (12 words)
> ```

In this version John preserves both the emphasis on causality and the conciseness of only 12 words. It is not as smooth as the first 12-word version, because it includes an embedded phrase, but it is both clear and concise.

Finally, by considering redundancy at the rhetorical level, John may question whether or not he needs the phrase *to the supplier* in the context of the whole piece of writing. Since the cable would obviously be returned to the supplier, and would not be returned by the ordering office anyway, John deletes the phrase.

> ```
>         This cable, being specially made, cannot be
> returned. (9 words)
> ```

John has gained conciseness and not cost himself any clarity by making all his decisions within his working context.

EXERCISES

1. Examine the other sentences in John's memo. Are they clear and concise? If not, follow a process similar to that applied to the second sentence to generate more concise sentences. Be prepared to explain each change you make. Is the shortest version always the best? Are the more concise versions generally clearer as well? Are the shortest versions always the clearest? (John's other sentences are listed below.)

   a. Therefore, I think you should use another more standard cable.

   b. This way you could still use the cable even if the thing you think you want it for does not work out.

2. Apply the instructions in question 1 to the following paragraph:

```
        To obtain the necessary geological data for
analysis, we utilized a seismic shot pattern of
exploratory drill analysis. The seismic shot methodology
we favored over the shock wave method due to being easier
to do and being able to be done in more various areas.
However, the seismic shot methodology is accurate to a
depth of 1500 feet and under our testing conditions
generally and usually seemed to be a reliable, accurate,
and efficient measurement system.
```

COHERENT

Once the writer has crafted clear and concise sentences, he can consider coherence. In a coherent document the sentences and paragraphs join together smoothly, allowing the reader to progress easily from point to point.

Coherence is achieved at two levels. First, the writer makes sure that the ideas do flow from point to point logically. Once the writer is convinced that the ideas follow one another clearly, then she uses various language devices to emphasize that orderly flow of thought. Unfortunately, some writers try to disguise poor thinking with smooth-sounding linguistic devices. However, *no* devices of language can substitute for clear and orderly relationships among a document's parts.

Some major devices a writer may use to signal the logical flow of her ideas follow:

- ▶ Transitional words and phrases
- ▶ Key words, synonyms, and pronouns
- ▶ Parallel sentence structure
- ▶ Sentence combining
- ▶ Organization

Each of these devices signals where the writing is going or is about to go. They function like road signs that show the driver the shape of the road ahead.

Transitional Words and Phrases

The writer uses transitional words or phrases to indicate relationships such as cause and effect, opposition, time, and conjunction. By placing the transitional word or phrase between two ideas, the writer shows the relationship of the ideas. For instance, consider these two sentences:

I made the best decision I could.

I should have followed the Norris policy.

As they stand, the two sentences are not coherent. Their relationship is not clear. In fact, at least two possible relationships could apply between these two sentences:

- Time: The first sentence took place in the past, and the second sentence took place later than the first and still holds true.
- Opposition: The *decision* in the first sentence and the *Norris policy* in the second are opposing; between the times of the first and second sentences, the writer changed his mind about the right decision.

The writer striving for coherence will use transitional words or phrases to link the two sentences together clearly:

I made the best decision I could **at the time, but now** I see I should have followed the Norris policy.

At the time and *now* indicate a time relationship between the two parts of the sentence; *but* indicates an opposing relationship.

Writers choose transitions to fit the relationships between the sentences, rather than choose transitions first and mold sentences to fit later. Molding sentences to fit transitions results in the smooth but false coherence mentioned earlier. A few common relationships and some transitional words and phrases that fit each are listed in table 8–1. It does *not* list all transitions, because coherence results from a habitual concern for indicating relationships; it cannot be achieved by memorizing a list of words and phrases and blindly picking one to stick between two sentences. Like every part of the writing process, coherence is a principle, not a mechanical action.

KEY WORDS, SYNONYMS, AND PRONOUNS

The writer uses these three devices to create patterns of related words and phrases woven through a piece of writing to give it texture and flow.

KEY WORDS: engineers shore	The life of an engineer on an offshore oil rig is much more demanding than anything the onshore engineer knows. Lack of material and decreased emotional resources confront most offshore engineers at every turn.

Synonyms and pronouns establish the same sort of network to tie the prose together:

Table 8-1. Transitions

If you want your reader to	Use a word or phrase like this
Refer back to something earlier	as we have seen; on the whole; as mentioned earlier; as stated previously; as I have said
Look ahead to something later	then; next; finally; to sum up
See a causal relationship	the result; in conclusion; because; consequently; accordingly; hence; thus
See a time relationship	now; then; soon; finally; at the same time; thereafter
See a place relationship	here; at this point; below; beside; behind; outside; inside
Compare two or more things	similarly; just as
Contrast two or more things	nevertheless; on the other hand; however; despite; on the contrary; conversely; although; yet; but; unless; whether
Be prepared for an illustration	for example; for instance; to illustrate

SYNONYMS:
72 hours = stint
workers = personnel
out of temper = frustration
offshore = on a platform 10 miles out in the ocean

Often on duty up to 72 hours in a row, offshore personnel get out of temper by the end of their stint. This frustration causes many workers to desperately need the rest and relaxation that just are not available on a platform 10 miles out in the ocean.

PRONOUNS:
he
his
it

Consider, for example, Mark Robinson, a welder on a 50-man offshore crew. By the end of his third tour of duty on the rig, he felt he never wanted to return to it.

A writer often uses key words, synonyms, and pronouns together in a single passage. Furthermore, other transitional words and phrases such as those listed in table 8-1 may also be used along with key words, synonyms, and pronouns. List all the types of each device you can find in the following passage:

```
     The first possible location is 200 yards offshore in
Wanship Township, Range 23. To use this location, we
would have to build a road from U.S. Highway 180, two
miles southeast to the shoreline. Also, a docking
facility would be required at the end of the road. The
docking facility would house a boat to transport workers
and supplies to the platform.
     This alternative has several features working
against it. First, the cost of the new road would be
approximately $800,000. Second, rain would make it
impassable three months out of the year, unless we spent
another $1.1 million to upgrade the road's quality.
Finally, according to Fred Gwynne, this particular drill
site is probably only marginal anyway. He feels that an
onshore site closer to the environment of interfingering
sands and shales will probably cost less to drill and
provide a better payback also.
     Therefore, we recommend rejecting the first possible
drill site.
```

Let's look again at John Clann's memo about the telephone cable. When John examined his memo for coherence, he found a few places he could improve, especially between the last two sentences.

```
     Therefore, I think you should use another more
standard cable.
     This way you could still use the cable even if the
thing you want it for does not work out.
```

When John tried to make these two sentences more coherent, he discovered that they were not too clear or concise either, so he worked on clarity and conciseness first, coming up with two revised sentences:

```
     Figure 8 cable can be used only for special
applications.
     A more standard cable could be used for many
different applications.
```

Now that his sentences are clear and concise, John turns his attention to coherence, joining the two sentences with an effective transition.

> Since the figure 8 cable can be used only for
> special applications, perhaps we should order the more
> versatile rural ''C'' wire instead.

At this point, John's memo reads:

> Purchase order #2103 calls for a special item:
> 10,000 feet of figure 8 telephone cable with a three-
> eighth inch support wire. This cable, being specially
> made, cannot be returned. Since the figure 8 cable can be
> used only for special applications, perhaps we should
> order the more versatile rural ''C'' wire instead.

Compare the revised version with John's original version.

> Your purchase order #2103 for 10,000 feet of figure
> 8 telephone cable with three-eighth inch support wire is
> a little strange.
>   This cable will have to be specially made, which
> will make it impossible to be returned to the supplier.
> Therefore, I think you should use another more standard
> cable. This way you could still use the cable even if the
> thing you think you want it for does not work out.

How is John doing on clarity, conciseness, and coherence? Are there further improvements he can make?

Parallel Sentence Structure

Another device for assuring coherence is parallel sentence structure. Put simply, the writer organizes her sentence as a series of parallel items that make the passage easier to read, remember, and act upon. Of course, the parallel structure is ineffective and even misleading if it is merely mechanical, i.e., if the ideas put into parallel form are not really parallel. Genuinely parallel content must precede the creation of a parallel sentence pattern. Also, even when the parallel content is genuine, the best sentence for the context might not be one in a parallel form. As always, the writing process simply cannot be reduced to a series of blindly followed steps.

Without changing the idea at all, the effective use of parallel sentence structure changes a difficult-to-read jumble into an easy-to-read sentence. Consider the following two versions:

```
     The area has been heavily drilled in the past twenty
years. The number of successful wells in the area has
dropped drastically. The most recent geological survey
was unfavorable. The recommendation is not to purchase
leases in Flint County.
```

```
     We are opposed to acquiring any leases in Flint
County because of recent heavy drilling, unsuccessful new
well starts, and an unfavorable geological survey.
```

The second passage is in parallel structure, and the writer has also achieved clarity and conciseness. Can you improve it even more?

Here is another example of a sentence without parallel structure and a version with parallel structure.

```
     The new procedure will increase the quality and
timeliness of our service to our customers. It will also
make our programming staff more productive. Finally, with
our new procedure, we can have a central point where
production problems can be monitored.
```

```
     Implementing the new procedure will allow us to
improve the service to our customers, increase the
efficiency of our programming, and monitor the problems
in our production.
```

Sentence Combining

Coherence is not just a quality to look for within a sentence or between two sentences. Ideally, coherence should pervade an entire piece of writing. Sentence combining is one way to achieve coherence throughout a document. Using this technique, the writer recasts many short, choppy, poorly related sentences into a few longer, but coherent, sentences.

Many inexpensive books of sentence combining exercises are readily available at most bookstores. Or the writer may create his own sentence combining exercises by recasting passages of short choppy sentences in rough draft form into longer more coherent sentences. Or the writer may break down a passage of long, complicated sentences into its constituent short sentences and then experiment with putting the parts back together again in different combinations. Many possible right ways exist to combine the short sentences. Ultimately, the best choice depends on the exact rhetorical context in which the sentence is working. Done in isolation, sentence combining yields only a set of different possibilities, many of which seem equally effective. However, the writer generating multiple versions of a passage within a specific document does have a rhetorical context and hence can make a final decision on the most effective version.

A typical sentence combining exercise, in isolation, follows:

> Following are groups of three sentences each. For each group, write two different combinations that join two of the three original sentences. Then write one sentence that combines all three of the original ones.

Example
1. The hitchhiker was throwing rocks at passing cars.
2. The policeman gave a ticket to the hitchhiker.
3. The policeman's car was hit by a rock.
4. The policeman gave a ticket to the hitchhiker who was throwing rocks at passing cars.
5. The policeman whose car was hit by a rock gave a ticket to the hitchhiker.
6. The policeman whose car was hit by a rock gave a ticket to the hitchhiker throwing rocks at passing cars.

Exercises
1. The ranger's boat patrols the river.
2. The ranger is determined to stop being easy on poachers.
3. Poachers are killing beavers.

4.
5.
6.

1. The woman is from New York.
2. The man is older than the woman.
3. The man's friend is from New Jersey.

4.
5.
6.

Now follow John Clann as he applies sentence combining to a rough passage in another of his memos:

> There is currently a surplus car in the Rock River car pool, unit #2709, a 1979 Chevy Impala, which on February 10, 1985, unit #2709 had an odometer reading of 67,230 miles and is getting old, so we need to dispose of it to a used car broker who will probably find it valuable enough to buy.

First, John identifies all the individual sentences inherent in the one long sentence he has written. (If John had written a passage of short and choppy sentences, this step would have already been done.)

1. There is a surplus car.
2. The car is in the Rock River car pool.
3. The car is unit #2709.
4. The car is a 1979 model.
5. The car is a Chevy Impala.
6. The car had an odometer reading.
7. The odometer reading was done on February 10, 1985.
8. The odometer reading was 67,230 miles.
9. The car is getting old.
10. We should dispose of the car.
11. A used car broker will find the car valuable.
12. A used car broker will probably buy the car.

Next, John must organize the short sentences into logical groups. In this case, he can identify the groups easily: sentences 1–5, 6–8, and 9–12 fit together.

Let's look at just one group of sentences, 9–12, to see some of the combinations John can generate. Note that John does not have to use every short sentence in generating his new versions.

```
Because the car is getting old, we should dispose of it
to a used car broker.
```

```
We should dispose of this old car to the used car broker
who finds it most valuable.
```

```
Some used car broker is sure to take this old car off our
hands.
```

```
We should dispose of this old car while it is still
valuable enough to interest a used car broker.
```

No doubt John could generate still other versions. The most important points about this generation process are

1. John can compare multiple versions of the same basic idea to find exactly the right one for his rhetorical context.

2. In the process, John will probably have more insights into the subject itself. For example, the idea of interest that John generated in the last sentence was not in any of the twelve short sentences, nor in John's original draft.

EXERCISE

Work on John's other two groups, 1–5 and 6–8, to generate several versions for each. Imagine that John is writing to the Rock River office, which wants to keep the car. In this case, which versions from all three groups should John use? Write John's memo to the Rock River office.

Now imagine that John is writing to the head office, which has a standing policy of disposing of all cars over three years old or with over 60,000 miles on them. Now how will John's memo read?

Effective Organization

A final aid to coherence is effective organization, both within and among paragraphs. Unlike the previously mentioned devices for attaining coherence, organization often involves a total restructuring of the document. For most writing tasks in business, industry, and government, the following principles of good organization hold true.

Within Document   Considering all the paragraphs, put the most important idea in the first paragraph, the next most important idea in the next paragraph, and so on.

Compare the following two versions for effective organization and resulting levels of coherence.

> In response to your letter of May 10, 1985, I have studied the question of the proposed Roosevelt Dam across the Snake River. The question of how to get the county a more permanent and steady water supply has been of great concern for many years. Perhaps the proposed Roosevelt Dam will be the answer.
>
> However, the Blackfoot Indians are worried about their burial grounds, which will be flooded if the dam is built. Quite often environmental groups and even the Idaho Historical Society have filed suits supporting the Indians. So it appears that the Roosevelt Dam will not work out.

> Anyway, the Bitterroot Landfill is also dangerously
> close to the proposed site. Taking all the problems
> together, I guess the county will just have to keep
> looking. The Blackfoot Indians will sure be glad to know
> that their burial grounds will not be flooded. I'm sure
> we can find another site somewhere away from burial
> grounds and landfills.

> After careful study of the relevant data, I have
> concluded that the proposed Roosevelt Dam across the
> Snake River is not acceptable. The difficulties with the
> proposal are both environmental and historical.
> Environmentally, the proposed site is less than two
> miles downstream from the Bitterroot Landfill. Recent
> studies show that the landfill is leaching toxic
> substances throughout the surrounding area. Thus, one of
> the primary purposes of the dam, to provide an improved
> water supply throughout the county, would be defeated by
> the possibility of the water being contaminated by toxins
> from the landfill.
> Historically, the proposed site is a little over
> sixteen miles downstream from the Blackfoot Indian tribal
> burial grounds. The dam would raise the water level
> approximately 35 feet up to 25 miles upstream, putting
> the burial grounds under about 25 feet of water. Tribal
> officials, environmental groups, and the Idaho Historical
> Society have all filed suits against the proposed dam.
> Thus, I recommend that the county abandon the
> Roosevelt Dam and continue its search for another site
> that does not create such serious environmental and
> historical difficulties.

The first version uses some transitions to keep it flowing, but the overall pattern of development is weak, mainly because it does not flow from most important to next most important point as in the second version.

Within Paragraphs Considering each paragraph, follow one of two general patterns.

1. The first sentence promises something that the rest of the paragraph fulfills (most important point first).
2. The first sentences lead up to the point stated at the end of the paragraph (most important point last).

The following two paragraphs, both based on John Clann's second memo, illustrate these two general patterns.

> Unit #2709 in the Rock River car pool should be disposed of immediately to the highest bidding used-car broker. The car, a 1979 Chevy Impala, is 3 years over the 3-year guideline, and 7,230 miles over the 60,000-mile guideline, as of February 10, 1985.

> The Rock River car pool currently has a 1979 Chevy Impala, #2709, with 67,230 miles on it. Company policy says all cars should be disposed of upon reaching 3 years of age or 60,000 miles. Therefore, we should sell the car immediately to the highest bidding used-car broker.

These two versions of John Clann's memo are equally coherent, even though they follow different patterns of development. Thus, they illustrate that even though the most important to least important pattern is usually preferred in business, industry, and government, it is not the only pattern available to you. For instance, sometimes you may know you have an audience hostile to a proposal you want to make. In such a situation, it is better to build your case point by point, coming out with your overt statement at the end, only after you have had a chance to convince your audience. You do not want to turn them off with a bold opening statement. For instance, if you were trying to convince an employer to purchase a new copying machine, and you knew she hated to spend money, you would certainly not start out with

> I recommend that we purchase a CopyMaster 9000 with collator, for $6750.

Instead, you would first establish the need for a copier, then move into the features of this particular copier, and conclude with the punch line:

> Therefore, I recommend that we purchase a CopyMaster 9000 with collator; although it will cost $6750, it will pay for itself in only six months at current use levels.

In summary, coherence results from the writer's careful efforts to provide continuity and orderly progression in a document. Coherent writing is clear, concise, and readable, because every idea follows naturally from the previous ideas and flows naturally into the next as well. A coherent piece of writing keeps the reader reading without any pauses or misunderstanding. To achieve coherence, the writer can incorporate many techniques: transitions, key words, synonyms, pronouns, parallel sentence structure, sentence combining, and paragraph organization.

EXERCISES

1. Which of John Clann's versions of the Rock River memo would work best for the sympathetic audience? Which for the hostile audience? Why?

2. Read the following document and comment on its coherence. Where are the exact places it fails to cohere? Using any of the techniques presented, rewrite the document to make it more coherent. If the passage has any problems in clarity or conciseness, improve these areas as well. Be prepared to explain any changes you make.

> On December 17, 1984, we notified the Army Corps of Engineers concerning the bank degrading in the Pearl River. Currently the condensate produced in Port Vicks is carried via pipeline to a holding facility on the Pearl River. The condensate is loaded on to a barge.
>
> The need for the bank degrading occurred when part of the bank, supporting a loading facility piling, started to wash away. The piling was a support for the pipe. The pipe runs from the storage tank to the barge. A new piling was sunk 200 feet from the original, being washed away. This information was gained from Merribeth Turner of the Pearl River loading facility.
>
> I believe that we did provide adequate notification of our actions. Also, our actions were justified by the situation.

SUMMARY

The most desired qualities of good writing in business, industry, and government are clarity, conciseness, coherence, and correctness. Clarity, conciseness, and coherence have been discussed in this chapter.

Clarity ensures that the reader knows exactly what the writing's purpose is. The writer achieves it by 1) deciding exactly what he wants to say; 2) selecting language that states the meaning without ambiguity; and 3) shaping that meaning to fit the implied audience and situation. **Conciseness** is the lowest possible ratio between content clarity and length, the shortest writing that is also clear. The writer achieves it by selecting the least wordy sentence structures, cutting redundant or unnecessarily complicated words, and making sure the resulting passage is still clear in its rhetorical situation. **Coherence** keeps sentences and paragraphs joined together smoothly, allowing the reader to progress easily from point to point. The writer achieves it at two levels. First, the writer makes sure that the ideas do flow logically from point to point. Once the writer is convinced the ideas follow one another clearly, she uses various techniques, such as transitions, key words, synonyms, pronouns, parallel sentence structure, and sentence combining to emphasize that orderly flow of thought.

FOR FURTHER READING

Bartholomae, David. "Teaching Basic Writing: An Alternative to Basic Skills." *Journal of Basic Writing* 2 (Spring/Summer, 1979): 85–109.

Britton, James. *Language and Learning.* Harmondsworth, England: Penguin Press, 1970.

Christensen, Francis and Christensen, Bonniejean. *Notes Toward a New Rhetoric,* 2nd ed. New York: Harper and Row, 1978.

Coe, Richard. *Form and Substance: An Advanced Rhetoric.* New York: John Wiley and Sons, 1981.

Daiker, Donald; Kerek, Andrew; and Morenberg, Max. *The Writer's Options: College Sentence Combining.* New York: Harper and Row, 1979.

Emig, Janet. "Writing as a Mode of Learning." *College Composition and Communication* 28 (May 1977): 122–28.

Halliday, M.A.K. and Hasan, Ruqaiya. *Cohesion in English.* English Language Series No. 9, London: Longman, 1976.

Karrfalt, David. "The Generation of Paragraphs and Larger Units." *College Composition and Communication* 19 (October 1968): 211–17.

Meade, Richard and Ellis, W. Geiger. "Paragraph Development in the Modern Age of Rhetoric." *English Journal* 59 (February 1970): 219–26.

Rodgers, Paul. "A Discourse-Centered Rhetoric of the Paragraph." *College Composition and Communication* 17 (February 1966): 2–11.

Winterowd, W. Ross, ed. *Contemporary Rhetoric: A Conceptual Background with Readings.* New York: Harcourt Brace Jovanovich, 1975.

9

Correctness

I n addition to being clear, concise, and coherent, effective writing is also correct: it follows the basic rules of the language, including grammar principles and mechanics conventions. Grammar involves concepts such as subject-verb agreement, proper word forms, and correct verb tenses. Mechanics include conventions such as correct spelling and accurate punctuation. The writer usually concentrates on correctness only after making the document clear, concise, and coherent. Then the writer has something worth giving the painstaking effort that absolute correctness demands.

BEING CORRECT

Many writers believe that being correct is unimportant. If the content is good, the writer reasons, the reader will overlook grammar and mechanics. Unfortunately, the opposite is often true—if the grammar and mechanics are not correct, the reader does not pay any attention to the content, no matter how good it is. For example, job candidates have been rejected because of too many spelling errors, and recommendations have been misunderstood or ignored because of punctuation errors.

> Being correct is not all-important, but it *is* important.

Changing Usage

The writer aims to be letter perfect so the reader sees only the writing's content so that the issue of correctness never comes up. However, correctness is not always an absolute matter. For instance, some people use the spelling *judgement,* while others use *judgment.* Most dictionaries list both spellings. Some purists insist that *data* is a plural word, which it is in Latin, and demand the form *The data are* . . . . But the form *The data is* . . . , although not correct, is probably used more often than *The data are* . . . . Thus, most dictionaries list *data* as plural, but note that it is often used as singular. Not long ago it was taboo to end a sentence with a preposition or to neatly split an infinitive. But today many handbooks, and even more people, do not insist on these rules anymore. To give an opposite illustration, 600 years ago the poet Geoffrey Chaucer could correctly write:

He nevere yet no vileynye ne sayde.

Or in word-for-word modern English:

He never yet no villainy not said.

But today, writers would never use double and triple negatives because they are considered incorrect.

These sorts of questions fall under the general heading of usage (but check your dictionary for the correct spelling of *useable*!). What is considered correct usage simply changes over the years. Some writers, ahead of their time, use forms currently considered incorrect, but those forms become correct within a few years. Other writers, behind the times, obstinately cling to forms that sound old-fashioned to everyone else, forms the user insists are correct (everyone else is ruining the language by lowering standards). Such forms may have been quite important in their day. For instance, most U.S. citizens born before 1930 probably remember having the proper usage of *shall* and *will* pounded into their heads. Once crucial, this distinction is no longer observed or even remembered. (See if you can find a handbook that mentions it; and if you do find the rule, check the book's date of publication!)

Given this constantly shifting set of rules for correctness, the wise writer plays it fairly safe by

- Finding out what is considered absolutely necessary to be thought correct today. To do so, the writer consults a reliable and up-to-date handbook. Two good ones are Corbett's *Little English Handbook* (Scott, Foresman) and *The Little, Brown Handbook* (Little, Brown).
- Carefully observing correct usage. Do not be the first person to coin a new usage or the last one to drop an obsolete usage.

Usage is a little bit like fashion; tie widths and skirt lengths change. Although a woman is not naked in an out-of-date skirt, she may draw attention as though she were. Usage changes, too, and the working writer tries to follow those changes to some extent. Thus, the writer needs to have and use a few simple tools: a good dictionary, an up-to-date handbook, a listening ear, and an observing eye. Using these tools, the careful modern writer avoids double negatives, does not worry about splitting an infinitive, and is utterly unconcerned about the distinction between *shall* and *will*.

Since correctness is both important and slippery, the writer must know the audience. Many business and government agencies publish detailed style manuals for their employees. If you are employed by such an employer or if you write regularly to one, get a copy of the style manual and use it. Similarly, many individuals have firm opinions about certain usage rules. If you write to such an individual often, try to find out his particular standards and honor them. Again, every writer should have and use a good dictionary and handbook to answer questions about spelling, abbreviations, hyphenation, punctuation, and other common concerns. Different dictionaries and handbooks may offer different advice, but by selecting one of each for general use, the writer can at least be consistent.

Acknowledging that usage rules sometimes change does not make correctness impossible to attain. After all, there is nearly universal agreement about many usage rules, such as the double negative. In such cases, the agreed upon form should definitely be followed. A discussion of some basic usage rules and some common usage problems follows. The discussion certainly does not exhaust the subject, for if it did, you would not be motivated to get a good handbook for yourself. However, it does sketch out the fundamentals you need to be correct.

GRAMMAR

Beginning with the Greeks and Romans, grammar was thought of as a set of absolute rules prescribing all aspects of correct linguistic behavior. Many of these rules, such as the prohibition against splitting infinitives, were originally based on parallels with Latin grammar. More recently, however, grammar has been defined as a systematic accounting of how language *is* rather than as a set of rules for how it *should be.*

Some of the most important and agreed upon principles of current English grammar follow.

Subject-Verb Agreement

The subject of a sentence is either singular or plural. The verb of the sentence must agree with the subject in number: a singular subject demands a singular verb; a plural subject demands a plural verb.

> The engineer**s** survey_   the documents.
> The engineer_   survey**s** the documents.

As long as the sentence is simple, the writer usually has no problem with subject-verb agreement. However, more complicated sentences sometimes cause difficulty. A few rules covering these complications follow:

1. *Collective nouns are singular.* Collective nouns have plural meanings but are grammatically singular:

> The engineering *staff* survey**s** the documents.
> The *furniture* **is** ugly.

Other collective nouns include such words as *equipment, faculty,* and *committee.*

2. *Two singular nouns joined by "and" are plural:*

The engineer and the lawyer **survey** the documents.

3. *Two singular nouns joined by "or" are singular:*

The engineer or the lawyer survey**s** the documents.

4. *With a singular noun and a plural noun, the verb agrees with the noun closest to it:*

The engineers or the lawyer survey**s** the documents.

The engineer or the lawyer**s** survey the documents.

5. *A prepositional phrase is not a subject and is not involved in subject-verb agreement:*

The position_   of the companies **is** excellent.

The friend**s** of my client **are** scary.

Verb Tense

Generally speaking, the most important rule about verb tense is to keep it consistent. Unless the meaning of the sentence or paragraph demands a change in tense, keep the tense the same throughout.

When the engineers **studied** the proposal, they **found** out what they **needed** to know.

When the engineers **study** the proposal, they **find** out what they **need** to know.

However, the principle of consistency still leaves unanswered the question of which tense to select in the first place. Usually the rhetorical context determines the choice of tense for a particular piece of writing; however, a few general rules can be stated.

1. *Sentences referring to completed events or beliefs no longer held are put in the past tense.*

During the experiment, the white mice **ran** the wrong way in the maze.

Early scientists **did** not understand the circulation of the blood.

Columbus believed the earth **was** flat.

2. *Sentences referring to events still in progress or beliefs still held to be true are put in the present tense.*

The sun **rises** in the east.

The data **indicate** that saccharin **is** a carcinogen.

The experiment **is** progressing on schedule.

3.   *References to written reports, whether your own or someone else's, are put in the present tense.*

This report **covers** the period from 1919–1927.

Table 6 **shows** the results of last year's experiment.

According to Smithson's report last week, the greatest health risk **is** smoking.

Sometimes these guidelines become contradictory. For instance, if you refer to a completed experiment cited in another author's written report, rule 1 suggests the past tense, but rule 3 suggests the present. In such cases, no rule can substitute for intelligent consideration of the rhetorical context, and common sense. In the context of reporting experimental results, you would write:

According to Smithson's report, the smokers **had** more instances of lung cancer than the nonsmokers.

But in the context of giving the conclusion or overall findings of the experiment, you would write:

According to Smithson's report, the smokers **have** more instances of lung cancer than the nonsmokers.

Finally, in choosing verb tense, as in applying almost any grammatical rule, remember George Orwell's last rule for good writers: "Break any of these rules sooner than say anything outright barbarous." [1]

Even verb tense consistency, generally a good rule to follow, should be broken on occasion:

Now that I **am** thirty years old, my early experiments **do not** seem nearly as important as they **did** before.

Sentence Errors

Probably the two most common grammatical errors at the sentence level are the run-on sentence (or comma splice) and its opposite, the fragment.

---

[1]George Orwell, "Politics and the English Language," in *The Harper and Row Reader*, ed. Wayne Booth and Marshall Gregory (New York: Harper and Row, 1984), 142.

Comma Splice A run-on sentence squeezes two full sentences together as one, often joining them with a comma (hence the term *comma splice*):

The oil **rig blew** up, the **explosion killed** twenty men.

As this example shows, in a run-on sentence, a separate subject and verb appear on both sides of the comma. Conceptually, two related but distinct ideas are run together.

The comma splice may be corrected in many ways. As usual, the right correction depends on the rhetorical situation. Most simply, the comma can be replaced by a period:

The oil rig blew up. The explosion killed twenty men.

This version emphasizes the separateness of the two sentences, which is fine if the two events *are* separate, or the writer wants to make them seem as separate as possible. If, however, the two events are closely related and the author wants to stress that relationship, the period makes the passage choppy, or lacking coherence. A semicolon emphasizes the relationship between the sentences:

The oil rig blew up; the explosion killed twenty men.

This semicolon implies a close, but not necessarily causal, relationship between the two sentences.

Still another approach to run-on sentences is to change one of the two into a dependent clause:

When the oil rig blew up, the explosion killed twenty men.

The oil rig blew up in an explosion that killed twenty men.

In the first example, the writer emphasizes the explosion killing the men by putting that idea in an independent sentence and deemphasizes the oil rig blowing up by placing that idea in a dependent clause. In the second example, the writer achieves the opposite emphasis by placing *oil rig* in the independent sentence and linking *explosion* to the dependent clause. The right emphasis can only be determined from the rhetorical context.

Finally, other improvements to the run-on sentence combine the two original sentences into one sentence by changing one into a dependent phrase:

The oil rig's blowing up killed twenty men.

The oil rig blew up, killing twenty men.

Twenty men were killed in the oil rig explosion.

The alternatives are numerous. The good writer quickly goes beyond repairing a comma splice to generating alternatives in order to make the most effective choice. In other words, for the effective writer, correctness is never the only issue, or even the main issue, in choosing the final language. Too many correct possibilities exist to base the final choice only on correctness.

Fragment The fragment is just the opposite of the comma splice. It is less than a full sentence and hence often fails to express a complete thought:

> The exploding oil rig. (No verb)
> Killed twenty men. (No subject)

As these examples indicate, the fragment usually lacks either a subject or a verb and can be made into a sentence by adding the missing part:

> The exploding oil rig killed twenty men.
> The explosion killed twenty men.

Another type of sentence fragment has both a subject and a verb, but puts them in a dependent clause starting off with a word such as *while, during,* or *although:*

> While the rig exploded.
> Although twenty men were killed.

These fragments can be corrected by deleting the opening word:

> The rig exploded.
> Twenty men were killed.

However, this approach usually results in choppy sentences, as the two examples illustrate.

A better solution is to add a sentence to the fragment to complete the idea:

> When the rig exploded, the emergency crew was resting on shore.
> Although twenty men were killed, forty others escaped unharmed.

Thus, a comma splice is in effect two sentences, while a fragment is in effect a partial sentence. As with the comma splice, writers can correct the fragment in many different ways. To find the right one, the writer generates many alternatives and then carefully compares them against the demands of the rhetorical situation and against each other.

MECHANICS

Mechanics are conventions followed by writers in such areas as punctuation and spelling.

Punctuation

The various symbols used to indicate stress, pause, and intonation are referred to as punctuation marks. Like most matters of correctness, the rules for punctuation change over time. Some of the most important current punctuation rules follow.

Apostrophe   The apostrophe indicates the possessive case of a noun.

1.   *For most singular nouns or names the apostrophe is followed by an "s."*

> The boy's dog eats meat.
> She liked Smith's report.

2.   *If the singular noun or name itself ends in "s," the apostrophe is added after the "s" and a second "s" is not added.*

> The boss' dog eats employees.
> She liked Dickens' report.

(Some handbooks do give the writer the option of adding the second "s.")

3.   *If the noun or name is plural rather than singular, the apostrophe follows the "s."*

> The boys' dog eats bosses. (Two or more boys own the dog.)
> The Smiths' report is excellent. (Two or more Smiths made the report.)

4.   *When two nouns are joined by "and," the same rules apply, but only to the second noun.*

> John and Mary's first anniversary with Texaco is tomorrow.
> The Hatfields and the McCoys' feud is famous.

The apostrophe also indicates contractions. Although contractions are generally not favored in formal reports, some handbooks do not ban them absolutely:

Let's examine the data. Let us examine the data.

Here's the result. Here is the result.

One special case, the word *it*, causes lots of trouble for apostrophe users. *Its* is always the possessive form:

The well has **its** problems.

The exclusion in paragraph six is **its** weak point.

It's is always a contraction for *it is:*

It's going to be a great day.

The writer will always select the correct form of *its* if she asks whether or not the phrase *it is* can be substituted for *its*. If *it is* can be substituted, then *it's* is correct. The writer may be solaced by knowing that this is one of the few rules with no exceptions to worry about. *It's* always means *it is.*

Quotation Marks

Quotation marks are used to indicate inserted material, such as dialogue, citations from other sources, or special word uses.

1. *In American usage the period and the comma always go* **inside** *the quotation marks.*

The scientist was quoted as saying that "we will never solve the problem."

"We will never solve the probem," said the scientist.

2. *The colon and semicolon always go* **outside** *the quotation marks.*

I must question your "data"; personal opinions are too subjective to bear much weight.

The auditors have uncovered the following "procedural discrepancies": failing to cross-check tapes at the end of the day, and using the same individual to check the money both in and out of the safe.

3. *The question mark may go either outside or inside the quotation marks, depending on how much of the sentence is a question.*

What reputable engineer would say, "I don't care whether the bridge will be here five years from now or not"? (The sentence inside the quotation marks is not a question, but the whole sentence is.)

    The engineer asked, "Will the bridge be here five years from now?" (The sentence inside the quotation marks is a question, but the whole sentence is not.)

    Why can't anyone answer the question, "What causes cancer and how can we stop it?" (The sentence inside the quotation marks is a question and so is the whole sentence.)

Hyphens

    The hyphen indicates that two or more words function as one grammatical unit.

1. *Words functioning as one grammatical unit are joined by hyphens.*

    The **red-haired lady** stole the plans. (She is neither a *red* lady nor a *haired* lady, but a *red-haired* lady.)

2. *Words not functioning as one grammatical unit are not joined by hyphens.*

    The **ugly old man** is my boss. (*Ugly* and *old* each modify *boss:* the boss is ugly and the boss is old.)

    The **sharply rising prices** hurt the economy. (The adverb *sharply* modifies the adjective *rising;* it does not modify *prices.*)

Hyphens should also be used in the following situations:

    Numbers less than 100: **Fifty-six** students failed the test.

    Fractions: You must use a **three-quarter-inch** wrench for that job.

Other Punctuation Marks

Often punctuation marks indicate pauses, pitches, and stresses normally indicated by voice modulation in the spoken language. The semicolon, the colon, the dash, and the comma all link sentences and sentence parts together in varying degrees of looseness or tightness.

Semicolon Mainly, the semicolon joins together independent clauses not already joined by a coordinating conjunction (*and, but, or, nor, for, yet, so,* etc.).

The semicolon indicates that the sentences on either side are closely related, yet could stand alone grammatically:

> The surgeons went in without any prejudices; they came out without any illusions.

Words other than coordinating conjunctions, such as *however, then, furthermore,* and *thus,* can also be placed between two independent sentences by means of a semicolon.

> The surgeons went in determined to save a life; however, they were unable to fulfill their goal.

Colon The colon has two structural features: to the left of the colon is a complete sentence; to the right of it is a specific enumeration or illustration of the sentence on the left.

> Only six of our Travis County wells are producing **enough oil:** B-6D, B-7D, B-8D, C-10D, D-10D, and D-11D.

Dash The dash indicates a comment on or reevaluation of what went before.

> We rushed into the Kemmerer leases—and quickly regretted it.

The writer can also use a pair of dashes to mark off an inserted phrase in a sentence. Such dashes indicate a high degree of pause or stress on the inserted clause.

> The new office manager—who we later found out was not new at all—quickly set everything up exactly the way she wanted it. (The most emphatic insertion)

The writer can lessen the degree of pause or stress by replacing the dashes with parentheses, or make the insertion the least emphatic by replacing the parentheses with commas.

> The new office manager (who we later found out was not new at all) quickly set everything up exactly the way she wanted it. (Less emphatic insertion)
>
> The new office manager, who we later found out was not new at all, quickly set everything up exactly the way she wanted it. (Least emphatic insertion)

Comma Certainly no mark of punctuation is more common than the comma, and probably no mark of punctuation is more commonly misused either. Some writers want to stick in commas everywhere, while others have outlawed the comma altogether. Rarely is either extreme justified.

Generally speaking, the comma marks a shift in direction of the written sentence, or a slight pause in the sentence if it were spoken.

1. *A comma sets off an opening word or phrase in a sentence.*

Normally, we do not hire any temporary help.

Besides miscalculating all the profits, Stenson helped himself to some excess inventory.

For the first time in the study, the trip gate functioned as it was supposed to.

When the customer misses a payment, a late charge is assessed.

Each of these sentences can be rewritten to eliminate the introductory phrase or clause, which eliminates the pause in the sentence, and thus the need for the comma.

We do not normally hire any temporary help.

Stenson miscalculated all the profits and also helped himself to some excess inventory.

The trip gate functioned as it was supposed to for the first time in the study.

A late charge is assessed when the customer misses a payment.

2. *A comma sets off a clause placed at the end of a sentence, if that clause marks a definite shift in the sentence and it couldn't stand alone grammatically.*

A late charge must be assessed, unless the customer applies for an extension.

The bridge collapsed quickly, as though a bomb had hit it.

3. *A comma is used between two independent clauses joined by a coordinating conjunction (and, but, or, nor, for, yet, so, etc.).*

The inspector refused to pass my car, and I think he was right to do so.

Smith was hired to turn the company around, yet this has been our worst quarter ever.

However, the comma is not used if the two clauses have the same subject.

The environmental specialist did not protect the environment and lied to protect the company.

4. *Commas generally separate items in a series.*

The environment was safe, the company was making a profit, and the stockholders were getting big dividends.

We need supervisors who are fair, understanding, and reliable.

5. *Commas set off an adjective clause if the additional information in the clause is not necessary to specify the noun being modified, but only adds extra information about the noun. If the information in the clause is necessary to identify the noun itself, then the commas are not used.*

All personnel **who have not yet taken vacation time this year** are eligible for a special bonus.

In this case the adjective clause *specifies* certain individuals in the group *personnel.* Hence the commas are not used.

My boss, **who is a real stickler**, would never allow us to have a slush fund.

In this case the adjective clause adds extra information, but does not specify who the boss is. (*My* already does that.) Hence the commas are used.

Here are two more examples.

The Arab oil cartel, **the most powerful economic force in the seventies**, caused the gasoline panic of 1974.

The Arab oil cartel is the pressure group **that most powerfully affected the world's economy in the 1970s.**

Spelling

The English language is notorious for its inconsistent spelling. The same letters do not always sound the same. Often cited are the letters *ough*:

- tough   =   **tuff**
- cough   =   **coff**
- though   =   **tho**
- thought   =   **thaw**t

The vowel sounds also give many spellers problems:

- independence or independance
- acquaintance or acquaintence
- correspondence or correspondance
- resemblance or resemblence

In each of these cases, the correct spelling is in the first option; two use **e** and two use **a**, yet the syllables sound identical to most speakers.

A writer can become a better speller by applying two principles:

1. Whenever you have the slightest doubt about a word's spelling, look it up in a good dictionary.

2. Don't try to tackle the whole spelling problem all at once. Every writer has a certain few words, usually fewer than fifty, that cause the most trouble and that come up constantly because they are related to the subjects the writer writes about. Keep a list of these words and concentrate on memorizing them a few at a time—say five a week. Most people cannot memorize fifty words at once but can memorize five at a time. In ten weeks, you will have internalized some of the fifty original words. Because you use them frequently, your number of spelling errors will decrease, thus allowing you to concentrate even more heavily on the few that remain.

SUMMARY

Effective writing uses clear, concise, coherent, and correct language. While striving for such language at all times, the writer actually concentrates on these qualities when revising and editing.

Language includes both form and content—what is said and how it is put. Effective revision and editing change not only the form of the document, but its very substance as well. Even the editing processes discussed in this chapter, such as fixing a spelling error or a grammatical mistake, often include not just window dressing, but substantive changes as well. The writer's ability to monitor and rewrite the language of initial drafts, to come up with the best possible language, is crucial to the success of the final version. All too often an excellent document has been ignored because of problems with correctness that should have been repaired before the document was ever submitted.

EXERCISES

1. Examine the language in the following documents. Referring to specific passages in each document, analyze how clear, concise, coherent, and correct the language is in each. When necessary, improve the language. Be prepared to justify your improvements.

```
        Per our earlier telephone conversation attached you
will find a Xerox copy of our check #301 in payment of
your invoice #2271. As you can see, this check pays the
invoice you are saying is not paid. We therefore request
that you acknowledge the invoice is paid.
```

These comments are expressed in reference to your letter of February 27, 1985, addressed to me at Hillyard Shipping, concerning the timing and amount of our rate increase to take effect June 1, 1985. It is our opinion in consultation with legal counsel that commission guideline #31-756A can in no wise be utilized to preclude us from our constitutionally guaranteed right too raise our rates. Five years ago we had a similar rate increase without hearing anything from the commission so I'm sure we'll have no problem this time around.

TO: All Staff
FROM: Jim Clarke, Section Chief
Date: January 21, 1976
Re: Equipment Inventory

Please give me a list of all company equipment you are using at home, such as

        computer terminals
        telephone couplers
        typewriters
        filing cabinets

For each piece of company equipment, please provide the following information:

        model number
        serial number
        company property control number

In order for us to complete our portion of the company-wide inventory, I need to have the above information no later than Monday, January 31, 1976.
        Thank you.

---

2. Select any three magazine or newspaper articles you wish and analyze them exactly as you have analyzed the passages in number 1.

3. Select one of the three articles in number 2 and rewrite it completely, not merely improving the existing language, but providing new language whenever needed. Submit your new passage along with the original article.

4. Chapters 7 and 8 presented several situations for analysis. Select one and write the document the situation requires. Make sure your language is clear, concise, coherent, and correct.

FOR FURTHER READING

Baker, Sheridan. *The Complete Stylist and Handbook,* 2d ed. New York: Harper and Row, 1980.

Corbett, Edward P. J. *The Little Rhetoric Handbook.* New York: John Wiley and Sons, 1977.

Crews, Frederick. *The Random House Handbook,* 2d ed. New York: Random House, 1977.

Francis, W. Nelson. "Revolution in Grammar." *Quarterly Journal of Speech* 40 (October 1954): 299–312.

Hacker, Diana and Renshaw, Betty. *A Practical Guide for Writers.* Cambridge, Mass.: Winthrop, 1979.

Herndon, Jeanne. *A Survey of Modern Grammars.* New York: Holt, Rinehart and Winston, 1970.

Hodges, John and Whitten, Mary. *Harbrace College Handbook,* 9th ed. New York: Harcourt Brace Jovanovich, 1983.

Meade, Richard. "Who Can Learn Grammar?" *English Journal* 50 (February 1961): 87–92.

Ong, Walter. "Hostility, Literacy, and Webster III." In *Aspects of American English,* 2d ed. Ed. Elizabeth Kerr and Ralph Anderman. New York: Harcourt Brace Jovanovich, 1971, 109–15.

Weaver, Constance. *Grammar for Teachers: Perspectives and Definitions.* Urbana, Illinois: NCTE, 1979.

Womack, Thurston. "Teachers' Attitudes Toward Current Usage." *English Journal* 48 (April 1959): 186–90.

UNIT III

Writing Effective Reports

10

Beginning

K nowing about writing is not the same as being able to write. The knowledge you gained in the first two units of this text still has to be translated into specific action. That's what the last section of this book is all about. This chapter presents the types and sources of the writing assignments that come to a writer during a working day. Also, it points out what a writer takes into account as he considers how to begin responding to a situation. Finally, it examines the process by which a writer sets a scope for the document from the very beginning.

GETTING STARTED

Few people enjoy writing. It just is not fun to sit at a desk, trying to put words on paper. Why do people do it then? Because they have to. Most writing assignments come to the writer from outside, and in the working world at least, they come with a sense of urgency, demanding that the writing be completed right now—or even yesterday. Here is a typical writing situation in business, industry, and government and a look at what it demands.

> Roy Machado is an inside salesman for an electrical distributor. Six months ago he sold a dozen repeaters to the Beaver Creek Telephone Company. The engineer for the telephone company has just informed Roy that six of the repeaters did not work when they were installed.

The critical difference between *this* situation and the situations in the first sections of this text or the situation you usually face in the writing classroom, is that the telephone company engineer does not overtly ask Roy to do any writing. He simply dumps a problem on Roy, a problem he expects Roy to solve on his own. He does not care how Roy solves it; he probably does not even want to know what Roy plans to do. All he wants is to have six functioning repeaters delivered right away.

Roy's impetus thus comes from outside, but his communications strategy must come from inside—the telephone engineer cannot and will not help him. Roy must consider writing several letters. Then, for the letters he chooses to actually write, he must figure out a strategy and get the writing done.

First, Roy probably wants to write to his customer, the telephone company, promising to take the bad repeaters back and have them replaced immediately. Next, and equally important, Roy must write to his supplier, explain about the bad repeaters, and request two things: a return for credit of the six bad repeaters and a new order for six replacement repeaters to be shipped at once, direct to the customer. When planning strategy, Roy must decide whether he wants to put both requests into one communication or keep them separate. Keeping them together will make the situation more clear to the supplier. Separating them will probably result in the six replacement repeaters being delivered faster, but that leaves the exchange for credit to be worked out later, which could cause a problem for Roy if the supplier makes trouble about the return. Roy could be stuck with six bad repeaters the supplier will not take back and a bill for six new repeaters the customer will not pay.

Finally, Roy might also need to write several in-house memos: 1) to the warehouse authorizing receipt of the six bad repeaters when the customer delivers them, and 2) to the branch manager explaining why six repeaters are lying around the warehouse and how Roy will get rid of them.

Notice how different Roy's writing tasks are from the writing assignments usually given in school. No one assigns them. No one comes to Roy's desk and says, "Machado, write a 600-word essay describing a repeater," or "Roy, write a ten-page research paper on the technology of repeaters." In fact, no one demands that Roy write anything. Roy could telephone his orders in to the supplier and could stop by the warehouse and the branch manager's office to talk to them. Why write anything at all?

MOTIVATION FOR WRITING

Roy writes at least some of the documents because the situation demands it. For instance, as he considers whether or not to write a letter of reassurance to his customer, Roy realizes that his livelihood depends on good customer relations. Of course, he has just made a firm telephone commitment to his customer, but he knows that the engineer who called him is just one employee of the telephone company. Roy wants to have something in writing that everyone in the telephone company can see; he needs to reassure not only the engineer, but also people he does not even know. The telephone engineer does not demand such a letter from Roy—he just wants the repeaters—but Roy wants him to have it. Unlike many students in a school writing class, Roy writes because he really wants to communicate. Roy does not do assignments; he communicates in writing. So Roy sits down to write a letter to his customer. It is not fun—he'd rather be sailing—but he is genuinely motivated and that is the key to writing effectively.

Different Motivations

Before we follow Roy on one of his letters, let's look briefly at the motivations existing behind typical written communications in business, industry, and government. Often a combination of forces motivates a single piece of writing. For instance, Roy wants to send a memo to the warehouse because the customer has already sent the six bad repeaters on their way. From the customer's point of view, sending the repeaters is justified: the repeaters are bad and the telephone company buys through distributors instead of ordering their own repeaters precisely to avoid hassles on returns. From Roy's point of view, they are beyond his control. He did not want them or know about them until they were already on their way, but now he has to deal with them. So the repeaters on their way to the warehouse motivate Roy to write.

Yet this is not Roy's only motivation for writing. Roy also knows that the warehouse foreman gets very upset about unexpected things demanding entrance into his well-ordered warehouse. Good relations with the warehouse are vital to Roy's ability to get things shipped out to his customers as quickly as possible. Any problems between Roy and the warehouse cause Roy difficulty. So Roy wants to warn the warehouse that the repeaters are coming, assure them that return authorization is on the way, and explain that the repeaters will not be in the way for long. Finally, Roy decides to *write* to the warehouse foreman, because if he went out to talk to the foreman, it would make the communication seem out of the ordinary, a special request. Roy intends to write a business-as-usual memo, in an attempt to minimize the special nature of the request.

Roy's motivation for writing to the warehouse foreman or the customer contrasts with his motivation for writing to the supplier. One factor is the same in both cases: the bad repeaters. However, Roy is especially motivated to write to his supplier about the bad repeaters because his customer has already returned them. In this case, two motivating factors interact and reinforce each other, so Roy probably writes to the supplier right away. Actually, he almost certainly calls the supplier as soon as he hangs up the phone with his customer. The supplier surely will give return authorization, but Roy wants to protect himself by putting his request in writing. Then he can send a copy to his own branch manager and the customer.

But what has all this motivation got to do with Roy's actual letters? By recognizing what motivates him, Roy may see how to start his letters or what strategies to use. For instance, in his follow-up letter to the supplier, Roy's motivations suggest at least two possible openings.

He may stress the six bad repeaters:

```
Dear Supplier,
     Six of the repeaters on purchase order #2369 have
proven defective. . . .
```

Or he may stress the dissatisfied customer:

```
Dear Supplier,
     Our customer, the Beaver Creek Telephone Company,
has informed me today that six of your repeaters that we
supplied on purchase order #2369 have proven
defective. . . .
```

> An understanding of how the *situation* got started can sometimes help the writer decide how to get the *writing* started.

Levels of Formality and Familiarity

Roy must also consider formality level as he begins his letters. He assesses the rhetorical situation he faces. Is he writing to subordinates, peers, supervisors, or some combination of them? Is he writing to an audience he knows well, not at all, or somewhere in between? These audience criteria interact subtly to determine a letter's formality level. For example, Roy should address his customer as someone between a peer and a superior. He wants the customer to feel that Roy serves him and not vice versa. On the other hand, Roy should perceive his supplier as someone between a subordinate and a peer. He wants to keep things friendly with the supplier, but also be firm so he can succeed in getting the action he needs from the supplier.

These general audience considerations influence the formality level Roy adopts as most effective for each letter. With his customer, Roy wants relative informality, to emphasize that everything is under control with no need for alarm. However, Roy does not want to be too informal because that might give the impression he is taking his customer's problem lightly. For the same basic reasons, Roy wants to approach his customer as a relatively well known friend. If he were to distance himself with an "I don't know you" attitude, the customer might think Roy was trying to get out of an obligation. On the other hand, if he is too friendly, the customer may think Roy is trying to play on the supposed friendship as an excuse for poor customer satisfaction.

Roy's letter to the supplier has different constraints. Roy needs to take a serious and businesslike approach to the problem, so he moves toward relative formality. And he will forego a friendly tone in favor of the more impersonal. When Roy attempts a first draft of his letter to the supplier, he writes:

```
Armory Telephone Supply
1600 Mission
San Francisco, CA 94101


Dear Sirs:
     You have a big problem on P.O. 2369. Six of the
repeaters are no good and the customer is mad as hell
about it. You'd better make good on them right away.


                              Sincerely,

                              Roy Machado
                              Roy Machado
```

Roy's letter is clear (in a sense), and certainly concise, coherent, and correct. It might even get the job done this time, but it would certainly ruin Roy's relationship with the supplier, because it is off base in terms of motivation, formality, and familiarity.

Roy was shooting for a portrayal of his audience as between subordinate and peer, but the tone of phrases like "you have a problem" suggests a totally subordinate role for the supplier. Roy wanted a relatively formal tone, yet phrases like "mad as hell" are informal. Finally, Roy's goal was to treat the supplier as a fairly unknown entity, yet phrases like "you'd better make good on them" suggest that the supplier knows exactly what Roy has in mind by *make good*. In short, Roy's letter would not necessarily get the job done in the short-term, and would certainly hurt his long-term relationship with the supplier. Roy knows he will have to deal with this same supplier on later orders, or his customers will find other distributors who can still order from this supplier. Customers may use distributors for convenience, but they are loyal to suppliers as well.

Therefore, Roy writes several more drafts of his letter to the supplier, trying to find the exact combination of audience, formality, and familiarity that will get the immediate job done and perhaps even improve his relationship with the supplier.

EXERCISES

1. Examine the following letters. Is Roy's letter getting any closer to the qualities he is aiming for? Which of the following versions do you think is the best so far?

```
Armory Telephone Supply
1600 Mission
San Francisco, CA 94101
Attn:  Ken Griffey



Dear Ken:
     Old pal, I really need your help on this one.
Hodgkins at BC Telly is pissed off about six repeaters he
says are no good. Can you ship out six new ones right
away? I'll collect the six bad ones and we can check them
out and decide what to do with them later.


                              Sincerely,

                              Roy

                              Roy Machado
```

Armory Telephone Supply
1600 Mission
San Francisco, CA 94101
Attn: Ken Griffey

Dear Mr. Griffey:

On our purchase order 2369, dated October 6, 1984, you supplied twelve repeaters to the Beaver Creek Telephone Company. Recently their service manager called us to report that six of the twelve were defective. Please ship an additional six of the A-59 type repeaters to the Beaver Creek Telephone Company and issue us return authorization for the six defective units so that we may send them back to you for credit. Your promptness in handling this request may save us both a good customer.

Sincerely,

Roy Machado

Roy Machado

Armory Telephone Supply
1600 Mission
San Francisco, CA 94101
Attn: Mr. Kenneth Griffey, Claims Adjuster

Dear Sir:

Our relationship with Armory Telephone Supply Company has always been cordial and efficient. However, a recent unfortunate situation may cause us to have to reevaluate our relationship.

Specifically, our client, Beaver Creek Telephone Company, recently purchased from you, through our good offices, twelve A-59 type repeater units for use in telephone lines. For your reference, the said repeaters were ordered on purchase order number 2369, dated on the sixth day of October, 1984.

On December 9, 1984, Mr. Chester (Tex) Hodgkins, chief line maintenance engineer at Beaver Creek Telephone Company, regretfully reported to us the demise of six of your units. He requested (and we second his request) an

immediate reimbursement for the six inoperative repeater
units and furthermore an immediate resupplyment of six
new units in proper functionality.
    We here at Zap Electric Supply urge your most rapid
and efficacious satisfaction of Mr. Hodgkins' dual
requests. Ultimately, the well-being of our corporate
enterprises will be determined by the alacrity with which
we respond to the trials and tribulations of our mutual
clientele.

                              Yours in efficient service,

                              Raymond Machado

                              Raymond (Roy) Machado
                              Interior Salesman

a. After looking at these three examples and discussing their good and bad points, try your hand at writing a final draft for Roy.

b. Write a draft of Armory Telephone Supply's response to Roy.

c. Have a little fun by parodying the style of one of Roy's less effective letters on some other piece of writing you are working on.

d. Write a draft of one of Roy's other letters, such as the one to the branch manager or the warehouse foreman.

2. Below are two more situations that demand writing, but no specific assignments would be made to any of the individuals involved. For each situation, a) list the specific documents the writer might consider writing, b) indicate the motivations causing the writer to consider writing the document, c) indicate your assessment of the relationship of the writer and the audience and the desired levels of formality and familiarity, and d) write a draft of the document you think the situation most strongly demands.

Sarah Fleming works in the corporate purchasing department of a major company. She has been buying tubular steel from one supplier, but this morning Frank Smith, a salesman with a competitive supplier, has just given her a much lower price on tubular steel.

Terry Sanders works for the Flagstaff Ranger District of the Coconino National Forest. He has just finished a three-day tour of the Schnebly Hill area, has noticed an abundance of heavy underbrush, and has documented approximately two million board feet of overmature timber. The summer season, with its very high risk of forest fire, is just around the corner.

SETTING THE SCOPE

The famous naturalist John Muir once stated, "When we try to pick out any-thing by itself, we find it hitched to everything else in the universe."[1] The writer certainly feels the interconnectedness of the nearly infinite number of possibil-ities inherent in every situation. The writer wants to say everything, yet time presses. Deadlines rush up. And writers learn that readers rarely want reports or letters to have everything that could be included. As a famous wall poster has it: "You just told me more than I wanted to know." Or, as one frustrated supervisor said of his new engineers and their reports, "They don't know what to include and what to leave out—to them everything is relevant or nothing is." Writers need to learn how to set the proper scope for their writing, and how to do so as early in the writing process as possible.

Many writers flounder around for days and even weeks because they do not know the exact dimensions of the problem they are working on. When the pressure to produce becomes too great, they wind up taking a shotgun ap-proach—a blast in the general direction of the problem. Such an approach only partially hits the target and includes considerable wasted effort.

Informational and Directional Notes

Often when an engineer or businessperson is confronted with a situation demanding communication, she begins making notes that can eventually be expanded on and incorporated into the final written document. Such notes, whether in longhand on legal pad paper or typed neatly on 3 × 5 cards, are a form of prewriting, as discussed in chapter 6. In whatever form, these notes fall into two general types: informational and directional. The difference is that between substance and direction, both essential to almost any written docu-ment. The informational note contains facts, data, or evidence of many kinds. It says something verifiable. The directional note points out a strategy, angle, or approach for investigation. It presents an opinion or conclusion. A good writer uses both sorts of notes throughout the writing process. They especially help at the start, as the writer attempts to establish a scope for his project.

EXERCISE

Which of the following notes are informational and which are directional?

a. Company policy is that Henry Douglas must be contacted to approve all orders over $5,000.

b. Last month we handled $9,567.63 worth of goods returned for credit.

---

[1]This quotation is from John Muir's journal, as cited in David Brower, ed., *Gentle Wilderness* (New York: Ballantine, 1968), 146.

c. Inventory records indicate twenty-five 8-ft. ladders in stock.

d. In our experiment, the black teal was found to eat an average of 16 prawns per hour.

e. Our inventory of #10 wall covers is too high. We must have a sale to reduce inventory.

f. The black teal is clearly the culprit behind the dramatically reduced yields at the prawn farm.

Planning

Usually, the writer cannot go directly from a collection of notes to a rough draft in one step. Instead, the writer needs a plan. Such a plan includes a clear understanding of the planned document's scope and its likely pattern of development.

Such a plan can be outlined by carefully piecing together patterns of meaning inherent in the informational and directional notes. In general, a single directional note relates quite naturally to several supportive informational notes. Each combination of directional and informational notes makes a single unit. Various combinations of these units can be put together to create a final document with a specific scope that matches both the rhetorical situation and the available information. You can see this process in action in the following situation.

T.K. Lassiter is the quality control officer for outside contracts entered into by a national department store chain at its head office. Her job is to check up on the work of certain outside contractors to make certain that their performance is up to the standards in their particular contract. She has been gathering data for some time on the performance of the Top Job Janitorial Company, which has a janitorial contract to service the head office complex.

First, T.K. knows what the contract specifications are and has them written down in her logbook.

Toilet Rooms
- Damp wipe doors, stalls, and partitions—daily
- Sweep and damp mop floor—daily
- Spray buff tile and linoleum areas—weekly
- Wet mop and scrub tile and linoleum floors—quarterly
- Polish all chrome and fixtures—quarterly
- Wash walls—twice yearly

Offices
- Dust all flat surfaces—daily
- Vacuum all carpeted areas—daily

- Clean and polish all flat surfaces—weekly
- Empty trash containers—twice weekly
- Dust light fixtures—quarterly
- Wash walls—twice yearly

Hallways
- Vacuum—daily
- Clean drinking fountains—twice weekly
- Spot clean carpets—monthly
- Shampoo carpets—quarterly

T.K. also made the following observations in her logbook on March 9:

- chrome in toilet rooms not polished
- drinking fountains polished
- office light fixtures quite dusty
- carpets very spotted
- tile and linoleum sticky and dirty
- dust in corners and on some desks
- trash overflowing
- walls not washed
- hall OK

In this case, the contract specifications provide the essential direction for T.K.'s observations. Her job is to observe the specific areas covered in the contract and make accurate factual notations of what she sees, along with appropriate recommendations. Her observations should be informational, providing verifiable support for her recommendations, which are directional. She cannot do her job well without using both informational and directional notes.

Her notes for March 9 indicate a good ability to observe, but not much ability to set a scope for her observations. As a result, her notes are not usable. She has included a little of everything, all mixed up in two lists without any order. Is the situation bad enough to file a formal complaint against the janitorial service? She cannot tell from her notes, because they provide too little order and scope for her to discern exactly what kind of case she has.

Let's imagine instead that her notebook for March 9 looked like this:

Offices
- light fixtures quite dusty
- carpets spotted
- dust in corners and on some desks

Toilet Rooms
- tile and linoleum sticky and dirty
- chrome not polished
- trash overflowing
- walls not washed

These notes can help her decide first, if she will file a complaint, and second, what the possible grounds for that complaint are. She has kept her notes strictly informational, eliminating judgments such as "hall OK." She has also ordered her observations under headings, which enable her to see where the problems are and are not. Finally, she has eliminated areas such as the hall, where there is nothing to complain about. She can now clearly see the scope and extent of the problems, and thus make a judgment about whether or not to issue a formal complaint. If she does decide on the complaint, she has the evidence well-ordered and ready. The contract specifications provided the direction, and her own observations provided the information.

EXERCISE

Select a particular audience for T.K. Lassiter and write a first draft of the document demanded by her situation and her notes.

Narrowing the Topic

In T.K. Lassiter's situation, as is usually the case on the job, the possible documents are inherent in the circumstances. However, school assignments are often given in terms of a broad subject or theme for the student to write about. Sometimes the teacher even assigns the dreaded research paper on some general topic, such as *the environment*. Not having a real situation compelling her to write, the student often flounders around in such a monstrous topic. However, you *can* grapple with the monstrous topic and win. You narrow the topic until you arrive at a specific question you actually want to know the answer to. Then, you may want to communicate your answer to someone. See figure 10–1 for how to narrow a topic.

The student can thus arrive at a viable question to write about through the process of narrowing a topic, even without having a compelling reason to write. Professional writers, however, rarely need to make up an assignment; plenty of situations demanding communication arise all by themselves. Ideally, even the student actually faces situations that demand writing, but if not, the narrowing method can help the student generate a manageable topic.

EXERCISE

For each of the following topics, arrive at a narrowed question, suitable for writing about in roughly twenty pages:

a. students
b. women's rights
c. health
d. biology

TOPIC	POTENTIAL PAGES
Environment	5,000
Pollution	2,500
Air Pollution	1,000
The role of automobile exhaust fumes in air pollution	500
The effect of basic engine design on the level of exhaust fumes	100
Can the Wankel engine reduce automobile exhaust fumes?	20

Figure 10–1.   Narrowing a Topic

SUMMARY

In most on-the-job writing situations, the writer is given no assignment, but instead must sort out on his own what possible communications might be made in a given situation and which ones actually will be made. This decision will be partly based on the exact motivation for writing. Once the writer decides which documents to write, which to communicate some other way, and which not to communicate at all, she must also decide on an audience strategy, including appropriate levels of formality and familiarity.

With at least an initial strategy in mind, the writer must consider the scope of the document. The writer gets insight into the proper scope by considering the directions or main ideas of the document and the available support or facts. The scope of the document may be defined as the purposes appropriate to the situation, together with all the necessary factual information to support those purposes.

CASE IN POINT

Instructions

One of the documents a new worker most frequently refers to is a set of instructions for her new job. Like any document, the set of instructions is written to fulfill the demands of a particular situation. The writer of a set of instructions must consider purpose and audience, and then set an appropriate scope for the document itself.

Most instructions are intended to give the reader the information required to perform some task. The situation behind the instructions may be summarized as follows:

1.   The writer is presumably an expert in performing the task at hand. At the very least, he knows more about the task than the reader does.

2.   The writer's superior knowledge implies that the instructions are not written as an argument, but as the transmission of information.

3.   The audience is presumably attempting to complete the task by referring to the instructions. Because the audience plays the operator role, most instructions have a narrow scope. The audience is usually not interested in background or justification, but simply in getting the steps necessary to perform the task. Since these readers do not know much about the task, they need the utmost clarity, and the writer needs to be sure not to skip steps or make assumptions that the reader will not be aware of.

4.   The particular situation behind most instructions implies the following typical features:

a.   The imperative or command form of language communicates instructions in the most brief and direct way.

b.   Graphic aids are often essential and must be tightly integrated into the text.

c.   The writer cautions or warns the reader when the task is especially dangerous or difficult. When appropriate, the writer tells not only *what* to do, but also *why* and *how*.

d.   Headings and subheadings often identify major sections of the text.

e.   Most written instructions contain the following parts:

(1)   The Introduction: sets author, audience, and purpose for the instructions

(2)   Equipment/Materials: lists the equipment (items that can be reused) and the materials (items that cannot be reused)

(3)   Main Body: a step-by-step factual description of the separate actions making up the task

(4)   Conclusion: a brief summary of the whole

The introduction and conclusion are normally used when writing for a novice audience, but in many on-the-job situations, they are skipped.

Instructions for Hanging a Door

For the average do-it-yourselfer, hanging a new door is not a simple project. The goal is worthwhile: to make the door tight fitting without binding, and to save yourself some money in the process. But certain skills are required to accomplish the goal: you must work accurately within fractions of an inch, and be patient as you get closer and closer to success. If you can do these things, you probably can wind up with a tight fitting door and some extra dollars.

Equipment and Materials You do not need a whole tool chest for the job, but you should have the following ready:

- The door itself
- Hinges
- Heavy screws (½″ × 1″)

- Claw hammer
- Plane
- Screw driver
- Pencil

Hanging the Door First, you must fit the door properly.

1. Remove any weather stripping from all four sides of the door frame.
2. Take out the door saddle.
3. Try to fit the door in the opening.
4. If any sides are too wide, use a pencil to mark the approximate amount to take off.
   WARNING: If you have to take off more than one-quarter inch, divide the amount in half and take each half off opposite sides of the door. Otherwise, the door will hang crookedly.
5. Use the plane to shave the door down to the pencil marks.

GO SLOWLY!! REMEMBER:
YOU CAN ALWAYS TAKE MORE OFF,
BUT YOU CANNOT PUT IT BACK ON AGAIN.

Then, you must mount the hinges.

6. Once the door fits perfectly, mark the spots where the hinges go on both the door and the jamb.
7. Place the top hinge about 5″ below the top of the door and the bottom hinge about 12″ from the floor.

The Final Fit Fit the door in the frame for one last test. Looking from the inside, the clearance should be at least one-sixteenth and not more than one-eighth of an inch. If this is so, then screw in the hinges, first on the door, and then into the frame. If you have done the job right, the door should be tight but not binding. Now enjoy the satisfaction of having done the job well and of having some extra money to spend.

WRITING ASSIGNMENTS

1. Find a set of instructions and write an evaluation of them based on the principles presented in this chapter.

2. Based on your evaluation, rewrite the instructions referred to in question 1. Be prepared to explain your changes.

3. Prepare your own set of instructions based on the principles presented in this chapter.

FOR FURTHER READING

Berthoff, Ann. "From Problem-Solving to a Theory of Imagination." *College English* 33 (March 1972): 636–49.

Chase, Stuart. "How Language Shapes Our Thoughts." In *Speaking of Words,* edited by James MacKillop and Donna Cross. New York: Holt, Rinehart and Winston, 1978.

Coles, William. *Composing: Writing as a Self-Creating Process.* Rochelle Park, N.J.: Hayden, 1974.

D'Angelo, Frank. "A Generative Rhetoric of the Essay." *College Composition and Communication* 25 (December 1974): 388–96.

Hartwell, Patrick. "Teaching Arrangement: A Pedagogy." *College English* 40 (January 1979): 548–54.

Odell, Lee and Cohick, Joanne. "You Mean, Write It Over in Ink?" *English Journal* 64 (December 1975): 48–53.

Pitkin, Willis. "Discourse Blocks." *College Composition and Communication* 20 (May 1969): 138–48.

Rose, Mike. "Rigid Rules, Inflexible Plans, and the Stifling of Language: A Cognitivist Analysis of Writer's Block." *College Composition and Communication* 31 (December 1980): 389–401.

11

Sources of Information

After determining the basic type of report or document the situation calls for, the writer must find the necessary information. For most routine on-the-job writing problems, writers can go to the telephone or the company files to get information on the exact dollar amount from a week-old quotation, pipe specifications, a promised delivery date for a given product, a contract's precise language, etc. However, for many larger professional documents, such as decision packages, major proposals, and marketing analyses, as well as many longer student reports, writers need to consult published materials. Published materials can come from many sources: manufacturers' technical sheets and sets of instructions, advertising materials and other marketing tools, and pamphlets of all sorts, to name just a few. But the most consistently useful source of excellent and plentiful information is a good library, where the writer can find books and periodicals.

Fortunately, modern information systems do not restrict you to libraries within your immediate area. Through interlibrary loan you can get access to materials in libraries thousands of miles away. Also, the computer age has arrived at most larger public and university libraries. Sophisticated research tools, available at nominal cost, can save hundreds of hours by searching indexes and files. Besides their greatly increased speed, these computer research tools are more efficient than any individual working by hand could ever hope to be. Some computer systems can generate a list of potential sources on a given subject, while others can transmit an entire document from one library to another. Transferring an entire book is expensive, but the cost is worth it when the book cannot be obtained in any other way.

Whatever the special capabilities of some libraries, any library offers many basic resources to the writer in business, industry, and government. However, no matter how much information a library contains, if the library user cannot find anything, the material is useless. Once you find material, you need a system for recording its location to guarantee your own later access to it. The readers of your study may also want to find the materials you used. To record such sources uniformly, the bibliographic note has been devised. Each time you find a source of information you might want to use later in your piece of writing, record all the information about it in one of the following forms:

▶ Book:
   Author's last name, author's first name. *Title of book.* City of publication: Publisher, Date of publication.

   Smithson, Joseph. *The Facts of Oil Refining.* New York: John Wiley & Sons, 1982.

▶ Book with two or more authors:

> Smithson, Joseph and Harris, Martin. *The Drake Discovery.*
> San Francisco: Macmillan, 1976.

▶ Subpart of a larger book with an editor:

> Nielson, Ralph. "Success Can Be Yours in the Franchise Busi-
> ness." In *Financial Security for the Eighties.* Tom
> Frankel, ed. New York: Penchant Press, 1980, 56–76.

▶ Magazine or periodical:

> Author's last name, author's first name. "Title of article." *Title of maga-
> zine or periodical* Volume (Date): Pages of article.

> Clive, Henry. "The Last Chance for the Northern Slope." *Oil-
> man's Quarterly* 35 (1982): 34–48.

The basic book and magazine or periodical formats remain constant despite small differences in publication particulars. One of these four formats can be used for almost any book or magazine necessary for writing. A few additional specialized and unusual forms, such as those for newspapers or television programs, are listed in appendix II.

EXERCISE

Figures 11–1 through 11–3 contain titles and content pages from various books and magazines.[1] For each source, write a proper bibliographic note. When you see more than one possible note, select one of the possibilities.

---

[1]Book title and copyright pages from Donald D. Spencer, *The Illustrated Computer Dictionary* (Columbus, Ohio: Charles E. Merrill Publishing Company, 1983). Copyright © 1983 by Bell & Howell Company. Reprinted by permission. Magazine table of contents from *Radio-Electronics* 48 (October 1977): 3. Copyright © by Gernsback Publications. Reprinted by permission. Book title page and table of contents from *Symposium on Foods: Carbohydrates and Their Roles,* ed. H. W. Schultz, R. F. Cain, and R. W. Wrolstad (Westport, Conn.: The AVI Publishing Company, Inc., 1969). Copyright © 1969 by the AVI Publishing Company, Inc. Reprinted by permission.

Published by
Charles E. Merrill Publishing Company
A Bell & Howell Company
Columbus, Ohio 43216

This book was set in Palatino and Moore Computer.
Production Editor: Rex Davidson.
Cover Design Coordination: Tony Faiola.
Cover Photos: Ampex Corporation; Richard Feldman, National Institute of Health, Bethesda, Maryland; The Goodyear Tire and Rubber Company; Honeywell Information Systems; MATRIX Instruments, Inc.; and Tektronix.

Library of Congress Catalogue Card Number: 83-60392

International Standard Book Number: 0-675-20075-X

1 2 3 4 5 6 7 8 9 10—86 85 84 83

Printed in the United States of America

Figure 11-1 (continued)

Revised Edition

THE
ILLUSTRATED
COMPUTER
DICTIONARY

DONALD D. SPENCER
Computer Science Consultant

CHARLES E. MERRILL PUBLISHING CO.
A Bell & Howell Company
Columbus   Toronto   London   Sydney

Figure 11-1

Radio-Electronics®

THE MAGAZINE FOR NEW IDEAS IN ELECTRONICS

Electronics publishers since 1908

OCTOBER 1977 Vol. 48 No. 10

ON THE COVER

Special music effects just your style? Then try building the Phlanger—it's a honey of an effect generator, and you use it with your hi-fi system. Complete details start in this issue on page 42.

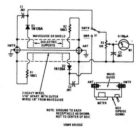

SWR BRIDGE is only one of 3 inexpensive CB test meters. . . . see page 40

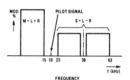

THIS IS A PROPER FM signal. A misaligned FM tuner will destroy it. Restore the good sound by realignment. . . . see page 50

Radio-Electronics, Published monthly by Gernsback Publications, Inc., 200 Park Avenue South, New York, NY 10003. Phone: 212-777-6400. Second-class postage paid at New York, NY and additional mailing offices. One-year subscription rate: U.S.A., U.S. possessions and Canada, $8.75. Pan-American countries, $10.25. Other countries, $10.75. Single copies $1.00. © 1977 by Gernsback Publications, Inc. All rights reserved. Printed in U.S.A.

Subscription Service: Mail all subscription orders, changes, correspondence and Postmaster Notices of undelivered copies (Form 3579) to Radio-Electronics Subscription Service, Box 2520, Boulder, CO 80322.

A stamped self-addressed envelope must accompany all submitted manuscripts and/or artwork or photographs if their return is desired should they be rejected. We disclaim any responsibility for the loss or damage of manuscripts and/or artwork or photographs while in our possession or otherwise.

Figure 11-2

Symposium on Foods:
Carbohydrates and Their Roles

The fifth in a series of Symposia on foods held at Oregon State University

Editor **H. W. Schultz, Ph.D.**
Head, Department of Food Science and Technology
Oregon State University
Corvallis, Oregon

Associate Editors **R. F. Cain, Ph.D.**
Professor, Department of Food Science and Technology
Oregon State University
Corvallis, Oregon

R. W. Wrolstad, Ph.D.
Assistant Professor, Department of Food Science and Technology
Oregon State University
Corvallis, Oregon

THE AVI PUBLISHING COMPANY, INC.

Westport, Connecticut

1969

Figure 11-3

Contents

Figure 11-3 (continued)

> Once you start to work on a project and locate sources, record all informa-
> tion about each source's publication in the proper bibliographic form, *before*
> *you do anything else.*

Now that you know how to record any book or magazine's bibliographic
information, you need to know how to find books and magazines to record.

THE CARD CATALOG AND THE READERS' GUIDE

Two old standbys, guaranteed to help you find books and magazines, are the
card catalog and the Readers' Guide. The card catalog is the library's index to
its own collection of books and nonprint media, such as films and tapes. Of
course, the card catalog covers only materials in the library—if the library is
small, then the card catalog may not help you much. On the other hand, if you
find something in the card catalog, you know you can get it eventually. Remember that the card catalog lists only books and nonprint media; it does not index
any periodicals (magazines, journals, and newspapers). For the writer in the
working world, periodicals are often the best sources. Therefore, no matter how
simple your research project is, do not make the card catalog the full extent of
your research effort. Use the card catalog for all you can get out of it, but plan
to go beyond it.

The Readers' Guide indexes general periodicals, hence its official name:
The Readers' Guide to Periodical Literature. A *periodical* is a publication that
appears at regular intervals, such as a daily newspaper, a weekly or monthly
magazine, or a quarterly journal. The Readers' Guide has the same strengths
and weaknesses as the card catalog. Because it is a general index, it does not
index specialized sources. For instance, the Readers' Guide indexes *Time* and
Life magazines, but not *Water and Sewage Works.* You cannot research a
subject in depth if you use only sources found in the Readers' Guide. On the
other hand, because the magazines indexed in the Readers' Guide *are* general,
most libraries subscribe to nearly all of them. Thus, if you can find something
in the Readers' Guide, chances are you can find it in the library. As a rule,
however, the materials indexed in the Readers' Guide are on the introductory
level. As with the card catalog, the writer in business, industry, and government
should use the Readers' Guide for all it is worth, but not overly depend on it.
The technically oriented researcher has to go beyond the Readers' Guide.

EXERCISE

To review your knowledge of the card catalog and the Readers' Guide, a few sample
entries with the important parts indicated are given in figure 11–4.[2]

---

[2]Sample entries from *Readers' Guide to Periodical Literature* (New York: The H.W. Wilson
Company, 1983), 395. Copyright © 1983 by the H.W. Wilson Company. Material reproduced by
permission of the publisher.

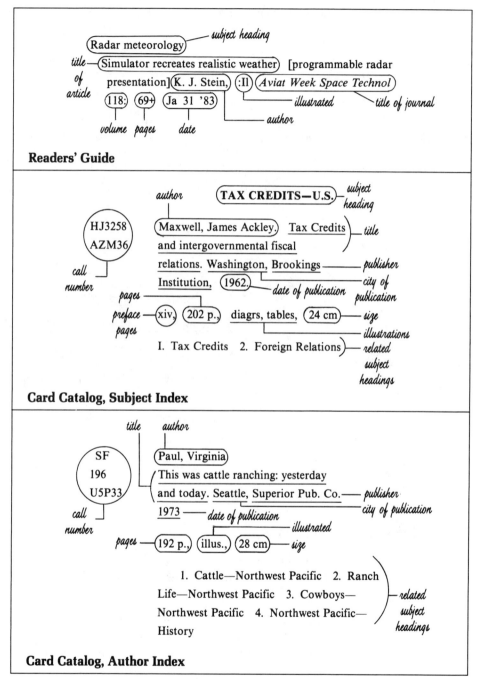

Readers' Guide

Card Catalog, Subject Index

Card Catalog, Author Index

Figure 11–4

Now, indicate what each of the circled and numbered items is on the examples in figure 11–5.[3]

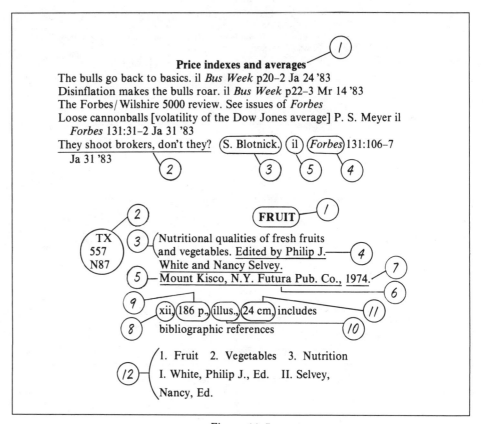

Figure 11–5

THE REFERENCE SECTION

The first place the technically oriented writer can find valuable material is the library's reference section. In general, the reference section contains two different types of sources:

- Books of broad, wide-ranging interest, such as encyclopedias or almanacs. These books are usually part of a set or series.
- Books containing specialized or highly technical information on one narrow topic, such as *The Encyclopedia of Textiles* or *Energy Technology Handbook*.

[3]Sample entries from *Readers' Guide to Periodical Literature* (New York: The H.W. Wilson Company, 1983), 457. Copyright © 1983 by The H.W. Wilson Company. Material reproduced by permission of the publisher.

If you do not know much about the subject you are writing about or if you do not even have a subject yet, start with the first type of source. Reading a good encyclopedia article on oil refining can give you many leads for further information and a sense of whether to continue working on that subject. Writers in business, industry, and government usually do not use encyclopedias or almanacs because they already know the subject quite well and hence do not need a general introduction. For the student or novice on the job, though, the encyclopedia can be a helpful springboard into the more scholarly and technical sources of information.

Students and professional writers alike can use the other kind of book found in the reference collection: the specialized and highly technical source books of particular fields. In general, these books provide easy access to essential information in a given discipline. Such information is comparable to a table of logarithms for a mathematician or a table of monthly mortgage payments at various interest rates for a banker. The reference collection contains similar works relevant to virtually every field of human endeavor. A library's card catalog indexes all items in the reference collection, so you can find your specialization by using the card catalog subject index and checking for cards that have *reference* or *reference collection* on them. To give you an idea of both the range and the depth of such works, introductory pages from two typical reference collection sources, *The Heat Transfer Data Book* and *The Energy Technology Handbook,* are shown in figures 11–6 through 11–8.[4]

As you can tell from the tables of contents, these are not the books to read while curled up in front of a cozy fire! In fact, these are not books to read at all. Instead, you refer to them for specific pieces of information that you need for something other than just information or general interest. The information in these books is basically raw data, without a context. Writers supply contexts by referring to the rhetorical situations or problems causing them to write. The writer comes to the reference work armed with a specific purpose, audience, and authorial stance, all of which enable him to select the significant specific data for that context. The writer uses the problems or questions generated in prewriting as a guide to what is significant and what is not. *Significance* is of course not an absolute term, but relative to the particular problem or situation behind the writing.

Ideally, the student also comes to the reference section with a specific problem or set of questions in mind. However, if a student has no idea what to write on or has at best only a vague topic, such as *solar energy* or *coal mining,* she may skim through an appropriate reference work to find something more specific to write about. The range of subjects in the areas of business, industry,

[4]Preface from *The Heat Transfer Data Book,* ed. Deborah A. Kaminski (Schenectady, N.Y.: General Electric Company, 1982), i. Copyright © 1982 by the General Electric Company. Reprinted by permission. This preface explains *The Heat Transfer Data Book*'s intended uses and audiences. Table of contents from *The Heat Transfer Data Book,* ed. Deborah A. Kaminski. (Schenectady, N.Y.: General Electric Company, 1976), 1. Copyright © 1976 by the General Electric Company. Reprinted by permission. Partial table of contents from *Energy Technology Handbook* (New York: McGraw-Hill, 1977), v–vi. Copyright © 1977 by McGraw-Hill Publishing Co. Reprinted by permission.

HEAT
TRANSFER
DIVISION

PREFACE

Purpose of These Data Books

This Heat Transfer Data Book and the companion volume, the Fluid Flow Data Book, have been prepared to serve the needs of design and development engineers. The objective has been to provide a convenient collection of information, relatively general in applicability, on those aspects of heat transfer and fluid flow found by long experience to require frequent consideration and application in design and development work.

Unusually comprehensive, worldwide sources of information have been drawn on for obtaining the information and data collected in these data books. The heat transfer staff in what is now the General Electric Research and Development Center has been continually screening both the world's published literature and internal General Electric technical reports and memoranda since 1925 in the subjects here covered. Outside heat transfer experts have also contributed or consulted, as appropriate, including contribution of entire new sections.

These data books are intended primarily for the engineers who are not specializing in heat transfer. For this reason attention is directed to the limits of validity of each of the formulas presented, references are given to the literature for information outside these limits, and numerical examples of calculations illustrating use of many of the correlations in the data books are presented.

The Data Books are also valuable to the heat-transfer and fluid flow specialist, because of their convenience, broad scope, and accessibility to much information not included in readily available literature.

Generalized performance relations — particularly correlations in dimensionless form — are the most common type of information presented here. the equations, however, are not directed primarily to design of particular products, but rather to provide fundamentals.

Provision for Annual Additions of New and Revised Pages

The use of a three-ring binder for each volume has permitted addition — each successive year — of new information, as well as revisions for updating and for misprint corrections in older material.

The criteria for the selection of future updated material will continue to be those which have been used for compiling the current Data Books, as explained below.

Criteria for Selection of Subject Matter

Several different criteria have been, and will continue to be, used for selection of new material or for revision of earlier material, for these data books.

The most common selection criterion is the absence, in the many widely known textbooks, of information adequate for current engineering application needs.

Another criterion for inclusion of information is the need to provide a more comprehensive coverage of a topic than is available in most textbooks.

A third type of justification for inclusion of information is to identify our choice of one preferred correla-

tion, for a commonly encountered physical process, among several alternative correlations — mutually inconsistent to greater or less degree — already available in the literature.

When these data books were first issued in 1943, their major content was a collection of data on thermal properties of materials. These data books were issued then as additional volumes of a set of already existing other "Data Books" on other properties of engineering materials. The Heat Transfer and Fluid Flow Data Books became an independent set of documents some years later. The original numbering system for the sections of these books has been retained, however, in order to maintain consistency with the numbering sequence of other proprietary publications. As a consequence, the Fluid Flow Data Book thus still has its sections numbered G401 through G409, and the Heat Transfer Data Book has its sections numbered G501 through G516.

After a Section was initially issued, minor revisions have — in many cases — been issued from time to time as pertinent new information or need for clearer explanation came to the attention of the editors. Major revisions, based on a thorough reconsideration of the subject of an entire Section, have been undertaken at less frequent intervals.

Accordingly, the pages of the present version carry dates ranging from 1943 to the present. The presence of an old date does not imply that no later information exists, but rather that serious practical need for incorporation of that later information has not come to the attention of the editors.

With respect to numerical data on thermal properties of materials (Sections G513-G515). An extensive collection of thermal properties data has become available in 1970-77 from Purdue University. It is known as the "TPRC Series — Thermophysical Properties of Matter" edited by Touloukian and Ho and is published by Plenum Publishing Corp. It now comprises 14 volumes. The availability of this collection of data, as well as the existence of a computerized data bank at TPRC, has reduced our incentive for extending the comprehensiveness of the data in our own Data Book.*

In addition to the compilations of actual data, in our Data book and in the TPRC Series volumes, there has been available for many years' also a TPRC "Retrieval Guide," also edited by Touloukian, for identification of substantially all published references containing data on thermal properties. That "Guide" is itself identified as Ref. 162 on page 7 of Section G515.2 of our Data Book.

The collection of data in our Section G513-G515 continues, however, to be a convenient collection of data on many materials commonly used in electrical products. The data include, furthermore, many unpublished values obtained by routine tests in General Electric laboratories.

*Information on the availability of TPRC data and cost of a search can be obtained by calling 1-800-428-7675, toll free.

Figure 11-6. Preface from *The Heat Transfer Data Book.*

| Heat
Transfer
Division | NUMERICAL METHODS
CONTENTS | Section **501.1**
Page 1
June 1976 |

GENERAL ⚙ ELECTRIC

Figure 11-7. Contents page from *The Heat Transfer Data Book.*

Overview of Contents

For the detailed contents of any subsection, consult the title page of that subsection. The alphabetical index is at the end of the book.

Contents

Figure 11–8. Partial table of contents from *The Energy Technology Handbook*.

and government is evident even in the incomplete list of some reference titles that follows:

- *The Encyclopedia of Physics*
- *International Dictionary of Geophysics*
- *Chemical Encyclopedia*
- *Industrial Toxicology*
- *Clinical Toxicology of Commercial Products*
- *California Manufacturer's Register*
- *Consumer Complaint Guide*
- *Engineering Materials Handbook*
- *ASTM Standards in Building Codes*
- *Automobile Engineers Reference Book*
- *Fire Protection Handbook*
- *Solar Institute of America Sourcebook*
- *World Directory of Wood-based Panel Products*

Undoubtedly your own library has some of these, but not others. In addition, your library probably has many useful reference collection works not listed. More important than exactly what books are in the collection is how well you learn to use the ones that are there. Most reference books have instructions on how to use them in the preface. Reading and following these instructions will increase your efficiency.

THE SPECIALIZED INDEXES

The specialized indexes to periodicals also provide a source of highly specific information on any given subject. These indexes work basically just like the well-known Readers' Guide, but instead of indexing a wide range of subject matters shallowly, they index a narrow range of subject matter deeply. Each specialized index indexes *only* the periodicals from a narrow field. The Readers' Guide indexes *Time* and *Life,* but a specialized index indexes periodicals such as *The Journal of Radiographic Medicine.* Hence, from the many specialized indexes available, only one or two are useful for any given subject. However, those one or two should be *very* useful. The general indexes certainly have their place in the library, but in almost every case, the technically minded writer finds many more valuable sources listed in the specialized index.

Specialized indexes exist in every field from art to zoology. For the writer in business, industry, and government, an excellent example of a useful specialized index is the *Applied Science and Technology Index*. A sample is shown in figure 11–9.[5]

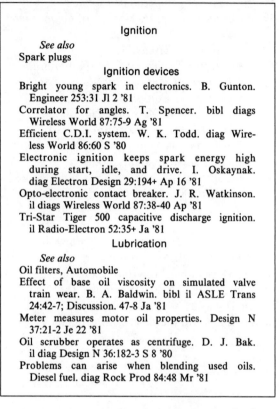

Figure 11–9.   Example from the *Applied Science and Technology Index*.

As the sample shows, the *Applied Science and Technology Index* is organized by subject headings, with numerous subheadings breaking down the main headings into fine gradations. Individual articles appear under each specific subheading in a code similar to that used in the Readers' Guide.

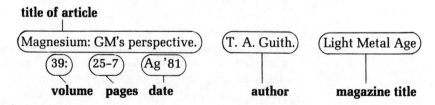

Once a writer selects an article that seems promising, and decodes the publishing information, he needs to determine whether the library has the necessary periodical for the exact date required. Most libraries hold their periodicals in two different forms: bound volumes, in the regular stacks along with the books on the same subject, and microforms, usually in a separate room equipped with special machines necessary to make the film readable. If the periodical you want is on microfilm, there is no use looking for it in the stacks, and vice versa. Every library has a printed listing of the periodicals it holds, which gives you all the information needed to find the periodical if it is in the library.

> *Business Conditions*
> HC107.A14B9
> (1957–1968)
> Superseded by *Economic Perspectives*

The listing indicates that the library holds the magazine *Business Conditions* in bound form, from 1957–1968, and that in 1969 the magazine changed its name to *Economic Perspectives*. The long number beginning with *HC* is the magazine's call number. You use this number to find the magazine's location, just as you do with a book call number.

> *Chemical Marketing Reporter*
> Oversize
> HD9650.1.C486
> v. 203–208 (1973–1975)
> v. 209–   (1976–   ) microfilm

Here, the listing indicates that the library holds only volumes 203–208 in bound form. Since 1976, the library has put volumes of the magazine on microfilm. This particular magazine is also larger than usual; its bound volumes can be found on special *oversize* shelves at the call number indicated.

> *Accounting Review*
> HF5601.A6
> v. 1–50 (1926–1975)
> v. 56–   (1981–   ) microfilm

Note that the library's holdings of the magazine are interrupted by a five-year gap. Before this gap, the magazine is in bound form; after this gap, it is on microfilm; but during this gap, the magazine's issues are not in the library at all.

Although your library's listing of its periodical holdings may not look exactly like the entries just examined, the basic information contained in it will be the same. The periodical listing has one goal, to help you find the magazine you want as quickly as possible. Also, remember that some libraries place the most recent issues of their magazines in a reading room where they are available unbound. After about a year, these magazines are sent either to be bound or microfilmed. Hence, magazines about a year old are sometimes unavailable for a few months while they are being bound or microfilmed.

Normally, neither professional writers nor students can accomplish much by skimming through articles found in specialized periodicals. The information is simply too technical and context-specific. To effectively use the specialized periodicals, the writer must have a list of specific questions, find articles whose titles indicate information bearing on those questions, and finally read the articles themselves, taking out only the information needed to answer the questions.

A list of a few of the most useful specialized indexes for writers in business, industry, and government follows, including a brief listing of some specific periodicals indexed in each.

- *Biological and Agricultural Index*
  - *Advances in Agronomy*
  - *Biochemical Genetics*
  - *Canadian Journal of Botany*
  - *Journal of Environmental Quality*
  - *Quarterly Review of Biology*
  - *Limnology and Oceanography*

- *Industrial Arts Index*
  - *Brick and Clay Record*
  - *Illuminating Engineering*
  - *Rock Products*
  - *Machine Design*
  - *Journal of Aeronautical Sciences*
  - *Public Roads*
  - *Railway Age*

- *Applied Science and Technology Index*
  - *Architectural Record*
  - *Journal of Engineering for Industry*
  - *Corrosion Science*
  - *Design Engineering*
  - *Textile Research Journal*
  - *Plastics World*
  - *Nuclear Engineering International*
  - *Noise Control Engineering*
  - *Wireless World*

Your library will probably have these specialized indexes and other useful specialized indexes as well. However, the key to how useful these specialized indexes are to you lies in how many of the periodicals listed are actually in your library. If your library has a great collection of indexes but a poor collection of periodicals, you will generate a tantalizing list of unavailable titles. Of course, armed with such a list, you can go to other libraries or use the services of interlibrary loan. Today, as long as your time and money hold out, there is never really a dead end—only more intriguing possibilities.

EXERCISE

In which of the following specialized indexes do you think you would probably find articles relevant to the following topics of study?

Specialized Index	Topic of Study
Index Medicus	Waste Water Treatment
Population Index	Consumer Fraud
Accountant's Index	Commercial Logging
The Environment Index	Zero Population Growth
Business Periodicals Index	Cyrokinetics
Index to Legal Periodicals	Japanese Cars in the U.S.

ABSTRACTS

Abstracts are another excellent source for useful articles. They work like the specialized indexes, but have an additional feature: they include a description of each article listed. Like the specialized indexes, each of the abstracts contains lists of articles arranged under specific subject headings. Also, each of the abstracts covers only a narrow range of subjects, indexing only specialized periodicals. Thus, they are detailed and technical in comparison to the more general sources. For example, figure 11–10 shows a section of a table of contents from a typical abstract, the *Energy Research Abstracts*.[6]

04	**OIL SHALES AND TAR SANDS**	05	**NUCLEAR FUELS**
01	Reserves and Exploration	01	Reserves
02	Site Geology and Hydrology	02	Exploration
03	Drilling, Fracturing, and Mining	03	Mining
04	Oil Production, Recovery, and Refining	04	Feed Processing
05	Properties and Composition	05	Enrichment
06	Direct Uses and By-Products	06	By-Products
07	Health and Safety	07	Fuels Production and Properties
08	Marketing and Economics	08	Spent Fuels Reprocessing
09	Waste Research and Management	09	Transport and Storage
10	Environmental Aspects	10	Marketing and Economics
20	Regulations	20	Waste Management
		30	Environmental Aspects
		40	Health and Safety
		50	Regulations

Figure 11–10. Example from contents of *Energy Research Abstracts*.

---

[6]Partial table of contents from "Subject Contents," *Energy Research Abstracts* 6, no. 16 (1981): v. Copyright © by Energy Research Abstracts. Reprinted by permission.

Abstracts such as *Energy Research Abstracts* give not only bibliographic information about each source, but also a short paragraph that summarizes the article's content. This short paragraph is an abstract, as explained in chapter 3. So instead of having only the article's title to go by, the writer has a brief summary of the content. Using the abstract, the writer can accurately predict which articles are worth looking up and reading. Hence, the writer wastes no time searching for articles with useful sounding titles that turn out to have no value. A sample entry from *Energy Research Abstracts* is shown in figure 11–11.[7]

> **23314** **(DOE/NASA/20485—7) Laboratory evaluation of a Pilot Cell Battery Protection System for photovoltaic applications.** Cataldo, R.L.; Thomas, R.D. (National Aeronautics and Space Administration, Cleveland, OH (USA). Lewis Research Center). 1981. Contract AI01-76ET20485. 15 p. (CONF-810812—16). NTIS, PC A02/MF A01.
> From IECEC conference; Atlanta, GA, USA (9 Aug 1981). The results of laboratory tests performed on a Pilot Cell Battery Protection System, for use in photovoltaic power systems, shows this as a viable method of storage battery control. This method of limiting battery depth-of-discharge (DOD) has several advantages including: (1) temperature sensitivity, (2) rate sensitivity, and (3) state-of-charge (SOC) indication. The pilot cell concept is of particular interest for stand-alone photovoltaic power systems.

Figure 11–11. A sample entry from
Energy Research Abstracts.

To use the abstracts effectively, the writer must have a fairly good idea of the document's eventual shape and content. Articles indexed in abstracts are so technical and specific that writers undecided about their document's scope and structure cannot effectively use either the abstracts or the articles. Such writers should go back to more introductory material, use it to select a specific focus, and then move on to the specialized indexes and abstracts. By first defining their purposes, audiences, and authorial stances, they can usefully read detailed technical material.

To show you the range of abstracts found in most libraries, a list of some well-known abstracts (and a few less well known ones, too) follows:

- *Chemical Abstracts*
- *Applied Mechanics Abstracts*
- *Energy Research Abstracts*
- *Microbiology Abstracts*
- *Nuclear Science Abstracts*
- *Nutrition Abstracts and Reviews*
- *Water Resources Abstracts*

---

[7]Sample entry from *Energy Research Abstracts* 6, no. 16 (1981): 3091. Copyright © by Energy Research Abstracts. Reprinted by permission.

- *Wood Industry Abstracts*
- *Meteorological and Geoastrophysical Abstracts*

EXERCISE

Which of the listed abstracts would probably include references to articles on the following subjects: *city planning, garbage dumps, wind power generators, corrosion in pipes, earthquakes?*

GOVERNMENT DOCUMENTS

For good or ill, the U.S. government is the single biggest publisher by volume in the world. Every month, thousands of reports, periodicals, proceedings, and books come off the government presses, and much of the information is relevant to writers in business, industry, and government. The government indexes its voluminous output in two main locations: *The Index to Government Periodicals* (for regularly scheduled publications) and the *Monthly Catalog of U.S. Government Publications* (for individual works not published as part of a regular series). These specialized indexes both contain lists of specific materials, arranged under appropriate subject headings and subheadings. But neither of the government indexes uses abstracts, so the writer has only the article title to go by.

In *The Index to Government Periodicals,* the subheadings are alphabetical according to subject and article title, as shown in figure 11-12.

HYPERTENSION
Heading off heart attack. Lana Ott. il Soldiers 35 2 37-41 F 80-100
Health education program for weight reduction in a hypertension
    clinic. Donna Hafeman Hill and Roberta Madison, ref, tab Pub
    Health Rep 95 3 271-275 My-Je 80-146
Hypertension control programs in occupational settings. Michael
    Alderman and others, ref Pub Health Rep 95 2 158-163 Mr-Ap
    80-146
Management of the hypertensive patient. John T. Reppart, tab Med
    Serv Dig 30 3 22-23 My-Je 79-229
Nurse- and automatic machine-measured blood pressure readings: a
    comparative study. Laurie K. Glass and others, ref, tab Pub Health
    Rep 95 4 382-385 Jl-Ag 80-146
Pharmacy students wage campaign against hypertension. il Synergist
    8 3 49 Wint 80-128
Please don't pass the salt. Esther Peterson, Black N Dig np Je 16
    80-020
Public pressure checker. il NASA Act 11 9 20 S 80-072
Salt shakes up some of us. Louise Fenner, il FDA Cons 14 2 2-7 Mr
    80-045

Figure 11-12. A sample entry from *The Index to Government Periodicals.*

The government has its own filing code for each of its periodicals, which is not like the system used in the rest of the library. As a result, government periodicals are usually housed in a separate section of the library. To find a particular periodical, the writer must look in the front of *The Index to Government Periodicals.* See the sample code index in figure 11-13.

Nav Civ Eng—Navy Civil Engineer, D209.13: quarterly
Nav Lifel—Navy Lifeline, D207.15: bimonthly
Nav Res Logistics Q—Naval Research Logistics Quarterly, D210.12: quarterly
Nav Res Rev—Naval Research Reviews (ceased publication D '78), D210.11: monthly
Nav War Col Rev—Naval War College Review, D208.209: bi-monthly ○
Navigator—Navigator, D301.38/4: triannually
NOAA—NOAA, C55.14: quarterly
Nuclear Safe—Nuclear Safety, Y3.N88:9: bimonthly
Occup Outl Q—Occupational Outlook Quarterly, L2.70/4: quarterly
Opport II—Opportunity II, CSA1.11: quarterly×
Our Pub Land—Our Public Lands, I53.12: quarterly
Outd Rec Act—Outdoor Recreation Action (ceased publication 1977), I66.17: quarterly
Overseas Bus Rep—Overseas Business Reports, C57.11: irregular

×   Not on list of periodicals sent to Depository Libraries.
○   Not distributed by Government Printing Office; may be available from issuing department or agency.

Figure 11-13. Sample code index from *The Index of Government Periodicals.*

With the proper code, exact date, volume, and pages all noted, the writer can go to the shelves in the government documents section and find the item in question. Thus, the writer goes from subject index, to code list, to specific article, ending with some reading on the subject at hand, as in the following article from the *Navy Civil Engineer.*

In the *Monthly Catalog of U.S. Government Publications,* the first level of subheadings indicates the particular government agency publishing the material, such as the Department of Energy or the Department of Transportation. Under each department name the writer finds articles relevant to that department. Figure 11-14 shows an example section from the *Monthly Catalog of U.S. Government Publications.*

The code system for the *Monthly Catalog of U.S. Publications* is simple. The same basic code is used as for the government periodicals, but since each book or publication is unique, each is coded separately right along with its entry in the subject headings. Hence, there is no code list at the front. The writer can go from the title of the article and other bibliographic information directly to the book shelves.

> **United States. Federal Aviation Administration.**
> **Office of Environment and Energy.**
>> Biennial report prepared in accordance with the strato-
>> spheric ozone protection provision, section 153(g), of the
>> Clean Air Act amendments of 1977 /, 83-8098
>
> **United States. Federal Aviation Administration.**
> **Office of Systems Engineering Management.**
>> An Analysis of runway-taxiway transgressions at controlled
>> airports /, 83-8097
>>
>> Cost analysis of the discrete address beacon system for the
>> low-performance general aviation aircraft community /,
>> 83-8101
>
> **United States, Federal Aviation Administration**
> **Systems Research and Development Service**
>> Cost analysis of the discrete address beacon system for the
>> low-performance general avaiation aircraft community /,
>> 83-8101
>
> **United States. Federal Election Commission.**
>> FEC disclosure series., 83-8243

Figure 11–14. An example from the *Monthly Catalog
of U.S. Government Publications.*

As with all other specialized sources of information, the writer needs to
have a good idea of his direction before the government documents can be of
much use.

EXERCISE

Review the Elk Hills article. What question or questions might a writer be trying to
answer if she found this article relevant? Make a brief outline for a document that
could use the article on Elk Hills. Indicate the passages from the article that would be
relevant and indicate where those passages would fit in the document's outline.

OTHER SOURCES OF INFORMATION

Especially in business, industry, and government, books and magazines found
in the library are by no means the only, or even the best, sources of information.
Professionals on the job also depend heavily on interviews and privately printed
documents, such as manufacturers' data sheets, advertising materials, and in-
house newsletters.

Elk Hills!

Cdr Gordon R. Gilmore, CEC, USN

Vast new oil resources opened at Naval Petroleum Reserve.

In 1976 Congress passed the Naval Petroleum Reserves Production Act, which mandated that the Navy bring the production of each Reserve to its maximum efficient rate with the oil to be sold commercially through competitive bids.

Today Elk Hills is the third largest producing field in the country just behind Prudhoe Bay in Alaska and the East Texas field. It is probably the most active field in terms of construction, well drilling and other associated development.

The Reserves, now administered by the U.S. Department of Energy, have been extensively developed in recent years with additional processing, storage and distribution systems whose construction has been supervised by the Naval Facilities Engineering Command and the Navy's Civil Engineer Corps.

A first look at Elk Hills is not particularly inspiring. Ultramarine walking beams with yellow "horse heads" form the pumping units for the shallow wells and supply what little color there is to the barren hills. In the distance, a drilling rig towers over the landscape. Roads snake around and over the hills—some are paved, while others remain gravel or sand. The surfaced roads were built originally by the Seabees during World War II. They aimed their bulldozers at the hills, scraped a ribbon out of the sand, rolled a bit, laid some asphalt, and that became the road network used to this day. Over 33 miles of paved and secondary roads were completed before the Seabees were transferred to the urgent needs of the Pacific Theater of war.

A county highway bisects the Reserve from south to north. Near this road between the flat desert and gently sloping hills is the newly constructed crude oil tank farm. Five 10.5 million-gallon tanks wait for crude oil storage. The total capacity is 1.25 million *barrels* of crude. The tanks are 210 feet in diameter and 40 feet high. They have floating roofs with double seals to retain gaseous vapors and avoid degradation of the environment. This is probably one of the largest tank farms ever built under NAVFAC supervision. A short distance from the tank farm are 12 smaller tanks used for separation of oil, water and other foreign material prior to delivering the oil to commercial buyers.

Passing the tank farm and climbing to the top of a slight rise, tall silver towers gradually grow out of the desert. These are the fractionating columns for the existing gas processing plant which was constructed in 1951 but not placed into operation until 1976. The plant is now processing an average of 94 million cubic feet of gas per day (MMCFD) at full capacity. Behind the plant is a liquid storage facility where the butane, propane and liquid natural gasoline, extracted from the gas as it travels through the plant, is stored and delivered to buyers.

Adjacent are two new gas processing plants under construction, each with a capacity of 100 MMCFD. Included in the construction NAVFAC is building another liquid products storage facility and a truck loading facility. These new gas processing plants are low temperature separation types where the temperature of the gas is reduced to about −10°F to enhance extraction of the butane, propane, etc. The recovery efficiency of products will be much better than that experienced in the existing plant which uses an absorption process.

Between the new plants and the existing one is a recently completed high pressure injection facility with three gas-fueled, 5500 hp compressors. As the gas leaves the processing plants, its pressure is increased to about 3500 pounds and it is then transferred through gas lines to wells where it is injected into the oil reservoir gas cap for pressure maintenance. Currently, the major producing reservoirs at the Reserve have enough pressure for the oil to flow to the surface. However, as oil is produced this pressure is reduced. The gas is reinjected to maintain pressure and keep the wells flowing as long and as efficiently as possible.

The high pressure injection facility was an urgent project required for an immediate increase in oil production. Erection of the plant began in early July 1978 and around-the-clock construction operations resulted in completion in November 1978.

The gas that is being processed and then reinjected is called associated gas because, rather than coming from actual gas wells, it comes to the surface with the oil. At the surface, the oil and gas are separated with the gas going to the plants for processing and the oil transferred to small field tanks and then to the larger settling tanks prior to sale.

The oil comes primarily from the Shallow Zone at 3,000–4,000 ft. drilled depth and the Stevens Zone from 5,000–9,000 ft. drilled depth. Over 43 million barrels have been sold during the past year, two-thirds of which came from the Stevens Zone. Recoverable oil is estimated at 1.2 billion barrels with over a trillion cubic feet of recoverable gas.

There are other producible zones, one of which is particularly interesting. The Carneros Zone is found between 9,000–10,000 feet drilled depth and while not as prolific as the Shallow or Stevens Zones, it produces a gas condensate which is so light it could almost be burned directly in an automobile as it comes from the ground. In the old days, before high performance cars, it *was* used directly for fuel by some oil field workers.

Since the majority of the oil produced flows to the surface its production expense is minimal. The Elk Hills crude oil contains very little sulfur and is of high quality. It is an excellent crude for refining, with Shallow Zone crude noted for its lubricating oil content and the Stevens crude noted for its high gasoline content.

"The objective is to get the oil out and a side benefit is the extraction and sale of the liquid products encompassing butane, propane and liquid natural gasoline," explains LCDR Jerry Newton, CEC, USN, project engineer. "With additional gases scheduled for processing as the new plants become operational, there will be a tremendous quantity of liquid products to handle. Design is underway on a rail-loading facility east of the community of Taft, south of the Reserve. The products will be transferred by pipeline, then loaded in rail cars for transfer to market areas."

The land proposed for the rail loading facility belongs to the Bureau of Land Management (BLM). At the present time an environmental study is underway to assess the impact of construction on the surrounding environment and to develop any mitigating measures necessary.

The present wave of construction is progressing at a rapid pace with shift and overtime work utilized when needed to meet critical schedules. The program is estimated to cost about $600,000,000 and is almost evenly split between NAVFAC and Williams Brothers Engineering Company, the current operator/contractor for the Reserve, which, by the way, is currently administered by the Department of Energy (DOE). The DOE has about 60 civil service employees and eight naval officers managing the Reserve. Chevron USA owns about 20 percent of the Reserve and participates in its management through a unitization agreement with the Government.

It is interesting to note that during World War II, women comprised about half of the work force. Their job was like their male counterparts to keep the machinery running and the field producing around the clock.

At all hours of the day they drove their trucks over lonely, muddy roads, in rainy weather and through fog-ridden nights to ensure that production was maintained.

In 1973 when the initial oil embargo rocked the country, Elk Hills was only partially developed and basically in a caretaker status under the watchful eye of the Congress. In a short six years, oil production has increased from below 5,000 BOPD to over 160,000 BOPD and the facilities are being constructed to enable a production rate of over 200,000 BOPD in 1980. This Reserve is playing a vital role in offsetting the growing energy supply problem. Our future will depend on using our energy resources wisely while alternate sources of supply are being developed.

Interviews

The world is full of people who know more about any given subject than you do. Often these experts have never published anything, but their knowledge can be invaluable. To tap into their expertise, however, you need to master the techniques of interviewing.

Effective interviewing consists of the following essential features.

Preparing for the Person   Find out as much as you can about the person you are going to interview before you even try to set up the time and place. Occasionally a thorough background study may convince you not to interview the person at all. In that case, you save valuable time for both of you. Usually though, a thorough background study makes your interview more productive because you know more about what you want to ask and what the person can answer. You should try to find out at least the following about the people you are going to interview:

1. Job title and responsibilities
2. Likes and dislikes
3. Education level
4. Relationship to subject matter
5. Relationship to others in the subject matter area
6. Relationship to the document you are in the process of writing

You can learn these and similar things from many sources. If your interviewee is famous enough, he or she may be written about in a published biographical source, such as *Who's Who* or *Biography Today*. For less exalted personages, telephone conversations with fellow workers, secretaries, and colleagues can be informative.

Preparing for the Subject   Make a list of the exact questions you want to ask your interviewee. Nothing is less productive than going into an interview with no idea of the information you need. To know what information you need, you should gather some knowledge of the subject and your approach to it before interviewing. In other words, books, magazines, and other printed sources discussed earlier should be consulted before interviewing begins. Then you do not waste interview time gathering information already available from printed sources. Also, you make yourself knowledgeable enough to ask intelligent and probing questions. Many interviewees are insulted and uncooperative if they go to the trouble to give you an interview and then you use it to ask questions they know can be easily answered from published sources. In such a situation all you establish is that you are either too lazy or too unintelligent to talk to.

Of course, you should be able to go beyond your prepared questions should the interview move in directions you did not anticipate. Even so, a list of intelligent, pertinent, and well-stated questions provides an effective starting point.

Effective interview questions take a wide range of forms; however, they do share a few characteristics:

- They are open-ended, to encourage the person to expand on the subject. Several yes/no questions will usually not generate as much information as one probing open-ended question.
- They are stated clearly, in simple, nonambiguous language. Appropriate technical terms are fine, but jargon used to impress should be avoided.

Preparing for the Setting   Once you know all you can about the person you are interviewing and once you have studied your topic and your approach well enough to have a good list of clearly stated, open-ended questions, you must make the physical arrangements for the interview itself.

First, you must arrange the time and place of the interview. You want to accommodate the interviewee as much as possible, because the person's comfort is important to a productive interview. If possible, arrange to conduct the interview on the person's home turf. He will probably be more comfortable there and may have access to relevant materials that would not be available anywhere else. The interview should be private, where you can both be seated, physically comfortable, and as free from disturbances as possible. Thus, although you may want the interview on the interviewee's home turf, you may *not* want it in his or her office. The telephone is the worst distraction of all, one which the interviewer has no way to counter.

Before you set the exact time for the interview, indicate the approximate amount of time you think the interview will take. If you do not do so, you may find your interview scheduled at the time set, but with someone else's interview exactly fifteen minutes after yours. Then the focus is on rushing to get it over, both you and the interviewee are distracted, and the interviewee will probably give very short responses, considerably decreasing the interview's productivity.

Preparing to Record   You should also prepare some effective way to record the interview. If the interviewee consents, you can use a tape recorder, but it should be as small, quiet, and inconspicuous as possible. The interview's being taped should not become the focus of the conversation or set its tone. However, the tone of a taped interview usually moves toward more formality and less frankness.

Always have a backup system of plenty of paper and a few pens (also an effective system to begin with). Be sure to have a clipboard, because you cannot assume you will have a conveniently placed table to write on. As with the tape recorder, you want your notetaking to be as inconspicuous as possible. Do not try to write every word the interviewee says; if you do, you will be writing, not engaging in a conversation. No one likes to talk to someone who is busy doing something else. Ultimately the interview's quality is determined by how effectively you start and maintain the conversation. You cannot be effective if you are writing all the time and making the interviewee wait for you and worry about the accuracy of all you are writing down.

Be certain that throughout the interview you understand what is being said and keep accurate track of it all. If you use a tape recorder, your recording problems are over. If you take notes, be sure they are clear, accurate, and understandable. Be cautious about using abbreviations or other shorthand methods of recording that seem clear at the moment but will not later. The ultimate goal of the interview is to leave it with the maximum amount of relevant information recorded in an accurate and retrievable form.

Preparing to Listen, Not to Talk The ideal interview is a friendly conversation between two equals, one of whom (the interviewer) subtly guides the discussion's direction and records what the other says without the other being aware of the guiding or the recording. Of course, such an ideal is not usually possible in actual practice; however, the interviewer can work toward the ideal by beginning the interview with small talk and moving gradually into the real subject. The interviewer wants to put the interviewee so much at ease that she never consciously realizes an interview is taking place. Of course, you should not try to be too clever or sneaky; the interviewee is probably a busy person who will resent lengthy and irrelevant small talk.

Such small points as knowing the person's name, looking directly at him or her, and using a lively tone of voice (not overbearing, but not dead either) help establish a relaxed atmosphere. Here, in the opening moments of the interview, your preparation really pays off.

Try to keep the interviewee talking and you listening as much as possible, especially as the interview progresses. Asking open-ended questions, maintaining an interested look on your face, and concentrating on the interviewee's answers rather than on your next question encourage the person to talk. Again, preparation is essential. If you have no idea what your next question is, it is hard not to think about it.

An occasional nod and an "I understand" can also keep the conversation moving along. Also, when appropriate, puzzled or expectant looks, or phrases like "and then?" or "how?" may keep the interviewee talking. Above all, avoid creating lengthy or clever rejoinders to what the other person is saying. You want to get the interviewee's answers, not provide final answers to the questions posed. In general, save your opinions for when you are rich and famous and some aspiring youth is interviewing you!

Also, remember to keep your questions and language at an appropriate level for the person being interviewed. You want to impress the person with your interest in the subject, with how well you are prepared to listen and appreciate, *not* with how clever or intelligent you are. Avoid stilted, high-flown jargon; such "impressive" language only makes the interviewee doubt your understanding of the subject or your purpose in asking for the interview. Your purpose is to get the other person to talk, not to impress that person with your own talking.

You must be alert for any signs that the interviewee is bored, nervous, embarrassed, or feeling negative about the interview. Such negative attitudes are detrimental to the interview because they often make the interviewee less talkative than usual. Try to make *everything*—from the physical setting to the questions you ask—comfortable and relaxed.

Preparing to Direct On the other hand, you want the interviewee to answer the questions you ask. You may need to gently steer the interview back to the subject. Having a carefully prepared list of questions and a clear understanding of your purposes can help you recognize when the conversation is going off target.

Documenting the Interview The recording or set of notes you have at the end of the interview should be usable just like any other source of information. It is not that different from a book, magazine, or pamphlet. Therefore, record all the pertinent bibliographic information just as you would for any other source. For an interview, include at least the following:

- Name and title of person interviewed
- Date and place of interview

Other special facts about the interview, for example, that it was done as part of a convention, can also be recorded. It is always easier to record extra information and not use it than to need information several months and many miles later. A typical bibliographic entry for an interview follows:

> Interview with Gary Smythe, President of Avocando Products, Ltd., at the Detroit Home Products Show, Detroit, Michigan, July 4, 1982.

EXERCISE

Imagine you are trying to decide whether to buy a stereo with a normal turntable or one with a linear turntable. You know a lot about the normal turntable, but you cannot get much information about the relatively new linear turntable. So you plan to interview Ted Thomas, president of a small company marketing the new linear turntable in your area. What background information should you gather on Mr. Thomas? What questions do you want to ask him?

Privately Printed Documents

Much of the best information available on technical subjects is not mass-produced. Such materials include in-house publications aimed at company employees, sales literature and other advertising materials aimed at potential buyers, and specifications and other technical data aimed more at the engineer than the consumer. Such information is usually available from only two sources: the company itself or the sales outlet. If you can visit manufacturing plants, head offices, or other work places, you can often pick up brochures and technical descriptions. Many companies maintain private libraries containing information unavailable elsewhere. Access to such collections is more often than not restricted, but it never hurts to ask. Also, a company may give you some sales literature, just to get rid of you and keep you from asking too much about the library. As always in research, the more you can find out ahead of time about what your source actually has available, the more likely you will be to get some of it. If you ask for "some information," you will probably get nothing. If you make a specific request for a particular document or type of information, you are more likely to get it.

Going to a sales outlet is usually much easier than going to a head office or manufacturing site. Of course, information is severely limited too; because sales literature is intended to sell, it is often less objective and factual than most other sources of information. But it is readily available and free. As long as you do not accept it as the whole truth and nothing but the truth, sales literature can be useful. A good researcher never accepts any one source of information as the whole truth anyway.

EXERCISE

Two pages from a sales brochure are shown in figures 11-15 and 11-16.[9] What questions might this document help a researcher answer? What specific passages would fit into specific parts of an outline for a written document? Try to find some other examples of privately printed documents.

SUMMARY

Once the writer has analyzed his purpose, audience, and authorial stance, he knows what information he needs to complete that piece of writing. The next step is to find that information. The professional writer has two major sources of information: the library, for published sources, and live interviews, for unpublished sources. Using either source of information requires special skills, which may be divided into two subskills: preparing and recording.

In the library, preparing means finding likely titles of articles and books by using the indexes and catalogs. At this stage, recording means writing down bibliographic information about the proposed source of information.

---

[9]From *What is Gore-Tex® expanded PTFE?* (Newark, Del.: W.L. Gore and Associates, Inc., 1980), 1-2. Copyright ©1980 by W.L. Gore and Associates, Inc. Reprinted by permission.

What is GORE-TEX® expanded PTFE?

GORE-TEX® expanded PTFE is a microporous structure with a matrix of nodules interconnected by fibrils. The photomicrograph below shows a typical configuration and the open pore construction. The degree of porosity (0-95%) and the pore size can be controlled permitting the fabrication of materials to fit specific end use requirements.

GORE-TEX expanded PTFE retains all of the excellent properties of ordinary PTFE and adds important additional properties as well.

Typical Properties
Polytetrafluoroethylene

- Chemically inert—unaffected by all common chemicals.
- Low coefficient of friction.
- Useful through wide temperature range (−450°F to 550°F).
- Non-flammable
- Non-aging
- Weather durable

Typical Properties
GORE-TEX PTFE

- Controllable pore size
- Hydrophobic—air permeable
- Low cold flow
- Less creep
- Low shrinkage
- High strength

TYPICAL POROSITY/
PORE SIZE RELATIONSHIPS

Relationship of porosity (%) to density (g/cm³)

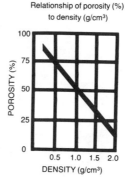

Relationship of porosity (%) to largest pore size (μ)

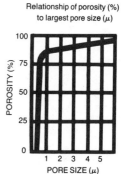

TYPICAL AIR PERMEABILITY/
WATER ENTRY
PRESSURE RELATIONSHIPS

Air Permeability $= \dfrac{V \cdot H}{t \cdot A \cdot P}$

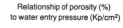

Relationship of porosity (%) to water entry pressure (Kp/cm²)

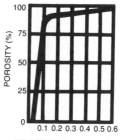

AIR PERMEABILITY (Metric Units)

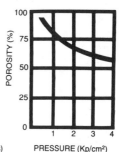

PRESSURE (Kp/cm²)

V = Volume of air (cm³)
H = Thickness of film (cm)
t = Flow time (sec)
A = Area (cm²)
P = Pressure (cm Hg)

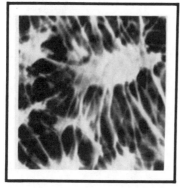

The illustration on the front cover is from a stained glass window designed by Willet Studios of Philadelphia, Pa. and depicts the GORE-TEX® structure magnified 12,000 times. The window is installed in the lobby of Gore's Elkton, Maryland offices.

Figure 11–15

Rainwear

GORE-TEX® Laminate is waterproof yet vapor permeable. When manufactured in thin membrane-like sheets and laminated between layers of cloth, it becomes an excellent material for outdoor equipment, such as garments, tents, and sleeping bags. In any high exertion outdoor sport, such as backpacking or skiing, reliable waterproof garments are required. They must offer protection from wind, cold, and rain but not at the expense of weight or

discomfort. In normal rainproof equipment of coated fabrics, perspiration can condense inside a garment and cause the wearer to become wet, cold, and uncomfortable. Garments of GORE-TEX Laminate, however, keep external water from penetrating while allowing internal water vapor to escape. This factor has accounted for the tremendous acceptance of GORE-TEX Laminates by consumers and a wide variety of outdoor equipment and garment manufacturers. Garments of GORE-TEX Laminates for bicycling, motorcycling, skiing, canoeing, jogging, golf, boating and sailing are now either in production or under consideration by leading manufacturers. W. L. Gore & Associates does not produce garments or equipment of GORE-TEX Laminates. Rather, they are the sole producer and patent holder on both GORE-TEX expanded PTFE and the laminating process. The unique combinations of the properties found in GORE-TEX PTFE have widespread potential for all outerwear applications, plus industrial and medical uses as well.

Figure 11–16

For a live interview, preparing means devising the exact questions to ask the person being interviewed and setting up physical arrangements for the interview. Recording the interview means using a tape recorder or paper and pencil to capture the main ideas of the interview.

Occasionally, you may find privately printed materials in a company library, or you may be given such materials in an interview. The basic activities of preparing and recording apply, however, to all information used in your writing, no matter what its source.

CASE IN POINT

The Informative Report

Many written projects only transmit information, and argue no point. In such a case, the writer's purpose is to gather information and pass it on. The most logical organization for such a report is to start with the most important information and work toward the least important information. Chronological order can sometimes work effectively in the report of information. For instance, to write a set of instructions telling someone how to make or do something, begin with the first step and go on through the whole process from beginning to end. Still another effective organization is spatial (organized in terms of physical space). A brief informative memo, with the main point placed in a spatially organized graphic aid, follows:

On July 26, 1985, George Moscone and I accompanied Jill Parker, Project Biologist for the Weyerhauser Corporation, on a field inspection of the Longview Forest Preserve.

We confirmed the existence of three large burn areas, apparently lightning set, as follows:

	Location	Extent	Salvageable
Area I	3 mi. east of Miller's Falls	25,000 acres	none
Area II	centered around Jasper	50,000 acres	50 percent
Area III	NW shore of Friese Lake	35,000 acres	90 percent

A type of informational report often required on the job is the progress report. As the name implies, the purpose is to inform others of the status of a particular job or project.

The progress report usually has the following sections:

1. Introduction
2. Project description, including statement of preplanned schedule of work and/or expense
3. Statement of work completed and/or money spent to date
4. Statement and schedule of work still remaining
5. Appraisal of situation

A sample progress report follows:

My current project, under the direction of Mr. Fred deSilvius, is to design a cable TV descrambler, capable of decoding various coded signals, such as ONTV, Spotlight, Showtime, and Home Theatre Network. The schedule established by Mr. deSilvius calls for the descrambler to be completely operational and marketable by August 1, 1985. All necessary materials are available right here in the shop, so no outlay of money is anticipated for the project.

Work Completed to Date

1. On May 19 I tested the descrambler on the Spotlight cable channel. By turning up the gain control on the TV board, Spotlight became unscrambled, but reception was poor.

2. On May 28 I added a 1000-ohm resistor across R16 and changed the LM301 op-amp to an updated version, LM301AP. The result was clear reception of the Spotlight cable channel.

3. On June 7 I tested this improved descrambler on the Home Theatre Network. By adjusting the gain, I received this channel quite clearly.

4. On June 9 I added a rotary switch and placed various gain resistors on each solder lug. The result was a descrambler capable of decoding and receiving many pay TV channels at the turn of a switch.

Work Remaining

I plan to experiment with various additional gain settings and resistors in an attempt to further refine the quality of the reception achieved by the descrambler and the quantity of stations it can decode. I anticipate no difficulty in completing this project well ahead of schedule.

An extended example of the informative report, a status summary prepared by a panel of experts, follows on pages 238 through 244. This document aims to summarize the current state of knowledge about a popular food additive.

WRITING ASSIGNMENTS

1. Prepare an informative report. This could be a progress report, a status summary report, instructions on how to make or do something, or any other written document in which you simply report information, not argue a point.

2. With the help of your teacher, if necessary, select a topic you would like or need to write about over the next few weeks or months. Next, prepare a written outline of questions about that topic. These questions should take into account the types of problems discussed in chapter 1, as well as the rhetorical situation discussed in chapters 2 and 3. Then, devise a strategy for finding the information demanded by the questions. Record all published sources in proper bibliographic form and make a full list of questions for any interviews you plan. Finally, start gathering all the information you can.

FOR FURTHER READING

Barzun, Jacques and Graff, Henry. *The Modern Researcher.* 3d ed. New York: Harcourt Brace Jovanovich, 1977.

Chen, Ching-Chin. *Scientific and Technical Information Sources.* Cambridge, Mass.: MIT Press, 1977.

Cunningham, Donald. "Bibliographies of Technical Writing Materials." *The Technical Writing Teacher* 1 (Winter 1974): 9–10.

Harris, John S. "Technical Writing Practice." *Engineering Education* 60 (February 1970): 491–92.

Herner, Saul. *A Brief Guide to Sources of Scientific and Technical Information.* 2d ed. Arlington, Va.: Information Resources, 1980.

Maltha, D.J. *Technical Literature Search and the Written Report.* New York: Elsevier-North Holland, 1976.

McCormick, Mona. *The New York Times Guide to Reference Materials.* New York: Popular Library, 1982.

Palic, Vladimir M. *Government Publications: A Guide to Bibliographic Tools.* Washington, D.C.: Library of Congress, 1975.

Ricks, Don. "Teaching Documentation in the Technical Writing Class." *College Composition and Communication* 21 (May 1970): 196–98.

Monosodium glutamate (MSG)

A Scientific Status Summary by the Institute of Food Technologists' Expert Panel on

Food Safety & Nutrition and the Committee on Public Information

One of the most common natural amino acids, glutamic acid and its salts have a long history of use in foods. The acid itself is used to adjust the acidity in foods and the various salt forms are used to enhance flavor. The sodium salt, usually called MSG (for monosodium glutamate), is by far the most widely used glutamate, although potassium, ammonium, and calcium glutamates have been used in low-sodium formulations as salt substitutes.

The use of MSG in food goes back to the Oriental cooks of antiquity, who used a seaweed called seatangle to make a stock. This stock added a richness to the flavor of foods cooked in it. The link between the seaweed flavor improvement and glutamate (first isolated in 1866) was discovered by Professor Kikunae Ikeda of the University of Tokyo in 1908. He demonstrated that the seaweed (*Laminaria japonica*) contained generous amounts of glutamate and that *it* was the seaweed component responsible for food flavor enhancement. The Japanese began production of glutamate almost immediately, although 30 years passed before it was produced in North America, from corn and wheat gluten. Today, MSG is produced in the United States from sugar beet molasses, in a fermentation process similar to that used in making yeast or sauerkraut. (Kirk-Othmer, 1978). Alternatively, MSG may be extracted directly from sugar beets.

Glutamate is ubiquitous in nature and is present in both food and the human body, either as one of the amino acid building blocks of protein and peptides, or in its free form. The glutamate bound into a protein structure has no flavor enhancing properties—only the free form has that, and then only the "L isomer." Protein-rich foods such as human milk, cow's milk, cheese, and meat have a high content of bound glutamate, while most vegetables contain little, because of their low protein content. However, many of these vegetables—such

as mushrooms, tomatoes, and peas—do have high levels of free glutamate. In fact, some investigators have suggested that this explains the effectivenss of mushrooms and tomatoes in enhancing the flavor of other foods, in much the same way as seaweed. The glutamate content of some representative foods is shown in Table 1.

In the 1940's, Hac and co-workers (1949) demonstrated that fresh young peas and sweet corn contained more free glutamic acid than more mature vegetables harvested from the same field. They suggested that the amount of glutamic acid present in vegetables was proportional to their rate of growth. Furthermore, they demonstrated that even short cooking times depleted the glutamate in these vegetables.

In addition to being abundantly present in food, glutamate exists as part of the human body itself, in both free and bound form. The human body contains 14 to 17% protein, of which about one-fifth is glutamate. An adult weighing 70 kilograms (156 pounds) contains, on the average, 2 kilograms (4.4 pounds) of glutamate in his protein.

The free form of glutamate is also present in the digestive system, the blood, and other organs and tissues in varying levels. For example, the free glutamate concentration in the brain is about 100 times as high as in the blood. Total circulating free glutamate available for the body's use is about 10 grams (1/3 ounce). Total body turnover in intermediary metabolism is estimated to be 5 to 10 grams per hour. The total content of free glutamate in the human body is illustrated in Table 2.

As previously mentioned, the major use of MSG in food processing or cooking in the western world is as a flavor enhancer—in soups and broths, sauces and gravies, and flavoring and spice blends, as well as in a wide variety of canned and frozen meats, poultry, vegetables, and combination dishes—rather than to add a flavor of its own. Results of taste panel studies on processed foods indicate that a level of 0.2-0.8% of food, by weight, gives the best enhancement of the natural flavor of food. For cooks

Table 1. *Glutamate Content of Certain Foods*[a]

Product	Percent of protein in food	Percent of glutamate in protein	Protein-bound glutamate (grams per 100 grams of food)	Free glutamate (grams per 100 grams of food)
Cow's milk	3.5	23.4	0.819	0.002
Human milk	1.4	16.4	0.229	0.019
Camembert cheese	17.5	27.4	4.787	0.600
Parmesan cheese	36.0	27.4	9.847	0.600
Eggs	12.8	12.4	1.583	0.023
Chicken	20.6	16.1	3.309	0.044
Beef	18.8	15.1	2.846	0.033
Pork	15.2	15.3	2.325	0.023
Peas	23.8	23.5	5.583	0.200
Corn	10.0	17.7	1.765	0.130
Tomatoes	1.0	23.8	0.238	0.140
Spinach	2.3	12.6	0.289	0.039

[a]From Baker, et al., 1977; Giacometti, 1979; and International Glutamate Technical Committee, 1974

Table 2. *Free Glutamate in Adult Humans*[a]

Organ/tissue	Free glutamate (gm)
Muscle	6.
Brain	2.25
Kidney	0.680
Liver	0.670
Blood plasma	0.040
Total	9.640

[a]From Giacometti, 1979

in home or restaurant kitchens, this translates to about one-half to one teaspoonful per pound of meat or per four to six servings of vegetables, casseroles, soups, etc.

There appears to be some variability from one person to another as to their preferred optimum level of use. Some recipes call for MSG in the food preparation, followed by additional MSG at the time of serving to "season to taste." Since MSG is readily soluble in water, recipes often call for dissolving it in the aqueous ingredients of products such as salad dressings before they are added to food. In the Orient, MSG is often used in amounts sufficiently large that its own characteristic flavor comes through; the Japanese call this "umami," often translated as meaning "tastiness."

The free glutamate consumed daily as MSG typically equals about 1/1000th of the total gluta-mate present in the body, including that in the body's protein. Individual consumption ranges from a low of approximately 1/2 to 1 gram per day in the United States to a high of approximately 3 grams per day in Taiwan (Giacometti, 1979; NAS, 1979). On the average, about 20 additional grams (2/3 ounce) of naturally occurring glutamate are ingested each day as a part of normal food consumption—most of which is bound to protein. The ratio of protein-bound MSG and free MSG ingested each day varies with food habits, of course, depending on protein consumption and MSG use.

The exact mechanism by which MSG exerts its flavor enhancing abilities is not known, despite extensive work. The quality of the taste effect brought about by use of MSG is different from the four basic tastes—sweet, sour, salty, bitter. Also, it does not simply *increase* the intensity of the four basic tastes. Some studies suggest that MSG's effect on food flavor involves two basically different mechanisms: how tightly the flavor enhancer is bound to the taste receptor sites on the tongue, and how accessible these receptor sites are (Cagan, 1979). According to this research, glutamate binds preferentially to the taste receptors and to certain other food-flavor enhancing components. Other studies have shown that MSG has no effect on aroma but tends to enhance perception of a taste, and thus increase its intensity (Yamaguchi and Kimizuka, 1979).

ACUTE AND CHRONIC TOXICITY STUDIES

Because of its use in food, glutamate's acute and chronic toxicities have been studied extensively. Special toxicological studies have also been done. The acute toxicity of glutamate is low. The LD_{50} for mice—the dose at which half the test animals die— is 19.9 gm/kg body weight for L-MSG when the mice are fed an aqueous solution with a stomach tube (Ebert, 1979b). Translated to a 70-kg man, this dose amounts to more than three pounds.

Chronic feeding studies, which involve feeding the test substance to experimental animals daily for a two-year period of time or longer, have been completed in rodent and non-rodent species (Ebert, 1979a). There was no evidence of chronic toxicity or carcinogenicity (ability to induce cancer) in rats and mice when MSG was fed over a two-year period at dietary levels of either 0.4% or 4% on an "as consumed" basis. Long-term feeding studies on pure-bred beagle dogs were carried out with diets containing MSG at levels of either 2.5, 5 or 10% by weight (Owen et al., 1978). Two controls were used: the first received a diet with no test compound added, the second received the control diet plus 5.13% sodium propionate to determine the effect of the *sodium* in MSG. The test did not reveal any adverse effect on mortality rate, body weight gain, general behavior, ophthalmological findings, dermatology, blood chemistry, or on gross or histopathologic findings.

GLUTAMATE: THE FETUS AND YOUNG CHILD

Placental Transfer The question has been raised as to whether the fetus *in utero* would be exposed to glutamate concentrations higher than those normally found, following ingestion of MSG by the mother.

In one study, enough MSG was administered to pregnant non-human primates to raise the glutamate levels in the maternal blood stream to 40–50 times normal (Pitkin et al., 1979). The primate placenta proved to be a virtually impregnable barrier, apparently capable of metabolizing large amounts of glutamate.

In addition, it is apparently impossible to raise blood glutamate concentrations to those high levels by dietary means alone. Stegink et al. (1975) had to resort to injecting MSG solutions directly into the mother's blood stream to obtain comparable levels

when they studied offspring of MSG-treated mothers for brain damage. They looked specifically for lesions in the arcuate nucleus of the hypothalamus, and found that none was present.

In another series of studies on the possible elevation of glutamate levels in mothers' milk following the ingestion of MSG, Stegink and co-workers (1972) administered 0.1 gm of MSG per kg body weight. The glutamate level in the lactating mother's *blood plasma* increased almost sevenfold, but the levels in their milk were not significantly affected. Later studies confirmed these results (Baker et al., 1979).

In the late 1960's, the consuming public voiced concern over the possible effects of glutamates fed to infants and small children. At the time, MSG was being added to baby foods in pureed vegetables and meat products, for the same reason as it was used in the adult diet—to enhance their flavor. Because of the concern expressed by the public, baby food manufacturers in both the U.S. and Canada voluntarily stopped using the additive in late 1969. (It was never used in pureed fruits, cereal products, or infant formula.)

GLUTAMATE AND THE CENTRAL NERVOUS SYSTEM

Olney and others have demonstrated that glutamate can be markedly toxic to the central nervous system of laboratory animals (Olney et al., 1969, 1970, 1972). In some species, obesity, sterility, and other effects may also result. As with other components in food-stuffs which have been shown to affect the central nervous system and the endocrine glands—such as aspartic acid, cysteine, and related compounds— large doses and high concentrations not common to foods are required. Laboratory animals will usually not eat these large doses voluntarily—they must be administered by injection or tube feeding (gavage). The smallest dose of MSG which will bring about these effects ranges from 0.7 gm/kg in 10-day-old mice to 2 gm/kg in 23-day-old mice, markedly greater than the amounts used in foods eaten by man.

Moreover, the toxic effects appear to apply only to particular species. While the central nervous system findings originally reported by Olney have been corroborated by a number of research laboratories (Lemkey-Johnston et al., 1972), several other laboratories disagree with his findings. They found no evidence of central nervous system damage in the non-human primate following oral, subcutaneous or dietary administration of MSG at doses of up to 4 gm/kg (Abraham et al., 1971, 1975; Newman et al., 1973; Reynolds et al., 1971; Wen et al., 1973).

GLUTAMATE: SAFETY ON FEEDING

A number of laboratories have attempted to explain why different species of animals respond differently to glutamates, as well as why the human being fails to show central nervous system damage. Takasaki and co-workers (1979) concluded that many factors affect the potential damage to the nervous system of even the most sensitive species, the mouse. These factors include the metabolic capacity of the test animal, the dose, the concentration of the dose and the way it is administered. These investigators demonstrated that when glutamate was injected into a mouse, brain damage occurred with smaller doses than when the test animal was tube fed. They also showed that sensitivity decreased as the mice got older.

It is important to note that large doses of MSG were required to induce brain damage. While World Health Organization authorities recommend a maximum daily oral intake of MSG of 0.15 gm/kg body weight for man, the smallest dose which produced negative effects in 10-day-old mice was 0.4 gm/kg, using intraperitoneal injection. When force feeding was used instead of injection, 0.7 gm/kg doses were required before brain damage occurred. When the mice were older—23 days—the doses required to cause central nervous system damage increased to 0.7 gm/kg and 2 gm/kg following subcutaneous injection and forced feeding respectively.

The method of administering MSG doses to mice also affects the peak levels reached in their blood plasma. For example, when infant mice were dosed with an MSG solution by forced tube-feeding, their peak plasma levels of glutamate were only about one-fourth as high as the peaks in mice who were given the same dose by subcutaneous injection (O'Hara, 1979). When a larger dose of MSG was eaten (voluntarily) as part of a commercial laboratory ration, the changes in plasma glutamate levels were minimal.

A number of studies of dietary ingestion of MSG, sometimes in massive doses (up to 46 gm/kg body weight per day), have shown no harmful effects on the hypothalamus (Heywood et al., 1977; Takasaki, 1978; Takasaki et al., 1979). Similarly,

fetuses and newborn rodents of *parents* receiving massive doses of MSG in food were unaffected (Semprini et al., 1974), as were several animal species in other tests (Wen et al., 1973).

Steglink and co-workers (1979) measured plasma glutamate levels in humans of varying ages following ingestion of a high protein meal to which MSG had been added, either at the levels actually consumed by 90% of the population, or at the higher "Acceptable Daily Intake" (0.15 gm/kg as defined by FAO/WHO 1979). A control group ate the same high-protein meal with *no* added glutamate. These studies showed that when other foods were eaten with MSG, the peak plasma glutamate levels were drastically reduced. Peak levels reached when WHO's Acceptable Daily Intake was consumed in the high-protein meal were only slightly elevated in comparison to the control meal. When an aqueous solution of MSG *alone* was administered at that dose, however, peak plasma glutamate levels were 12 times as high as those in the control group.

Many other animal studies have shown the importance of considering not only dose but also the concentration of test solution, the route of administration, and the age of the experimental animals in evaluating the safety of glutamate for man.

THE "CHINESE RESTAURANT SYNDROME"

In addition to the published scientific studies of MSG, a number of anecdotal or case history reports have appeared describing its effects on humans. The effects reported are often tightness, warmth, tingling, and a feeling of pressure in the upper part of the body, sometimes after eating Chinese food (Schaumburg et al., 1969). While many different ethnic foods have been reported as causing reactions, the phrase, "Chinese Restaurant Syndrome," caught on in the general press and with consumers.

Contemporary research on such response to glutamate in individuals with idiosyncracies of metabolism has followed two lines. The first involved the use of survey questionnaires with various groups in an attempt to estimate accurately the overall incidence of glutamate sensitivity in man. The second approach used typical biochemical and physiological studies, in an attempt to determine *how* glutamate might cause a reaction in sensitive humans.

Survey studies by Kerr and co-workers (1979, a,b) showed that some portion of the U.S. population will react adversely to any of a wide variety of ethnic dishes. According to Kerr, one or two percent of the general adult population may react negatively to MSG, compared to previously reported estimates of up to 25 percent of the population. These differences appear to be at least partly related to differences in questionnaire design (Kerr, et al., 1977).

Another study examined the minimum concentrations of MSG needed to induce effects in susceptible people, and concludes that when MSG is added to food at a concentration of 0.75% it is "extremely unlikely that any of the symptoms will be experienced by even a demonstrably sensitive individual" (Kenney, 1979). Furthermore, even doubling the use level to 1.5% resulted in only a few individuals being affected. Kenney postulated that the response to glutamate in sensitive individuals may involve stimulation of receptors in the esophagus, or be linked to reflex esophagitis (similar to heartburn).

OTHER DIETARY ASPECTS

The presence of MSG in a food is of interest to consumers wishing to control their sodium intake from two standpoints. Since it is the sodium salt of glutamic acid, its sodium content must be considered in evaluating the total amount of sodium ingested from all sources. On the other hand, since MSG's molecule contains only 12 percent sodium (compared to the 40 percent in table salt), its flavor-enhancing properties may sometimes be substituted for salt,

with a consequent reduction in total sodium ingested. Table 3 illustrates a day's menu and typical amounts of MSG used for seasoning. The meals in this menu contribute approximately 0.5 gm of sodium from the MSG, or about half the sodium allowed per day on a moderately restricted sodium diet (up to 1 gm). If low-sodium versions of all the foods shown in the menu plan were used, and no further sodium were added, the meals described would be well within the limits of a "moderate" sodium diet.

If *no* added sodium is permitted in the diet, there are also several commercially available forms of glutamic acid which are derived from non-sodium salts (calcium, potassium or ammonium). For further information on sodium see the IFT Scientific Status Summary on "Dietary Salt."

REGULATORY STATUS

Although glutamate is encountered extensively as a natural component of food and in human metabolic pathways, when it is used as a food additive it is regulated by a variety of government agencies. Because of its efficacy as a food flavor enhancer, MSG is specifically authorized in the Standards of Identity of many foods under Title 21 of the United States Code of Federal Regulations (CFR), but its presence must still be disclosed on the label. Among such foods are mayonnaise, french dressing, canned tuna, and breaded shrimp.

Recently, the Select Committee on GRAS Substances, commissioned by the U.S. Food and Drug Administration, issued a supplement to their report

Table 3. *Contribution of Sodium to the Diet by Use of MSG[a]*

Meal	Food	Typical portion	MSG use level	Sodium from MSG (gm)
Breakfast	Sausage	1 oz	0.4% (0.113 gm)	0.014
Lunch	Ground chuck	4 oz	½ tsp/lb (0.625 gm)	0.077
	Green beans	1 cup	½ tsp/4 servings (0.625 gm)	0.077
Dinner	Soup, canned or dehydrated	8 oz	0.5% (1.134 gm)	0.139
	Chicken	6 oz	½ tsp/lb (0.938 gm)	0.115
	Corn	1 cup	½ tsp/4 servings (0.625 gm)	0.077
			Total 4.059 gm	0.499 gm

[a]From Glutamate Association, 1978

on glutamates. Monosodium glutamate was re-classified to a more liberal status than that originally proposed (from category 3 to 2). The opinion of the Select Committee reads, "there is no evidence in the available information on . . . [all common forms of glutamate] . . . that demonstrates, or suggests reasonable grounds to suspect, a hazard to the public when they are used at levels that are now current and in the manner now practiced. However, it is not possible to determine without additional data whether a significant increase in consumption would constitute a dietary hazard" (FASEB, 1980).

The report goes on to state that there may be some persons who will react to relatively small doses of MSG because of metabolic idiosyncracies, and that research is underway on this phase of glutamate evaluation.

In Canada, MSG is considered to be a food *ingredient* which has functionality as a seasoning and flavor enhancer. Hence, it may be used at levels consistent with "Good Manufacturing Practises," provided its presence is declared on the label of prepackaged foods.

In short, MSG is a good additive which serves as a useful flavor enhancer. It occurs naturally in a wide variety of foods. In fact, one of its main functions as a food additive may be to restore the natural glutamate lost during storage, processing or cooking. At the levels now used, it has been shown to be safe for use by the general public in places which Professor Ikeda never envisioned.

REFERENCES

Abraham, R., Dougherty, W., Golberg, L., and Coulston, F. 1971. The response of the hypothalamus to high doses of monosodium glutamate in mice and monkeys. Cytochemistry and ultrastructural study of lysosomal changes. Exp. Mol. Pathol. 15:43.

Abraham, R., Swart, J., Golberg, L., and Coulston, F. 1975. Electron microscopic observations of hypothalami in neonatal rhesus monkeys (Macaca mulatta) after administration of monosodium-L-glutamate. Exp. Mol. Pathol. 23:203.

Baker, G. L., Filer, L. J., and Stegink, L. D. 1977 . Plasma and erythrocyte amino acid levels in normal adults fed high protein meals: Effect of added monosodium glutamate (MSG) or monosodium glutamate plus Aspartame (APM). Fed. Proc. 36:1154.

Baker, G. L., Filer, L. J., and Stegink, L. D. 1979. Factors influencing dicarboxylic acid content of human milk. In

"Glutamic Acid: Advances in Biochemistry and Physiology." Raven Press, New York, N.Y.

Cagan, R. H., Torii, K., and Kare, M. R. 1979. Biochemical studies of glutamate taste receptors: The synergistic taste effect of L-glutamate and 5'-ribonuleotides. In "Glutamic Acid: Advances in Biochemistry and Physiology." Raven Press, New York, N.Y.

Ebert, A. G. 1979a. Dietary administration of L-monosodium glutamate, DL-monosodium glutamate and L-glutamic acid to rats. Toxicol. Lett. 3:71.

Ebert, A. G. 1979b. Dietary administration of monosodium glutamate or glutamic acid to C-57 black mice for two years. Toxicol. Lett. 3:65.

FAO/WHO, 1979. "Guide to the Safe Use of Food Additives." (CAC/FAL 5-1979). Food and Agriculture Organization of the United Nations, World Health Organization, Rome, Italy.

FASEB, 1980. "Evaluation of the Health Aspects of Certain Glutamates as Food Ingredients." (Supplemental Review and Evaluation SCOGS-37A). Life Sciences Research Office, Federation of American Societies for Experimental Biology, Bethesda, Md.

Giacometti, T. 1979. Free and bound glutamate in natural products. In "Glutamic Acid: Advances in Biochemistry and Physiology." Raven Press, New York, N.Y.

Glutamate Association, 1978. MSG and sodium in the diet. Atlanta, Ga.

Hac, L., Long, L., and Blish, M. J. 1949. The occurrence of free L-glutamic acid in various foods. Food Tech. 10:352.

Heywood, R., James, R. W., and Worden, A. N. 1977. The *ad libitum* feeding of monosodium glutamate to weanling mice. Toxicol. Lett. 1:151.

International Glutamate Technical Committee, 1974. The remarkable story of monosodium glutamate. Washington, D.C.

Kenney, R. A. 1979. Placebo-controlled studies of human reaction to oral monosodium-L-glutamate. In "Glutamic Acid: Advances in Biochemistry and Physiology." Raven Press, New York, N.Y.

Kerr, G. R., Wu-Lee, M., El-Lozy, M., McGandy, R., and Stare, F. J. 1977. Objectivity of food symptomatology surveys. Questionnaire on the "Chinese restaurant syndrome." J. Am. Diet. Assoc. 71:263.

Kerr, G. R., Wu-Lee, M., El-Lozy, M., McGandy, R., and Stare, F. J. 1979a. Prevalence of "Chinese restaurant syndrome." J. Am. Diet. Assoc. 75:29.

Kerr, G. R., Wu-Lee, M., El-Lozy, M., McGandy, R., and Stare, F. J. 1979b. Food symptomatology questionnaires: Risks of demand-bias questions and population based surveys. In "Glutamic Acid: Advances in Biochemistry and Physiology." Raven Press, New York, N.Y.

Kirk-Othmer—Encycl. of Chem. Tech. (1978), 3rd Edition, Vol. 2, M. Grayson, Ed. John Wiley & Sons, New York, N.Y.

Lemkey-Johnston, N. and Reynolds, W. A. 1972. Incidence and extent of brain lesions in mice following ingestion of monosodium glutamate (MSG). Anat. Rec. 172:354.

National Academy of Sciences 1979. Survey of industry on the uses of food additives (NTIS #PB 80-113418). Food and Nutrition Board, NAS-NRC, Washington, D.C.

Newman, A. J., Heywood, R., Palmer, A. K., Barry, D. H., Edwards, F. P., and Worden, A. N. 1973. The administration of monosodium L-glutamate to neonatal and pregnant rhesus monkeys. Toxicology 1:197.

O'Hara, Y. 1979. Relationship between plasma glutamate levels and hypothalamic lesions in rodents. Toxicol. Lett. 4:499.

Olney, J. W. 1969. Brain lesions, obesity and other disturbances in mice treated with monosodium glutamate. Science 164:719.

Olney, J. W. and Ho, O-L. 1970. Brain damage in infant mice following oral intake of glutamate, aspartate or cysteine. Nature 227:609.

Olney, J. W., Sharpe, L. G., and Feigin, R. D. 1972. Glutamate-induced brain damage in infant primates. J. Neuropathol. Exp. Neurol. 31:464.

Owen, G., Cherry, C. P., Prentice, D. E., and Worden, A. N. 1978. The feeding of diets containing up to 10% monosodium glutamate to Beagle dogs for two years. Toxicol. Lett. 1:217.

Pitkin, R. M., Reynolds, W. A., Stegink, L. D., and Filer, L. J. 1979. Glutamate metabolism and placental transfer in pregnancy. In "Glutamic Acid: Advances in Biochemistry and Physiology." Raven Press, New York, N.Y.

Reynolds, W. A., Lemkey-Johnston, N., Filer, L. J., and Pitkin, R. M. 1971. Monosodium glutamate: Absence of hypothalamic lesions after ingestion by newborn primates. Science 172:1342.

Schaumburg, H. H., Byck, R., Gerstl, R., and Mashman, J. H. 1969. Monosodium glutamate: Its pharmacology and role in the Chinese restaurant syndrome. Science 163:826.

Semprini, M. E., Conti, L., Ciofi-Luzzatto, A., and Mariani, A. 1974. Effect of oral administration of monosodium glutamate (MSG) on the hypothalamic arcuate region of rat and mouse: A histological assay. Biomedicine 21:398.

Stegink, L. D., Filer, L. J., and Baker, G. L. 1972. Monosodium glutamate: Effect on plasma and breast milk amino acid levels in lactating women. Proc. Soc. Exp. Biol. Med. 140:836.

Stegink, L. D., Reynolds, W. A., Filer, L. J., Pitkin, R. M., Boaz, D. P., and Brummel, M. C. 1975. Monosodium glutamate metabolism in the neonatal monkey. Am. J. Physiol. 229:246.

Stegink, L. D., Filer, L. J., Baker, G. L., Mueller, S. M., Wu-Rideout, and M. Y-C. 1979. Factors affecting plasma glutamate levels in normal adult subjects. In "Glutamic Acid: Advances in Biochemistry and Physiology." Raven Press, New York, N.Y.

Takasaki, Y. 1978. Studies on brain lesions by administration of monosodium L-glutamate to mice. II. Absence of brain damage following administration of monosodium L-glutamate in the diet. Toxicology 9:307.

Takasaki, Y., Matuzawa, Y., Iwata, S., O'Hara, Y., Yonetani, S., and Ichimura, M. 1979. Toxicological studies of monosodium L-glutamate in rodents: Relationship between routes of administration and neurotoxicity. In "Glutamic Acid: Advances in Biochemistry and Physiology." Raven Press, New York, N.Y.

Wen, C. P., Hayes, K. C., and Gershoff, S. N. 1973. Effects of dietary supplementation of monosodium glutamate in infant monkeys, weanling rats, and suckling mice. Am. J. Clin. Nutr. 26:803.

Yamaguchi, S. and Kimizuka, A. 1979. Psychometric studies on the taste of monosodium glutamate. In "Glutamic Acid: Advances in Biochemistry and Physiology." Raven Press, New York, N.Y.

12

Critical Reading and Notetaking

Before the writer can do any critical reading and notetaking, two other jobs, discussed in earlier chapters, must be well underway:

1. The writer must have a fairly good idea of the structure and scope of the document being worked on. Such knowledge includes an accurate understanding of the situation behind the document—purpose, audience, and authorial stance—and a detailed list of questions and subquestions, the answers to which provide the material necessary to compose the document.

2. The writer must have a good list of available sources containing the information necessary to write the document. Such sources include books, magazines, interviews, and any other places the writer suspects good information might be found.

PREPARING TO READ

The effective reader has prepared well, bringing to the reading both an understanding of the subject matter and plans for using what he expects to find. If a writer begins to read without knowing what to look for, she should expect to find nothing! You will probably not find anything if you do not know what to look for. Imagine a game in which you are told to find *it,* and then are turned loose with no clue whatsoever as to what *it* might be. How quickly do you think you would find *it*?

Yet many writers read with no more idea of what they are looking for than the game player looking for *it.* The following examples demonstrate the importance of a writer's knowing what to look for before reading.

Tom Carleton is an oil company geologist. Every month he receives a list of available reprints of recent articles published by the Society of Mining Engineers. Included in the most recent list is the following title: "Stratabound Tungsten Deposits in Metamorphic Terrains: Stratabound Scheelite Deposits of Northeast Brazil." Tom is interested in tungsten, and he knows his company is always looking for new sources of the precious metal; however, he works in Texas, not Brazil, so he figures the article is not useful for him and does not order it.

Sheryl Ritt is an oil company geologist in the same city as Tom Carleton. She too is interested in tungsten. Particularly, she has been trying to find better sources of the rare metal. As a result, she has done considerable research into the areas where tungsten is most likely found, and is currently trying to locate such areas for her company to lease. She knows tungsten is normally found in three major areas: 1) volcanic-sedimentary areas, 2) metamorphic-sedimentary areas, and 3) alkaline lake brines. She has not heard of "stratabound" tungsten deposits, but she knows "metamorphic terrains" are a likely location for tungsten deposits. She decides to check further into this matter of "stratabound" tungsten deposits by looking up the abstract of the article in her company library.

The last sentence of the abstract causes her to order a copy of the entire reprint: "While such stratabound tungsten deposits are considered rare in North America, the hypotheses developed in this paper may open new areas for exploration."

Sheryl's ability to bring understanding and direction to her reading has made her an effective reader, and led her to an article she otherwise might not have bothered to check.

> Good readers bring meaning to the page; they do not just take meaning off the page.

EXERCISE

The title page of the reprint Sheryl ordered is shown in figure 12–1.[1] It is not exactly a book or a periodical. Find the example most like it in the sample entries in appendix II and devise a correct bibliograhic form for the reprint.

Working Outline of Questions

Ideally, before the writer begins to look for information, he has a specific idea of what information he seeks. You can organize this search by making a working outline of questions. For instance, George and Mary Barnes are considering buying a water softener for their home. They want to do some research before deciding whether to buy. Before doing any reading, they devise the following set of questions to guide them:

Major Question	Should we buy a water softener for our home?

Sub-questions	1. What does a water softener cost?
	   a. initially?
	   b. after installation?

---

[1] From J.C. Reid, "Stratabound Tungsten Deposits in Metamorphic Terrains: Stratabound Scheelite Deposits of Northeast Brazil." Preprint number 83-128. Published by the Society of Mining Engineers of AIME, Littleton, Colorado. Used by permission; all rights reserved.

SOCIETY OF MINING ENGINEERS
OF
AIME
CALLER NO. D, LITTLETON, COLORADO 80127

PREPRINT NUMBER
84-426

COMPUTER SIMULATION OF TAILINGS POND OPERATION
AND
SPREAD SHEET ANALYSIS FOR WASTE MANAGEMENT OPRIMIZATION

Jack O'Hearn

Morrison-Knudsen Company, Inc.
Boise, Idaho

For presentation at the SME-AIME Fall Meeting
Denver, Colorado - October 24-26, 1984

Figure 12-1. Title page from a reprint.

2. What are the financial benefits of a
   water softener?
   a. reduction in the use of soap and detergents
   b. plumbing and fixture value retained
   c. other benefits

3. Do the financial benefits outweigh the costs?

4. What health factors are involved with soft water?
   a. absence of calcium and magnesium
   b. cleaner clothes
   c. taste and odor of water
   d. other

5. Do all the benefits outweigh all the costs?

George and Mary did not make this list up out of thin air. They did some general reading, talked informally to friends who had water softeners, and thought about what they wanted. Furthermore, they do not consider this list finished; they know they may have more questions to ask. Rather, this is a working list, designed to be expanded as they find other relevant points they did not consider before. On the other hand, once they begin reading, if they discover that some of their planned points are not as significant as they had thought, they can cut an area out of their research. So although they do not have a final organization yet, they are further ahead than if they had just dived into the subject and started reading without knowing what to look for.

EXERCISES

1. Generate a list of subquestions for the following major questions:
   a. For building automobiles, is an assembly line more or less efficient than an assembly team?
   b. Are artificially sweetened soft drinks dangerous to your health?
   c. How can companies protect themselves from computer fraud?

2. For each of the questions in number 1, which indexes would probably provide relevant materials? Generate a list of at least five articles, five books or parts of books, and five other sources (interviews, sales literature, etc.) for each of the questions in number 1. In each case, how many of these sources are readily available to you?

3. Generate your own major question, one you would like to devote a good deal of time to over the next few weeks or months. Next, perhaps after some preliminary reading of introductory material if necessary, generate a list of at least five subquestions you think are important to answer in order for you to answer the major question. Finally, locate at least ten specific sources of information, all immediately available to you, on this major question and its subquestions.

The writer with a specific question, a plan for answering that question, and sources of information to fulfill that plan, is ready to read and take notes. In the working world of business, industry, and government, the specific question to write about is often inherent in the worker's situation. But the plan and the sources of information usually have to be figured out, by carefully analyzing the rhetorical situation and searching the library and other possible sources of information.

Recording What You Read

Armed with a question, a plan, and sources of information, the writer still needs a good recording system. If the writer loses the information she gathers, its relevance is rendered useless. A good recording system has several important features:

1. Each separate piece of information can be traced quickly and easily to its original source.
2. Each separate piece of information can be quickly and easily organized into meaningful patterns in relationship to all the other pieces of information.
3. Each pattern can be quickly and easily modified as further gathering of information makes changes necessary.

Evaluate some possible ways to record information by seeing how well they each stack up against the goals listed. First, one may think that a natural and simple way to record information is to start listing everything you read on a piece of paper. But how well does this system work?

Miller Fitzmaurice is director of personnel for a large electronics firm. Competition for the best talent is high in the business, and recently Miller's company has lost some of its top brains to other companies. Top management is upset at losing these people, but say they cannot compete with other companies' salary offers. The president wants to know, "What are we going to do about this?"

Miller has generated the following plan to attack the problem and found some good sources of information:

Major
Question   What reward system can management implement to both motivate outstanding employees to stay with the company *and* hold salaries down to a reasonable level?

Sub-
question
Areas

1. Outline the problem
    a. High salaries
        1. desired by employees
        2. offered by other companies
    b. High profits
        1. desired by stockholders
        2. undercut by high salaries

2. Raises
    a. Employees do equate salary with the value
        the company places on them.
    b. Guidelines for raises
        1. What constitutes minimum job
            responsibilities?
        2. What is over and above minimum and
            hence deserves a raise?

3. Bonuses
    a. As rewards for outstanding performance
    b. As incentive for doing more than the minimum
    c. As incentive for staying with the company

Miller reads several articles, interviews the company vice-president, and scans two books. His resulting sheet of notes looks like this:

Before asking for a raise, find out the relative level of salaries in your field.

Women are generally viewed as passive and easily coerced into accepting less money than they deserve.

Sometimes a raise request is really a request for a promotion.

A.K. Jones = $75K   Tally Ho Corp.

Jan Lamb = $89K   Burry, Inc.

Sales up in Smedley's division 78%

Foreman's job description does not include system design work, only operation

Pay in ways besides money

Set up fixed number of bonuses per division

Set up fixed dollar amount per division and let each divide it up as it sees fit

---

Miller's note sheet is not going to do him much good. First, he does not indicate where any of these ideas are coming from. Miller can easily fix this problem by adding a short note to each idea, telling its source:

> *Sales up in Smedley's division 78%—Corporate Report for 1983, p. 37.*

Such a note after every separate piece of information makes the total quite bulky, but Miller can lessen that by grouping his notes according to source, thereby recording the name of the source only once:

> *1983 Corporate Report*
>
> *Sometimes a raise request is really a request for a promotion. p. 4*
> *Sales up in Smedley's division 78%. p. 37*

If Miller goes one step further and lists his source in full bibliographic form, then he has his source information completed.

However, the clarity of the sources is accomplished at the cost of the clarity of the patterns among the pieces of information. In the example just cited, both points are from the same source, but they are not closely related, and they do not fit under any one heading in Miller's working outline. Yet Miller's use of a single sheet for his notetaking forces him to place these two ideas side by side because they happen to come from the same source. Miller can only indicate relationships among specific pieces of information by some system of lines, arrows, and notations, which will quickly become a real mess— hard to read and impossible to use. Miller wants to retain the clarity of his sources and also group his ideas according to subject matter, that is, according to his working outline. Furthermore, if Miller decides to change his working outline, he wants an easy way to change the relationships among his individual pieces of information.

A Note Card System

What Miller needs is a note card system, the key points of which are as follows.

1. Each note is recorded on its own individual 4 × 6 note card. To allow complete flexibility to reorganize the various notes in any order, the writer must be careful to place only *one* idea on each card. This way, any one idea can be placed in any relationship to any other idea; the writer can make almost instant changes merely by reshuffling the cards to fit a newly discovered relationship.

2. To solve the problem of source attribution for each note card, a separate 3 × 5 bibliography card is made for each source. Each bibliography card is given an identifying letter or number that the writer then places at the top of every note card drawn from that source. The bibliography card contains a full entry for the source, in proper bibliographic form.

3. Also at the top of each note card, the writer places the exact page or pages from which the note is drawn.

4. A final item at the top of each note card is some reference to the writer's working outline, so that he knows where he wants to put the piece of information in the final document.

5. Underneath the note itself, at the bottom of the 4 × 6 note card, the writer places his own comment, if any, about the note. For instance, the writer may want to point out a relationship between the note on this card and a note on another card. Or the writer may want to draw an inference from the note— his own idea, based on the note, but not actually contained in it. The writer must not confuse his own ideas with related ideas taken from other sources. To avoid such confusion, the writer's own ideas are always placed in square brackets.

A complete note card and a bibliography card using this format follow.

Bibliography Card (3 × 5)

> A
>
> Tellis, Marlene. <u>Women in Work</u>. New York: Lippincott, 1980.

Note Card (4 × 6)

> A, p. 35.   1. a. 1. High salaries desired by employees
>
> Women are generally viewed as passive and easily coerced into accepting less money than they deserve.
>
> [This may be the general view, but it is not accurate in my experience. The article by Alice Ossler also indicates that today women are no longer so easily pushed around.]

Even when you know the best format for note cards and bibliography cards, you still must determine when to take a note and when not to. Also, what does one put in the note and what does one leave out? Finally, are there different sorts of notes for different purposes?

First, remember you are taking notes for a specific purpose, the document you are writing. Therefore, you should take a note only when you read something that seems related to one of the points you plan to make in your piece of writing. As you take the note, you may or may not know exactly *how* you will use it; in fact, you may not use it at all. But since you cannot know whether you will use something while you are still in the notetaking process, take down everything that relates and worry about how to fit it in later.

Also remember that your vision of your document will probably change as the research proceeds. Notes taken at the beginning may not fit the document's final shape. Taking a note on everything that seems related as you read may mean you discard some notes later, but that is better than later wishing you had taken certain notes.

> A good writer works from an abundance of material, which can be cut down for improved clarity and conciseness.

Better to have to cut good material than to have to fill space with empty words.

As you read, however, you want to discover *good* material, not just large volumes of information. An effective reader, then, considers the following points throughout the information gathering process.

1.   *How up-to-date is the information?* Most information in technical fields has a short useful life. New discoveries, as well as changes in outlook, occur constantly. Therefore, the researcher should read the most recent information first and read with increasing skepticism as sources become less recent. The researcher should start with books and articles from the current year and move backwards in time for approximately five years. Sources older than that should be examined only if they have been referred to as worthwhile sources in the more recent literature.

2.   *How reliable is the source of information?* The researcher needs to be aware that every source has biases and preconceived points of view that may color the information it contains. The effective reader does not necessarily ignore information coming from a questionable source, but does take the source's attitudes into account when evaluating the information provided. About each source, the reader should consider qualifications for providing information on a particular point, methods and facilities used to gather and report the information, and degree of awareness about alternative points of view. Specifically, then, the effective researcher checks into the credentials of every source. The more impeccable the credentials, the more credence can be given to the information; the more questionable the credentials, the less weight can be safely placed on the information.

3.   *How specific and detailed is the information provided?* The researcher looks above all for concrete data on which to base conclusions. A book or article that says exactly what the researcher wants to hear but offers no concrete data is of considerably less value than a source that has relatively little commentary but offers considerable factual data. Often the best sources of information are not originally written with the researcher's point in mind at all, but contain specific information the researcher can use to support her own ends. Thus the researcher does not look so much for sources that agree with her as for information upon which to ground her own point of view.

4. *How relevant to the researcher's overall purpose is the information?* Often the researcher will read sources containing fascinating information on the general topic. However, this information may not be directly relevant to the researcher's piece of writing. In such cases, the researcher may be tempted to reorganize the writing to include the information or, even worse, to just stick the information in somewhere. The researcher must remember that his first priority is to support the case at hand, not to include all the best information. In other words, the *best* information is the most relevant, not necessarily the most interesting.

EXERCISE

Examine the following sources of information and comment on their probable usefulness for the major question indicated. What limitations does each source present?

a. *Major Question*   Should I drop engineering and go into the acting profession?
   Source   The *Hell-Hole of Acting,* by the Reverend James Dunnsdale, copyright 1909.

b. *Major Question*   What is the ideal computer, if any, for a small business to invest in?
   Source   "Those New Mini-Computers: Are They Worth the Cost?" *Business Review Weekly,* July 24, 1972.

c. *Major Question*   Can wind power offer a viable energy alternative?
   Source   "Thirteen Reasons to Go Solar," published by the Solar Arts Manufacturing Company, 1983.

d. *Major Question*   How much capital would be required to get into a fast food franchise on Southern Avenue in Las Vegas, Nevada?
   Source   "Franchising vs. Starting Your Own: A General Guide for the Potential Investor," by Hal Stinson, owner, BigBuns Hamburgers, Inc.

e. *Major Question*   How can we lessen the danger of hydrogen sulfide explosion at the Baytown refinery?
   Source   "My Most Dangerous Moment: The Night the Pump Reversed," *Reader's Digest,* May, 1980.

Once the writer figures out what information to put down on the note card, she must choose the type of note she wants to make from the four basic types of note cards. Each has its particular form and use. Definitions of each follow, including examples taken from "Elk Hills!" in chapter 11.

The Summary Card   For this sort of note, the writer wants only the source's main idea. Exact details are not important for the writer's purpose. Because the summary note captures just the source's main idea, it is much shorter than the original material. For instance, the writer may reduce a ten-page article to one sentence, or a book to a short paragraph. To make these changes, the writer must change the language of the original to his own words. Because it is unusual for a writer to be interested in a source's main idea but not its details, summary notes should account for only about ten percent of the total number of cards.

The Paraphrase Card   For this kind of note, the writer is interested in the source's details. While the main idea may also be important, the writer focuses on the particular, individual points made in the original material as it moves from paragraph to paragraph or even from sentence to sentence. The paraphrase note is thus roughly the same length as the original material, perhaps a little shorter. For instance, the writer may reduce a long sentence in the original material into a short sentence for the note. Or, the writer may want to use her own language to make the point fit more smoothly into the document being written. In paraphrasing, the writer should be careful to change the original's language into her own language. It is tempting to retain much of the original's language; however, to do so constitutes plagiarism, which should be avoided at all costs. If you are ever unsure about whether you have changed the original author's language enough to avoid plagiarism, then you should change it some more until you are sure. Plagiarism can result in legal action against the plagiarizer, so do not take chances with it. Usually, you can figure out language of your own that is just as good as the original author's anyway.

The paraphrase is the most likely form in which to record your notes. If you aren't sure how to record a given note, use a paraphrase. About fifty percent of the note cards should be in paraphrase form.

The Quotation Card   For those few times when the author's original language is so striking or close to perfect that any change will harm the idea's effectiveness, then quotation is the best choice. To make a quotation card, simply copy the words of the original source *exactly*, word for word, on your note card. Be sure to use quotation marks at the beginning and end of your note so that later on you will remember that this note is a direct quote and not just a paraphrase.

Several special conventions are associated with the use of quotations. The writer should observe these on the note card, rather than waiting until the final typing of the paper to change the quotations into proper form. Do it now, and save trouble later. The conventions are of two sorts: those dealing with deleting material from a quote and those dealing with adding material to a quote.

If you want to quote only part of a sentence, or if you want to leave some material out between two sentences, you must use a series of spaced periods (. . .) called ellipses. Simply indicate that you have left material out by replacing it with a series of three spaced dots. For instance, if the original sentence reads,

> Less well known are those which have been classed as "strata-bound and allied deposits," a category erected by Hosking (1971),

but you want to stop your quotation after the word *deposits*, then the correct way to quote this statement would be

> "Less well known are those which have been classed as 'strata-bound and allied deposits' . . . ."

In this case the fourth dot is not part of the ellipsis, but the period on the sentence itself. Or, if the deleted part of a quotation comes out of the middle of the sentence, then only three dots are used for ellipsis.

If you need to add some words to a sentence you are quoting, enclose those additions in square brackets. Then the reader knows the enclosed words are not part of the quotation. For instance, sometimes a writer wants to quote a sentence that uses a pronoun. The referent is clear in its original context, but not clear when taken out of context and placed in your document. The writer explains the pronoun in such a case:

> "In clastic rocks, he [Wiendl] noted that tungsten is as abundant in sandstones as in shale."

Square brackets are also used when the original material contains an error of some sort, or does not fit smoothly into your document's context. The error or problem may be repaired in one of two ways. Either fix the problem, but place the fixed word or words in square brackets, or leave the error, but place the designation [sic] immediately after it. (By the way, [sic] means *intentionally done so,* not *sick!*) For instance, the following sentence could be repaired in either of two ways:

> In many deposit, the volcanic components are apparently lacking. (Sentence as it appears in original)

> "In many deposit[s], the volcanic components are apparently lacking."

> "In many deposit [sic], the volcanic components are apparently lacking."

Occasionally, you may want to change a word, and may do so by using square brackets:

> "In many [locations], the volcanic components are apparently lacking."

Two words of warning about using ellipses and square brackets. First, both are used *only with quotations*. Second, neither should be overused. That is, if a sentence needs a lot of ellipses and/or square brackets to quote it, then it probably should not be quoted at all. Use a paraphrase instead. Your quotation cards should number no more than twenty percent of your total.

The Data Card   This note card is a quotation of numbers. Many times readers come across numerical information in the form of tables, charts, graphs, etc. Often this information is the most valuable part of an article or book, and the part that the writer most wants to incorporate into his own document. To do so, simply treat the table, chart, or graph as you would any other piece of information. Take a bibliography card on the source of the information, fill out the top of the note card just as you would any other note card, and then copy the table onto the card exactly. The data card simply quotes numbers. Such cards should number no more than twenty percent of your total, but they may be an important twenty percent.

The Notetaking Process

To see the notetaking process in action, let's consider the following note cards, taken from "Elk Hills!" in chapter 11.

Bibliography Card

F

Gilmore, Gordon R. "Elk Hills!" *Navy Civil Engineer* 19 (Spring 1979): 3–6.

Imagine that the writer is preparing an informational report on U.S. energy reserves. Following are some of his note cards.

Summary Note Card

```
┌────────────────────────────────────────────────────────────────┐
│                                                                  │
│                                                                  │
│                                                                  │
│   F, p. 3            IA, oil storage facilities                  │
│                                                                  │
│   The Elk Hills oil reserve, now administered by the U.S.        │
│   Department of Energy, is the third largest producing field     │
│   in the country.                                                │
│                                                                  │
│                                                                  │
│                                                                  │
└────────────────────────────────────────────────────────────────┘
```

This card has several problems. Two passages, all but the first five words of the sentence, are direct quotations. Dangerously close to plagiarism, the card is not really a summary at all. Furthermore, the page cited is the cover page for the article, not the page the information is on.

A better summary card would be

Summary Note Card

```
┌────────────────────────────────────────────────────────────────┐
│                                                                  │
│                                                                  │
│   F, pp. 3–6           IA, oil storage facilities                │
│                                                                  │
│   Developed during World War II, the Elk Hills refinery is now   │
│   a major oil and gas producer. In the past few years its        │
│   capacities have been considerably expanded, with still         │
│   more expansion both planned and underway.                      │
│   [This rapid growth is typical of the U.S. oil industry over    │
│   the past thirty years. It reflects the greatly increased       │
│   consumer demand for more oil and oil products more than        │
│   anything else.]                                                │
│                                                                  │
│                                                                  │
└────────────────────────────────────────────────────────────────┘
```

If the writer is interested in some of the article's details, then use paraphrase note cards:

Paraphrase Note Card

```
F, p. 4              IA(2), oil storage capacity

Elk Hills capacity = 1.25 million barrels of crude oil
[This is a large amount, but not a drop in the bucket should a real crisis come.]
```

A good paraphrase card; compare it with the following card:

Paraphrase Note Card

```
F, p. 5              II.C. (3), modern technology
                              high pressure injection

The high pressure injection facility was an urgent project to increase oil production. The
plant began in early July 1978 and around-the-clock construction finished in November
1978.
[It's amazing what motivation can do!]
```

In this case, the note itself is far too close to the original. It is a clear case of plagiarism, since no quotation marks are used. Also, the writer's comment at the bottom of the card is probably useless. If you cannot think of a comment, do not put one down. You may see something more significant about the point when you are writing.

Another paraphrase card follows:

Paraphrase Note Card

F, p. 3   IV, B who profits from
                 the high cost of oil

The oil from the Elk Hills refinery is sold commercially to private companies who make all the money on it.
[The government may be getting a cut or kickback on this, too.]

This note's form is fine, but an objective analysis of the article's first paragraph and the writer's paraphrase of it will show that the author claims things about the article that simply are not there. The writer has a purpose to prove and is determined to do it even if it means distorting the article. Of course, any careful and objective reader will discover this dishonesty and hold it against the writer. In fact, it could even call the writer's honestly made points into question.

Quotation Card

F, p. 6   III, A Ownership

"The land proposed for the rail loading facility belongs to the Bureau of Land Management (BLM)."
[Perhaps since the land is already under government control, the country as a whole could benefit from it faster in case of emergency.]

This card itself is done correctly, but the passage chosen seems unworthy of being quoted, since it is not stated in a particularly striking way. The point should have been made with a paraphrase card.

"Elk Hills!" does not have any sections calling for a data card and probably nothing needing a quotation card either.

EXERCISE

Examine the article about electrification. Then

a. Describe a rhetorical situation for which this article might be valuable.

b. List a major question and related subquestions relevant to the rhetorical situation described in answer to part a.

c. Take notes from the article, producing at least six note cards. Each should help answer one of the subquestions you generated in part b. Use all four types of note cards.

Finishing the Notetaking

How many notes does the writer need? Of course, no absolute answer to this question exists. But remember that a good writer works from an abundance of material. Certainly the writer needs note cards for every section planned in the final document. Of course, information may not be available on a given point. Then the writer must decide whether leaving the point in, unsupported, will help or hinder the document's overall purpose. Often it is better to restrict the report's scope to points you feel confident about, rather than stay with a broad scope you cannot cover adequately.

Periodically, the writer should stop during the notetaking process to take stock. For example, you can organize all the cards so far into groups according to the proposed outline. Are all the points in the outline being researched? If so, you know the outline is holding up well. If some points are not being researched at all (have no note cards), then perhaps the outline needs to be changed to reflect the direction the research seems to be taking. If you think the outline cannot be changed, then you must redouble your efforts to find information for the parts neglected so far.

The reading and notetaking process is over when every point on the outline is represented by at least several high quality, correctly written note cards. This happy event will probably result from extra scrounging after sources, much careful reading and accurate notetaking, and some reducing and/or changing of the original outline's scope.

Electrification talk is getting more serious

Interested railroads are ready to work with the FRA to study how a nationwide network of electrified rail lines could be shaped, financed, and operated. Primary goal: achieving fuel security.

Some major U.S. railroads are serious about electrification—at least about discussing its major aspects with the federal government. Surfacing recently at a conference sponsored by the Federal Railroad Administration, the railroad seriousness will remain a matter of public record worthy of attention from FRA under the Reagan presidency.

Also worthy of attention will be arguments in favor of electrification, especially in view of another matter the new Administration must consider, namely the national need for greater energy independence.

Southern, Conrail, Union Pacific, and Burlington Northern have all at one time or another undertaken their own studies of electrification. At an Oct. 22 meeting in Kansas City, high-ranking representatives of those roads told Federal Railroad Administrator Jack Sullivan that they were willing to take part in joint studies of specific crucial aspects such as financing, which no carrier could handle on its own. Spokesman for the carriers told *Railway Age* on Nov. 5 that the commitments remained intact.

ASPECT: GREEN

In Kansas City, Sullivan phrased the conference's major question as follows: "Assuming that we could overcome the capital barrier, would you undertake a serious discussion of an electrification program?" He got unqualified yesses from John K. Kenefick, UP president; Thomas J. Lamphier, BN transpor-

tation division president; John L. Sweeney, Conrail senior vice president; and Walter W. Simpson, Southern vice president-engineering. Some other railroads represented at the meeting have since expressed interest in working with the FRA.

As a result, FRA staffers are organizing four working groups to study: (1) the shape of an electrified system; (2) its financing; (3) technical and operating elements; and (4) interinstitutional elements such as environmental impact. In charge of assembling these study panels is Lou Thompson, who has been directing improvement of the Northeast Corridor for FRA.

"Electrification is an idea whose time, everybody realizes, is coming as much as it ever will," Thompson says. "It's time to get on with it and figure out whether there is a way to do it. The FRA has gone about as far as it can go with this, and now it's time for us to be dealing directly with the railroads. Otherwise, we're not going to get good answers to our questions."

Rail industry involvement will be crucial not only for analyzing but also for promoting electrification among energy alternatives. As Sullivan says: "Part of our getting together is to prepare our case for a known technology and known benefits. We have to get input from the railroads to really make a solid case."

FRA studies have centered on a 26,000-mile system of main lines handling 30 million gross tons or more a year. The system represents nearly 14% of all route miles but handles more than 50% of all rail tonnage, based on 1978 figures. Electrifying those 26,000 miles would mean that railroads' yearly oil consumption would drop by 56 million barrels, according to FRA. That's about half of current annual consumption.

THE GOAL: POWER SECURITY

"In the event of a petroleum shutoff, the rail system would be largely insulated," Sullivan says. That security seems to rank higher in proponents' minds than the savings in overall national petroleum use, because the rail industry already accounts for less than 2% of national consumption. Electrification could reduce that share to about 0.6%.

As BN's Lamphier says: "We have been very serious about electrification because we're more concerned about availability of diesel fuel than we have been about its price. The independence idea is very attractive to us."

An insulated rail system, however, would be free to handle increased traffic from fuel-short trucks as well as to continue handling its own loadings. "Apparently, during World War II, the Pennsylvania Railroad increased the flow of traffic over its electrified network by about 40%," Thompson says. "If the electrified network that we're talking about did that, the fuel savings would more than double because of the shift of traffic from trucks. So you can't look only at the rail mode's low percentage of fuel consumption. You have to look also at the truck mode's high percentage as reduced by greater reliance on a secure rail system."

FRA studies project a 14% return on investment for the 26,000-mile network over a 29-year period. Net annual savings would total $1.5 billion, for cumulative savings of $43.7 billion on total capital investment of $14.9 billion.

At the Kansas City meeting, Sullivan and Thompson cautioned that the shape of an electric network still needs a lot of study. Refining the configuration would be the duty of the planning panel, whose members would first have to define the criteria for deciding which lines would be electrified. Thompson says the FRA system proposal would be refined so that a working draft would be available for the panel's pondering. The panel then would try to produce a "quantitatively justifiable" system, one that could survive attempts to change it for purely political reasons.

FINANCING THE SYSTEM

The key panel, however, will be the one dedicated to producing a financial mechanism for a project that at first glance seems staggering in cost. The

Net Investments and Savings Due to Electrification

Category	
Route miles	26,000
Traffic (MGTM/Y)	945,800
Investments (million $):	
Catenary	6,040
Substations	2,620
Signal and communications	4,400
Civil reconstruction	1,660
Electric locomotives	5,240
Total investments	19,960
Credits (diesel locomotives)	−5,060
Total capital requirement	14,900
Annual costs and credits (million $):	
Diesel locomotive replacement	−281
Diesel energy	−1,500
Electric energy	1,110
Diesel locomotive maintenance	−1,360
Electric locomotive maintenance	409
Catenary maintenance	114
Net annual savings	1,510
Economics:	
Cumulative savings (29 years)	43,790
ROI	14%

largest single element would be the catenary system, estimated to cost more than $6 billion. The government would have to share the burden, but in such a way as to guarantee a recovery of its funds. One way would be a sort of variable user charge, based on kilowatt hours used, for payback to a federal revolving fund.

"We have to find a mechanism that permits payback on a basis that does not appear immediately on a railroad balance sheet," Thompson says. "Each segment could be financed by a revolving fund. Knowing the capital cost when completed and projected traffic levels, you would calculate the electrical energy needed, divide that into the traffic, and reach a prorated payment to be made for each kilowatt hour. Cost/traffic calculations would lead to the amount to be added to the monthly electric bill as payback to the revolving fund.

"The important thing is that this would take the payments off the railroads' balance sheets and convert them from fixed charges to user charges variable with the traffic. That's exactly the situation now enjoyed by the trucks and barges."

Thompson emphasizes that such a mechanism needs a lot more study, for administrative as well as functional reasons, but he sees it as probably the only workable plan. He also sees it as a way to deal with each railroad as a contractor, as the Federal Highway Administration deals with states on the Interstate system. That way, the government role remains more palatable than, for example, its role in Northeast Corridor renovation.

As for the term of payback, railroads could choose between 10 and 20 years. "According to estimates that we have, a ten-year payback schedule would result in nearly all the saving from electrification going for payback," Thompson says. "A 20-year schedule would have about half the savings going to the revolving fund and the other half accruing immediately to the rail industry."

OPERATING THE SYSTEM

As for the technology/operations panel, a major concern would be the signal and communications systems for an electrified network, differing from those for diesel operations. Addressing this major-cost element, the panel would also address a major-savings element, the reduced cost of maintenance for electric locomotives. At the Kansas City meeting there was wide agreement that maintenance savings would be significant, though there are differing estimates of just how significant. This panel, Thompson says, would attempt to answer all the questions for people who've never run an electric railroad.

One thing they won't have to answer are questions about electrification's fundamental technology. "There's nothing particularly exotic, or difficult, or even unfamiliar about it," Thompson says. "That doesn't mean it can't be made better, but there is just no argument remaining that electrification won't work or that it depends on major new technological advances for success.

"Many other countries are way ahead of any scale of electrification that we would ever be likely to discuss for the U.S. One good example is the Soviet Union, which runs an electrified railroad that basically runs the rest of the country. They are increasing the size of that system by about 600 miles a year. They regard the technology as proven enough for them to structure their economy around it." Supporting that viewpoint at the Kansas City

meeting was a technical panel consisting of AAR, FRA, and rail industry representatives.

ECONOMICS OF THE SYSTEM

The fourth study group would address interindustry or interinstitutional problems, especially those of the utilities. One question would be the utility industry's ability to handle increased demand from an electric rail system. In Kansas City, rail officers told Sullivan that utilities in their territories foresee no great supply problems. Agreeing was Blair Ross, an official of American Electric Power Co. and a long-time advocate of rail electrification.

Utilities, however, would face capital outlays for new units, transmission and distribution facilities, and traction substations. There would be state regulatory problems, too, along with environmental concerns.

But perhaps the biggest task of this panel will be to determine and defend the economics of railroad electrification, in the face of other alternatives for national energy security. One man who has been working on this issue for several years is Robert K. Whitford, a member of Purdue University's automotive traffic center. In August, Whitford completed a study for the U.S. Transportation Department that said rail electrification, using existing technology, is cost competitive with synthetic fuel plants now and "should be considered by the United States as a potential national investment of equal priority."

Such things as construction of synthetic fuel plants, gasohol production, and improvement in automobile fuel economy are limited in investment level by technology and other constraints, Whitford says. "In addition, the full output of synthetic fuel plants will be needed to supply automotive needs for a very long time to come. Railroad electrification provides another reasonable, economically compatible, fuel-conservation alternative without new technology constraints."

That, essentially, was Whitford's message at the Kansas City meeting, too, where he outlined the investments and savings of electrification along with those of alternatives such as shale oil, coal liquefication, biomass (grain), and automobile efficiency. He also compared the technology risks for each alternative, as well as energy efficiency and social/environmental impact.

FRA'S FINDINGS

FRA's own studies stem from the well-known preliminary report, "A Prospectus for Change in the Freight Railroad Industry," published in October 1978 in response to requirements of the 4R Act. An appendix of that report addressed the costs, benefits, and energy/environmental impacts of electrification as directed by section 901 of the Act. Findings were that certain route segments were likely to benefit significantly, although national benefits, especially in lower petroleum consumption, would not be large enough to warrant government sponsorship of a major program of rail electrification. FRA, however, proposed to support further research, and one result was an update of the appendix evaluation of costs and benefits published in 1978 and based on 1976–77 realities.

Released in April, the update shows that estimates of net operating savings from electrification have more than doubled since the appendix evaluation was made (investment estimates have "approximately" doubled). "Railroad electrification is a mature, demonstrated technology, and is the only mode for intercity transport of goods and people that can be shifted from liquid petroleum-based fuel without the need for additional technology development," the update said, before concluding that government support of a demonstration project is warranted. "While the demonstration project may also provide stimulus to other railroads to electrify, it is prudent that a more defined policy be developed by the FRA to provide incentives to electrification which are consistent with the expected social benefits," the update concluded.

The update also cites a major study completed last year by Gibbs & Hill, showing that electrification of Conrail sectors east and west of Harrisburg is technically and economically feasible. Discussing that study at the Kansas City meeting, Garry Collins, CR director of corporate planning, said the railroad has no doubts whatever about the economic benefits of the shift. One of the greatest benefits, he said, would come in reduced locomotive maintenance. Another would be in fuel-cost savings, which Collins said had likely been underestimated.

OTHER STUDIES

Another major study is under way, that of partial BN electrification, by Arthur D. Little. BN's Lamphier says the study already has shown that return on investment might be even higher than estimates by FRA for electrification in general.

Of a study in the early 1970s by UP, Kenefick says: "It looked quite interesting, but the price tag was $500 million, so we put the project aside. If the price tag had been lower, we certainly would have made a more detailed study and we probably would already be putting up the wires."

Southern, too, was an early studier, especially of its main line between Atlanta and Cincinnati. "We have never really stopped studying it," Harold H. Hall, SR president and chief executive officer says. At Kansas City, Simpson said Southern basically agrees with FRA on the benefits in general, but would like to see better analysis of locomotive maintenance savings in particular.

THE COST PROBLEMS

While agreeing on the potential for savings, the railroaders also agree that the potential costs are cause for some sober thinking, indeed. A good summary of those costs comes from Purdue's Whitford: "The major cost of electrification occurs in two categories: namely, in the fixed plant required to achieve electrification and in electric locomotives. The largest of the fixed plant costs per route mile is the catenary. Other costs involve the upgrading of the utility (both its generation and transmission capacities) to meet the added power requirements, substations to mate the power from the utility to the catenary, burying the communication and signal cables to reduce the effects of noise and interference, and the civil reconstruction necessary to ensure adequate clearance for the catenary.

"A conservative estimate of the fixed plant cost, according to recent, actual engineering data, appears to average about $500,000 for each route mile of single track and $800,000 per route mile of double track. In the second area of investment, the cost of electric locomotives on a per-horsepower basis, appears to be equal to or slightly below the diesel equivalent." He cites price tags of $900,000 for a 3,000-hp diesel locomotive with an 18-year life and $1.2 million to $1.5 million for a 5,100-hp electric locomotive with a 30-year life. He also cites electric locomotive capability of traveling 187,500 miles a year, compared with 125,000 miles for diesels, and a 25% higher general availability rate for electrics.

Such statistics are part of the reason for FRA's estimate that reduced locomotive maintenance could account for as much as 62% of the savings to be achieved by electrification, compared with about 26% from reduced energy costs. Churning out such estimates have been, among others, Curt H. Spenny and Frank L. Raposa of the Transportation Department's transportation systems center. They have the analytical tools that will be available to members of the industry-government working groups that Thompson is organizing.

But the railroaders have the experience needed for further analytical pursuits. "From here on out, if the idea's going to be developed it's got to be a joint effort," Thompson says. "It's got to have a lot of industry participation or it will never have the kind of credibility that it will need in order to move forward."

Thompson sees the panels as oriented toward "essential homework" on aspects of an idea whose merits, he says, are "essentially nonpolitical."

SUMMARY

Before the writer can read effectively, he needs to generate a working outline consisting of a major question and its related subquestions. The rhetorical situation behind the writing should determine the exact shape of these questions. The writer must also prepare for reading by generating a list of possible sources of information on the subject, including books, magazines, interviews, government documents, sales literature, and anything else one can uncover.

Once prepared to read effectively, the writer must use a high quality recording system. Such a system ensures that every piece of information is attributed clearly to its original source and easily organized into effective patterns along with all the other pieces of information that the writer gathers. The best system for accomplishing these tasks is a note card system. Four basic sorts of notes can be taken with this system: summary, paraphrase, quotation, and data.

When the writer has note cards on every point in the outline, he can stop taking notes, at least for the moment, and start writing the paper.

CASE IN POINT

The Evaluative Report

Because the writer should monitor the quality of sources and information while they are being gathered, one frequently writes an evaluative report during the course of a research project. In on-the-job situations, evaluative reports are also a way to assess the worth of a new or potential item or service. An evaluation does not have to take up a whole document though. Frequently, evaluative subsections are located within a larger document.

In an evaluation, the writer judges the value of something and offers concrete evidence to support the evaluation. The evaluative report usually contains the following parts:

1. Introduction.

2. Statement of criteria the evaluation is based on. Defense of these criteria if necessary.

3. Point by point comparison of the thing being evaluated with the criteria.

One sort of evaluative report involves making a judgment about whether something will work in a given situation. Typically, the writer discovers a method for doing something, which she then applies to a different situation to see if it will work then, too. For instance, reread the two-part article on acoustic emission testing in chapter 4 and then study the following evaluative report:

An Evaluation of
''Acoustic emission testing of FRP equipment—I and II''
for possible application at our Fresno plant

MEMO TO: Fred Jones
MEMO FROM: Gordon Pym
RE: Acoustic Emission Testing

Introduction
    We have had many quality control problems with our nonmetal containers. As most of these are made of some sort of composite material, we have been looking for a low-cost, reliable, and nondestructive test for such materials. Two recent issues of Chemical Engineering discuss just the test we may have been looking for. All references in the evaluative report that follows are to
    Fowler, T.J., and R.S. Scarpellini. ''Acoustic emission testing of FRP equipment—I.'' Chemical Engineering, October 20, 1980, 145-148.
    Fowler, T.J., and R.S. Scarpellini. ''Acoustic emission testing of FRP equipment—II.'' Chemical Engineering, November 17, 1980, 293-296.

Criteria
    As the authors explain, any good testing method must be nondestructive, must identify all defects, and must keep plant downtime to a minimum (p. 145). These qualities are especially hard to obtain in working with relatively fragile materials such as the composites we use in our plant. In part I of their presentation, the authors show exactly how composite materials behave acoustically when placed under stress (pp. 145-148). First, the authors define acoustic emissions, using a

clear graphic aid to make certain the reader understands
the basic principles and what to look for in the stress
waves that result from the application of stress to the
material (p. 145). The authors then move into the
behavior of composite materials under stress and again
use graphic aids effectively to show the reader exactly
what to look for in such a test. Using this general
information, we can apply these same sorts of tests to
our own situation.

Point by Point Comparison
        In part II the authors get into specific sorts of
tests for specific applications. Of interest to us are
the vessel and tank tests (pp. 294-295). The data
presented seem to clearly indicate that faulty vessels
and tanks can be detected using acoustic emissions
testing, and that most of the defects can be repaired so
the vessel or tank can still be used. Hence, the
criterion of nondestructiveness is met.
        Judging from the data presented, the acoustic
emissions test also meets the second criterion,
reliability. Generally speaking, test data indicate that
vessels and tanks passing the test are reliable, and that
flaws are detected even in some vessels and tanks
appearing to be all right after a visual inspection.
        Unfortunately, the authors do not present any
specific information on the third criterion of a good
testing method, cost. Thus, although acoustic emissions
testing appears to be an accurate and reliable testing
method, we have to find out more about its cost before
attempting to use it here.

Often an evaluation is not the entire document, but is embedded within a larger context instead. For instance, the article that follows on page 270 presents a process for measuring resin penetration into wood and concludes with a brief evaluation of the process.

WRITING ASSIGNMENTS

1. Select any article you have read in your initial research and write an evaluation of it, based on the following criteria:
   a. How well written is the article itself?
   b. How useful will the article be for the subject or situation you are working on?

2. Evaluate the memo from Mr. Pym to Mr. Jones using the criteria presented in chapter 1.

3. Write an evaluation similar to one of the documents used in this chapter. That is, evaluate a process for doing something in terms of how well it could be applied to a purpose of your own.

Method for measuring resin penetration into wood

M. S. White; G. Ifju; J. A. Johnson

Abstract

Knowledge of the depth of penetration of resin adhesives into wood may be needed in studying the properties of wood-adhesive joints. A method for measuring penetration depth is described. It involves the addition of meta-bromo phenol to the resin, removing thin sections near the glue joint after curing, radiation of the sections, and counting of γ-ray emissions.

There is evidence in the literature that penetration of adhesives into wood increases the bond strength between joined surfaces. Assessing the effect of this penetration on the properties of wood-adhesive joints is, however, a difficult task. Measuring penetration is difficult because, due to irregularities in the wood surface, penetration may vary considerably from point to point. This effect has been demonstrated by Hare and Kutscha (1) and Nearn (4). Figure 1 is a schematic representation of the adhesive/wood interphase profiles described. Many low-molecular-weight substances ranging from solvents (7) to vinyl monomers (2), and macromolecules (9) including urea- and phenol-formaldehyde resins (6,8) will penetrate wood. Hare and Kutscha (1), Quirk, Kozlowski, and Blomquist (5) and Smith (8) showed evidence of resin penetration and Nearn (3,4) reported that capillary penetration may be related to apparent interfacial failure.

A number of sophisticated techniques have been used with varying success to detect resin near gluelines in a wood-adhesive joint. However, these techniques have yielded largely qualitative information on the depth of penetration of adhesives into the wood. Thus, the objective of this study was to develop a quantitative technique for measuring adhesive penetration into wood around glue joints.

From M.S. White, G. Ifju, and J.A. Johnson, "Method for Measuring Resin Penetration Into Wood," *Forest Products Journal* 27 (July 1977): 52-54. Copyright © 1977 by Forest Products Research Society. Reprinted by permission.

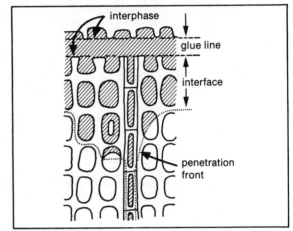

Figure 1. *Schematic representation of a wood-adhesive bond formed on the tangential surface of a softwood.*

METHODS

The substrates for this study were southern pine earlywood and latewood with microtomed surfaces. The adhesive, a resorcinol-formaldehyde resin, was applied to the surfaces at about 10 percent equilibrium moisture content. The resin was labeled with bromine (Br) by adding to it a known amount of metabromo phenol in a manner similar to that used by Smith (8). The resin was applied to the surfaces, and pressure was applied for 72 hours at room temperature.

Serial microtome sections on the order of 20 to 40 mm thick were then cut, starting about 0.5 mm on one side of the glueline and continuing through the adhesive joint to approximately the same distance on the other side. Care was taken to orient the plane of microtoming parallel to the plane of the joint. This procedure was similar to that used by Quirk, et al. (5). The position of each section with respect to the glueline was recorded.

Neutron activation analysis (NAA) was used to measure the Br in each section. This involved radiating the sections in a nuclear reactor and then counting the γ-ray emissions from the Br isotopes produced by the capture of thermal neutrons. Since the amount of Br in the tagged resorcinol was known, both from gravimetric and NAA determinations, the amount of resin in each section could be calculated from the Br concentration. A total of 22 bonds were analyzed each with 30 to 40 microtome sections for NAA.

RESULTS AND DISCUSSION

Data Analysis

Figure 2 is a typical plot of Br concentration in wood sections taken serially across a wood joint. The curve is quasigaussian with a flat top indicative of pure resin at the center of the glueline.

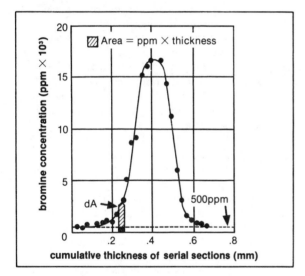

Figure 2. *Typical plot of bromine concentration in the vicinity of bromine-tagged resorcinol resin bond between southern pine latewood surfaces.*

Neutron activation analysis of southern pine wood without resin gave a background count equivalent to 18 ppm Br. Thus one would expect the Br concentration around the glueline to fall to this value. Figure 2 shows, however, that the concentration curve leveled off at about 500 ppm on either side of the glueline and remained at this level out to at least 0.5 to 0.8 mm from the gluebond. Two possible explanations for this result are: a) that the resin

penetrated deeply into the wood through certain tissues or b) that gaseous Br liberated from the resin during polymerization penetrated the wood. Microscopic observations of a few tangential sections after microtoming showed the presence of resorcinol-formaldehyde resin in some ray cells but most consistently in the fusiform ray cavities at depths of 600 μm and even beyond. Hare and Kutscha (1) have also demonstrated this phenomenon in eastern spruce plywood joints. Following this observation, a few specimens were prepared in which radial wood surfaces were glued together. In the radial specimens the ray tissues should play no role in conducting liquid resin into the wood. Neutron activation analysis of sections removed at various distances from the bonds between radial surfaces showed somewhat less than 500 ppm bromine but still substantially more than the 18 ppm previously determined for wood alone, indicating that ray cells are not the sole—and probably not even the major—route of penetration.

A comparison between the Br content of the fresh resin formulation and the polymerized resin in the bonds after 72 hours revealed that approximately 10 percent of the Br was lost during curing. Smith (8) also reported liberation of small amounts of Br from metabromo-phenol mixed with phenol-formaldehyde resin formulation during curing at high temperatures. We found that when small southern pine blocks with their end-grain surfaces epoxy-sealed were suspended over curing brominated resin for 72 hours, all sections of the blocks attained approximately 500 ppm Br content as revealed by NAA. Apparently the high vapor pressure of Br at room temperature causes the Br liberated during curing to diffuse rapidly into the blocks.

In order to compare penetration results, data such as those in Figure 2 were plotted in a normalized, cumulative form as shown in Figure 3. The sigmoid curve was obtained by dividing the incremental areas (shaded vertical bars in Fig. 2) by the total area and integrating over thickness.

The thickness of the glueline between the substrate surfaces was measured microscopically and located on the Br-concentration curve at the point on the abscissa corresponding to 0.5 cumulative Br concentration on the ordinate. The half-thickness of the glueline measured microscopically was then marked on each side of the midpoint, indicating the boundaries of the glueline. The intersections of these

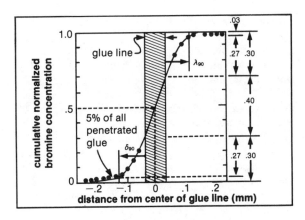

Figure 3. *Cumulative normalized bromine concentration as a function of distance around a gluebond of southern pine latewood surfaces.*

Table 1. *Mean Penetration Depth (δ_{90}) of Resin around Southern Pine Earlywood and Latewood Adhesive Bonds as Related to Reaction Time Prior to Application of Resin*

Reaction time (hr.)	Depth of penetration			
	Earlywood		Latewood	
	Mean (µm)	Range (µm)	Mean (µm)	Range (µm)
0.00	260	(20)	143	(0)
0.50	285	(30)	—	—
1.50	280	(40)	145	(60)
2.50	150	(30)	140	(80)
3.50	123	(30)	102	(40)
4.25	48	(0)	32	(10)

boundaries with the cumulative curve were used to determine the fraction of the resin included in the glueline (0.40 of the total applied in Fig. 3). It may be seen, in Figure 3, that resin concentration asymptotically approaches zero. Thus, it is impossible to measure accurately the full depth of penetration; that is, the depth of penetration that accounts for all of the resin applied to the wood. As an alternative, we decided to determine those depths that account for 90 percent of the resin, on each side of the glueline, that has penetrated the wood. These are indicated, in Figure 3, by δ_{90}.

Evaluation of the Method

In order to test the sensitivity of the method, southern pine blocks were glued together using the Br-tagged resin that had been allowed to polymerize for different periods of time before application. Partial polymerization increases the viscosity of resin adhesives, and this in turn, influences penetration. Table 1 is a summary of the results obtained by gluing together earlywood-to-earlywood and latewood-to-latewood assemblies using six different resin "reaction" times. Each tabulated penetration value is the average of two individual determinations.

First, it should be noted that penetration of resin into earlywood was deeper than into latewood, probably reflecting anatomical differences between earlywood and latewood. This difference in penetration may, in part, account for the low bond strength known to develop between latewood surfaces of southern pine. Second, increasing reaction time prior to the application of the resin resulted in decreasing penetration, the decrease becoming appreciable only after 1.50 hours' reaction time. This indicates that penetration is closely related to resin viscosity. Both of these effects were expected. However, this is the first quantitative demonstration of these effects for a synthetic resin adhesive used by the wood industry.

The procedure outlined in this paper may seem laborious and complex. However, the use of simple computer programs made the calculations quite simple and quick. Furthermore, measurement of resin penetration into wood by this method does not necessarily require a nuclear reactor since the Br content could be measured gravimetrically rather than in terms of radioactivity. In the case of urea-formaldehyde resins, simply measuring the nitrogen content of the sections may give accurate estimates of resin concentration. The real value of the method lies in the quantitative information it can yield. It makes possible, for example, calculation of resin concentration at various depths in the substrate if the rate of glue spread and the glueline thickness are shown.

REFERENCES

1. Hare, D. A., and N. P. Kutscha. 1974. Microscopy of eastern spruce plywood gluelines. Wood Sci. 6(3): 294-304.

2. Matsyama, M., N. Shirashi, and T. Tokota. 1972. Polymerization of monomers with the cell wall of wood. Makuzai Gakkaishi 18(10):489–494.
3. Nearn, W. T. 1965. Wood-adhesive interface relations. Official Digest 37(485):720–733.
4. ———.1974. Application of the ultrastructure concept in industrial wood products research. Wood Sci. 6(3): 285–293.
5. Quirk, J. T., T. T. Kozlowski, and R. F. Blomquist. 1968. Contributions of end-wall and lumen bonding to strength of butt joints. USDA Forest Service, Forest Prod. Lab., Res. Note FPL-0179. 12pp.
6. Rice, J. T. 1965. The effect of urea-formaldehyde resin viscosity on plywood bond durability. Forest Prod. J. 15(3):107–112.
7. Shirashi, N., K. Sumizoura, and T. Tokota. 1973. The interactions of wood with organic solvents. Makuzai Gakkaishi 19(5):241–249.
8. Smith, L. A. 1971. Resin penetration of wood cell walls—Implications for adhesion of polymers to wood. Dissertation, SUNY, College Forestry, Syracuse Univ., Syracuse, N.Y. 175 pp.
9. Tarkow, H., W. C. Feist, and C. F. Southerland. 1966. Interaction of wood with polymeric materials-penetration versus molecular size. Forest Prod. J. 16(10):61–67.

FOR FURTHER READING

Comprone, Joseph. *Teaching Form and Substance: A Left-Handed Guide to Teaching Students to Read and Write.* Dubuque, Iowa: William C. Brown, 1976.

DeBeaugrande, Robert. "Linguistic Theory and Composition." *College Composition and Communication* 29 (May 1978): 134–40.

Flower, Linda. "Writer-Based Prose: A Cognitive Basis for Problems in Writing." *College English* 41 (September 1979): 19–37.

Gebhardt, Richard. "Imagination and Discipline in the Writing Class." *English Journal* 66 (December 1977): 26–32.

Gunderson, Doris, ed. *Language and Reading.* Washington, D.C.: Center for Applied Linguistics, 1970.

Hirsch, E. D., Jr. *The Philosophy of Composition.* Chicago: University of Chicago Press, 1977.

Kolers, Paul. "Experiments in Reading." *Scientific American* 227 (July 1972): 196–203.

Stauffer, Russell. *Directing the Reading-Thinking Process.* New York: Harper and Row, 1975.

Williston, Glenn. *Understanding the Main Idea, Middle Level.* Providence, R.I.: Jamestown Publishers, 1976.

13

Logical Thinking and Organization

Anticipation grows; relief is on the way; the end is in sight. The writer finishes the process of gathering information and thinks, "At last I'm ready to make a piece of writing out of all this."

But a few more tasks still stand between the information gathered and the final product. The first problem the writer needs to tackle is organization. With the information all together for the first time, only now can the writer see everything that is going into the document. Only now can the writer make final organizational plans.

What the writer has at this point is a working outline and material to fill in that outline. In some cases this material has come from published sources, or from other kinds of sources outside the writer's own experience. In such cases the writer has a full and correctly written bibliography card for each source. In other cases, the writer supplies all the information from his own experience, so bibliography cards are unnecessary.

In any case, unless the document is very simple, the writer has placed each piece of information on a single note card. Even if all the information is from the writer's own experience, the note cards are still a good idea, because they allow the writer to organize the many separate pieces of information quickly and efficiently, and to experiment with many different patterns of organization without having to start all over with a new set of notes each time.

When confronted with many individual pieces of information, the writer must consider both the order in which to arrange them and that arrangement's logic. First, two logical patterns of arrangement and then two organizational patterns will be discussed.

The writer has two basic patterns of logic to choose from. She may use specific pieces of information to support a general conclusion, or she may use general principles to establish a specific conclusion. Of course, the two patterns may also be combined in various ways within any one document or within a single section. Before looking at some of the possible combinations, let's look in some detail at each of the general patterns of logic and their related organizational patterns.

INDUCTION: FROM SPECIFIC TO GENERAL

The organizational pattern known as induction works from the most specific facts to more general conclusions. The individual facts serve as evidence for the correctness of the general conclusion, which itself cannot be proved. An example of induction is shown in figure 13-1.

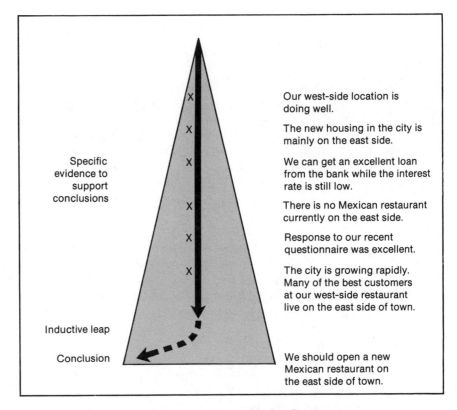

Specific evidence to support conclusions

Our west-side location is doing well.

The new housing in the city is mainly on the east side.

We can get an excellent loan from the bank while the interest rate is still low.

There is no Mexican restaurant currently on the east side.

Response to our recent questionnaire was excellent.

The city is growing rapidly. Many of the best customers at our west-side restaurant live on the east side of town.

Inductive leap

Conclusion

We should open a new Mexican restaurant on the east side of town.

Figure 13–1. Example of induction.

Observe these points about this particular inductive pattern:

1. Although the example lists seven points in support of its conclusion, those points do not prove the conclusion is correct. The inductive pattern merely indicates an increasing degree of probability, not absolute certainty. In other words, the Xs signifying individual supporting points never get all the way to the horizontal line that marks the conclusion. An inductive leap is always required. Of course, the more good evidence presented, the shorter that dangerous inductive leap has to be.

2. In the inductive pattern, the more factual and verifiable the evidence is, the more probable the conclusion becomes, assuming that the evidence does in fact support the conclusion.

3. The inductive pattern is open to question in three different ways:

▶ We may demonstrate or argue that the facts are sound, but they point to a different conclusion.

We should open *any kind* of restaurant on the east side of town, not necessarily a Mexican one.

▶ We may call into question one or more of the alleged facts being used to support the conclusion.

> Most of our best customers live on the west side of town, not the east side.

> The city's growth is tied to the copper industry, which is about to enter a severe slump, in turn causing the city's growth rate to slow down.

▶ We may present new facts, unrelated to any of the support points in the original pattern.

> There will be a new city and county tax rate schedule, aimed especially at curbing growth on the east side.

> Within the next two years this new schedule will cause a dramatic rise in the taxes on any east side commercial property.

In terms of organization, the inductive pattern is present any time a paragraph or document starts out with specific supporting points and ends with broad concluding points, as in the following example:

```
     Over the past five years we have lost holdings at
Thistle, Payson, and Mt. Pleasant. These losses have
reduced our arable land a total of 23 percent. As a
result, over the past five years our total output has
dropped 15 percent, and our profits have dropped 10
percent. This coming year we face the loss of at least
part of our Lehi and Pleasant Grove holdings. In all
probability these losses will cause further drops in both
outputs and profits.
     We have owned the Wood's Crossing parcel since 1966.
During all these years the land has lain fallow, probably
making it some of our most productive land at this time.
     Because of these facts, this office recommends that
the Wood's Crossing acreage be put into production next
year.
```

EXERCISES

1. Examine the following passage.

```
The following list includes the key facts about the
recent death of my daughter:

   1. At the time of the accident, Mrs. Johnson's car
      was out in the street down which my daughter was
      coming.
```

```
     2. My daughter tried to stop in time, but was unable
        to do so because Mrs. Johnson pulled out so
        suddenly.
     3. The damages to my daughter's bicycle were
        extensive.
     4. The weather was good, and Mrs. Johnson cannot
        blame the accident on any extenuating
        circumstances.
     5. The police were not called because Mrs. Johnson
        tried to get away as soon as she could from the
        scene of the accident.

Therefore, Mrs. Johnson is liable for damages in the
death of my daughter.
```

a. Is the above argument arranged in an inductive pattern? How smoothly does the argument flow? How might you rearrange it to flow more smoothly?

b. Is the above argument a good one, i.e., how probable is it? How much of an inductive leap does it require?

c. If you were on Mrs. Johnson's side, how would you go about attacking this argument? List as many specific ways as you can.

d. Create an inductive argument for Mrs. Johnson's side of the story.

2. Examine any newspaper or magazine you wish. Find an article or passage containing an inductive pattern used as support for some conclusion. A newspaper's editorial page is a likely source. Then answer questions a–c in number 1 for that passage.

3. Think of any piece of writing you have to do that demands an argument in support of a conclusion. Devise an inductive pattern to support the point you are trying to establish.

DEDUCTION: FROM GENERAL TO SPECIFIC

The deductive pattern is in many ways the opposite of the inductive. In the deductive pattern, the general points, called premises, are established first and the conclusion is the logical result of putting the premises together. Let's look at the diagram at the top of the next page.

Some of the most crucial points about the deductive pattern are

1. Since the conclusion in a deductive pattern is the logical outcome of putting the premises together, it establishes proof or certainty rather than probability. If the deductive pattern is set up correctly, the fact that the conclusion follows can be demonstrated with mathematical certainty. Any deductive

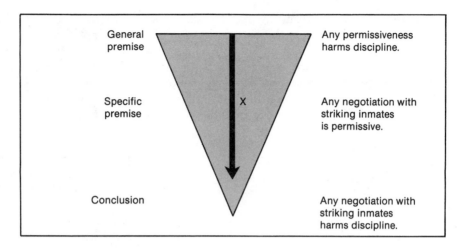

pattern in which the premises and the conclusion are related correctly is called *valid.*

A fun way to check validity is with a Venn diagram. Each of the three parts of a typical deductive pattern is used to draw a pair of interrelated circles, through which the validity of the whole pattern can be checked. See the Venn diagram for the deductive pattern just presented.

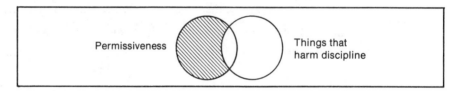

The shaded area indicates that nothing is present therein. The only part of the *permissiveness* circle left is the unshaded part—the part overlapping the *things that harm discipline* circle. In other words, anything left in the remaining part of the *permissiveness* circle automatically becomes part of the *things that harm discipline* circle.

Now add the diagram for the sentence, "Any negotiation with striking inmates harms discipline."

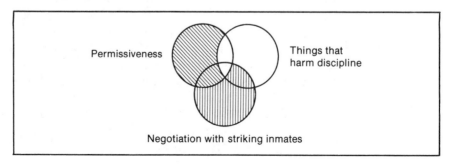

As the resulting diagram shows, everything left inside the *negotiation* circle is also inside the *permissiveness* circle, and nothing left inside the *negotiation* circle is also outside the *harms discipline* circle. Or in other words, the conclusion, "Any negotiation with striking inmates harms discipline," is a valid conclusion from the two given premises.

The Venn diagram can detect an incorrectly set up or invalid deductive pattern. Consider the following deductive pattern:

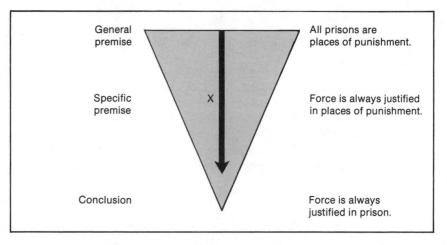

This deductive pattern seems valid; however, a Venn diagram for its three statements looks like this:

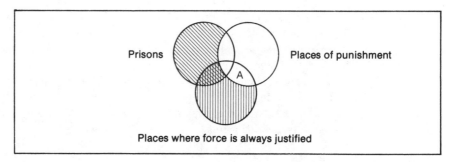

As you can see in the Venn diagram, there is one small area labeled *A* left *inside* the *places where force is always justified,* but *outside* the *prisons* circle. Hence, the deductive pattern is not valid in this case. It is important to note that the statement "Force is always justified in prison" is not necessarily disproven. This particular deductive pattern is proven not to be a valid support for the statement, but we have said nothing about the truthfulness of the conclusion itself. Deductive patterns work with truth not in the absolute sense, but strictly within the context defined by their own premises.

2. The proof or certainty of a deductive pattern is, therefore, completely dependent on the correctness of the premises. That is, a deductive pattern may set up a valid relationship within itself and still not be true, simply because one or more of the premises are not true. As the reader examines a deductive pattern, she must be careful not to be so impressed by the validity of the argument that she fails to see that one or more of its premises are not true.

3. The truthfulness of the deductive pattern is open to question in two basic ways:

▶ We may demonstrate that the deductive pattern is not set up correctly, i.e., that it is invalid.

▶ We may attack the alleged truthfulness of one or more of the premises. Then, even if the deductive pattern is admittedly valid, the argument as a whole is still worthless.

In terms of organization, the deductive pattern is present any time a passage starts with a broad statement and narrows down to specific supporting points. Notice that the deductive pattern of organization might not contain only deductive logic. In fact, a paragraph or a passage might be organized deductively (from large to small), and yet not have any deductive arguments in it at all. Organization refers to the order in which items are presented. Argumentation refers to the logical flow of the argument from support or premise to conclusion. It is perfectly possible to have one type of organization and another type of logical argument in the same passage. Consider the following example:

```
        My fellow citizens:
The time has come for us, the citizens of Tavis, to rise
up and put a stop to the constant car accidents caused by
the students here at the university. Our neighbors in
Canyon Heights, only five miles away, have far fewer
accidents than we do, and a much lower accident rate as
well. We all know that all college students are drunk and
unruly, and it is these kids who are causing the extra
accidents.
```

This passage is deductively organized because it states its conclusion in the opening sentence, and uses the rest of the paragraph to cite specific support for that conclusion. The passage also uses a deductive argument, that is, a pair of premises, which if accepted, undoubtedly yield the conclusion the author of the passage argues for.

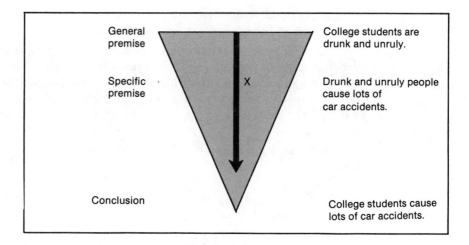

This deductive argument is valid:

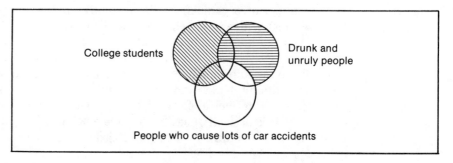

However, you might want to call into question the two premises. If either one or both of the two premises can be shown to be untrue, then the whole argument is defeated. The argument may be valid internally, but is just not true because it is based on false grounds.

EXERCISES

1. Examine the following passage and answer these questions:

   a. Is the above passage arranged in a deductive organizational pattern? How smoothly does it flow? How might you rearrange it to make it flow more smoothly?

   b. Point out both an inductive argument and a deductive argument in the memo.

   c. Is the deductive argument in the memo a good one, i.e., a valid one? Is it based on true premises?

   d. Is the inductive argument in the memo a good one, i.e., how big an inductive leap is required?

```
MEMO TO:  A.W. Able
MEMO FROM:  Georgette Babington
RE:  Recommended purchase of typewriters

After careful study of several different models
available, it is my recommendation that we order six of
the Delta 404X electric typewriters. My reasons are as
follows:

    1. The 404X is a little more expensive than the
       others, but you always get exactly what you pay
       for.
    2. The 404X is superior to the other models in the
       following particulars:
               a. twice as much memory
               b. better service contract
               c. faster delivery
               d. easier to learn to use
```

2. Examine any newspaper or magazine you wish. Find an article or passage containing a deductive pattern used as support for some conclusion. A newspaper's editorial page is a likely source. Then answer questions a and c in number 1 for that passage.

3. Think of any piece of writing you have to do that demands an argument or a proof of a point. Devise a deductive organizational pattern to support the point you are trying to establish. You may use any combination of inductive and deductive logic to support your point.

COMBINING INDUCTIVE AND DEDUCTIVE PATTERNS

The inductive and deductive patterns can be used together to form a powerful argumentative team. Inductive and deductive patterns can be used side by side, as in the memo concerning the 404X typewriter. An argument can also employ induction and deduction simultaneously, as part of one argumentative chain of reasoning, as in figure 13-2.

As you can see from the diagram, the above argument has the validity and airtightness of a good deductive pattern, and its major premise, usually a potential weak spot for a deductive argument, is protected by a solid inductive pattern leading up to it.

One can hardly attack this argument at the deductive level. It is certainly valid, and furthermore, the second premise, that the proposed plant is designed as a nuclear plant, is simply fact. Of course, you can disagree with the first deductive premise, but right away you are on enemy ground, since you have to

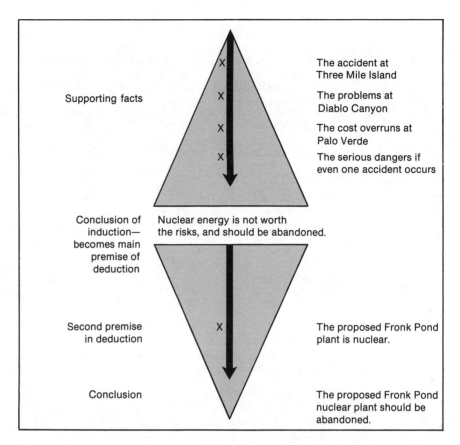

Figure 13-2. Argument employing both inductive and deductive reasoning.

at least comment on or rebut the inductive argument presented as evidence for the premise. An argument with an inductive pattern supporting the major premise of a deductive argument has an effective organizational scheme.

EXERCISES

1. Examine each of the following arguments and state whether each is inductive, deductive, or a combination. Then state whether the organizational pattern is inductive, deductive, or a combination. Finally, state for each how effective you think the argument is, and tell how you would attempt to counter it.

   a. Watch out for that car. The driver is a woman.

   b. The doctor found you have a temperature of 103, a swelling of the extremities, and nausea. You must have malaria.

   c. There can be even prime numbers, because 2 is even and it is prime.

d. Students at Atford High are poor sports. Two of their players were thrown out of last night's basketball game.

e. Over the past 10 years 30 different oil companies have tried to hit oil in that county. Not one has succeeded. Therefore, I don't think that is a good county for oil, and we should not lease any property there.

2. Think of a subject of your own and a rhetorical situation in which that subject is taking place. Now devise a combination inductive/deductive argument to support a point concerning this subject. If you were the opponent of this argument, what countering devices or arguments could you use?

LOGICAL FALLACIES

Whenever you are working with the logical patterns of induction and deduction, you should be careful not to commit an error in logic. Certain errors are so frequently made that they are grouped together as logical fallacies.

> A wary reader is alert to such fallacies, and a wise writer avoids them.

Many logical fallacies have been identified over the centuries. They may be given slightly different names and shapes by different writers, but they can always be divided into three major groups: fallacies resulting from a misuse of induction, fallacies resulting from a misuse of deduction, and fallacies based on a substitution of emotions for any attempt at logic at all.

Fallacies of Induction

The Hasty Generalization   The writer bases her conclusion on too little evidence. Because the volume of data is low, the probability of the conclusion is small.

> We hired an engineer from Kuwait once and his English was terrible. All foreigners are poor in English.

To protect against the charge of hasty generalization, you must prove that the sample does represent the total population from which it is drawn. Because modern pollsters have reliable sampling methods, they can accurately predict election results with less than one percent of the votes counted—if that one percent of the counted votes is drawn from sample precincts known to be representative.

The Nonsequitur There may be enough data, but they do not lead to the stated conclusion. *Nonsequitur* simply means *it does not follow.*

> Every time I get nervous about money, I start eating doughnuts and get sick. I must be allergic to doughnuts.

Often the best way to demonstrate a nonsequitur is to show a different conclusion following from the same data.

> Perhaps the nervousness makes me sick, not the doughnuts.

The Post Hoc A special type of nonsequitur, post hoc is short for *post hoc, ergo propter hoc,* or *after this, therefore because of this.*

> Over the past five years we have seen a dramatic increase in the suicide rate. During the previous five-year period, we documented a dramatic rise in the number of people eating out at fast food places. Thus, poor quality food is making people miserable.

The mistake the writer makes here is to assume that because event B follows event A in time, therefore event A causes event B. But of course, the two may be totally unrelated, or event A may be an umbrella phenomenon masking the true cause of event B. In fact, causation is notoriously difficult to prove.

> As soon as he was elected, taxes went up. Therefore, he must have broken his campaign promise and raised taxes.

Fallacies of Deduction

Faulty Classification The writer asserts incorrectly that the second premise falls into the class generalized in the first premise. But the specific instance may *not* fall into the same class as the general premise, as in the following example:

> Sugar is safe for people to eat. My diabetic uncle is a person. Therefore, it is safe for my uncle to eat sugar.

Equivocation This is a special type of faulty classification. The writer uses the same word or words in his premises, but they change meanings from one premise to the other. Thus the argument may look valid, but the second premise does not actually fit the reality of the first—it fits the name only.

> Aunt Thelma is a very busy person. Busybodies should be ostracized from good society. Aunt Thelma should be ostracized from good society.

Begging the Question   Sometimes, instead of presenting a specific instance of a general class, the writer simply restates or assumes the truthfulness of the general premise. Such an argument is mere circular reasoning, or assuming the truthfulness of the point supposedly being proven.

> I don't really want to quit smoking, because if I did, I would be able to.

Fallacies of Emotion

The Red Herring   Sometimes when the argument gets rough, the writer may simply try to change the subject altogether. Raising a false or irrelevant issue is called a red herring.

> The drinking age should be lowered to sixteen. Sixteen-year-olds are people, too!

Red herrings have several variations.

The Ad Hominem   Instead of debating the issues, the writer may attack the person being debated. Name calling is a simpler name for this fallacy.

> We need pay no attention to Jones' argument on the city sales tax—he has been divorced four times.

Bandwagon   Instead of debating the issues, the writer may assert that everyone already agrees. "Everyone's doing it" and "get with it" are popular forms of this fallacy.

> Thirty-seven other states have ratified it already—it must be good.

Appeal to _____   The writer may play on almost any emotion by appealing to it instead of to the logical merits of the situation being debated. Such an argument is aimed not at the issues involved, but directly at the reader's emotions. Appeals to emotions are often extremely effective, but they are not logical. Appeals to country loyalty, pity, racial prejudice, sexual stereotype, or just plain sex, are a few of the many possible emotionally based appeals. Similarly, the writer may try to hide the weakness of his argument under an emotional tone, such as humor, bravado, sarcasm, or irony.

> My fellow Americans, let us resist, as did our forefathers at Valley Forge, the evils of the dole. Any red-blooded American would.

EXERCISE

Using magazines or newspapers, find examples of at least three of the logical fallacies discussed. Advertisements, editorials, and letters to the editor are especially good places to check for such fallacies.

OTHER PATTERNS OF ORGANIZATION

Induction and deduction are especially helpful logical patterns for use in argumentative contexts. However, other patterns of development can be effective in informational contexts, although useful in argumentative contexts as well.

First, the chronological pattern is based on a simple time framework. For instance, to describe the history of something, the writer would naturally employ a chronological pattern of development. In argumentative contexts, an introductory section giving the history of the conflict is the place for a chronological pattern.

Second, in the spatial pattern of development, the document is organized around a physical sense of space. For example, a writer reporting on the inventory in a warehouse might move spatially, from row to row or section to section in the warehouse. Again, primarily a pattern useful for informative situations, the spatial organization is sometimes needed in an argumentative context as well. For instance, Mrs. Johnson's quarrel with the dead girl's parents might be decided by a carefully organized spatial account of the scene of the accident.

In addition to the four general patterns of development discussed in chapter 4 (thesis, original research, problem/solution, and theory/application), and the four patterns discussed so far in this chapter (deductive, inductive, chronological, and spatial), several others are possible:

- Cause to effect
- Effect to cause
- Steps in a process

Just as there is no absolutely correct pattern of argumentation, there is no absolutely correct pattern of development. The writer must examine carefully the rhetorical situation, including the purpose, audience, and authorial stance, and select the pattern of development that best fits the situation.

However, a few generalizations can be made about when and where to use some of the organizational and argumentative patterns. Business, industry, and government much prefer the deductive organizational pattern. Unless there is a good reason not to, the writer should get the major point in front of the reader right away, usually in the first sentence. Then the most important supporting detail should come next, and so on until all the points are covered.

The crucial opening sentence should never be wasted with empty phrases such as the following:

> This is a report of our attendance at the meeting with the Philby group.
>
> I would like to respond to your letter of May 25.

If the writer needs to inform the reader of the letter's context or background, he can do so in a subject or reference line, thus freeing the document's first sentence for a clear and forceful statement of the main idea:

```
Mr. Tom Chambers
Colab International Corp.
Memphis, Tennessee 23804

RE:  May 25th meeting with the Philby group


Dear Mr. Chambers:
    Our subcommittee unanimously agrees that we should
proceed with the proposed merger with the Philby group as
soon as possible. The reasons for our recommendation,
worked out at our recent meeting with the Philby
representatives, are as follows:
```

One situation often calls for the inductive pattern: if the writer faces an argumentative situation and a hostile audience, it may be best not to start right off with a statement sure to raise the audience's disapproval. It might be better to build your case inductively, point by point, before hitting the audience with the punch line. In other words, you sneak up on the enemy.

But for all informative writing and for argumentative situations in which the audience is *not* known to be hostile, the up front, deductive pattern is best. Also, certain audiences want the deductive pattern. For instance, an executive audience almost always requires it. A busy executive does not have time to read all the details of a lengthy report, so she wants to get right to the main point, which is usually placed at the beginning in the form of an executive summary or abstract. The executive's job is to make decisions, and in most cases she has already made a decision when she finishes reading the abstract or summary, especially if that decision is a negative one.

Conversely, the technician or operator, who carries out the instructions of others, does not want to make any decisions. The operator does not want to exceed his authority, even to make a correct decision, and is especially vulnerable if caught making an incorrect one. Hence the natural reaction is to avoid decisions altogether. So this audience wants clarity, with the overall point of the directions stated at the start and then the details following in an orderly inductive list. In this situation, the list of facts does not support any conclusion, as in an argument, but simply lists the step-by-step instructions needed to do the job. Thus, the chronological or spatial pattern is probably the best organizational choice.

When selecting a pattern of organization, remember that the demands of the purpose, audience, and authorial stance must come before any attempted application of a general rule. The writer should never choose a pattern merely because it fits the general rule better.

> In effective writing, what works in the specific situation is the thing to choose.

CREATING ORGANIZATION

Once the writer has gathered all the information, she should check the working outline to see how well it holds up. Sometimes the proposed organization fits the gathered information well, but more often, the writer finds at least some places where the old organization does not fit the new information.

Schematically, the situation the writer faces at this point looks like the following diagram. In this working outline, each X represents a note card containing one idea.

    I. X X X
       A. X X X X
       B. X
       C. X X X X X
       D. X X X

   II. A. X X X
       B. X X X X X X
       C. X X X

  III. A. X X X X
       B. X X X X X

  IV. A. X X X X
       B. X X
       C. X X X

The writer can see that things are going well. Every point in the working outline has at least one note card to support it. The writer may be worried about points IB and IVB, because they have only one and two note cards respectively. The writer has several choices about these two possibly weak areas. He can read the note cards and decide that although they are small in quantity, they are large enough in quality to support the point. Or the writer may decide to gather more information on those two points to generate a little more support. Or the writer may combine the weak sections with other stronger sections. Or, of course, the writer may delete the weak areas altogether.

Similarly, the writer may be concerned about the order of the sections now that all the information is gathered. Perhaps I and II ought to switch places, or IA and IB, or even IIB and IIIA, etc. The writer must confront every possibility with the same basic question in mind: does it fit the rhetorical situation in the best way or not? If the writer has done the job correctly up to now, the information can be easily switched around, and organizational patterns can be tried on for size. When the information is all in and the organization is all set, the writer can finally write a draft.

The Organizing Process

By tracing the organizing process step by step in the following example, you can see its important contribution to the overall content and shape of the final product.

> The time has come for us, the citizens of Tavis, to rise up and put a stop to the constant car accidents caused by the students here at the university. Our neighbors in Canyon Heights, only five miles away, have far fewer accidents than we do, and a much lower accident rate as well. We all know that all college students are drunk and unruly, and it is these kids who are causing the extra accidents.

A committee of students was assigned by the university to investigate these charges and respond. The committee's initial organization and preliminary collection of information looked like this:

```
Working Outline
    I. What has caused the townspeople to accuse the
       students of being responsible for the accidents?

          Relevant Note Cards

          X Population of Tavis = 8,000
          X Population of Tavis during school months =
            15,500
          X Population of Canyon Heights = 16,500 year
            round
```

```
            X Accidents in last five years in Tavis
              = 150
            X Accidents in last five years in Canyon
              Heights = 38
            X 130 out of the 150 accidents were during the
              school months


  II. Who is actually involved in the accidents?

            Relevant Note Cards

            X 70 of the 150 accidents involved students
            X 94 of the 150 accidents involved townspeople
            X 80 of the 150 accidents did not involve
              students
            X 56 of the 156 accidents did not involve
              townspeople

 III. Are there other factors besides students causing the
      high number of accidents?

            Relevant Note Cards

            X Both cities have a hard winter with snow and
              ice on the roads often during the same months
              the students are in school
            X In Tavis the basic speed limit in unposted
              zones is 35 MPH
            X In Canyon Heights the basic speed limit in
              unposted zones is 25 MPH
```

Upon seeing all this information together, the students quickly decided to do a little more information gathering from police accident reports. Then they established the following general outline for their document:

```
    I. The reasons the townspeople have blamed the
       students for the high number of accidents (deductive
       organization)
   II. Facts about those involved in the accidents
       (inductive organization), with conclusion that since
       more townspeople were involved in accidents, they
       were also more responsible
  III. A counter proposal to explain the responsibility for
       the accidents (inductive argument)
   IV. A suggestion for bringing down the number of
       accidents without removing the students (combination
       of inductive and deductive arguments)
```

The final outline of the students' report, including relevant notes, is as follows:

I. The townspeople have some evidence for blaming the students for the high number of accidents
   A. The populations of Tavis and Canyon Heights are roughly the same during the school year
   B. During the last five years, Tavis has had 150 car accidents, while Canyon Heights has had only 38
   C. Of these 150 accidents, 130 happened during the school year

II. Significant facts about involvement in the accidents
   A. Of the 150 accidents, 80 involved students
   B. Of the 150 accidents, 94 involved townspeople
   C. Since more townspeople than students were involved in the accidents, it follows that they must be more responsible

III. Another possible explanation for the high number of accidents
   A. Of the 38 accidents in Canyon Heights, none involved cars going over 35 MPH in an unposted zone
   B. In Canyon Heights, the speed limit in unposted zones is 25 MPH
   C. Of the 150 accidents in Tavis, 134 involved cars going over 35 MPH in an unposted zone
   D. In Tavis, the speed limit in unposted zones is 35 MPH
   E. The evidence suggests that the higher unposted speed limit in Tavis is more dangerous than that in Canyon Heights, and is therefore causing the high number of accidents

IV. The high number of accidents in Tavis will be improved by lowering the speed limit, not by getting rid of student drivers
   A. The evidence shows that the Tavis unposted speed limit is dangerous
   B. Dangerous speed limits should be changed
   C. The Tavis unposted speed limit should be changed
   D. Since more accidents involved the higher unposted speed limit than involved students, that speed limit is a more likely cause of the high number of accidents than are the students

By comparing the three versions of the students' report, you can clearly see how the organizing process improved both the content and the structure of the final document. First, the students used a working outline to guide their search for information. Second, they looked carefully at the information they had gathered, and made appropriate adjustments in their working outline. Finally, they gathered some very specific additional information, generated a final organization for their report, and put all the necessary information into the final outline. The final report was not radically different in structure from the original working outline. Most of the information the students gathered was used in the final report. But in the cases of both the outline and the information, the students did not hesitate to make the changes that they saw would improve the report. Careful planning *and* effective changes in the plan make a well-written report.

SUMMARY

The effective writer generates a working outline and gathers information to fill that outline. As the information gathering process proceeds, the writer may change the outline and search for different pieces of information. When all the information appears to be gathered, the writer examines both the information and the outline to see how well the two line up.

In general, the writer has two basic argumentation logics to select from. The inductive argument moves from specific to general and the deductive argument moves from general to specific. Inductive argumentation may be called into question by denying some of the alleged facts supporting it, by demonstrating that the same facts could support a different conclusion, or by bringing new facts to bear on the conclusion. The deductive argument may be called into question by showing that its premises have been put together incorrectly (making it invalid), or by attacking the truthfulness of the premises.

An organizational pattern refers merely to the order in which items appear, not to their logical relationships. An inductive organizational pattern starts with evidence and builds up to a conclusion. A deductive organizational pattern starts with the conclusion and then supports it with evidence.

In general, the deductive organizational pattern is preferred in informational writing and in argumentative writing directed to a nonhostile audience. The inductive pattern may be the best choice for cases of argumentative writing directed to a hostile audience. Other patterns especially useful for informative writing include chronological, spatial, cause-effect, and steps in a process.

Various logical fallacies are associated with inductive reasoning, deductive reasoning, and emotional nonreasoning. The inductive fallacies include hasty generalization, nonsequitur, and post hoc. The deductive fallacies include faulty classification, equivocation, and begging the question. The emotional fallacies include red herring, ad hominem, bandwagon, and appeals to almost any emotion.

Once the writer has arranged the best possible information in the most effective logical and organizational pattern, he can begin a draft. However, *best possible* is definable only in terms of the purpose, audience, and authorial stance inherent in the situation behind the writing.

CASE IN POINT

The Decision Package

The writer working with logical patterns of development is usually arguing a point, not merely passing on information. One of the most common argumentative formats used throughout business, industry, and government is the decision package.

In it, the author tries to convince some authority to take the action recommended by the decision package. In this format, the author is in the position of having superior knowledge about the recommendation, but of needing the power or authority to carry out the needed action.

Hence the decision package is inherently argumentative, and makes full use of both the inductive and deductive patterns and arguments. Most companies have their own specialized decision package formats, tailored to the specific requirements of their particular business. The following format is a generalized plan taken from several different sources.

Format for Decision Package   The decision package should provide detailed information on each of the following points.

▶ State the purpose or objective of the package.

▶ If the proposed action is presently being accomplished in some other way, indicate what that way is.

▶ State the specific action necessary to implement this package.

▶ State whether this package can be accomplished through a one-time effort, or would require ongoing support.

▶ If this package would require ongoing support, state the exact nature and amount of that support.

▶ State the benefits of adopting this package.

▶ State other possible ways of accomplishing the purpose or objective of this package.

▶ State the consequences of not adopting this package.

An example of a decision package using this general format follows.

THE COMPANY CAFETERIA

A Decision Package

1. Purpose

The purpose of this decision package is to urge the Newburn Manufacturing Company to build a cafeteria on the plant grounds.

2. Present Situation

Presently there is no place on the plant grounds for employees either to purchase or to eat their lunches. As a result, all employees have to travel several miles, either to eat their lunch at the park or to buy lunch at a fast food place. Employees are consistently late in returning from lunch. Furthermore, employees tend to congregate in cliques rather than develop the spirit of cooperation and togetherness that we would like to see.

3. Implementation

Starting a cafeteria on the plant grounds would require

- construction of a cafeteria building, including all appliances and other facilities necessary to operate a cafeteria

- provision for initial start-up capabilities, including all materials, food, and personnel necessary to begin serving lunches to approximately 200 employees

4. Support

The basic construction of the cafeteria would be a one-time expense of approximately $150,000. An initial, one-time start-up fund of $50,000 would be necessary to provide the cafeteria with equipment, food, supplies, and personnel, according to the following schedule:

equipment (silverware, hand appliances, bowls, trays, tables, chairs, etc.)	$25,000
food (two months' worth of staple items, plus the first months' worth of perishables)	$5,000
supplies (nonrenewable items, such as napkins, soap, cleansers, etc.)	$2,500
personnel (one month's salary and benefits for eight employees)	$12,200
emergency contingency fund	$5,300
one-time initial start-up funds required	$50,000

Once the cafeteria got going, it would be self-supporting, generating enough revenue to pay its own operating expenses.

5. Ongoing <u>Expenses</u>
    The approximate ongoing monthly expenses associated with the cafeteria would be as follows:

<u>maintenance</u> <u>and</u> <u>janitorial:</u> The present plant custodial contractor has indicated he would be glad to take over the janitorial work on the new cafeteria for an additional 15 percent over his current wage $700
<u>food:</u> average cost of food to the cafeteria per meal served is $0.75 times 200 meals per day times 20 days per month $3,000
<u>personnel:</u> seven individuals at an average salary of $10.00 per hour for 20 hours per week $5,600
<u>benefits:</u> 25 percent of the salaries $1,400
<u>accountant/bookkeeper</u> (including benefits) .. $2,500
<u>total</u> <u>monthly</u> <u>operating</u> <u>expenses:</u> $13,200

<u>Income</u> <u>generated</u> <u>from</u> <u>the</u> <u>cafeteria</u>
Average meal price per worker equals
$4.00 per day <u>times</u> <u>200</u> <u>workers,</u> <u>times</u>
<u>20</u> <u>days</u> <u>per</u> <u>month</u> $16,000

6. Benefits <u>of</u> <u>Adoption</u>
    Newburn Manufacturing Company will benefit in two ways from the construction of the new cafeteria. First, we will reduce late returns to work after lunch. Second, we will foster an attitude of cooperation and company loyalty among employees by showing them we are willing to invest in their well-being.

7. <u>Alternatives</u>
    We could reduce late returns from lunch by adopting a more strict set of penalties. But such an action would cause confrontation between management and employees and work directly against the spirit of company loyalty we wish to foster. We could try to develop company loyalty and spirit by sponsoring athletic teams and having other activities after work. However, many workers have families or other reasons for wanting to return home immediately after work, so organized activities might create the cliquishness we are striving to avoid.

8. <u>Consequences</u> <u>of</u> <u>Not</u> <u>Adopting</u>
    If we do not build the cafeteria we will continue to experience late returns from lunch and a decline in company spirit that harms the company.

WRITING ASSIGNMENT

Think of some problem you are now having that might be solved if someone in authority would take the proper action. Or, imagine such a situation you might encounter in the future. Prepare a decision package you think will get the problem solved.

FOR FURTHER READING

Boley, Tommy. "A Heuristic for Persuasion." *College Composition and Communication* 30 (May 1979): 187–91.

Cohen, Morris and Nagel, Ernest. *Introduction to Logic.* New York: Harcourt Brace Jovanovich, 1962.

Copi, Irving. *Introduction to Logic.* 6th ed. New York: Macmillan, 1982.

Estrin, Herman. "Teaching Report Writing." *Civil Engineering* 38 (December 1968): 64–65.

Howell, Wilbur. *Logic and Rhetoric in England, 1500–1700.* New York: Russell & Russell, 1961.

Larson, Richard. "Problem-Solving, Composing, and Liberal Education." *College English* 33 (March 1972): 628–35.

Schnure, Wilmer. "An Engineer Teaches English." *Journal of Technical Writing and Communication* 4 (Fall 1974): 279–84.

14

Integration of Personal and Borrowed Materials

When writing a longer report, especially one based on considerable outside material, the writer must find a way to smoothly connect the opinions and conclusions she makes with the facts and other borrowed materials she has gathered through research. At the outset of this integration procedure, the writer faces a working outline that incorporates note cards (designated by an X) under each heading:

I. X X X
   A. X X
   B. X X X
   C. X X X X

II. X X
   A. X X
   B. X X

III. X X X X
   A. X X X
   B. X X
   C. X X X X
   D. X X X X

LEVELS OF ORGANIZING

The basic structure of the paper is set by the working outline, which has developed over the course of generating the paper. The note cards under each heading must also be organized so that each of the report's individual sections has its own logical flow or development. Any pattern that organizes a whole report can also be used to organize sections or paragraphs of a report. By arranging the note cards into exactly the right order, the writer winds up with a report that is not only organized in general terms, but one in which every borrowed idea or fact is introduced at just the right point. This crucial organizing process has three levels, the factual, the transitional, and the commentary, as the following example shows.

```
Major Point:  Utah's grazing lands must not be called upon
              to support more animals than are healthy for
              the land itself.
Working Outline and Note Cards
(Induction)          I. Utah has a serious overgrazing problem
                        X 800,000 cattle in Utah
                        X 1,000,000 sheep
                        X 1,500,000 overgrazed acres today
                        X 3,500,000 overgrazed acres predicted
                          by 1990
(Induction)         II. Eroded lands are more subject to costly
                        floods
                        X 1953 Springville flood
                        X flooding is proportional to
                          precipitation
                        X floods start in small areas in canyon
                          heads
(Deduction)        III. Vegetation helps prevent erosion
                        X vegetation holds topsoil in place
                        X topsoil helps prevent erosion
(Induction)         IV. Utah's grazing lands must not be called
                        upon to support more animals than are
                        healthy for the land itself
                        X too much grazing damages vegetation
                        X fewer animals lead to more vegetation
                          and vice versa
```

Factual Level

On the factual level, the note cards are organized into effective patterns of support based on the overall outline. Schematically, the document looks like the following diagram:

```
                    I. X
                       X
                       X
                       X
                   II. X
                       X
                       X
                  III. X
                       X
                   IV. X
                       X
```

If the report were written as a compilation of these organized facts, it would be logical and consistent, but it would also be choppy and hard to read.

```
       There are 800,000 cattle in Utah. There are
1,000,000 sheep in Utah. There are 1,500,000 acres of
overgrazed land in Utah today. By 1990 there will be
3,500,000 acres of overgrazed land.
       A flood caused major damage in Springville in 1953.
A flood is proportional in devastation to the
precipitation that has fallen. Floods start in small
areas in canyon heads. Eroded lands are more subject to
costly flooding.
       Vegetation holds topsoil in place. Topsoil helps
prevent erosion. Vegetation helps prevent erosion.
       Too much grazing reduces vegetation. Fewer animals
increase vegetation. Utah's grazing lands must not be
called upon to support more animals than are healthy for
the land itself.
```

Transitional Level

Clearly, this version of the report is not acceptable, yet it covers all the main points and does so in an organized way. The transitional level is missing; the report lacks movement from one point to the next. When the note cards are related to one another by transitions, the report looks like the following:

$$
\begin{array}{rl}
\text{I.} & X \\
 & X \\
 & X \\
 & X \\
\text{II.} & X \\
 & X \\
 & X \\
\text{III.} & X \\
 & X \\
\text{IV.} & X \\
 & X \\
\end{array}
$$

If the writer adds transitions to the report, it then reads like this:

```
       Utah is big in size, but it still has an
overpopulation problem. The excess is not in people but
in animals. There are over 800,000 cattle in Utah, with
an additional 1,000,000 sheep. The Utah Environmental
Association says that today there are 1,500,000 acres of
overgrazed lands in Utah. They also say that by 1990
3,500,000 acres will be eroded.
```

EXERCISES

1. Identify each of the transitional devices used in the revised paragraph.

2. The revised paragraph is considerably improved. However, it still has some problems with conciseness and correctness. Rewrite the paragraph to make it even more effective.

3. The report contained three more paragraphs without transitions. Revise each to include transitional devices.

Commentary Level

The paragraph with transitions is considerably better than the one without; however, it still lacks something. The report does not seem to be going anywhere. It is merely a smoothly organized set of facts. The writer has drawn no conclusions and offered no opinions. This situation can be corrected by adding the commentary level. The writer intersperses his own opinions and conclusions among the ordered and related note cards, as shown in the following schematic.

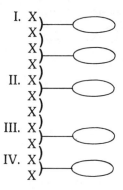

The report with the writer's comments added would then read:

> Despite its relatively large size, Utah suffers from an overpopulation problem. The excess is not in people, but in animals. Over 800,000 cattle and 1,000,000 sheep gobble the grass like locusts. The Utah Environmental Association claims that already 1,500,000 acres of Utah are overgrazed to the point of erosion. By 1990, they predict that 3,500,000 acres will be badly eroded.

A considerable improvement over the paragraph with only transitions between the facts, this paragraph gives the reader a sense of the writer's purpose shaping the entire passage. The transitions are much improved and the rhetorical effectiveness of the paragraph is greatly enhanced.

EXERCISES

1. Identify the writer's comments in the last version of the sample paragraph. (Sometimes even one word can be a comment.)

2. The report contained three more paragraphs without writer's comments. Revise each to include writer's comments.

Integrating Graphics

Whenever possible, the writer wants to gather her supporting facts together in tabular or graphic form. At the same time, the writer wants to preserve the smooth functioning of the factual, transitional, and commentary levels. Consider the following short section from a larger report:

```
Cebu City--Case Study
      In addition to the facts I have already presented as
a cause of riots, I would like to present the case study
of the 1959 riot in Cebu City. An excellent source, it
not only includes relevant information about the rioters
themselves, but also includes survey results of Cebu City
blacks about their evaluation of the disorder's causes.
Moreover, relevant facts about the white rioters are also
added.
```

EXERCISES

1. Point out the facts, transitions, and comments in the sample paragraph.

2. This paragraph introduces the section that follows. How well does it serve this function? Indicate specific passages that serve introductory functions.

Next, the writer integrates a table.

```
           Upon being asked what they deemed the main causes of
the riot, many blacks emphasized that inequalities in
opportunities for jobs, education, and housing were the
major factors. Table I shows the percentage of blacks
claiming that job opportunities are growing too slowly,
there is discrimination in employment, and there is
higher unemployment among blacks than nonblacks. In
addition, blacks cite a lack of equal educational
opportunity and equal housing.
```

Table I
Percentages of Blacks Stressing Various
Phases of Poverty as Cause of Riots

Cause	%
Lack of Equal Opportunity	80%
Higher Unemployment	75%
Lack of Educational Opportunity	60%
Lack of Adequate Housing	70%

Source: Jones, 69.

This paragraph uses effective transitions, and clearly points the reader to relevant facts, gathered conveniently in the table. The only missing element is the writer's commentary. What is the reader supposed to get out of these facts? How does the information presented in the table relate to the overall purpose of the writer's report? These questions should be answered in the writer's commentary, but since the paragraph includes no writer's commentary, the reader cannot find any particular relevance in the presented facts. The reader has to figure out for himself what the relevance is, or the reader may give up and see no relevance in the facts.

The writer tries a different approach in the next paragraph.

The blacks claim that poor employment and educational opportunities cause the riots. Their claim is upheld when the educational and employment histories of those arrested are considered. In the Cebu City report, as seen in table II, sixty-four percent of those blacks arrested (over thirty years old) were employed less than full time; sixty-six percent had less than a high school education. The table also shows that fifty-five percent of the white persons arrested (over thirty years old) were underemployed and fifty percent were undereducated. This is strong evidence that any people, regardless of race, can resort to violence to bring a desired change to their lives.

Table II
Employment and Education of Persons
Arrested in Relation to Age and Race

	Black		White	
	0-30	30+	0-30	30+
Employment				
Full-time	44	36	35	45
Less than full-time	56	64	65	55

	Black		White	
	0–30	30+	0–30	30+
Education				
High school grad	48	34	45	50
Non-high school grad	52	66	55	50

Source: Jones, 70–71.

This paragraph concludes with a strong writer's comment, which clearly indicates the conclusion the writer wants the reader to come to, based on the supporting facts in the table. However, most of the space in the paragraph is used to write out in prose the figures presented graphically in the table. In the earlier paragraph, the writing about the facts was reserved for making generalizations, not for writing out numbers already appearing in a far more accessible format in the table. Thus, the above paragraph shows an improvement in writer's commentary, but is a weaker version in handling the facts.

Let's look at still another paragraph that attempts to integrate facts and conclusions:

Earlier it was stated that the young are most affected by poverty. That would imply that they would also perform a major part in most riots. This theory can be supported by reviewing the age statistics of those arrested in the Cebu City riot. As table III indicates, the majority arrested were in the younger age brackets. But the crucial point for my thesis is that this pattern holds true for both blacks and whites. Thus, it seems that age, and not race, is the significant factor behind the riots.

Table III
Age Distribution of Those
Arrested in Relation to Race

Age	Black	White
10–15	30%	20%
16–25	45%	55%
26–35	10%	8%
36–45	9%	8%
45+	6%	9%

Source: Jones, 58.

In this paragraph we have the ideal combination of facts and commentary. The paragraph ends with a strong and clear writer's comment. Most of the paragraph is given over to drawing generalizations from the facts, which are themselves presented in tabular form. The prose does not contain written out numbers that already appear in an easier-to-read format in the table. Neither are the facts left all alone with no conclusion drawn.

Finally, look at the conclusion to this brief section.

> The foregoing data indicate underemployment and undereducation are more significant factors than race in predicting who will participate in a riot. The underemployed and/or undereducated person--not the white or the black person--is the likely participant. In evaluating the Cebu City riot, Jones declared that access to the mainstream system and its economic advantages is a high priority for all people, white or black.[18] As established in the beginning of this report, discontent and frustration can lead people--any people--to use violence as a way to free themselves from the chains of ignorance and poverty that hold them.

In this concluding paragraph the writer sums up the arguments made throughout the report. Specific facts are not presented in the conclusion. The writer does cite his primary source in the footnoted sentence, but this citation is to Jones' opinion, not to factual material. The section concludes with a strong statement of the overall purpose of the report. The reader does not doubt what the section was intended to show and how the facts were intended to support the writer's commentary.

EXERCISES

1. Go back through all the paragraphs of the report on causes of riots. Indicate which passages are on the factual level, which are on the transitional level, and which are on the commentary level.

2. Select any article or part of a book you wish. Examine your selection carefully paragraph by paragraph. Indicate exactly which passages are on the factual level, which are on the transitional level, and which are on the commentary level. Does every paragraph have to have facts, transitions, and commentary? If you find a passage that seems to need facts, transitions, or commentary, rewrite the passage and add the necessary items.

DOCUMENTATION

One sentence in the last paragraph of the report on the Cebu City riot ended with footnote number 18, used to indicate where the reader could go to find Jones' statement in its original context. The tables were referenced as well with the author's name and page number just underneath. Referring your reader to the sources used in your report is called *documentation*. Generally speaking, you should document all materials from any source outside yourself; you give proper credit for the materials you borrow. Failure to document properly is called *plagiarism* and amounts to stealing. In some cases, it is a legally punishable crime, and many teachers punish it with an *F*.

Besides these negative reasons for documenting, however, there are several positive reasons. First, you protect yourself. The borrowed facts and opinions you present are someone else's, not yours. If some error is found in those facts or opinions, that error is not yours, but your source's. Second, you help your reader by providing documentation. If your reader is interested in the subject, she can gain further valuable information by studying your sources, but if you do not indentify those sources, she cannot study them. Remember how grateful you were for the source leads you came across as you gathered information? Documentation is simply the way writers pass leads on to each other.

The three generally accepted methods of documentation are known as the parenthetical, the footnote, and the endnote. In business, industry, and government, writers usually choose the parenthetical, although the others are used also.

The Parenthetical Method

In this method, whenever the writer introduces any material from an outside source, he simply places the author's last name, date of publication, and page number of the original source in parentheses at the end of the sentence (just *before* the period). If the reader wants to look up this source, she turns to the bibliography (sometimes called list of references cited), finds the source listed with that particular author and date, and notes the full bibliographic information. This way, the report's text is not clogged up with full-scale bibliographic references.

```
        Roy T. Hurley, a former Ford Motor Company
executive, generated support for the company projects by
bringing in new technical ideas like the Wankel engine
(Norbye 1971, 161).
```

The related bibliographic entry would look like this:

Norbye, Jan P. *The Wankel Engine*. Radnor, Pa.: Chilton Book Company, 1971.

Many published sources that use the parenthetical method do not indicate the page number, only the author's last name and the year. Although common, this variation does not help the reader. In the example given, the writer cites a book of at least 161 pages. If the page number for the information is not indicated, how can the reader find it? Obviously, only by searching through the whole book, a needless inconvenience for the reader looking for specific information.

The Endnote Method

The writer must know exactly which sentences are her own and which are borrowed. Borrowed sentences are ended with a slightly raised number (*after the period*). No other source information is included in the text of the report. This system's obvious advantage is that the text remains free of documentation that can clutter it and bog the reader down. To find the exact source of information, the reader has to turn to an appendix or list of references that lists all the endnotes by number. The endnotes have to run in a continuous series of numbers through the entire text:

> At the time, Chrysler had committed a large sum of money to a gas turbine car project that never developed into anything.[29]

The related endnote entry would look like this:

[29]Wally Wyss, "The Engine Detroit Couldn't Ignore," *Motor Trend*, November 1972, 72.

The endnote system has a few extra intricacies. First, since the system uses one continuous series of numbers, any time the writer cites the same source more than once, the total number of endnotes is multiplied. That is, in the parenthetical system, each source appears only once in the bibliography, no matter how many times it is cited in the text. But in the endnote system, if a single source is cited ten times, it will have ten different endnote numbers in the endnote list. To save at least some extra ink, only the first reference to a given source need have the full bibliographic information. All subsequent references may just show the author's last name and page number, like the parenthetical approach, except that the reader must trace his way up the line of endnote numbers to find the one with the same author.

[29]Wally Wyss, "The Engine Detroit Couldn't Ignore," *Motor Trend*, November 1972, 72.
[30]Norbye, 87.
[31]Norbye, 70-71.
[32]Wyss, 63.

Using the author's last name and page number for all subsequent references also relieves you of having to use the Latin system of *ibid.* and *op. cit.* Further details on the endnote system can be found in appendix II.

The Footnote System

The footnote system is just like the endnote system, with one major exception: instead of gathering all the references together in an appendix at the end of the report, the footnote system places each note at the bottom of the appropriate page (hence the name *foot*notes).

This system combines both the advantages and the disadvantages of the two other systems. The text itself remains uncluttered, with only numbers to interrupt the reader's flow. Yet the full bibliographic information is right on the same page as the borrowed material. The reader need only glance down instead of having to turn to the end of the text and scan a list. However, the footnote system causes problems for the typist, who has to struggle to make sure he stops typing text and starts typing footnotes with enough space left on the page. Miscalculations require retyping the full page. One such punishment usually makes the typist use one of the other methods. Likewise, printers suffer all sorts of practical difficulties from the footnote system, which is why almost all periodicals use either the endnote or the parenthetical system.

When to Document

The clearest answer to the question of when to document is to ask yourself if the material in the sentence came from you or from a note card. If the material came from a note card, then document it. If it came from you, or from one of your comments at the bottom of a note card, then do not document it. However, this answer, if taken too literally, can result in massive amounts of needless documentation. Thus, a better principle of documentation is

> Be certain your reader always knows who is talking in a sentence, you or your source.

To accomplish this identification, introduce every section of borrowed material with a clear transition, and end every section of borrowed material with a documentation form (either parentheses or a raised number). The transition should make it clear that someone other than the writer is about to speak:

> Dr. Cole feels that . . . .
> According to one source . . . .
> Bridger relates that . . . .

Naturally, the writer should use as much variety in these transitions as possible. By using this system, the writer can string together several sentences from the same source, with only one documentation form at the end:

```
        Dr. Cole thinks the new system will one day be the
    only system. As evidence, she cites studies done in
    England over the past fifteen years. These studies seem
    to offer conclusive proof of the Lancaster system's
    superiority (Cole 1983, 78).
```

Because the documentation occurs at the end of this example, everything in it should appear on page 78 of the original source by Cole. Notice the difference in the following passage:

```
        Dr. Cole thinks the new system will one day be the
    only system. As evidence, she cites studies done in
    England over the past fifteen years (Cole 1983, 78).
    These studies seem to offer conclusive proof of the
    Lancaster system's superiority.
```

Because the documentation occurs part way through the passage, the writer says the last sentence is his own comment about the material on page 78 of Cole. If the reader found that *Cole* made that comment on page 78, then the writer would be technically guilty of plagiarism. If the writer wants to give Cole credit for the opinion and also state that he agrees with it, then he should write the passage in the following way:

```
        Dr. Cole thinks the new system will one day be the
    only system. As evidence, she cites studies done in
    England over the past fifteen years. To Cole, these
    studies seem to offer conclusive proof of the Lancaster
    system's superiority (Cole 1983, 78). The available
    evidence indeed suggests that this superiority is real.
```

In this manner, a writer can introduce a lot of borrowed material without using large numbers of documentation forms. At the same time, though, the writer can be certain the reader knows exactly who is talking in every sentence. For an extended example of this system in operation, see the sample research report at the end of appendix II.

SUMMARY

In order to change an organized collection of note cards into a clear and coherent report, the writer must join the documented facts together using smooth transitions. Such transitions give the report coherence. In order to achieve clarity as well, the writer must add his own commentary throughout the report. This commentary points out the conclusions the writer wants the reader to draw from the facts presented. An effective piece of writing based on materials outside the writer's personal knowledge has discernible sections of fact, transition, and commentary.

In order to give proper credit for any material borrowed from others, the writer must use some documentation system. The usual system in business, industry, and government is the parenthetical system, in which the author's last name, the date of publication, and the specific page number appear at the end of the borrowed material. The reader finds the full bibliographic information by looking up the author's last name in the bibliography at the end of the report.

Two other documentation systems, called endnotes and footnotes, involve placing the bibliographic information for each borrowed idea in a numbered list. A number placed at the end of each sentence containing borrowed material directs the reader to the reference with the same number. In the endnote system the entire numbered list is placed in an appendix at the end of the report. In the footnote system the numbered list is broken up, with each entry placed at the bottom of the page on which the borrowed information appears in the report.

In order to avoid plagiarism and to help readers find further information from your sources, all borrowed materials should be documented in such a way that the reader can always tell whether any given sentence is from the writer or from an outside source. To accomplish this, the writer should introduce all sections of borrowed material with a transition and end all sections of borrowed material with a documentation form (either parentheses or a raised number).

CASE IN POINT

The Recommendation and Grant Proposal

One of the most common of all report forms in business, industry, and government is the recommendation. In the recommendation format, the writer frequently has to integrate her own opinions with data from other sources. Like the decision package, the recommendation format argues a point. Unlike the decision package, the recommendation is a relatively informal and personal document. Recommendations may take many forms, but they all have in common a carefully prepared argument, attempting to lead the audience to a certain course of action. Because they are argumentative and often aimed at a hostile audience, recommendations often use the inductive organizational pattern: the case is made point by point before the recommendation is made. The writer hopes to have done a good job of convincing the audience before it knows exactly what it is getting into. Or, at least the audience is willing to read the recommendation because it is not turned off by an immediate and unsupported purpose statement right at the outset. The recommendation usually includes the following major points:

▶ *Background Statement:* The writer tries to set up the conditions that demand action and concludes with a general statement of the action the report recommends.

▶ *Justification:* The writer presents specific points of defense for the recommended action.

▶ *Implementation Plan:* The writer delineates exactly how the recommended action would be brought about.

▶ *Budget Statement:* The writer specifies the cost of the desired action. (Notice how near the report's end this delicate subject is placed.)

▶ *Recommendation:* The writer makes a single, short, strong statement of the desired action.

An example of a recommendation using this general format follows on pages 314 and 315.

Another important recommendation that uses a slightly different format is the grant proposal. In this case, the author asks for money and possibly other kinds of support to carry out a project. The important sections of the grant proposal include the following:

Items about the Proposed Project Itself
▶ Relevance to the agency being asked to grant the funds
▶ Originality and overall value of the proposal itself
▶ Soundness of the proposal design and scope
▶ Availability of necessary facilities and support

Items about the Person Making the Proposal
▶ Education appropriate to the proposal
▶ Job experience appropriate to the proposal
▶ Performance record on previously funded projects

An example of a grant proposal follows on pages 316 through 322.

---

[1]This considerably shortened version of Gina Cantoni-Harvey's grant proposal is reprinted by permission of the author.

Recommendation for an Intensive Accounting Program

for New Employees at Gung Ho

1. **Background**

   1.1 For years the other two import/export houses in town have had highly successful intensive accounting programs for new employees. Those programs have brought additional income into those companies, and have made employees feel a loyalty to the company. Many published articles extol the virtues of such programs (Craig 1982; Blarney 1979; Grigorio 1976).

   1.2 Devin James has had extensive experience with previous employers in such a program and has laid the groundwork during the past four years for such a program here at Gung Ho.

   1.3 So far, the rapid turnover of employees and the seemingly high cost of such a program have kept us from seriously considering it.

   1.4 Now, with the company in a definite growth period, and with the addition of Megan White, who directed such a program at Wai Mei Imports for two years, the time has come to inaugurate an intensive accounting program for new employees at Gung Ho.

2. **Justification**

   2.1 The two major benefits of such a program are

   - increased accounting skills for all employees (Gregorio 1976)
   - less supervision from management (Blarney 1979)

   2.2 Additional immediate benefits include

   - attracting some of the excellent university graduates who now generally opt for other companies
   - keeping and training those employees who need better skills
   - keeping older employees abreast of the newest developments in the field

   2.3 With the full cooperation of corporate headquarters, we have just completed a survey of the employees' perceptions about such a program (James 1983). Of the 171 survey instruments returned, 152 employees answered yes to the following question (one of six on the survey): ''Would you be in favor of our offering an intensive accounting program for new employees?'' Most of the information learned from the survey also supported inaugurating such a program.

3. **Implementation**

   3.1 All new employees will have the opportunity to enroll in the program. The pilot program would prepare for 12 new employees a year. We already have an excellent and underused conference room on the second floor that would be perfect for this program.

   3.2 Both Devin James and Megan White have agreed to teach the first group for one hour a day each, in addition to their regular duties. They have drawn up a pilot six-week-long course that could be taught to 12 employees at a time. They are willing to teach this course once a year. In any given year, old employees could be substituted for new ones, at the discretion of each section chief.

4. Budget

   <u>4.1</u> As we already have the physical facilities and the teachers available, these items will not cost the company anything. Offering the course would require some secretarial support, but only a quarter-time person for the six weeks of the course. If the course were offered every year, the secretarial cost would be a nominal $800.

   <u>4.2</u> To run the program we would need minicomputers for each new student and one for the two teachers. Figuring a total of 12 new minicomputers at $2,000 each comes to $24,000.

   Thus, the program could be offered for under $25,000, and would more than pay for itself in increased employee productivity and morale.

5. Recommendation

   Gung Ho should now attract and retain the best young talent available and develop a means of providing ongoing training to established employees by inaugurating an accounting program for new employees.

To: Organized Research Committee
From: Gina Cantoni-Harvey

Organized Research Proposal: TEACHING ENGLISH TO MINORITY CHILDREN (book)

1. ABSTRACT

    I am applying for a twelve-month contract in order to complete a
book on Teaching English to Minority Children. I have presented much of
this material at various conferences and workshops, where it has been
well-received by teachers who work with children of limited English
proficiency, often without their having received appropriate training
for this demanding work.
    Leaders and educators of ethnic communities have become
increasingly aware of the need to upgrade the quality of English
instruction available to their children, but materials and techniques
intended for teaching English to foreigners are as inappropriate as
those developed for middle-class English-speaking youngsters. Teachers
must learn to modify and adapt available texts and procedures or create
their own.
    My book will offer a brief summary of the foundations of the
English-as-a-Second-Language theory and practice most applicable to a
minority situation, along with a large variety of sample lessons and
techniques. No such manual is yet available on the market, in spite of
the urgent need for one.

2. AIMS AND OBJECTIVES

    I intend to assemble the results of my extensive experience as
teacher-trainer, along with an analysis of current research-based
pedagogical theory and its implications, into a very practical manual
that should be helpful to all teachers working with one or more children
of limited English proficiency. Most methodology books that
claim to address the professional interests of teachers of English
to Speakers of Other Languages actually deal with the teaching of
English as a Foreign Language (EFL) and contain very little information
applicable to the teaching of English as a Second Language (ESL). These
two specialties, ESL and EFL, serve different clienteles having
different goals and characteristics. English is taught as a foreign
language all over the world to persons who, except when practicing
English, use their mother tongue both in and out of school. For them,
English is seldom needed as a medium of instruction; they learn math,
history, and other subjects in Arabic, German, Japanese, or whatever.
Foreign students attending British or American universities may, for a
limited time, rely exclusively on English for social and academic
purposes; when they return to their own countries, however, English
usually plays only a secondary role in their lives.

3. PLAN OF RESEARCH

My scholarly activity will consist of assembling into a book a selective summation of research findings about the characteristics of minority children and their learning strategies as well as about appropriate approaches to teaching them English to facilitate their academic success, along with descriptions of original techniques, lesson plans, and projects developed and field-tested by me and by people I have trained. I have already published some of the theoretical material in article form; it needs to be rearranged and completed.

The book, to be entitled Teaching English to Minority Children, will consist of five parts, each including several chapters. Part One will discuss research findings about second-language acquisition and about the characteristics of the target population. Part Two will give suggestions for expanding the child's ability to understand and produce oral and written English and learn academic subjects in English. Part Three will discuss the rationale for developing materials locally and suggest some specific products. Part Four will discuss the role of errors in language acquisition and how to deal with common grammatical problems. Part Five will discuss various pedagogical and professional concerns.

4. TIME LINE

Having obtained three hours of released time from the English Department for spring 1984 for the purpose of working on this manuscript, I shall by the end of this academic year have completed the final draft of one chapter from each of the Parts, as well as a detailed outline of the entire book. This material will be sent to outside readers, whose comments should be available to me in July 1984. During the summer of 1984, Summer Session II, I intend to visit summer programs and communities far away from Arizona to gather authentic material for additional cultural awareness lessons from Cuban, Puerto Rican, and Creole communities within the United States. During the academic year, 1984-85, I shall incorporate this material into the draft of Parts Two and Three. By visiting some of the Asian programs in Arizona and California I shall be able to round-off my ethnic sampling. A twelve-month contract will give me adequate time to complete the manuscript by June of 1985. I shall divide my teaching duties between the Fall and Spring Semesters and Summer Session I of 1985.

5. DISSEMINATION

Of the various publishers interested in publishing the book, I have tentatively given first choice to Teachers College Press of Columbia University. Papers related to this material have been invited at the Regional Teachers of English to Speakers of Other Languages Convention, Salt Lake City, October 14, 1983; the Arizona Teachers of English to Speakers of Other Languages, Regional Conference, December 4, 1983; the International Reading Association Regional Conference, January, 1984; and the Arizona Teachers of English to Speakers of Other Languages State Conference, April, 1984.

6. FUTURE PLANS

     1. I shall apply for a Mina Shaughnessy fellowship grant on the basis of my experience in working nation-wide with minority children over the past twenty years.

     2. I have been invited by Dr. Suzanne Shafer to serve as linguistic consultant on a grant on the education of minority children in Zimbabwe.

     3. Since minority issues are world-wide, the logical sequel to this book seems to be a manuscript aimed at a clientele beyond the United States--the children of African, South Indian, Middle East groups, etc., entering English language schools.

7. BUDGET

Twelve-month contract, 1984-85	
Full-time graduate assistant at the going rate	
Telephone, out-of-state	$120.00
Xeroxing, supplies, postage	480.00
Books	100.00
Travel: round trip to San Francisco	210.00
per diem	90.00
	$1,100.00

CURRICULUM
VITAE

DATE OF BIRTH: March 30, 1922
        PLACE: Gorizia, Friuli-Venezia-Giulia, Italy
                  Naturalized United States Citizen

EDUCATION: Liceo Torquato Tasso, Rome, 1940 (Valedictorian)
                  Doctorate, Letters and Philosophy, University of Rome
                      1943 (Summa cum laude)

LANGUAGES: Fluent: Italian, French, German, Spanish
                  Reading: same, plus classical Greek and Latin
                  Linguistic knowledge of several Native American
                      languages

FIELDS OF SPECIALIZATION IN TEACHING AND RESEARCH:
                  Language Pedagogy
                  Applied Linguistics
                  ESL Methodology
                  Materials and Curriculum Development
                  Cross-Cultural Communications
                  Bilingual/Multicultural Education
                  Native American Cultures and Education
                  Teaching of Reading
                  Values Research

EXPERIENCE: TEACHING AND ADMINISTRATION
                  Organizing and teaching intensive courses in English
                      as a Second Language after World War II
        1959-61   Latin and French, Farmington High School, New Mexico
        1960-63   French, New Mexico State University, San Juan Branch
        1963-68   Assistant Professor of French and ESL, Fort Lewis
                      College, Durango, Colorado
        1968-72   Associate Professor of Education and English,
                      University of New Mexico, Albuquerque; Director of
                      federally-funded programs for teaching linguistics
                      and ESL to teachers of Native Americans and
                      Mexican-Americans
        1972-79   Associate Professor of English, Northern
                      Arizona University
        1979-   Professor of English, N.A.U., Chair of Committee on
                      Teaching English as a Second Language

        Teacher Training Director in English as a Second Language,
                      Navajo Area, BIA, 1967-70
        Director, Navajo Summer Institutes in Linguistics and ESL
                      for Teachers, 1971-75
        Co-Director, National Seminars in Indian Education (jointly
                      sponsored by Southwest Educational Associates in
                      Research and the National Council of Teachers of
                      English), 1972-75
        President, SEARCH (Southwest Educational Associates in
                      Research), since 1970

OTHER PROFESSIONAL ACTIVITIES:

        President, AZ-TESOL (Arizona Teachers of English to Speakers of
          Other Languages, formerly Arizona Bilingual Council), 1980-81
        Member, NCTE Committee on Issues and Problems in ESL and
          Bilingual Education, and NCTE Committee on Programs and
          Curricula in ESL and Bilingual Education
        Consultant, providing technical assistance to schools and
          institutions serving Native American tribes and Spanish-
          American communities in the United States and Canada,
          1967-current
        Evaluator of bilingual programs, Spanish and Native American
        Invited member of People-to-People delegation of ESL and
          bilingual educators from U.S. to Cuba, 1980
        Member of study group on Socialist Education, People's Republic
          of China, 1981
        Member of professional organizations: International TESOL,
          SWALLOW, LASSO, NCTE, AZ-TESOL, American Anthropological
          Association, etc.

FOREIGN TRAVEL:

        Europe: Italy, Spain, France, Belgium, Luxembourg,
              Netherlands, Denmark, West Germany, Switzerland,
              Greece, Yugoslavia, Ireland, British Isles,
              Hungary, Austria
        America: Mexico, Cuba, Bahamas, Canada
          Asia: Japan, Hong Kong, Thailand, India,
              People's Republic of China

HONORS: Doctorate (Summa cum laude), University of Rome, 1943
        Educator of the Year, Arizona Bilingual Council, 1977
        President's Award, Northern Arizona University, 1983
        Phi Kappa Phi

SERVICE TO N.A.U.:

        Chair, English Department ESL Committee, 1972-present
        English Department Curriculum, Faculty Status,
          and other committees
        BME Committee, 1978-83
        Doctoral Committees, every year since 1973
        President's Ad Hoc Committee on Admissions, 1983

PUBLICATIONS: (see separate sheet)

PUBLICATIONS
(Abbreviated list)

The Italian Verb, David McKay & Co., London, 1965

Reports on progress in ESL on the Navajo Reservation, 1969, 1970, 1971

Helpful Hints for New BIA Teachers, rev., 1971

''On Navajo Area Teacher Training Programs,'' Education for American Indians, Spring, 1971

''Dormitory English: Implications for the Teacher,'' Southwest Areal Linguistics, ed., Garland Bills, San Diego, 1974

Co-Editor, Southwest Languages and Linguistics in Educational Perspective, San Diego, 1975

''Developing a Native Language and Culture Curriculum,'' Arizona Bilingual Council Newsletter, December, 1975

''Teaching Reading to Bilingual Children,'' ABC Newsletter, Spring, 1976

''Some Observations about Red English and Standard English in the Classroom,'' Studies in Southwest Indian English, ed., William L. Leap, Trinity University Press, San Antonio, 1977

''Selecting Books about Native Americans,'' Arizona English Teachers Bulletin, October, 1977

''A Model for Writing Cultural Awareness Lessons,'' AET Bulletin, 1979

''LEAL--True Language Learning,'' with M. F. Heiser, ABC Newsletter, Winter, 1977

''ESL and Bilingual Teacher Certification,'' TESOL Newsletter, June, 1979

''Update in ESL–Bilingual Teacher Certification,'' TESOL Newsletter, October, 1979

''ESL and Bilingual Teacher Certification,'' ORTESOL Journal, Vol. 1, 1979

''The Status of ESL in Bilingual Teacher Certification,'' The Linguistic Reporter, December, 1979

NINE STEPS to Establishing Certification for English as a Second Language in Your State, AZ-TESOL Occasional Papers, 1981

''Non-English-Speaking Students in a Regular Classroom: A Challenge for the Teacher,'' Conference Proceedings, Vol. 1, TEAL '81, TESL Canada, 1982

Co-Editor, Proceedings of SWALLOW TEN (Tenth Southwest Areal Languages and Linguistics Workshop), Trinity University Press, 1983

''ESP in Every Classroom: An Option for a Navajo School,'' Proceedings of SWALLOW TEN, eds., Harvey and Heiser, Trinity University Press, 1983

Contributor to American Indian Language Proficiency Assessment, Arizona State Department of Education, 1983

Teaching English to Minority Children (in preparation)

WRITING ASSIGNMENT

Select any situation for which you have a recommendation to make or a project to propose and write it following one of the general outlines provided here.

FOR FURTHER READING

Braddock, Richard. "The Frequency and Placement of Topic Sentences in Expository Prose." *Research in the Teaching of English* 8 (Winter 1974): 287–304.

Childs, Barney. "A College Course in Engineering Writing." *College English* 21 (April 1960): 394–96.

Harris, John S. "So You're Going to Teach Technical Writing: A Primer for Beginners." *The Technical Writing Teacher* 2 (Fall 1974): 1–6.

Orth, William. "An Approach to Better Technical Report Writing." *Engineering Education* 64 (January 1974): 278–79.

Rathbone, Robert. "Cooperative Teaching in the Technical Writing Class." *Journal of Engineering Education* 49 (November 1968): 126–30.

Stern, Arthur. "When Is a Paragraph." *College Composition and Communication* 27 (October 1976): 253–57.

Yale, Stanley. "Writing Courses for Engineers." *Improving College and University Teaching* 19 (Winter 1971): 60–61.

Appendices

I | Case Study of a Writer at Work

J ill Stone directs the plant facilities at a large manufacturing concern. Recently, her plant experienced an electrical failure that resulted in costly downtime for the entire operation. As director, keeping the plant running is Jill's primary responsibility, so she wants to know exactly what happened and how she can keep it from happening in the future. Then she wants to write a memo to her superiors, letting them know exactly what happened and how she can keep it from happening again.

INVESTIGATION AND INFORMATION GATHERING

Jill begins the writing process by considering the possible causes of the failure:

- Lightning-induced voltage flashover
- Short circuit, caused by
    Insulation problem
    Condensation of moisture

These are the main possibilities she can think of, but she keeps her mind open to others as she goes to inspect the switchgear where the breakdown occurred.

Inspecting the switchgear, she finds the following facts:

- Circuit breaker rated for 15KV and 600 amps

- Breaker and busway located in separate compartments of one box
- Bus bars connect breaker load terminals to busway compartment
- Breaker compartment is heated and air intake is filtered
- Busway compartment has neither heater nor ventilation filter
- Staining indicates that condensation of moisture has been occurring in the busway compartment for some time

From these facts Jill generates the following theory about what happened:

- Moisture in the busway compartment caused current leakage
- Arching was severe enough to open the fuses, causing the power failure

Based upon this theory, Jill formulates the following recommendations:

- Put heater in busway compartment to help eliminate moisture
- Replace bus bars with continuous cable from breaker terminals to transformer

RHETORICAL ANALYSIS

Jill can now ask herself about the shape of the memo she plans to write. Specifically, she wants to identify her stance, audience, purpose, and scope.

- *Stance*   Jill wants to be both convincing in her explanation and reassuring about a plan for preventing a reoccurrence.
- *Audience*   The main audience is her own supervisor, operations Vice President, Harold Green. Green is exacting and loves efficiency. He is upset that the plant went down in the first place. He will be less interested in knowing why it went down than in knowing it will not happen again. Jill will also write a memo to the technicians, telling them how to repair the damage, but that memo will be different from this one.
- *Purpose*   The main purpose is to get the recommendations adopted by management. Her secondary purpose is to avoid laying the blame on anyone else while not getting blamed herself.
- *Scope*   Jill plans two major areas, the past situation and its repair, and assurances for the future.

PREWRITING

Having a pretty good idea of what she wants to do in the memo, Jill decides to write out a first draft quickly, using the freewriting technique. In effect, the thinking and noting she has done up to now have served as heuristic devices. Writing very quickly, Jill generates the following first draft:

> This memo will explain the unfortunate power failure we experienced last Thursday. Condensation had been building up in the busway compartment. The breaker and busway are located in separate compartments within one metal box. The moisture caused current leakage, and ultimately arching, which became bad enough to open the fuses, and cause the power failure. This happened in a switchgear bus compartment, which has a circuit breaker rated for 15KV and 600 amps and supplied with current limiting fuses. Bus bars connect the breaker to the busway compartment from which a 15KV cable connects to the transformer. The breaker compartment has a heater and a filter over the vents, but the busway compartment has neither heater nor ventilation. My recommendations are to remove the insulating barrier, to add a heater, and to replace the bus bars with continuous cable. This will stop the condensation. If we get any switchgear similar to this in the future, we should check it over carefully before another accident happens.

ORGANIZATION

Jill's hasty freewriting has not generated an effective piece of writing, but it *has* generated something she can work on. She can begin to improve the organization by grouping similar ideas:

Introductory sentence
- This memo will explain the unfortunate power failure we experienced last Thursday.

Sentences giving observed facts
- The breaker and busway are located in separate compartments within one metal box.
- This happened in a switchgear bus compartment, which has a circuit breaker rated for 15KV and 600 amps and supplied with current limiting fuses.
- Bus bars connect the breaker to the busway compartment from which a 15KV cable connects to the transformer.
- The breaker compartment has a heater and a filter over the vents, but the busway compartment has neither heater nor ventilation.

Sentences giving interpretations of the observed facts
- Condensation had been building up in the busway compartment.

- The moisture caused current leakage, and ultimately arching, which became bad enough to open the fuses, and cause the power failure.

Sentences giving recommendations
- My recommendations are to remove the insulating barrier, to add a heater, and to replace the bus bars with continuous cable.
- If we get any switchgear similar to this in the future, we should check it over carefully before another accident happens.

Sentences justifying the recommendations
- This will stop the condensation.

With her large groupings established, Jill can organize these groups in two ways:

- Externally, putting each group of sentences into any relation she wants with regard to any other group.
- Internally, putting the individual items within each group into any order she wants.

For the larger, external organization pattern, Jill decides she is quite happy with everything except the end section. First, she decides to move her recommendations to the front of the memo. But before she does that, she decides that the two main recommendations are quite different. One tells what to do for the immediate situation and the other tells what to do in the future to help avoid the problem. To make the order more effective, she decides to move the general recommendation to the very end, and put the immediate recommendation up front, after the introductory sentence. She also decides to bring the justification sentence up front too, just after the recommendation it justifies.

For the internal organization, everything seems fine except the section on the observed facts. Jill decides to reorganize this section in a spatial pattern, moving from an overall view of the switchbox to the smallest internal parts. Doing this, she organizes the observed facts as follows:

This happened in a switchgear bus compartment, which has a circuit breaker rated for 15 KV and 600 amps and supplied with current limiting fuses.

Bus bars connect the breaker to the busway compartment from which a 15 KV cable connects to the transformer.

The breaker and busway are located in separate compartments within one metal box.

The breaker compartment has a heater and a filter over the vents, but the busway compartment has neither heater nor ventilation.

So at this point, her overall pattern is

- Introduction
- Immediate recommendations
- Justification for recommendations
- Spatially organized facts
- Interpretation of facts
- General recommendation

WRITING THE FIRST DRAFT

With an improved organization, Jill writes a first draft. She still writes fairly quickly, making no attempt to polish individual sentences or to ponder over exact word choices:

> This memo will explain the unfortunate power failure we experienced last Thursday. We can repair the damage this power failure caused by following two simple recommendations: removing the insulating barrier, adding a heater, and replacing the bus bars with continuous cable. This will stop condensation from building up inside the switchgear bus compartment, which has a circuit breaker rated for 15 KV and 600 amps and supplied with current limiting fuses. Bus bars connect the breaker to the busway compartment from which a 15 KV cable connects to the transformer. The breaker and busway are located in separate compartments within one metal box. The breaker compartment has a heater and a filter over the vents, but the busway compartment has neither heater nor ventilation. Most likely, condensation had been building up in the busway compartment for some time. The moisture caused current leakage, and ultimately arching, which became bad enough to open the fuses, and cause the power failure. If we get any switchgear similar to this in the future, we should check it over carefully before another accident happens.

ADDING GRAPHIC EFFECTS

With the facts organized to support the recommendations effectively, Jill now considers adding to the impact of the memo by highlighting certain parts. She decides to highlight the recommendations by listing them and using white space around them to make them stand out:

> This memo will explain the unfortunate power failure we experienced last Thursday.
> We can repair the damage caused by this power failure by following a few simple recommendations:

```
    1. Removing the insulating barrier,
    2. Adding a heater,
    3. Replacing the bus bars with continuous cable.

    These recommendations will stop moisture from
building up inside the bus compartment, which was the
ultimate cause of the power outage.
    The moisture was concentrated in the bus
compartment, which has a circuit breaker rated for 15KV
and 600 amps and is supplied with current limiting fuses.
Bus bars connect the breaker to the busway compartment
from which a 15KV cable connects to the transformer. The
breaker and busway are located in separate compartments
within one metal box. The breaker compartment has a
heater and a filter over the vents, but the busway
compartment has neither heater nor ventilation.
    The most likely explanation to explain the above
facts is that condensation had been building up in the
busway compartment for some time. The moisture caused
current leakage, and ultimately arching, which became bad
enough to open the fuses, and cause the power failure.
    The recommendations listed above will take care of
any immediate problems on this particular switchgear, but
as we receive similar switchgear in the future, we should
check it over carefully before another accident happens.
```

Note that in the process of inserting the graphics, Jill made several paragraph, sentence, and word changes. Many rewriting problems are automatically taken care of in these earlier stages in the writing process. That is why revision itself is saved until the end of the process.

REVISION

The memo is taking shape nicely. It is organized and shaped to make the key ideas stand out. Now Jill has a chance to review it carefully sentence by sentence, to make sure she has said exactly what she intended and to see whether her audience can follow it. Looking the memo over, Jill sees a few points that seem unclear or ineffective:

- The opening sentence seems weak. It is a shame to waste the first sentence just to state the subject.

  Solution: Place the subject in a reference line at the top of the memo and reserve the key opening sentence for the main point instead of a mere reference.

- The recommendations mention items that have not been explained or defined in the memo itself.

Solution: Write a new introductory sentence to state the circumstances of the power outage in simple, clear, and brief terms. Thus, move the justification up ahead of the recommendations.

- The second half of the memo seems bloated. Looking at the volume of information in the second half and thinking about her audience, Jill realizes that Mr. Green does not want to know all the technical details. In the second half of the memo she has slipped away from her administrative audience to a technical audience.

  Solution: Take most of the technical details out and use them later, in the memo to the operations staff, *after* she has received permission to implement her recommendations.

Jill pauses at this point to check out what she has written so far. Then she starts to rewrite her memo.

```
MEMO TO:  Harold Green
MEMO FROM:  Jill Stone
RE:  Recommendations to avoid future power outages

The ultimate cause of last Thursday's power outage was
moisture which built up in the insulating barrier between
the two compartments of a 15KV switchgear box. If we are
to avoid more power outages in the future, we must make
changes that will eliminate the build-up of moisture
anywhere in the switchgear box. I recommend that the
following actions be taken toward that end:

     1. Remove the insulating barrier where the moisture
        build up took place.
     2. Add a heater to the busway compartment, to keep
        the air dry so moisture will not build up.
     3. Replace the bus bars with continuous cable.
```

Reading this new version of the memo, Jill realizes that the third recommendation is actually different from the first two because it is designed to reduce the chance that arching will occur even if moisture does build up again. Only the first two recommendations directly address the problem of moisture build up itself. Jill therefore decides that the third recommendation belongs at the end of the memo with the other general recommendation. After making this change, Jill goes on to condense the second half as she had planned earlier. With all these changes, the memo looks like this:

```
MEMO TO:  Harold Green
MEMO FROM:  Jill Stone
RE:  Recommendations to avoid future power outages

The ultimate cause of last Thursday's power outage was
moisture which built up in the insulating barrier between
the two compartments of a 15KV switchgear box. If we are
to avoid more power outages in the future, we must make
changes that will eliminate the build up of moisture
anywhere in the switchgear box. I recommend that the
following actions be taken toward that end:

    1. Remove the insulating barrier where the moisture
       build up took place.
    2. Add a heater to the busway compartment, to keep
       the air dry so moisture will not build up.

    While the two recommendations above will take care
of the immediate problem, they do not address the larger
issue of why the problem happened in the first place. The
most likely explanation is that the moisture had been
building up in the busway compartment for some time. The
moisture caused current leakage and ultimately arching,
which became bad enough to open the fuses, and cause the
power failure.
    To guard against future power failure in the event
that moisture does build up again, I recommend the
following actions:

    1. Replace the bus bars with continuous cable.
    2. Check existing switchgear immediately to see if
       this problem is developing elsewhere.
    3. Make a regular policy of checking all new
       switchgear for this problem before it is
       installed.
```

EDITING

Jill is now confident that her memo is clear, concise, and coherent. She has placed her major points in visible positions, organized each detail to fit into exactly the right spot, and has eliminated extra information that was related, but not necessary, to her audience. Now that the memo says what she wants it to, she checks it over carefully, word by word, for language details. In other words, she edits and polishes for correctness and maximum effectiveness. She discovers there are still several changes she needs to make. Doing so yields the final version of the memo:

```
MEMO TO:  Harold Green
MEMO FROM:  Jill Stone
RE:  Prevention of Power Outages

     Last Thursday's power outage was caused by moisture
buildup in the insulating barrier between two
compartments of a 15KV switchgear box. The following
recommendations will greatly lessen the chances of
moisture buildup:

     1. Remove the insulating barrier where the moisture
        buildup took place.
     2. Add a heater to the busway compartment, so the
        air inside will stay dry.

     Since condensation had been accumulating inside the
busway compartment for some time, our environment may be
prone to moisture build up, which could take place again
despite our best precautions. The following
recommendations will decrease the chances of power
failure, even if moisture should build up again:

     1. Replace the bus bars in all existing switchgear
        with continuous cable.
     2. Regularly examine all new switchgear and make
        appropriate modifications before installation.
```

EXERCISES

1. In this appendix you have traced one document through several versions. Analyze the differences between these versions. Account for each change the writer made.

2. What further changes can the writer make to improve the final version even more?

3. Do you go through a similar process as you write your papers? Can you account for the changes you make?

4. For the next paper you write, keep careful track of all the changes you make as you go along. Hand in all the preparatory versions along with the final copy.

FOR FURTHER READING

Holder, Fred. "What to Look for in Technical Communicators." *Personnel Journal* 51 (October 1972): 737–41.

McCarron, William. "Confessions of a Working Technical Editor." *The Technical Writing Teacher* 6 (1978): 5–8.

Rohman, Gordon and Wlecke, Albert. *Pre-Writing: The Construction and Application of Models for Concept Formation in Writing.* USOE Cooperative Research Project N. 2174, East Lansing, Mich.: Michigan State University Press, 1964.

II Final Manuscript Preparation

For longer and more formal reports, you must be especially careful to follow the most exacting set of formats, designed to make your report appear its very best. However, no single correct or universally accepted format exists for technical reports. Instead, many different style sheets and guidelines are available. In addition, many individual companies and government agencies print their own guidelines and expect all employees to follow them. Various journals and magazines also have their own formats, and authors attempting to publish in them must observe those guidelines. With so many competing formats to choose from, the student should learn the following principles, rather than memorize any one format:

1. Obedience is better than sacrifice. (See 1 Samuel 15:22.) In other words, find out what format your employer, magazine, or teacher expects and follow that format carefully. The practicing writer, whether at school or on the job, quickly discovers that no one style sheet or guideline covers every possible situation. When faced with uncertainty, the writer should follow the second principle.

2. In the absence of official guidelines, common sense is almost always acceptable.

These two principles are far more important than any set of rules; however, to help you get started, this appendix presents a generalized report format, suitable for an academic setting. On the job, most elements of this generalized format will still be acceptable; however, a few will undoubtedly change.

Remember, obedience and common sense never go out of style.

TYPING DETAILS

The paper should be typed (on one side only) on high-quality, heavy, white, eight-and-one-half-by-eleven-inch paper. Eighteen- or twenty-pound bond is a good weight. Each page should conform to the following specifications.

Margins

The basic margin is one inch on all four sides. Establish this by placing your page numbers in the upper right corner, exactly one inch down from the top and one inch over from the right side of the paper. Move two lines down from the page number before starting the text itself. On pages that begin with a title or major heading, the text should start two inches below the top of the page, with the title or heading in between the page number and the start of the text.

Spacing

The report should be double-spaced throughout, with the following exceptions:

- Triple-space between the text and an indented quotation.
- Quadruple-space between the text and the title, which is placed at the top of the first page.

See the example in figure 1 for how a typed page should look.

You must be careful to consider what type of binding you use before you type the paper. Many bindings reduce the width of the page, which must be taken into account while typing. Readers hate having to pull pages apart to peer down into the binding in an attempt to read the first letters of every line. The margins should be one usable or visible inch.

Numbering

Pages should be numbered consecutively throughout the report, beginning with the first page of the text, and going on through the last page of the text. An Arabic numeral should appear in the top right-hand corner of every page, *except* the first page, which, however, is counted. Hence, the first Arabic numeral will

The Wankel Engine

Whatever happened to a novel idea that influenced some of
the world's best automotive engineers, caused millions of dollars
to be spent on its research and development, and was predicted by
many of the experts in the field to be accepted industry-wide by
1980?

This idea, which received more than passing interest, was
the Wankel rotary engine. Those interested in new technology or
the history of the automobile will want to know where the Wankel
engine came from, how it made its way into American industry, why
it became so popular, and above all, why it declined so suddenly.
This report will detail and document the meteoric rise and fall
of the Wankel engine.

Felix Wankel

Felix Heinrich Wankel, born on August 13, 1902, came from
the German village of Lahr, located in Germany's Black Forest.[1]
His first, and so far his only, biographer describes his childhood thus:

> When only 12 years old, early in World War I, young Felix
> lost his father. Later, after the war, Germany's poor
> economic conditions forced Felix to go to work directly out
> of high school. This brilliant engineer never had a day of
> advanced training.

Figure 1. An example of a typewritten page.

be 2, on the second page of the text. Pages before the first page of the text, such as table of contents, abstract, and list of figures, are numbered with lower case Roman numerals, located at the center bottom of each prefatory page. The title page is treated just like the first page of the text—it does not get a number, but it is counted as though it were *i*.

Binding

The entire report should be bound together in such a way that the pages turn easily and remain open to the desired page without having to be held. Because graphics may be placed on the back of a page, to face the following page of text, the binding should allow any two consecutive pages to lie flat side by side. The above stipulations eliminate staples, paper clips, and torn corners, and suggest the use of some form of loose-leaf binding.

THE PARTS OF THE FULL-SCALE REPORT

The formal report consists of the following introductory parts, each of which contributes to the reader's ability to get off to a good start with the report:

1. Letter of transmittal
2. Cover
3. Title page
4. Table of contents
5. List of illustrations
6. Abstract

The Letter of Transmittal

The letter of transmittal is a cover letter introducing the report and identifying the circumstances under which it was written. It may also include a brief statement of the report's purpose and scope, as well as any features likely to be of special interest to the audience. The letter of transmittal should be addressed to the primary audience, as in figure 2.

The Cover

To protect the manuscript, enclose it in a heavy cover bound together with the rest of the report. So that the reader may see at a glance what the report is all about, type the most important details, such as the title, the author, and the intended audience, on a gummed label and paste it neatly on the cover. The

19 Bonito St.

Long Beach, California 94007

Oct. 3, 1983

Mr. Teddy Philpot

Vice President, Operations

Golden West Drilling Co.

Bakersfield, California 95608

Dear Mr. Philpot:

As you requested in your letter of August 26, 1983, I have prepared the accompanying report to be issued to all drilling crews. The report explains the basic cause of torsional failures in tool joints and tells how to avoid them.

I hope that by circulating this report we can make all the crews aware of these failures and thus help prevent them from happening in the future.

If you have any questions, I will be in the Bakersfield office the week of October 20. I hope to see you then.

Sincerely,

Tom Frankel

Tom Frankel

Maintenance Engineer

Figure 2. Example of a transmittal letter.

cover is not numbered. Finally, the cover should be neat and eye-catching, without being flashy or gaudy. You want an attractive cover that encourages the reader to move inside the book.

The Title Page

The title page provides introductory information for the reader:

- Title of report
- Name of writer
- Name of primary audience
- Date

Like the cover, the title page should be attractive. The exact format of the title page is not crucial, as long as the result is neat and the relationships among items clear. In other words, it should be brief, balanced, and ordered. Figure 3 shows an example of a correctly written and arranged title page.

The Table of Contents

The table of contents should tell the reader exactly which items appear on which pages. Additionally, the table of contents makes the reader aware of the exact scope and organization of the report. Like the other introductory items, no absolutely correct form for the table of contents exists, but neatness and clarity are important. The table of contents should not attempt to go into too much detail. The relative importance of various sections can be indicated by many devices, such as indentation, capitalization, or a number and letter system as in the following example. Notice in figure 4 that the table of contents starts with the first item after itself, namely the list of illustrations.

The List of Illustrations

The list of illustrations is a table of contents for the graphic aids. The term *illustration* refers to any graphic aid in the report. Using the list of illustrations, the reader can turn instantly to any diagram, chart, picture, table, etc. A good rule of thumb is that if the report contains more than six graphic aids, include a list of illustrations. If it has six or less, the list may be omitted. Some lists of illustrations, such as the one in figure 5, distinguish between tables and all other graphic aids, which are called figures.

THE FEASIBILITY OF BUILDING AND USING A LOW-COST

HOME-BUILT LASER TO DEMONSTRATE

BASIC PHYSICS PRINCIPLES

Submitted to

Dr. Norman Tosh

Michigan Institute of Technology

by

Scott Marshall

Senior Electrical Engineer

March 30, 1980

Figure 3. Example of a title page.

TABLE OF CONTENTS

Figure 4. Example of a table of contents.

LIST OF ILLUSTRATIONS

Figure 5. Example of a list of illustrations.

The Abstract

Abstracts were discussed in detail in chapter 3. The abstract is a condensed version of the entire report, placed at the front of the text for the benefit of audiences who may not have time to read the full text. The abstract is normally the last prefatory item in the report. Figure 6 gives an example of an abstract.

The remaining parts of the report—the introduction and the appendices—were discussed in detail in chapter 3. Four different patterns for the main body were discussed in chapter 4. Additional details about some of the mechanical aspects of the final manuscript follow.

PLACING LONG QUOTATIONS INTO A REPORT

Occasionally, you may want to introduce a long quotation into your report. *Long* means any single quotation that takes over four lines in your report. Such long quotations are not placed in the text within quotation marks, as are short quotations. Instead, long quotations must be indented and set off from the rest of the text by a triple-space above and below. Long quotations are documented just like any other piece of borrowed information:

```
        Quarry discusses in some detail the advantages of
    the large, single-dish radio telescope:
 ⎡triple⎤
 ⎣space ⎦
        In order to detect a source with a certain flux
        density, one must provide enough collecting
        area, bandwidth, and integration time to yield
        sufficient energy from the source to outweigh
        the noise energy which also enters from nearby
        transmitters (Walters 1983, 45).
 ⎡triple⎤
 ⎣space ⎦
        In other words, the larger the dish, the narrower
    the bandwidth or the shorter the integration time.
```

MORE BIBLIOGRAPHY AND FOOTNOTE FORMS

In chapter 11 you were introduced to the basic forms for footnote and bibliography. Those forms are generally correct; however, occasionally you may run into a source that does not fit the general form. Following are some additional footnote and bibliography forms for some of the sources you may want to include in your report.

ABSTRACT

Torsional failures often occur at the tool joint during drilling operations. Previously, we have gone on the assumption that a torsionally balanced drill string would prevent torsional failures. However, during the past six months we have had a large number of failures, even with torsionally balanced drill strings.

Tests indicate that the failures are mainly associated with tool joints coated with a "slick" thread compound. Further tests indicate that a compound containing 40 - 50 percent metallic zinc and a sulphur content of less than .3 percent provides the greatest protection against failure.

The steps to minimize torsional failure are:

1. select a balanced drill string
2. use the 40-50 percent zinc thread compound
3. use a torque gauge
4. regularly check and service threads

Figure 6. Example of an abstract.

Newspaper

Footnote   [1]"New Cure for Cancer Studied Intensively,"
                            Los Angeles Times, 23 Aug. 1976, p. 1 col. 6.

Bibliography   "New Cure for Cancer Studied Intensively."
                            Los Angeles Times, 23 Aug. 1976, p. 1, col. 6.

Pamphlet

Footnote   [2]U.S. Dept. of Energy, *Fifteen Ways to In-*
                            sulate Your House for Under $100, Pamphlet 213
                            (Washington, D.C.: GPO, June 1968), p. 5.

Bibliography   U.S. Dept. of Energy. *Fifteen Ways to Insulate*
                            Your House for Under $100. Pamphlet 213.
                            Washington, D.C.: GPO, June 1968.

TV or Radio Program

Footnote   [3]Dan Rather, "Hypothermia," CBS News
                            (New York: CBS–TV, 15 Nov. 1978).

Bibliography   Rather, Dan. "Hypothermia." CBS News, New
                            York: CBS–TV, 15 Nov. 1978.

As you can see from these examples, footnote and bibliography forms remain basically the same as the general forms, even if the source is a little unusual. So when faced by an unusual source, just go to the general footnote or bibliography form, use your common sense, and make the unusual form fit as closely as possible into the general form.

All the principles of final manuscript preparation are at work in the following published article.

EXERCISE

Answer the following questions about the article, "The Dilemma of Flood Control in the United States." Support your answers with specific illustrations from the article.

a. Does the author use the following report formats effectively: abstract, introduction, references?

b. To whom does the report seem addressed? What is its major purpose? What is the author's attitude toward the subject matter? What specific situation might have caused the author to write this report?

c. Are the graphic aids effectively integrated into the text of the report?

d. Does the report end strongly and convincingly?

e. Does the author use effective sentence structure and word choice?

f. Are there any errors of mechanics, grammar, or punctuation in this report?

g. What factors keep you from writing a report like this one? What elements of this report can you duplicate right now, even as a student? Once you are on the job, what assistance will you require (and perhaps have available) to allow you to write reports like this one?

The dilemma of flood control in the United States

John E. Costa

Department of Geography
University of Denver
Denver, Colorado 80208

ABSTRACT

In spite of increasing annual expenditures for flood control, losses from flooding continue to rise in the United States. This seeming contradiction arises from over-dependence on federally supported structural solutions to flood problems. Nonstructural controls are initiated reluctantly at local levels of government because of constitutional questions, restrictions of local tax bases, lack of federal subsidies for nonstructural solutions, and the high costs of delineating flood hazard areas. The success of the National Flood Insurance Program is doubtful since only about five percent of the flood-prone communities in the United States have qualified for the regular program. Future reduction of flood losses is dependent upon increasing popular awareness of flood hazards and altering federal subsidy policies to reduce the impact of local land-use regulations.

INTRODUCTION

About seven percent of the total land area of the United States (excluding Alaska) is subject to flooding, and an estimated 22,000 communities including 6.4 million single family homes are located on this flood-prone land (U.S. Water Resources Council 1976). This represents about 0.5 percent of the total population. Since 1953 American Presidents have declared 500 major disasters; 75 percent of these were the result of flooding. An average of about 100 persons die each year from flooding in this country. This is an actuarial statistic that does not reflect the

From John E. Costa, "The Dilemma of Flood Control in the United States," *Environmental Management* 2 (July 1978): 313–22. Copyright © 1978 by Springer-Verlag New York Inc. Reprinted by permission of the publisher.

impact of single disasters. In 1972 alone nearly 500 lives were lost from floods in Rapid City, South Dakota; Buffalo Creek, West Virginia; and in the eastern United States from Hurricane Agnes. In spite of these figures, loss of life from flooding in the United States is small compared with some other countries. During one flood along the Hwangho River in China in 1887, 800,000 lives were lost.

Flood plains have traditionally been among the first topographic areas to be settled. This pattern of development occurs for a variety of reasons: alluvial land is fertile, flat, and easy to develop; the river offers a supply of water (surface or ground water) and an easy method of waste disposal; the river provides a transportation route; and the sand and gravel associated with streams yield readily available building materials. A recent study of the extent of development of flood-prone areas in 26 American cities, published by the United States Geological Survey, shows that flood-prone areas constitute an average of 16.2 percent of the urban areas in these cities and over half (52.8 percent) of these areas have been developed (Schneider and Goodard 1974). The federal government is presently spending over 800 million dollars annually on flood control, yet annual flood losses have increased fourfold since 1936, and are increasing yearly.

THE FREQUENCY OF FLOODING

An important aspect of understanding flooding hazards is the frequency and magnitude problem. Flood frequency analysis provides the basis for flood-plain zoning and many engineering structures such as culverts, bridge openings, channel capacities, and spillways. A flood frequency curve is a cumulative distribution relating the magnitude of a flood event to the frequency of occurrence. Large, catastrophic floods generally have a low frequency, while smaller floods such as bankfull flow occur much more often. Since stream flow cannot be predicted, frequency is expressed as the probability of a given discharge being equaled or exceeded in any one year. The reciprocal of the probability is recurrence interval, expressed in years. For example, the flow with a twenty percent chance of being equaled or exceeded in any year has a recurrence interval of five years, or:

$$\frac{1}{P} = \text{R.I.}$$

where P is the probability of a flow being equaled or exceeded in any one year, and R.I. is recurrence interval. Therefore, along any stream the chance of the one hundred year flood being equaled or exceeded in any given year is one percent.

There are two general methods for constructing flood frequency curves: mathematical curve fitting and graphical fitting. Mathematically fitted curves represent a selected frequency distribution that shows some agreement with flood data. Since there is no clearly superior distribution applicable to all steams, it is not easy to determine the proper frequency distribution to use in flood frequency analysis. The theoretical frequency distribution used in flood frequency analysis adopted by federal agencies is the log Pearson III distribution (Benson 1968).

Graphical fitting is simple, rapid, and assumes no particular frequency distribution. However, because data points are averaged by eye, different people draw different frequency curves. Each annual peak is assigned a recurrence interval or probability by the relationship:

$$\text{R.I.} = \frac{N + 1}{M} = \frac{1}{P}$$

where R.I. is recurrence interval, N is the number of years of record, M is the magnitude order number of the sample (the largest flood in N years is assigned M equals 1, the second largest flood M equals 2, and so on), and P is the probability of that flow being equaled or exceeded in any one year. After each flood has been assigned a recurrence interval, the data are plotted against the discharge for each flood event and a line is drawn by eye through the data points. As the length of record of stream flow increases, the sample size increases and we get a more representative picture of the true population of flows. Unfortunately, hydrologic design based on a short sample of stream flows may be inadequate as a consequence of human modifications (that is,

urbanization) or local short term climate changes during the life of the project. The San Carlos (Coolidge) Reservoir built on the Gila River, Arizona in 1928 by the Office of Indian Affairs is a costly example of a dam and reservoir that were overbuilt because of inadequate records. The design was based on 33 years of flow records, and the reservoir has never been filled to capacity (Hoyt and Langbein 1955).

The Kenwood Dam was built by the City of Denver, Colorado in 1935–1936 following a disastrous flood along Cherry Creek in 1933. It was designed to control a flood 2.25 times the largest historic flood in the basin, a seemingly adequate safety factor. The infamous storm of 30–31 May 1935 on the Republican River basin and adjoining areas occurred during the construction of the Kenwood Dam. All four major cells of this storm were within 120 miles of Cherry Creek and one cell was within 12 miles of the basin. Meteorological conditions indicated that any one of these cells could have centered over the Cherry Creek basin. If this had happened, the Kenwood Dam would have been destroyed. Even before its completion, the Kenwood Dam had to be considered under-designed and obsolete.

One of the temptations of flood frequency curves, whether mathematically or graphically fitted, is to extend the frequency curve beyond the period of record to make some statements about the probability of larger flows. Attempts to estimate the recurrence interval of extreme flood events from parameters derived from records of forty years are based on the assumption that the same mathematical distribution is valid well beyond the period of record, say for the 100, 500, or 1,000 year floods. The extension of the plotted curve beyond the period of record assumes that the curve keeps the same trend. This is often an unwarranted assumption because when data from streams with long flow records are fitted graphically, they commonly show changes in convexity and concavity. As a general rule, flood frequency becomes less and less meaningful when records are extended much past twice the period of record, no matter what method is used.

IDENTIFICATION AND PERCEPTION OF FLOOD HAZARD AREAS

A flood plain is defined as a relatively flat constructional landform, bordering a stream, that is inundated during times of high water that exceeds channel capacity. The active flood plain is that geomorphic surface under construction by the stream in its present hydrologic regime by lateral and vertical accretion. Commonly river valleys contain one or more benches or terraces in the alluvium. Strictly speaking, these terraces are abandoned floodplains that are no longer associated with the present stream regime. Data from a large number of streams all over the world indicate that the active flood plain of a river is inundated, on the average, every 1.5–2.0 years (Fig. 1).

Before flood-prone regions can be protected, a decision must be made on the acceptable level of risk. In upstream areas where agricultural land use dominates, design usually protects against the one percent flood or less. Further downstream where severe loss of life and property is possible, protection from the largest flood that could be expected from the most severe combination of meteorologic and hydrologic conditions that are characteristic of a particular region may be required. The Water Resources Council and the Federal Insurance Administration have adopted the "100 year flood" (one percent flood) as the design level of risk for the Federal Flood Insurance Program. This represents a compromise between the truly catastrophic floods of very rare probability and the more frequent flooding that continually causes small amounts of property damage. This choice seems very reasonable since nearly $\frac{2}{3}$ of all residential flood losses in this country are caused by floods with recurrence intervals of only 1–10 years (Funk 1969).

In many communities a detailed flood plain identification project is not necessary to inform the people that a flood hazard exists. Data concerning flood perception and awareness have been slow in developing, and inconclusive. However, several points are clear. Flood plain users tend to think floods can be completely controlled and consequent-ly have a unanimous belief in structural engineering solutions to flood problems. Most flood plain users do not understand the concept of return periods or recurrence intervals. A common misconception is that the "100 year flood" happens once every hundred years, not that a flood of such magnitude has a one percent chance of occurring during any given year. When a rare flood occurs that exceeds the design criteria of an engineering structure, the event may be ominously labeled an "Act of God" and liability floats away with the rest of the flood debris.

Flood awareness is most closely related to the frequency of occurrence and the personal experience of the individual (Fig. 2). However, the awareness of a flood hazard does not guarantee a rational response from the people endangered. In fact, persons who have been flooded have a tendency to return to the same dangerous areas, some cloaked with ill-conceived optimism that flooding will not happen again, others reluctant to leave familiar surroundings of family and friends (White 1961).

ALTERNATIVES IN FLOOD CONTROL

For those cities and communities located in flood-prone areas there are two general methods that can be used to abate a flood hazard: structural, and nonstructural (administrative) approaches. The first involves increasing the ability of streams and rivers to pass floodwaters within the boundaries of their channels. Combining the continuity equation $(Q = w \times d \times v)$ and the empirical Manning equation:

$$V = \frac{1.49}{n} R^{2/3} S^{1/2}$$ the discharge Q can be represented by:

$$Q = \frac{1.49}{n} R^{2/3} S^{1/2} wd, \text{ where}$$

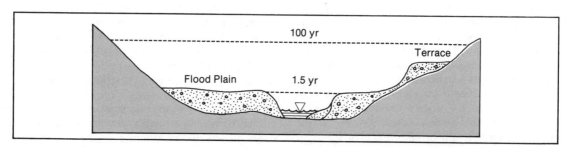

Figure 1. *Schematic cross-section of a river valley showing relative frequency of flooding.*

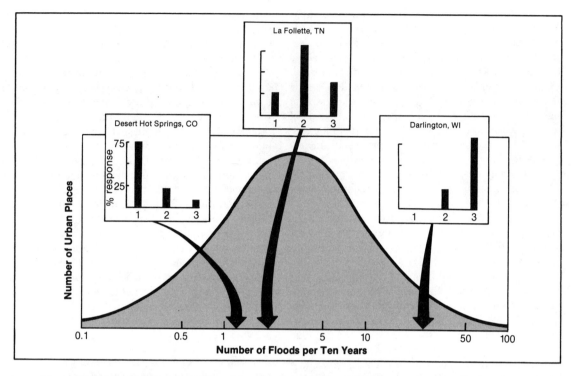

Figure 2. *Flood perception as measured by mitigating responses for three communities, each experiencing a different flood frequency. 1 = total ignorance (no response), 2 = hazard perceived, 3 = adoption of countermeasures (from Bauman and Kates, 1972).*

Q = discharge   R = hydraulic radius
w = width   S = slope
d = depth   n = roughness
v = velocity

This relation tells us that any combination of increasing channel velocity, slope, width, or depth, or reducing channel roughness, will allow more water to be discharged through the channel without overbank flooding. Levees, dikes, flood walls, embankments, channelization including straightening, deepening, and widening, and cleaning channels of obstructions such as trees, bars, debris, and paving channel bottoms, will all increase channel capacity.

An alternative structural method for protecting flood-prone areas is to retard floodwaters with dams, and release the waters gradually following the rainstorm. Whether a single large dam at the mouth of a large basin is better than a series of smaller dams on small headwater tributaries was

the center of the "flood control controversy" between the Corps of Engineers and Department of Agriculture (Leopold and Maddock 1954). The Flood Control Act of 1936 authorized both the Corps of Engineers and Department of Agriculture to engage in flood reduction activities. The Soil Conservation Service initiated a program of improved land management in headwater areas. Terraces, crop management, contour plowing, strip cropping, mulches, and controlled grazing were used to increase the infiltration and moisture storage capacity of upland soils. The general philosophy was to try to stop the water where it fell. After World War II, the SCS began construction of numerous small earth-fill dams along headwater streams controlling approximately $2.59\text{--}51.80 \times 10^3$ hectares (10–200 mi^2). Land management, plus these small check dams achieve about a $\frac{1}{3}$ reduction in runoff from small storms, but their influence decreases rapidly downstream. It is generally agreed that good land management practices conserve soil resources, reduce erosion and sediment yield, and increase agricultural yield, but the SCS headwater program had only a very small effect in reducing the impacts of major floods downstream. Consequently, as the structural program of the SCS expanded downstream to larger drainage areas, the Corps of Engineers felt that the benefits credited to their large structures along main channels would be reduced. The struggle between the SCS and Corps of Engineers for funding and domination of flood control programs centered on engineering works, not the value of land management as argued by Peterson (1954). The controversy is a moot question because both kinds of dams are designed to serve different purposes. Numerous small dams on headwater tributaries are advocated by the SCS to help control runoff from the small frequent floods that are most damaging to agriculture. These structures are not effective in controlling runoff from major rainstorms, as they are only designed to control floods of about 100 year recurrence intervals or less. Downstream construction of large dams is designed to mitigate big floods with a high catastrophe potential.

In the three decades between the passage of the Flood Control Act of 1936 and 1966, this country relied almost solely on engineering solutions to its flood control problems. The engineering (structural) approach has not been successful in reducing flood losses. Despite federal expenditures of 12 billion dollars on structural controls since 1936, annual flood losses have increased steadily from an estimated 1 billion in 1958 to 2 billion in 1972, 3.8 billion in 1975, and a projected 6 billion by the year 2000 (Table 1). There is no good evidence in the hydrologic record that flood frequencies or magnitudes are increasing (Hoyt and Langbein 1955), so the sharp rise in flood losses must signify increasing development of flood-prone areas spurred by unwarranted confidence in flood control structures.

Table 1. *Annual Flood Losses in Millions of Dollars (1975 Dollars)*

Land use	Upstream	Downstream	Total
Urban and built-up	$330	$990	$1320
Agricultural	$1130	$682	$1812
Other	$340	$378	$718
Totals	$1800	$2050	$3850

(from Goodard 1976)

It has been estimated that for every $6.00 spent by the federal government for flood control, $5.00 is spent by the public for expansion onto flood plains (Hanke 1972). Subsequent floods that exceed design criteria, or floods generated by storms in areas immediately below flood control structures contribute to the increased flood losses.

It must be borne in mind that flood control is as much a social and political problem as it is an engineering problem. There are no structural solutions to all floods, at least not within any presently conceivable limits of economic, technical, and political feasibility. Floods of rare magnitude will continue to inundate communities in low lying areas, and top or circumvent whatever structures are built. And they will do so with some regularity on a national scale. Consequently, instead of continuing a losing battle to control nature, efforts should be made to control man. This means grappling with the thorny problem of how the flood plain—the natural overflow channel of the stream—is used. The country is just beginning to face this issue squarely and halt the historic pattern of uncontrolled flood plain development. The Congressional report, "A Unified National Program for Managing Flood Losses" (Task Force) in 1966 changed the direction of flood control efforts by encouraging the use of nonstructural solutions to flood hazards. Nonstructural and administrative controls include zoning, statutes, subdivision regulations, building codes, urban renewal, tax assessments, warning signs and notices, flood proofing, and permanent evacuation (Liebman 1973).

The rights of state and local governmental units to regulate land use in flood hazard areas have been clearly established, provided regulations are reasonable and not arbitrary (Hogan 1963). However, federal and state initiatives in land-use controls have met stiff local resistance. There is some evidence that nonstructural and administrative controls might be more widely accepted if conceived and executed by local units of government (Geisler and Martinson 1976).

Unfortunately, nonstructural controls are initiated only reluctantly by local governments for a variety of reasons. Flood plain regulations to guide and regulate land use in flood-prone areas conflict with the basic rights of land owners to realize maximum profit from their lands as guaranteed by the Fifth Amendment. Even though the constitutionality of flood-plain zoning has been defended

(Dunham 1959) and is generally accepted in the United States (U.S. Water Resources Council 1971), local governments are strongly influenced by local land owners who are reluctant to perpetuate dilutions of Fifth Amendment protections. The constitutionality of the use of the banking function as a control measure has not been resolved. Flood plain regulations that restrict or prohibit developments reduce the tax base for local governments. In regions like Brazoria county, Texas, which contains 70 percent flood-prone areas, the impact on the tax base could be devastating. Since passage of the Flood Control Act of 1936 whereby the federal government assumed the initiative in abating flood damages, the most commonly utilized method of abating floods was some type of structural control. The present national policy allows flood plain owners to join together into flood control districts and jointly apply to the federal government for flood protection. Many federal agencies such as the Corps of Engineers, Bureau of Reclamation, and Soil Conservation Service have been eager to pump money and expertise into structural controls to protect flood-prone areas. The Flood Control Act of 1938 removed most of the cost-sharing provisions of the 1936 act; therefore communities have been overwhelmingly receptive to these structural controls because most of the costs were paid from federal funds. The costs of nonstructural approaches to mitigate flood damages are generally borne by local governments. The high costs of accurately delineating flood-prone areas may be beyond the budget constraints of many community governments. The most desirable approach to identifying flood hazard areas for flood plain management is the engineering hydrologic-hydraulic method of back water surface profiles (Wiitala and others 1961). Unfortunately, this method is expensive and time consuming, costing as much as $5,000 per channel mile (Dingman and Platt 1977).

In the absence of detailed engineering flood plain maps, several rapid, inexpensive alternative methods for identifying flood hazard areas are available for communities and regions awaiting or unable to afford expensive engineering studies. In some areas, lands periodically inundated by floodwaters will exhibit a zonation of vegetation, coincide with mappable soil boundaries, or contain distinctive morphologic evidence such as sand splays or berms

(Wolman 1971). High water marks, historical accounts, or air photos can retain the historic flood on record, which allows preliminary identification of hazard areas. It is difficult to document how much precision is compromised by these more economical and efficient surrogate methods. Since the standard hydrologic-hydraulic method is based on statistical data and probability, it can be considered no better than an approximation. A recent summary of this problem (Dingman and Platt 1977) concluded that various expedient methods of flood plain delineation can provide a hydrologically and legally sound basis for regulation. The utilization of expedient flood plain identification methods ought to be encouraged, so local governments can prevent further development in the flood plain while awaiting detailed delineation of flood hazard areas.

The cities of Rapid City, South Dakota and Denver, Colorado provide contrasting examples of communities that have adopted different approaches to flood hazard mitigation. Rapid City has almost completely eliminated the potential for future flood losses by the adoption of tough nonstructural regulations. Downtown Denver faces a large catastrophe potential from flooding, despite the presence of a large Corps of Engineers flood control dam just outside the city limits.

Following the June 9, 1972 flooding in Rapid City in which 238 people were killed, the mayor and city council would not issue building permits to rebuild in the flood plain. Instead, they used $48 million of federal aid and $16 million in local matching funds to move 1100 families and 157 businesses out of the flood-prone areas, and zoned the flood plains as parks and open spaces. The mayor of Rapid City said,

> "I think the first thing that we have to do is have the courage to say no to a developer. Say 'No, it's too damn close to the flood way. You can't build there,' and write a flood plain ordinance that has teeth in it where you can stop the guy. Some developers want to go in, build, make their dough, cut and run. You have to have the courage to say no to that potential investment in your flood way. That takes courage because the schools need the property tax base. Your county needs it. Your city needs it. Your municipality or special districts get their money from property taxes. They need to strengthen their tax base, but strength in the wrong place is wrong because it endangers life and property in the future." (Barnett 1975)

The Cherry Creek Dam and Reservoir, completed in 1950 by the Corps of Engineers, were designed to eliminate the flood hazard of Cherry Creek to the City of Denver. Two levels of reservoir development were initially proposed in 1943. The first level consisted of a single purpose flood control project and the second or ultimate level was planned as a multiple purpose flood control and irrigation project. The 85,000 acre feet of irrigation storage subsequently constructed into and reserved within the Cherry Creek Dam for use by the Bureau of Reclamation were never used, and in 1968 the space was returned to the Corps of Engineers for flood control allocations. Despite the enormous size and cost of Cherry Creek Dam, the flood hazard from Cherry Creek was not eradicated, only displaced into the adjoining drainage basin, Sand and Toll Gate Creeks.

The spillway for Cherry Creek Dam cuts across the drainage divide to Sand and Toll Gate Creeks. In 1947 a survey determined the value of lands and improvements along these creeks subject to flooding from Cherry Creek Reservoir emergency spillway discharges. The value was less than one million dollars. By 1958 this amount had increased to over $8 million, and by 1968 the value had increased again to over $86 million (U.S. Army Corps of Engineers 1972). From 1950 until today extensive development has crept up the flood plains of Sand and Toll Gate Creeks from Denver to the Cherry Creek Dam. The acquisition of necessary project lands, easements, and rights of way for the dam, reservoir, and spillway canal began right after the initial construction appropriation and were acquired by condemnation proceedings. However, land acquisition in Sand and Toll Gate Creeks for passage of water through the emergency spillway were postponed until the ultimate development stage. When the Bureau of Reclamation abandoned this project and in 1968 finally ceded the 85,000 acre feet allocated to it in 1943, it became apparent that nothing had been done to acquire and define the floodway through Sand and Toll Gate Creeks in the event of a spillway design flood. And so despite the additional 85,000 acre feet of reservoir storage reverted back to flood control in 1968, the Cherry Creek Dam is inadequate in its present condition because the spillway cannot be utilized without jeopardizing lives and property. Because of the lack of supportive nonstructural controls, encroachment has increased the potential flood damages and even forced revised operational criteria, which partially negate the initial benefits of the structure.

A POSSIBLE SOLUTION

The history of attempted flood control in the United States has been characterized by implementation of a variety of comparatively expensive engineering structures without adequate supportive land use planning. This single focus approach to flood control has proven over and over again to be unsatisfactory (White 1959). Despite all the efforts and expenditures to control flooding in the United States, annual losses continue to grow because construction is not supported by strict land-use regulations and controls. Once private land is "protected" by federally funded structural measures, the owners may realize large profits by developing the flood plain. Flood protection benefits for future development in areas protected by structures have even been used by the Corps of Engineers for economic justification of projects. While these structures may protect an area from the more frequent floods, development downstream may be subjected to catastrophe when floods in excess of design criteria occur.

Flood losses will never be reduced, or even stabilized, until the risk is transferred to local governments. If communities are reluctant to institute nonstructural controls, then the people who own flood plain lands and derive the benefits of expensive structures ought to contribute a bigger share of the costs. For example, the public costs of protecting flood plain lands in Denver, Colorado with structural controls amounts to $74,000/acre, exclusive of any development costs. At the same time undeveloped land outside of the flood plain was selling for about $3,000 per acre (Blewitt 1975).

One of the most successful local flood control programs ever initiated in the United States was along the Miami River basin in southwest Ohio. A tremendous flood along the Miami River in 1913 caused over 400 deaths and more than $100 million in damages. Rather than wait several years for federal aid, local citizens created the Miami Conservancy District with powers of eminent domain for the purpose of reducing the flood hazard in the valley. The district was locally formulated, privately organized, and privately financed by tax assessments on protected property. The flood solution consisted of 5 dry retarding dams that could store 841,000 acre feet. At that time (1915) there were no reservoirs built in the United States for flood control. Bonds were sold, and the retarding basins were completed in 1923 at a cost of $30 million. Flood peaks were reduced about 25 percent in Dayton, and today the district is free from debt and the dams provide valuable recreational areas (Hoyt and Langbein 1955).

Flood hazards are best mitigated by a comprehensive plan of action that must include a strong commitment to land-use planning and administrative controls in conjunction with structural controls. The basic responsibility for regulating flood plains lies with state and local governments (U.S. Water Resources Council 1976), yet this regulatory power conflicts with the desire for a healthy and expanding tax base. The most logical approach to encouraging local governments to regulate land use on flood plains is some kind of federal economic inducement.

In the search for a way to halt the rising cost of annual flood losses, the United States Congress passed the National Flood Insurance Act of 1968 (P.L. 90–448), which provided a 90 percent subsidy of flood insurance costs, available on a voluntary basis, for communities that agreed to adopt and enforce minimum flood plain management regulations set by the Federal Insurance Administration.

In its first year, only 4 of 22,000 eligible communities joined the program, with only 20 policies written. The Congress had not appreciated the slow and expensive task of flood plain identification, so on the heels of Hurricane Camille along the Gulf Coast in August 1969, the act was amended to include mudslide damage and to authorize an "emergency" phase for communities awaiting completion of detailed flood plain investigations. Although only minimal land-use regulations are required from communities in the emergency phase, these regulations are more than most communities had had in the first place and were a start in the right direction. In 1959 only about 50 examples of flood plain regulations could be documented in the entire country (Murphy 1958).

A second major deficiency in the NFIA was its voluntary nature. The sequence of flooding disasters in 1972 proved that a voluntary insurance

program would not work. In Rapid City, South Dakota, where 1100 homes were destroyed by the flood of June 1972, there were only 29 flood insurance policies. In Wilkes Barre, Pennsylvania, which was severely damaged by the tropical storm Agnes flood in June 1972, there were only 2 flood insurance policies. In 1973 the Congress passed the Flood Disaster Protection Act (P.L. 93–234), which required mandatory participation in the National Flood Insurance Program. No federal financial assistance or loans through federal reserve banks would be available for structures in flood-prone regions unless flood communities participated in the flood insurance program and flood insurance was purchased.

The National Flood Insurance Program and amendments are the most promising approach to flood plain management yet implemented by the federal government. By the end of 1976 there were over 850,000 policies sold, worth $25 billion. However, the most difficult phase of the program is transferring communities from the emergency program into the regular program. Unfortunately, this remains to be realized (Platt, 1976). Consequently, the success of the program remains in doubt (Fig. 3).

An alternative encouragement for local implementation and enforcement of land-use regulations in flood-prone areas would be to make federal funds available to replace lost property taxes in local communities. This could be partially financed with money saved by reducing the emphasis on struc-

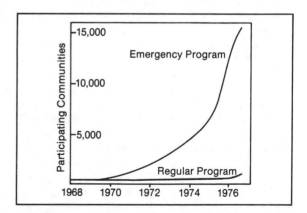

Figure 3. *Number of communities participating in the emergency and regular programs of the National Flood Insurance Program since initiation in 1968.*

tural controls, and the savings of annual maintenance costs. The federal government would repay to the local government the difference between current local property taxes and any income derived from the lands regulated for grazing, farming, or recreation. To minimize reductions in the multiplier effects of new developments or industry, the federal government might subsidize relocation in the community at a safer, but perhaps more expensive site. With these kinds of subsidies, local governments might be less reluctant to implement effective land-use regulations.

CONCLUSIONS

For the 22,000 flood-prone communities in this country, the Water Resources Council has adopted a "balanced view seeking neither abandonment nor full development of flood plains" (U.S. Water Resources Council 1976). The success of this goal may be heuristic, but the resolution of the flood control dilemma seems to center on two key points: perception, and federal policy. The country as a whole must realize that a dilemma exists, and people must be made aware of the hazard of their environment. Part of the ignorance of flood hazards can be traced to the former reliance on structural controls that perpetuated a false security because of reduced flood intervals. The availability of federal funds to support state, county, and municipal flood management regulations is a prerequisite for successful implementation of these programs. In the past, federal and state legislation for any type of flood control has been clearly linked to a recent flood disaster (for example, Rapid City). This reaction to crisis must be supplemented by annual support at a sufficient level so that long range flood plain management can be adequately introduced and enforced.

Those who occupy flood plains must become more responsible for the results of their actions, and less dependent on relief and rehabilitation. Besides subsidizing insurance for structures in flood-prone areas, federal relief and rehabilitation provide temporary housing, temporary mortgage and rental payments, food stamps, unemployment compensation, employment assistance, legal aid, and debris clean-up (Hanke 1972). Following the 1976 Big Thompson Flood in Larimer County, Colorado where 140 people died, land values in the floodway fell to 10–12 percent of their pre-flood values. This probably reflects the true value of this land when the risk of flooding is included in the price. However, property owners were reimbursed the full pre-flood market value of their land in an amendment passed with the Federal Land and Water Conservation Act of 1977. The land owners in the Big Thompson Canyon were participating in the National Flood Insurance Program but the county had not adopted the flood plain regulations necessary to qualify for the regular program.

All these relief measures are little more than inducements to move onto flood plains. The point is not to let people starve after a flood, but that social insurance implies a public right to have social control over private land use. Land-use planning, resisted when imposed from state and federal levels, has a chance of succeeding if local discretion is integrated into its management.

Finally, it should be noted that flood control does not mean flood elimination. Protection does not eliminate risk, it merely reduces risk to some acceptable level. The hundreds of millions of dollars spent annually on flood control are meant to prevent disaster, not stimulate land development. The false sense of security cast by the shadow of the huge dam has been a green light for development in flood plains. This means that losses will be even greater if and when flooding does occur. The struggle with flood losses will never be won until some prudent, tough decisions are made to transfer risk and responsibility to local governments. The alternative is to engineer and modify every stream and river in the country.

ACKNOWLEDGMENTS
I would like to thank Richard A. Walker, University of California, Berkeley, and Robert D. Sack, University of Wisconsin, Madison, for comment and discussion during preparation of this manuscript. The content, however, remains my responsibility.

LITERATURE CITED
Barnett, D. V. 1975. Luncheon address. Pages 15–31 in Proceedings of seminar on flood plain management. Urban Drainage and Flood Control District, Denver, Colorado. (ed. W. De Groot).

Bauman, D. D., and R. W. Kates. 1972. Risk from nature in the city. Pages 169–194 *in* T. R. Detwyler and M. G. Marcus, eds. Urbanization and environment. Duxbury Press, Belmont, California.

Benson, M. A. 1968. Uniform flood-frequency estimating methods for federal agencies. Water Resources Res. 4: 891–908.

Blewitt, R. I. 1975. The flood hazard cost of settling flood-plains. Flood Hazard News 5:4–5.

Dingman, S. L., and R. H. Platt. 1977. Flood plain zoning: implications of hydrologic and legal uncertainty. Water Resources Res. 13:519–523.

Dunham, A. 1959. Flood control via the police power. Univ. of Pennsylvania Law Rev. 107:1098–1132.

Funk, J. W. 1969. The flood potential and future flood problems. Pages 37–49 *in* M. D. Dougal, ed. Flood plain management, Iowa's experience. Iowa State Univ. Press. Ames, Iowa.

Geisler, C. C., and O. B. Martinson. 1976. Local control of land use: profile of a problem. Land Economics 52: 371–381.

Goodard, J. E. 1976. The nation's increasing vulnerability to flood catastrophe. T. Soil and Water Conservation 31: 48–52.

Hanke, S. H. 1972. Flood losses—will they ever stop? J. Soil and Water Conservation 27:242–243.

Hogan, T. M. 1963. State flood-plan zoning. DePaul Law Review 12:246–262.

Hoyt, W. G., and W. B. Langbein. 1955. Floods. Princeton University Press, Princeton, New Jersey. 469 pp.

Leopold, L. B., and T. Maddock. 1954. The flood control controversy. Roland Press, N.Y. 278 pp.

Liebman, E. 1973. Legal problems in regulating flood hazard zones. Amer. Soc. Civil. Engr., Hydraulics Div. 99:2113–2123.

Murphy, F. C., 1958. Regulating floodplain development. Dept. of Geography, Univ. of Chicago, Res. Paper 56, 216 pp.

Peterson, E. T. 1954. Big dam foolishness. Devin-Adair Co., N.Y. 224 pp.

Platt, R. H. 1976. The national flood insurance program: some midstream perspectives. Amer. Inst. Planners J. 42:303–323.

Schneider, W. J., and J. E. Goodard. 1974. Extent and development of urban flood plains. U.S. Geol. Survey Circular 601-J, 14 pp.

Task Force on Federal Flood Control Policy. 1966. A unified national program for managing flood losses. House Doc. 465, 89th Cong., 2nd Ses. U.S. Govt. Printing Office, Washington, D.C.

U.S. Army Corps of Engineers. 1972. Interim report on Sand and Toll Gate Creeks, Colorado. v. I and II, U.S. Army Engineer District, Omaha, Nebraska. 95 pp. and 12 Appen.

U.S. Water Resources Council. 1971. Regulation of flood-hazard areas to reduce flood losses. U.S. Government Printing Office. Washington, D.C. 578 pp.

U.S. Water Resources Council. 1976. A unified national program for flood plain management. U.S. Government Printing Office. Washington, D.C.

White, G. F. 1959. Action program for the states: a new attack on flood losses. State Govt. 32:121–127.

White, G. F., ed. 1961. Papers on flood problems. Dept. of Geography, Univ. of Chicago, Res. Paper 70, 228 pp.

Wiitala, S. W., K. R. Jetter, A. J. Summerville. 1961. Hydraulic and hydrologic aspects of flood plain planning. U.S. Geol. Survey Water Supply Paper 1526, U.S. Government Printing Office, Washington, D.C. 68 pp.

Wolman, M. G. 1971. Evaluating alternative techniques of floodplain mapping. Water Resources Res. 7:1383–1392.

FOR FURTHER READING

The Chicago Manual of Style. 13th ed. Chicago: The University of Chicago Press, 1982.
Style Manual. Washington, D.C.: U.S. Government Printing Office, 1982.
Williams, Joseph. *Style: Ten Lessons in Clarity and Grace.* Glenview, Ill.: Scott, Foresman, 1981.

III Oral Reports

Oral reports may not seem to belong in a book on writing. However, in business, industry, and government, the first result of a well-written report is often an invitation (or a command!) to present the material orally to some important people. Administrators like the oral format, because it allows them to ask questions and to get a feel for just how competent the presenter is. Sometimes the person with a great idea is not capable of carrying it out. So unless you want to spend your career writing effective reports that others sell to management, carry out, and get credit for, you must learn to deliver an effective oral presentation. Often the speaker has to make a presentation under extreme pressure, with a lot of money and prestige riding on the outcome.

An effective oral report is based on many of the same principles as an effective written report. Like written reports, oral reports are not made in a vacuum. Someone wants the report for a reason; someone will listen to the report; someone with a certain stance toward the material will make the report. In other words, oral reports are based on a response to a rhetorical situation, just as written reports are. However, the presenter of an oral report must not assume that the rhetoric of the oral format is the same as that for the written. Although oral presentations are often based on earlier written ones, they may demand considerable restructuring to fit the new situation. In addition to the old questions, the speaker should ask many new ones:

- How much time is allowed?
- Who is the audience?

- Why have I been asked to make an oral presentation?
- What are the physical facilities I will have to give the report?

TIME AND LENGTH

An oral report is often a drastic condensation of a successful written report. Usually, the oral report is delivered under strict time limitations, and administrators are notoriously impatient with long-winded presentations, often going so far as to noisily get up and stalk out. The presenter may experience some discomfort at continuing under such circumstances.

The key to condensing your report is to focus it. You cannot cover the full scope and the many details found in the written version. So you have to select one or two major points and make them clearly and forcefully. Naturally, the one or two points selected are determined by the situation behind the oral report. Remember that the situation may not be the same as it was for the written report; what was only a minor point in the written report may be the major point in the oral report.

THE CONTENT OF THE ORAL REPORT

The key to making points forcefully is to present the supporting data in a visible form, so that the audience can grasp at a glance what may have taken many pages in the written version. In an oral report, the data should appear visibly, so the speaker does not have to spend precious time presenting information. The spoken part of the presentation should focus on the conclusions, recommendations, observations, and other opinions that are supported by the visibly presented data.

In a written report, *all* the material is visible. The reader can turn back to a previous page or reread a difficult sentence over and over again if necessary. But in the oral format, the words are fleeting, invisible, and impermanent. The impermanence of the spoken word makes certain demands on the oral presenter.

Deductive Organization

The oral format mandates the deductive organizational approach. Make your main point very clear right at the outset, and then tie every supporting point into that main point. The listeners will be unable to follow a subtle or unclear organization. With the audience unable to stop the flow of words or reread sections, absolute clarity of organization becomes crucial.

Redundancy

The oral report needs redundancy. The presenter of an oral report usually wants the listeners to take a definite action as the result of the presentation. In fact, the oral report often comes about because the administrator liked the written presentation, but wants one last chance to check it over before approving it. To ensure that the audience both understands and takes the desired action, the oral reporter must repeat key points several times and make transitions overt, so listeners cannot get lost or become confused about the presentation's purpose. In a written report such repetition is redundant, but in an oral report it is necessary. The old saw, "Tell them what you're going to tell them, tell them, and tell them what you told them," is especially appropriate for an oral presentation.

Graphic Aids

The shortness of time and the inherent fleeting quality of the oral format make graphic aids a must. Because graphics are visible and semipermanent, they offer the oral reporter many of the advantages of the written format. Above all, they allow the oral reporter to refer to large masses of information without having to take the time to speak it all. Usually, this information is so detailed the listeners would never remember it even if the speaker did have time to say it all.

The graphic aid must be truly visible. Nothing is quite so frustrating or ridiculous as a graphic aid that only those in the first row can see. Thus, it must be oversized by normal standards.

Second, the graphic aid must be neat and clear. Remember, the listener is not just staring at the graphic aid. She is also listening. Therefore, the listener's full attention is not even on the graphic aid. So the graphic aid has to be instantly understandable, with a minimum of effort. If your graphic aid is too complex, you will lose your audience. They will stop listening to you because they will be too busy trying to figure out your graphic aid. Chances are they will not succeed, so you may lose them on both the spoken and the visible parts.

In fact, graphic aids can steal the show if you are not careful. It is best to put your graphic aids on a posterboard or an overhead transparency so that you can control when they are visible and when they are not. Ideally, the listeners only look at the graphic aid when you want them to. In other words, you have to control the graphic aids, rather than let them control your presentation.

In short, the oral report should have

▶ *Deductive Organization*
Main idea up front
Lots of transitions, so listeners keep track of
How far along presentation is
How point being discussed relates back to main point

▶ *Redundancy*
Main idea repeated several times throughout report
Strong introduction and conclusion
Restating main idea
Briefly recapitulating key supporting points

▶ *Graphic aids*
Supporting details
Put in graphic form whenever possible
Controlled so visible only when you want

THE DELIVERY OF THE ORAL REPORT

As with the written report, delivery is crucial. It is only slightly exaggerated to say that in an oral report, delivery is more important than content. Or perhaps, delivery *is* content, because in an oral report, the listeners focus at least as much on the deliverer as they do on the content being delivered. Naturally, this emphasis has several implications for the person giving the oral report.

The Role of Memory

Before the reporter can deliver the report at all, he must know the material cold. An oral presentation in front of powerful administrators is no place to wing it. Still less is it a place to freeze up. More than one oral presenter has been paralyzed by a combination of fright and lack of preparation. If at all possible, go to the room where you will present your report and practice it on stage. Then practice it over and over on your own.

Your goal in practicing is not so much to memorize your presentation as to become comfortable with it. The exact words do not matter nearly so much as a relaxed attitude, which can only come with confidence. As an old joke has it, a memorized or canned presentation will probably be deficient in three ways: "You read it, you read it badly, and it was not worth reading." The last thing you want is a stiff and formal appearance, which will simply put everyone on edge.

You should also practice your presentation to develop an accurate sense of how long it is. Often the time limit is rigid, and once on stage time has a way of moving quickly. It can be disconcerting to finish your introduction and have the vice president say in a firm voice, "Let's have a summary now, Smedley."

You must control your use of time to fit the limits set with the assignment. Because sticking to a set time limit is rare, your supervisors will notice that ability more than they will an extended speech, no matter what its quality.

The Performance Itself

If you have focused your presentation effectively, prepared clear and visible graphic aids, and practiced until you feel quite confident, then you are ready for the *performance* itself. Every presentation in front of a live audience is to some extent an act, and every presenter an actor. You must realize that your audience is giving you its full attention, even before you begin to speak. You want to appear calm and casual from the outset, to set a relaxed tone, both for yourself and your audience. Of course, you probably will not *feel* relaxed, but you have to look that way. A good trick for relaxing is to imagine, as concretely as you can, your audience sitting out there in their underwear. Such a thought will make you smile and forget your nervousness. The audience, seeing this, will relax with you, and they will never know they are sitting there half undressed.

Also, you must carefully choose your attire for the performance. You do not want to be caught wearing just your underwear! You should look clean and neat. Extremely formal wear is usually not appropriate, but informal wear is definitely out, too. Try to ascertain what your audience will wear and wear the same type of attire yourself. The bottom line is that you do not want your clothes to be the focus of attention in any way. The audience should see that you are dressed appropriately and not give the matter another thought.

Preliminaries A brief icebreaker makes an effective introduction to the oral report. This icebreaker may take almost any form: a joke, a quotation, a statistic, an anecdote. The only requirements are that it be lively, interesting, relevant, and brief. Absolutely avoid the tedious opening, such as "Today, my presentation is on . . . ." The opening should be lively and to the point, not dull. The opening should introduce the presentation, but not turn it off before it gets going.

The Main Body Once past the opening, launch right into the main point and on to the supporting points. Make sure the audience knows at the outset what you want them to do after the presentation is over. Catch their interest, give them a solid reason for listening to you, provide a context, and then, go to it. Prove your point so forcefully that your audience will get right up after your presentation, march purposefully down the hall, and do exactly what you said to do.

Focus and transition are the keys to the main body. Focus means that the oral reporter makes one or two points clearly and memorably, rather than four or five points that become confused and disorganized in the haste to get them all covered. Transition means that the oral reporter keeps the audience aware of the report's progress. The reporter indicates when one section of the report is over and what the next section will be. Because the audience for an oral report tends to lapse in and out of full attention, use focus and transition to minimize the effects of these lapses.

If you have organized your graphic aids carefully, you can almost organize your presentation around them. You can use them as cue cards, in effect, and simply deliver the talk around them—just talk them through. Such an arrangement has the added benefit of helping you not to forget anything. In fact, you will appear very organized to your audience when all you are really doing is looking at your own graphic aids to see what comes next. If you have practiced well, you will not need to have the whole presentation memorized word for word. Just use the graphic as a cue.

The Conclusion   Audiences tend to remember beginnings and endings most clearly, which puts an extra burden on the conclusion. The oral reporter wants to end with a flourish, reemphasizing the main point of the report and the key supporting details, but the conclusion is no place for totally new points. Instead, the conclusion should be the natural result of what has gone before. If the presentation has been effective, the audience should be anticipating the conclusion favorably throughout the report.

Physical Aspects of Delivery

The reporter has prepared hard for the presentation. It is tightly focused, transitions are well-planned, and graphic aids are prepared. Do not let all this earnestness go to your head, though. Even the most well-prepared presentation can be ruined by an overly formal or an overly informal delivery. Much of the formality or informality of the delivery can depend on physical aspects.

The first step toward an effective delivery is to relax. If you can maintain a relaxed *appearance,* you may actually start to *feel* relaxed. And when you are relaxed, you will deliver the report better. Everything in your delivery should aim to get your audience involved in your subject. Involvement comes from motion, in all its many forms. First, establish eye contact with everyone in the room. Keep your line of vision moving and make sure you look into everyone's eyes. Also, use hand gestures and feel free to move around in front of and even into the audience to keep the presentation from getting boring. Do not grip the podium tightly and hide behind it. Similarly, move your voice—use different pitches, speeds, and tones when appropriate. A monotone delivered by a cardboard dummy is deadly, no matter how good the content.

As you deliver your presentation, try to watch out for nervous mannerisms or pet phrases you tend to repeat. Many an otherwise excellent presentation has been completely ruined because the audience has been totally absorbed in counting *OK*s or *ummm*s. Other typical catch phrases to avoid are *and, for* *sure, you know, really,* and *uh.* Also, almost any habitual gesture can get locked in during a presentation. Hitching at one's pants, rubbing one's hands, scratching, or any other gesture repeated over and over can take the audience's attention off the presentation altogether. The point here again is not the specific gesture, but the constant repetition. The last thing you want is to draw the audience's attention to an irrelevant gesture or phrase.

SUMMARY

The effective oral report combines deductive organization, redundancy, and graphic aids with the delivery skills of memory, calmness, and involvement. The result is an effective and focused presentation which moves the audience to appropriate action.

EXERCISES

1. Attend any meeting at which someone gives an oral presentation. Write an evaluation of the presentation, divided into two main areas: content and delivery.

2. Prepare your own oral presentation, based on one of the written reports you have recently completed. Deliver this oral presentation to the other members of the class.

FOR FURTHER READING

Bryant, Donald C., et al. *Oral Communication.* 5th ed. Englewood Cliffs, N.J.: Prentice-Hall, 1982.

Ehninger, Douglas, et al. *Principles of Speech Communication.* 8th ed. Glenview, Ill.: Scott, Foresman, 1980.

Timm, Paul R. *Functional Business Presentations.* Englewood Cliffs, N.J.: Prentice-Hall, 1981.

Tracey, William. *Business and Professional Speaking.* 3d ed. Dubuque, Iowa: William C. Brown, 1980.

Index